THE FIRST COUNTERSPY

*Larry Haas, Bell Aircraft, and the FBI's
Attempt to Capture a Soviet Mole*

KAY HAAS

and

WALTER W. PICKUT

LYONS
PRESS

GUILFORD, CONNECTICUT

An imprint of Globe Pequot, the trade division of
The Rowman & Littlefield Publishing Group, Inc.
4501 Forbes Blvd., Ste. 200
Lanham, MD 20706
www.rowman.com

Distributed by NATIONAL BOOK NETWORK

British Library Cataloguing in Publication Information available

Library of Congress Cataloging-in-Publication Data
Names: Pickut, Walter W., author. | Haas, Kay, author.
Title: The first counterspy : Larry Haas, Bell Aircraft, and the FBI's attempt to capture a Soviet mole / Walter W. Pickut and Kay Haas.
Description: Guilford, Connecticut : Lyons Press, [2022] | Includes bibliographical references and index.
Identifiers: LCCN 2021044024 (print) | LCCN 2021044025 (ebook) | ISBN 9781493061563 (Hardback : acid-free paper) | ISBN 9781493061570 (ePub)
Subjects: LCSH: Espionage—United States. | Espionage—Soviet Union. | Espionage, American—Soviet Union—History. | Espionage, Soviet—United States—History. | United States. Federal Bureau of Investigation. | Haas, Larry. | Bell Aircraft Corporation. | National security. | World politics.
Classification: LCC JF1525.I6 P53 2022 (print) | LCC JF1525.I6 (ebook) | DDC 327.1273009—dc23/eng/20211202
LC record available at https://lccn.loc.gov/2021044024
LC ebook record available at https://lccn.loc.gov/2021044025

♾️™ The paper used in this publication meets the minimum requirements of American National Standard for Information Sciences—Permanence of Paper for Printed Library Materials, ANSI/NISO Z39.48-1992.

Contents

Part II: Lethal Consequences

Introduction

There was a time when nobody believed that machines heavier than air could leave the ground or that ether waves could carry sounds and pictures to distant places. The most learned of men didn't believe it. Only charlatans and troublemakers thought otherwise.

By the early twentieth century, scientists and engineers were starting to see things differently. They were the mavericks who would change the world. Larry Haas was one of those men.

Larry was an aeronautical engineer when taming the air still seemed like a miracle to many people. Propellers made winds that nature could not match and lifted sleek machines into the air. But that new wind could also do great damage.

Larry knew that because he designed and built engines for the propeller-driven warplanes of WWII. And then he helped create something even more powerful.

In the 1930s aviation was still so new that its pioneers were mostly self-taught men like Larry Haas. Haas banked on three skills. He had a knack for learning fast, he had a quick wit, and he could tell a lie that almost anybody would believe. In less than a decade after high school, that third skill propelled him from a humble milkman to the greatest heights in science and engineering cloaked in wartime secrecy. Unfortunately, it also launched him into espionage and brought injury and death to his family. Larry Haas's story has never been told. His story is also at the core of the Federal Bureau of Investigation's (FBI's) first ever investigation of a Soviet spy network operating inside the United States in which the Bureau used a civilian at the head of their spear. That story has also remained buried until now.

Soviets in America during WWII worked hard to learn all they could, a job made easier by the fact that they were wartime allies in the fight against Hitler's overwhelming forces. They needed new and invincible weapons against the enemies ravaging their homeland. With a thirst for power

1

growing alongside their desperation, the Soviets launched spies and moles deep into the American military-industrial complex in search for the secrets of ever-more deadly weapons yet to be unleashed.

Soviet spies had a thousand targets, but two of them topped their list. Priority one was stealing the secret of the atomic bomb. Priority two was to take home the secret behind jet-propelled warplanes. Hitler's 1941 Operation Barbarossa had demolished a vast swath of Soviet industry and crippled its once great air force in the opening days of the attack. Meeting their top priorities became an emergency for the Soviet Union. Such instant learning called for spies.

Sixty years later, Alexander Feklisov, an NKVD (the Soviet intelligence service) spy at the Soviet Consulate in New York City from 1940 to 1946, revealed in his memoir that in 1941 "Soviet networks in the United States were to concentrate their efforts on securing secrets of cutting-edge war technology."[1]

In the early 1940s, Soviet intelligence knew atomic and jet technologies were under top secret development in Germany. During WWII the Luftwaffe deployed its first jet fighters. The Soviets also knew their ally the United States, in league with the United Kingdom, was quickly and secretly catching up. The obvious choice, then, was for the Soviet Union to spy on the United States. Spies could hide in plain sight and steal what they wanted.

Soviet intelligence sent Andrei Ivanovich Schevchenko to Bell Aircraft in the United States to burrow into the American aircraft industry and take whatever he could. He posed as a legal representative of his country inspecting and buying thousands of Bell's conventional warplanes.

The FBI, soon suspicious of Schevchenko at Bell, recruited their first-ever civilian counterspies, Larry Haas, a top Bell engineer working at the heart of America's secret jet research program, and Leona Franey, the head librarian and custodian of secret documents at Bell's technical library.

The FBI told Haas to let himself be seduced by Schevchenko into his wide-ranging network of sub-agents throughout the American aircraft industry, then learn enough about Schevchenko to undermine and destroy him.

After two years of spy versus counterspy dueling, mutual seduction, and ultimately Haas's betrayal of Schevchenko to the FBI, the exposed and enraged Soviet uttered a threat that changed Larry Haas's life forever. Schevchenko's threat also turned out to be suicidal.

The Haas-Schevchenko case is unique—it is the first of its kind. Yet, despite its importance it has rarely been reported on beyond sparse footnotes and brief paragraphs in the historical records of WWII. A rare exception is found in historian Katherine A. S. Sibley's work,[2] though her research focused mainly on Soviet atomic bomb espionage. *The First Counterspy*, on the other hand, documents the Soviet's pursuit of their other great objective—American jet power. On the other hand, a 1956 history of the FBI authorized by Hoover appears to deny that the Haas-Schevchenko case ever happened.[3]

The First Counterspy is the story of "the first double agents operated by this Bureau within the Soviet espionage system in the United States during World War II," according to a June 8, 1949, memorandum from Assistant Director D. M. Ladd to Director J. Edgar Hoover.[4] The use of double agents against a wartime ally, the Soviet Union, violated important international precedents and created dissonance and controversy within the US government—conditions that severely complicated and ultimately defeated J. Edgar Hoover's conduct of this case. On the other hand, FBI counterespionage of all kinds against declared WWII enemies of the United States and the Allied Forces—Germany, Japan, and Italy—had been strong, effective, and enjoyed full US government and military support during the war.

A previous FBI anti-Soviet case that resulted in the 1941 conviction of Soviet intelligence agent Mikhail Gorin is not comparable to the Haas-Schevchenko case. The Bureau's Gorin investigation had been simple and relied only on informants, not on civilian counterespionage. Gorin recruited only a single American informant to learn about US naval defenses against Japan.[5]

A study of internal FBI communications during the Haas-Schevchenko case reveals that the Bureau was only starting to develop effective counterespionage methods during this investigation.[6] With the country's future at stake, all matters of national security took on an urgent character within the FBI. Agents, for example, often ran surveillance without Washington's approval—a technicality they deemed unnecessary. Approval was implicit in critical situations. Such practices were common, though poorly received at higher levels in Washington, even when successful in anti-Nazi spy cases.[7] As a result, such "on-the-job-training" in the Haas-Schevchenko case made it even harder for Hoover to warn the White House—reluctant to acknowledge an ally's malfeasance—of the new and rising Soviet danger.[8]

The unique nature of the Haas-Schevchenko case is matched by unique sources that made this book possible. Foremost is the personal experience of Kay Haas, Larry Haas's daughter, the last person alive who knows the story firsthand. As Larry's daughter, she was able to access the FBI's

WWII counterespionage archives (through the Freedom of Information Act—FOIA) specifically relevant to her father's case. These files (eighty documents, nearly four hundred pages) include a wealth of transcribed interviews between FBI agents and Larry Haas, including lengthy accounts of his conversations with Schevchenko. More than sixty pages of both public and secret interrogation records of the House Un-American Activities Committee (HUAC) also revealed previously unreported insights into the US government and military conduct of the case. In addition, Kay survived a succession of nearly fatal encounters with her father's enemies, abduction or assassination attempts, thus becoming an integral part of this saga herself. Her personal experiences and memories add new details to the FBI's probes into the Communist International (Comintern) Apparatus, as recorded in the COMRAP files, a six-hundred-page summary of all findings.[9]

The Central Intelligence Agency and the National Security Agency (CIA and NSA) files also reveal important aspects of this case in the more than 2,900 Venona files publicly disclosed in 1995.[10] Venona code breakers decrypted Soviet communications from WWII and the early Cold War years, revealing that Soviet spies had penetrated America's most highly classified programs to remarkable depths.[11]

Conversations depicted here come from many sources. The FBI transcripts quote numerous discussions between Schevchenko, Haas, and Leona Franey and her husband, Joseph, conducted with the FBI agents. These files also contain signed witness statements by Haas taken in post-contact interviews immediately following meetings between Haas and Schevchenko. In many transcripts Haas quotes Schevchenko directly.[12] In addition, we cite correspondence between FBI agents, Director J. Edgar Hoover, the Joint Chiefs, the Secretary and Undersecretary of State, the Secretary of War, the Attorney General, and others.[13] Some conversations are reconstructed (where noted) based on known dates, places, and participants, augmented by Kay Haas's recall of her father's many personal and detailed accounts.

Leona Franey's contacts with Haas and Schevchenko were also integral to this case and similarly well documented in the Haas-Schevchenko files. Leona was the first head librarian at the Bell Aircraft Technical Library, a newly established facility in October of 1942. At first, the library had nothing on its shelves except twenty-five books and four files containing National Advisory Committee on Aeronautics (NACA) reports for use by Bell's scientists and engineers. Leona quickly developed the library to a very high level.[14] It became a resource that Schevchenko found an irresistible trove of intelligence. Such quests as his—the search for forbidden treasures—require special traits and abilities in spy craft. As a result, the Haas-Schevchenko case has as much to do with the strengths and shortcomings of these two men as it has to do with their official status and the world events unfolding around them.

Among all the information sources used in the preparation of this book, however, one particular identity called for new investigation. This raised a question that the FBI itself apparently did not ask: Was there ever really a man named Andrei Ivanovich Schevchenko (*Андрей Иванович Шевченко*) acting as a Soviet agent in the United States?

All that is known about him before his arrival in the United States comes from one single document. In 1942, the Soviet government submitted the required PR-1 form to the US Secretary of State as prescribed in the Foreign Agents Registration Act protocols of 1938.

The document identified Schevchenko as a Soviet Union Purchasing Commission employee. Soviet citizens entering the United States during WWII, however, commonly used a fictitious cover name, especially if they were assigned undercover duties in addition to their professed legal jobs. Their true identity would remain secret should evasion or escape become necessary.

A 1952 House Un-American Activities Committee (HUAC) investigation revealed, "Soviets in this country were given so much freedom that even for a period of time this government did not make an attempt to ascertain the arrivals and departures of Russian personnel." Russians were eventually required to furnish personnel data, but compliance was left entirely to Soviet officials. "The result [was] that almost any information could be furnished, truthful or otherwise, and accepted."[15] COMRAP investigations never delved deeper into his identity than to add Andrei Schevchenko's nickname as "Andry" in one case.[16]

As a result, whether the name Andrei Ivanovich Schevchenko was a pseudonym or an authentic identity, the man was real. Within this account, the identity is accepted, though questions remain.[17]

The First Counterspy also examines the personal qualities needed in spy craft, failures traceable to the use of duress and threats in recruitment of agents, and the deployment of agents unsuited by nature to dangerous, clandestine work for which they were poorly trained. The moral and ideological strains on unsuited agents, especially in the face of the geopolitical turmoil of WWII, were important in determining the outcome of this case.

An inference that may be drawn from *The First Counterspy* is that any day's news stories may be only a plausible explanation of events, belying the complexities and deeper motives behind them. As a result, when daily news becomes history, it may be little more than a record of those plausible explanations. Deeper investigation is always more fruitful. *The First Counterspy* is such an investigation.

Though this case was a first, unique in many respects, it illustrates realities of domestic and international geopolitics that are timeless—an informative lens through which to view current events.

PART I

Seduction and Betrayal

Chapter One

Two New Arrivals

The First Arrival

As Larry Haas told his daughter Kay when he thought she was old enough to understand—and to no one else—his life had started with a lie. A family's culture marinates all who grow up in it, and truth was apparently an adjustable seasoning in the Haas family.

Haas was born on a rainy Friday morning, April 27, 1917, in the charity wing of Buffalo Columbus Hospital. His mother, Kay's grandmother, according to the story, was a twenty-year-old Native American woman named Nel, a member of the Seneca Nation of Indians, presumably of the Salamanca or the Tonawanda band. Her child's father, Loren Charles Haas, was not present for the birth. He was at home with his wife, Emma, and his daughter, Ethel.

Nel's child, given the name Frederick George Haas, turned the scandal into a family secret.

Larry's father had previously hired Nel to be a live-in housekeeper as a gift for his wife. Nel, previously destitute in the big city of Buffalo, New York, was paid in room and board. It was the only way Loren Charles's meager bakery accountant's salary could provide such a convenience for Emma. Nel was forced to raise her newborn as a Haas along with the three children Emma eventually had, Ethel, Robert, and Milton.

According to Kay Haas, Larry's birth mother died at the age of forty-two, a victim of poorly treated diabetes. That left Emma, as far as anyone else ever knew, the mother of four children. Nel's child eventually changed his name from Frederick George Haas to Loren "Larry" George Haas, strengthening the family link and honoring his father by seasoning his portion of the family history with a more expedient lie.

Among the siblings, only Larry had been told this story about his birth. Today, some Haas family members still doubt its truth, though some other family secrets follow a like pattern of expedient fictions.

Milton Haas, for instance, was mentioned in his mother's obituary but not in his father's, apparently to remove another embarrassment from history. As a teen, Milton set one of the costliest fires in the history of Buffalo up to that date.[1] Caught, convicted, and diagnosed as a pyromaniac, he spent the rest of his life in a mental institution mere blocks from his family home. His family, however, never saw, heard about, or spoke of him again, except for a seldom-told dark tale and the rarest of secret visits from his brothers, Larry and Robert.

Ethel, on the other hand, was not listed in her mother's obituary (but was named in her father's) though she had become an award-winning, nationally recognized tennis star. Ethel's problem was that stories had circulated through the family grapevine about her then-scandalous lifestyle choice of female romantic partners. Some thought of it as more than unsavory. As a result, Kay as a child was never allowed to be alone in Ethel's presence.

Milton and Ethel were therefor deemed as nonexistent. Family history, as far as possible, was made to comply with carefully crafted lies.

Larry Haas absorbed what he needed of his family's culture. Then, at the age of seventeen, after graduating from Buffalo's Bennett High School (PS 200) in 1934, he left home to set his own course.[2] He had earned pocket money in high school as a milkman touring Buffalo's suburbs six days a week long before sunrise. But now, he took work at better hours for higher pay as a bakery salesman where his father worked, at the Hall Baking Company on Fillmore Avenue in Buffalo. He used that year to devise a ten-year plan for his life. He decided his dreams would be the kind of fiction he could turn into fact. He planned a career ladder of his own design.

Following graduation, Larry audited a business course at the nearby Stratford Commerce School. In the spring of 1935, he enrolled in a one-semester aviation course at the Burgard Vocational School (PS 301), a place to which many aspiring young aviation enthusiasts were gravitating. Burgard's newest addition included a state-of-the-art, approved aviation training facility in a tower atop the school. It contained an aeronautical lecture room and a rooftop platform housing weather bureau and airport instrumentation. Larry devoured the course and studied far beyond its limits.

Then Larry's dreams took a predictable detour for a young man like him. He met a girl. Her name was Dorothy. She was a college student and the daughter of a wealthy Olean, New York, oil man. Larry and Dorothy started dating. She seemed a perfect mate—smart, beautiful, and a talented musician. On their first date, Larry told her he was on the way to someplace special.

"And where might that be?" she asked.

"Up," he said, his voice charged with excitement. "Straight up! The sky's not even the limit." He knew it was true, and she saw it in his eyes. He had that way about him. Nobody could resist it. Least of all, Dorothy. They married in 1937. In awe of her talent, Larry gave Dorothy a finely crafted piano as a wedding present, an instrument Kay still owns today. Kay was born in 1939.

In 1941, with a new family to support, Larry took a job that fit his personality and his needs, but not yet his long-range plans. He signed on with the Household Finance Corporation in Buffalo as a loan salesman. The company had recently invented a trendsetting word in the loan industry: *buymanship*. Larry discovered he had a knack for giving his clients a good case of it. He made borrowers feel like enlightened consumers, people skilled in the art of wise buying. After a private consultation with Larry Haas at Household, his customers had become different people.

Larry's persuasiveness, however, had an unusual quality. If his loans were not actually good for his customers, he would not close the deal. That set him apart from some others in the industry. Though he sometimes stretched the truth by promising to make their dreams come true, he always helped every client fulfill that promise. Larry Haas made what he had learned about truth—its flexibility—pay off for everyone.

The greatest beneficiary of that fact, however, would be his own future.

After only four months, Larry was so successful that he was given management of his own Household Finance branch in Lockport, New York. He was good at it but the work did not scratch his real itch for long. His dreams would not be put off.

Larry resigned from Household in June of 1942. He had convinced the Chevrolet Aviation Engine Corporation in Tonawanda, New York, that a good loan salesman could be an excellent engine test operator. Somehow the connection made sense when he said it. After all, he already had formal training in aviation, didn't he? He worked hard, learned fast, did good work, and made good friends at Chevy as another carefully calculated investment in his future.

After a year, he stepped up the ladder again to work for Glenn Curtiss and the Wright brothers at the Curtiss-Wright Aircraft Corporation of Buffalo. Once again, the more he learned, the more he grew into his ambition.

Dorothy, however, disliked his next scheme. She thought a steady job was better than chasing another dream. Unfortunately, her objection that day revealed a difference in their views about work and ambition that they never fully resolved.

Larry's newest scheme called for a jump from Curtiss to a lower-paying job at the Bell Aircraft plant at nearby Niagara Falls, New York, Bell's so-called Buffalo Plant. The thing was a sure loser in Dorothy's calculations.

"What's Bell got that Curtiss doesn't have? Except lower pay," she carped.

"Opportunity. That's everything."

"You think so? Put a bowl of that on the kitchen table and see if we can eat it for dinner." She folded her arms and bored a hole through him with her eyes.

"Any idea that's not a little dangerous isn't good enough to be called an idea," Larry said. He had worn that Oscar Wilde quote like armor for years.[3]

Larry's sights were now set on the apex of modern American aviation. He knew he could make his wit and his genius serve him well again. After all, the company's founder, Larry Bell, was a man like him; a risk-taker, smart, and bold. Without even finishing high school, Bell had started his own company only six years before with one small order for a gross of aircraft wing panels. Now he was captaining one of the nation's largest, most advanced aircraft corporations.[4] Haas had done his research and he had made his plan. It was, of course, a little dangerous.

He would apply at Bell over Dorothy's objections. The magic ingredient for pulling down this job was one he was uniquely suited to use. It would be his biggest lie ever.

THE SECOND ARRIVAL

On July 3, 1941, Andrei Ivanovich and Antonina Alexievna Schevchenka sat in their cramped kitchen, Moscow, USSR, listening to Stalin's appeal to Soviet citizens in the wake of Germany's June 22 massive, surprise attack on the Soviet Union. Hitler's Operation Barbarossa was the largest invasion force in the history of warfare—more than 3.8 million men-in-arms.

Within Stalin's message, however, Andrei heard the seeds of a plan that would take him, Antonina, and their young son to the United States eleven months later to join the fight for their homeland.[5]

Stalin's years in power brought death and catastrophe beyond measure to his enemies and his countrymen alike. One such disaster, however, is seldom mentioned in popular accounts. Stalin destroyed his own air force by what the few brave critics bold enough to speak of it called his own criminal inaction.

By January of 1941, the Soviet Air Force, the *Voyenno-Vozdushnye Sily* (VVS), was not the most modern military air force in the world, but it was the largest by a count of its aircraft. Six months later, however, it was almost totally demolished when Hitler betrayed Stalin's trust in the ten-year nonaggression pact they had signed on August 23, 1939. Stalin had ignored dozens of warnings from his own intelligence sources revealing Hitler's secret plans to attack.[6] Only a few officials in Moscow knew that damning truth when 170 divisions of Hitler's *Wehrmacht* stormed eastward across the Soviet borders. The Luftwaffe quickly obliterated thousands of Soviet warplanes before even a meager scattering could take to the air.[7]

Because Andrei was a 1939 graduate of the Aviation Institute of Moscow, and now a ranking engineer in the People's Commissariat of Aviation Industry,[8] he was one of the first to know about the predawn German attack and the failure that had allowed it.[9]

Stalin's thirteen-day delay in addressing the citizens of the Soviet Union about the catastrophe must have enraged Andrei even further. And worse, Stalin's call for patriotic zeal from his "brothers and sisters" ended with a threat of death to any citizen who gave less than their all—in case patriotism was not motivating enough.

Beyond all that, however, Andrei blamed Stalin for allowing his carefully planned future to be blown into flaming rubble on VVS airfields. Andrei had seen it for himself.

Three days after the invasion, hidden among the trees on a hillock overlooking an airfield somewhere beyond the Belarusian city of Minsk, Andrei felt his heart pound while he watched in horror. He had made an eight-hundred-kilometer cross-country dash westward from Moscow to see for himself. The airplanes he loved were being blown into flaming, mangled bits along a kilometer of runway under a sky filled with streams of German bombers. Their bombs were blasting new craters where moments before gleaming rows of aircraft had sat grounded by fuel supplies already in flames. He knew the same catastrophe was decimating every other Soviet airfield along three thousand kilometers of borderland stretching from the Baltic northward to Ukraine. Within a few days the world's most numerous air force was withered by four thousand once-flyable airplanes on dozens of ruined airfields.[10]

Andrei knew the Luftwaffe had been flying high-altitude photoreconnaissance missions over Soviet airfields since springtime. Stalin's inept industrial bureaucracy, however, had refused to admit that those flights foreshadowed a military threat. The Commissariat of Aviation and the VVS had been fuming, though privately, at the Moscow-based bureaucrats' impotence. Rollout of more modern aircraft and battle plans to deploy them had fallen years behind schedule, if there had been a schedule at all.

Now Andrei blamed Stalin as much as Hitler. He knew he was not alone in that, but few were bold enough or foolish enough to say so openly.

Back at home now from the western airfields, listening to Stalin's speech, one phrase started its own fire in Andrei's mind. Stalin had said, "All the best people in Europe, America, and Asia . . . sympathize with the Soviet government. In this great war we will have faithful allies in the peoples of Europe and America . . . Our war for the freedom of our fatherland will merge with the struggle of European and American people for independence and for democratic freedom."[11]

So, Andrei decided, he and Antonina would fight in the Great Patriotic War for Russia from America. He could best revenge the smoldering graveyard of his dreams from afar.

Within a year, Andrei Schevchenko's entry documents to the United States declared that he had been born in the Ukrainian city of Kharkov in the USSR and now worked for the Soviet government. Because of that, he identified himself to his new American allies as Russian. He was thirty-five years old by the time the *Myrmidon*, a Polish naval destroyer, sailed past the Statue of Liberty and into the port of New York on Friday morning, June 19, 1942.[12] With him were Antonina and their young son, Andrei Andreevich Schevchenko. This was the wartime posting Andrei had fought his way through the Soviet bureaucracy for—and won.

Andrei's entry permit, registered by the US State Department, identified him as an engineer in the Aviation Department of the Soviet

Purchasing Commission, Amtorg—the Americanization of its Russian name, *Amerikanskaya Torgovlya*.

The Soviet government had deployed Andrei to the assignment he had reckoned best suited his plans: Bell Aircraft at Niagara Falls, New York, where he finally arrived in July. Though Andrei did not know this yet, Bell was also where Larry Haas had finally reached the job he had dreamed of.

Nominally, Andrei inspected the P-39 and P-63 warplanes Russia was buying right off Bell's efficient, high-production assembly lines. But that groundbreaking Bell Aircraft mass-production system itself was one of Andrei's prime targets for theft. Nothing like it had ever been created before in the world. Bell Aircraft was building thousands of airplanes at previously unheard-of rates, auto plants such as Chrysler were turning out tanks and jeeps by the tens of thousands, and shipyards were doubling and quadrupling the shipbuilding capacity of every other production method in the world. The once-prodigious German manufacturing sector, even at its pre-war best, was now being swamped by American mass production methods. Andrei was a Russian engineer embedded in one of America's most productive high-technology plants. His opportunities at Bell promised astounding advances for Soviet manufacturing—if he could harvest them and send them home.

Andrei's post, however, did not carry diplomatic immunity of a kind that could protect him in such a task.[13] He considered that to be a dangerous oversight on the part of his other employer, Soviet intelligence—the employer his entry permit did not name.

In the United States, Andrei planned to remake himself into a suave gentleman of the world. He would use whatever American fashion could offer in creating his persona. He reckoned he would need to project such a presence, even on the plant floor at Bell. He was, after all, representing a nation many American intellectuals of his day believed to be at the vanguard of social and industrial evolution.[14] He accented his well-tailored, pin-striped suits with silk ties printed in art deco designs. He wore expensive, brown and cream, wingtip Oxfords, and in the summertime, a jaunty, white, straw fedora. In winter, he sported a black *ushanka* fur hat with its earflaps tied back "ski-style" no matter how biting the wind. Rather than the traditional rabbit or muskrat, however, Andrei's winter hat looked more like mink. He credited the Siberians with that fine innovation.

Andrei's demeanor came to match his style. He was well-spoken, urbane, and apparently used to exercising authority. He seemed at ease in high-ranking circles. As his English improved, Andrei deliberately slid his accent toward the exotic.

But he had not asked to be a spy. His passion was for aircraft. Nevertheless, he had been informed that every Soviet citizen in a foreign country was expected to report back anything of strategic value. That imperative was formalized for Andrei by being appointed to a high rank in the Soviet intelligence service, the *Narodny Komissariat Vnutrennikh Del* (NKVD), the People's Commissariat of Internal Affairs. This assignment created a dilemma. A spy's best camouflage is to look and act as unremarkable as possible, to hide in plain sight. Andrei's legal work at Bell, however, required him to fit in seamlessly with the upper echelons of capitalist society. He resolved his dilemma with a decision to look entirely unlike a spy. He managed to look too good to be one.

Of the two kinds of spies recognized since the profession began—legal and illegal spies—Andrei was to be the legal kind.[15] He had a legal reason to enter the United States and legal work to do. Schevchenko's job as an aircraft engineer[16] posing as a purchasing agent was to cover his attempts to steal what he could not buy. His espionage work was to be secret, deniable, and beyond legal restraint.[17]

Every Soviet citizen in the United States had this second job of observer-reporter.[18] But it takes more than orders to make one able to do a more advanced version of the job that called for special skills and temperament. This obedience-based model at the heart of Soviet espionage recruitment in that day was bound to backfire.

Illegal spies are shadowy figures who infiltrate the country undercover without permission. They remain unknown and unseen. Only their handi-work—things that explode, collapse, or fail spectacularly, intelligence that reaches an enemy's hands, or key people who die mysteriously—eventually hints at their existence. Sometimes they are "sleepers." They sit tight, harmless, doing nothing unusual for years until a long-awaited command morphs them into dangerous operatives. Sometimes they pirate closely held secrets that expose weaknesses even more dangerous than munitions and bombs.

Larry Haas's first meeting with Andrei happened in 1943.[19] It quickly grew awkward. Each man saw the other as disagreeable. In time, though, they discovered reasons to become friends. Larry and Andrei eventually traveled different paths professionally, but those reasons kept their friendship alive, though for both of them it was based on lies.[20]

Andrei looked enough like Larry that he could have been a family member, maybe a close cousin. Larry was twenty-eight years old, of average stature, though with a wiry, muscular physique. He had started to bald prematurely and looked closer to Andrei's age of thirty-five. People found the mischievous twinkle in Larry's eye and his ready smile as charming in an all-American way as Andrei's was seductive in the Continental manner. Larry dressed more casually. He could make any business suit look good, but when he did not need one, his style was more relaxed. Larry combined a folksy nature with an easy confidence that made him remarkably persuasive any time he needed to be. That skill was, of course, a family trait he always brought to work with him.

Larry Haas was not the first person at Bell Aircraft targeted by Schevchenko in his probe for confidential information.

Leona Vivian Franey[21] may have been the first. She was born on February 14, 1912. She had worked as a librarian at the Technical High School public library in Scranton, Pennsylvania, between September 1930 and July 1942. Based on that experience, she signed on as the first chief technical librarian at the Bell Aircraft plant on July 3, and she married Joseph John Franey on July 31, 1942.

Joseph was born on July 11, 1911, at Clarks Summit, Pennsylvania. He worked at the Glen Alden Coal Company in Scranton from 1929 until he was injured in 1932. From then until 1942, he worked as a truck driver and school custodian. But on May 19, 1942, he unknowingly made himself one of Schevchenko's future targets by taking a position at the Hooker Electrochemical Company in Buffalo, New York. Hooker contributed to the Manhattan Project by supplying chemicals used in building the world's first atomic bomb.[22]

In October or November 1943, Schevchenko had met Leona for the first time at the Bell library. On his first visit, Leona impressed him by spelling his name correctly, translating Cyrillic characters to English letters. He took a liking to her and developed an interest in her and her staff of four. He appreciated their kindness in the small number of ordinary library requests he made at first.[23] To express his thanks, Andrei gave Leona a few small gifts of candy and perfume.

At this time, Leona considered him unconventional but unremarkable. That would soon change.

CHAPTER TWO

One Big Lie

On Wednesday morning, March 31, 1943, Larry Haas opened his interview at the Bell Aircraft personnel office with his simple but carefully crafted lie.

"I have a university degree in aeronautical engineering," Larry told the hiring agent, "and Bell Aircraft is the right place for me. My name is Haas, Larry G. Haas."

Manpower was short and hiring practices were sometimes lax in terms of resume checking. Good workers had become hard to find with WWII raging on two fronts, now in its twenty-seventh month since Pearl Harbor.[1] Lawrence D. Bell, America's newest upstart aviation genius, had discovered, as had all aircraft manufacturers, that he needed more men than he could find.[2] He had to staff an entirely new, eight-million-square-foot aircraft plant beside the Niagara Falls airfield.[3] The world's appetite for his war-planes appeared insatiable.

Bell made up for the wartime manpower drought, at least in part, with his version of Rosie the Riveter. According to company archives,[4] as early as 1941, the workforce at the Buffalo plant averaged approximately 8,500 male workers and 150 female workers, though by 1945 the proportion of female workers far outpaced that number. Bell treated the women in his plants with pay equity and fair working conditions previously unknown in American industry. Whether this was purely magnanimous or meant to please their husbands on the battlefield and the US Army, is unclear. Nevertheless, men were still in high demand. Larry Haas made sure Bell's hiring agent would take special note of him.

Larry also bet that Bell was already looking beyond wartime needs. He was sure Bell was quietly, if not secretly, designing the next generation of superplanes to sell to the world. The commerce of peacetime would demand such aircraft. Larry planned on being part of that.

The words "university degree" and "aeronautical engineering" occurring in the same sentence made the personnel agent stop shuffling his papers and sit up straighter. His morning had just gotten better.

"I design power plants for airplanes," Larry said with calm self-assurance. "I build fast engines."

The agent picked up a freshly sharpened pencil, yanked a pad of lined paper out of a pile of forms perched on the corner of his desk, and nearly knocked it all to the floor. He wanted all the details he could get as fast as he could take them down.

Larry leaned in closer. He glanced right and left and spoke in a stage whisper as if he were sharing a deep conspiracy. He *could not* say more. His work at Curtiss-Wright had been so confidential, he shared, that it qualified as military service. Larry looked at the nameplate on the man's desk and said he was sure Mr. Parker understood such things.

Mr. Parker nodded knowingly. He was well aware such confidential work was also happening at Bell. It would also surely qualify Mr. Haas for a continued III-B deferment.[5] He opened a desk drawer, pulled out a file with a bright red tab, opened it, and ran his finger down a long list of names and numbers. After a thoughtful pause, he looked up with disappointment in his eyes. He apologized. It seemed Bell did not just now have an opening in any department that needed a man with Haas's qualifications.

But Larry already knew that. His research had also revealed that the kind of jobs that were actually open here would not need a check for college records. Once onboard in any position, Larry reckoned, he would be able to move up from within in a way that would by then make record checks appear unnecessary.

Larry simply smiled. He told Mr. Parker not to worry. He would in fact be delighted to take any job that would help with Bell's manpower shortage. That was fine music to Mr. Parker's ears. And then, Larry assured him, when *his* job opened up in aeronautics he would already be there. Didn't that sound reasonable?

Mr. Parker was not used to such a helpful applicant. He thought for a moment and decided that sounded just fine.

To seal the deal Larry filled out the paperwork for the kind of engineering position he wanted, just to save time later, of course. They decided to leave the transfer date open and file it away until needed. Whenever Bell and the army air forces needed "Please-call-me-Larry" Haas, he and his new friend Mr. Parker would be ready for them. No need to monkey with reporting a different draft status during such a short bridge between jobs.

Mr. Parker beamed. He spread the right papers across his desk. Larry printed and signed his name wherever Mr. Parker pointed.

Larry Haas had adapted his skill at imparting the *buymanship* he had perfected at Household Finance to one more customer. And just as he had also done at Household a few years back, he knew he would make this lie bear the honest fruit it promised.

On April 14, 1943, Larry took a service trainee job on the night shift in Bell's new aircraft plant.[6] He worked fast every night to finish his simple tasks and then headed for the plant's brand-new technical library. The library was not yet well guarded, except by Leona Franey and her small staff of librarians during the day. Larry read every textbook and technical journal he could find on aviation engineering. He smuggled the most complicated material home on weekends, where he could read all day by ignoring sleep if necessary. Larry also mined the library's confidential reports from NACA, the War Department, the Bureau of Ordinance, and whatever manufacturers of guided missiles with which Bell was collaborating. He was sure the file cabinets marked "Authorized Personnel Only" would soon be backed up with a lock, so he read fast.

One night in a small workroom at the back of the library, Larry discovered something that stunned him. He had only imagined its existence at Bell, but, in an instant, it raised his career plans to a new level. The files he found were stamped in bold, red capital letters TOP SECRET and prominently marked "Property of General Electric Corporation."[7] Larry opened the top file to page one. It unfolded to twice its width. He saw an engine of a sort he had never seen before. But unfamiliar as it was, he instantly knew he was looking at a powerful jet engine fully depicted in an exploded diagram detailed down to its rivets and wiring. Jet power was the dreamed-of holy grail of his age in the field of aviation. Larry had heard only rumors of its development for American warplanes. Before him lay proof that the real thing existed. His hands shook as he discovered Bell was working in collaboration with GE to build and fly America's first jet-propelled aircraft, most assuredly for use in the war. He carefully left everything exactly as he found it and stepped away imagining another new future for himself at Bell. It was beyond anything he had even dreamed of finding there.

The next day, Leona Franey was delighted to help the young man who had lingered after his night shift just to meet her. Leona could tell he was a rising star in Bell's firmament in spite of his maintenance uniform. Larry found her easy to engage in conversation about the library's holdings and how useful Bell's engineers had already found it. She explained that even the on-site Russian P-39 inspector, Mr. Schevchenko, had found it helpful since he arrived at Bell about two years before. More recently he had also sent his assistant, Nicolai Ostrovsky, to ask for general reading matter on aviation. Mr. Haas was certainly welcome to do the same.

But sensing a need for caution, Leona also told Larry that two gentlemen from the government had recently come to ask her about the Russian. They requested that she and her staff politely decline any such future requests from Mr. Schevchenko. They should tell him only that the material is out at this time. But she did not explain the full reason to Larry beyond the simple fact that certain material was for Bell engineers alone. The deeper problem, as Leona explained to the government men, was that Schevchenko's requests had escalated to reports stamped "Confidential" and "Secret." Sometimes his requests went so far as to include accession numbers beyond anything yet in Bell's own files. He wanted papers on swept-wing designs and supersonic research that neither she nor Bell's highest echelon of scientists had yet seen. Her suspicions deepened when the Russian's requests came with gifts of expensive chocolates, fine perfume, dinners, and theater tickets for her staff, herself, and her husband.[8]

Larry, on the other hand, enjoyed Leona's kind assistance. He had not, after all, asked for prohibited files or brought her gifts. He was simply a nice young man who wanted to study. Of course, unknown to Leona, Larry continued to supplement her help with his own nightly expeditions into her otherwise closely held domain.

Within a month Larry was ready to make his next carefully calculated move. He made a hard-to-refuse offer to his supervisor. If he could teach an in-house class in aeronautics for engineers and aircraft designers—a course focused on the assembly-line dynamics—it might strengthen the link between assembly-line workers and the engineers. Larry assured his supervisor that Mr. Parker in personnel already knew he was a university-trained aeronautical engineer just waiting for the right opening. Larry, of course, now had the lingo to go with his claim. Mr. Parker, of course, saw no need for further background checks because Larry's supervisor liked the idea.

Larry's answer came quickly. He was soon promoted to full-time technical instructor, class two, specializing in airplane power plants in the Bell Service Division.[9] Larry had employed his remarkable knack for learning in order to teach the most technical material as if he'd known all of it for years. After that, even beyond his few years at Bell, nobody ever questioned Larry's credibility or his credentials. He was living up to the promise of his one big lie. Honest con men always did that.

By the end of 1944, Larry's students included Stalin's Falcons, the elite, eager, and highly intelligent young Soviet fighter pilots who had been sent to the Unites States to learn all they possibly could before flying Bell's most lethal weapons into battle. They were becoming unparalleled killers in Bell's "Cannon on Wings." In their hands, the P-39 was remarkably deadly, even against Germany's most decorated air aces.

Soviet pilots found the P-39 highly effective against the Messerschmitt Bf 109, for example, and often found them superior to the Focke-Wulf FW 190 in the low altitude combat typical of the air war over western Russia. The Russian air group commander, Alexander Pokryshkin, infamous and feared among German fliers, however, was under intense pressure from Moscow to convert his regiment to the newest Soviet fighters, in particular to the Yak-3 and the La-5. But Pokryshkin hated the La-5 and complained that the Yak-3's firepower was too weak. He also reportedly held a strong personal dislike for aircraft designer Yakovlev. As a result, Pokryshkin and his fliers refused to give up their Bell P-39 Airacobras. They did, however, have to accept later Lend-Lease agreements prohibiting their use of the newer enhanced P-39, Bell's P-63 Kingcobras, against the Luftwaffe. The 63s were restricted for later use only against Japan.[10]

Stalin's Falcons had learned to kill by watching real falcons, hunters that dropped out of the sky fast and unseen from high and behind their victims. Using that as a guide, the diving Russian pilots blasted their prey out of the air with the P-39's armor-piercing T-9 cannon-fire and .50 caliber machine guns.[11] They outgunned the Luftwaffe every day and made headlines for themselves in the United States and in Russia. Soviet pilots racked up the highest individual kill totals by any US fighter type flown by any air force in the world.[12] They held off wave after wave of Nazi planes while the Soviet aviation industry was heroically rebuilding itself like the phoenix of legend.

In this way, after Germany's blitzkrieg invasion of the Soviet Union, Bell's aircraft fought blistering battles of vengeance against the Luftwaffe. Larry Haas's pride in his new role was topped only by his respect for these young Falcons.[13] He joined them in analyzing their combat experiences with Bell engineers for continual upgrades of the P-39.

Early in 1945 Larry took one more step up his new career ladder by joining Bell's top secret jet-power research team.

The jet age was about to take off. Strategic planners around the world knew that the first nation to rule the skies could dominate the planet. Larry knew he could help make that happen. Eventually, Andrei Schevchenko came to know that about Larry, too.

Larry had turned his one big lie into the truth. And he had kept his word to Dorothy.

Unfortunately, he could not have imagined the danger that lurked behind his dreams.

CHAPTER THREE

First Meeting

"I dislike Russians in general, and I dislike Schevchenko in particular,"[1] Larry Haas told Larry Bell at the end of the day on August 4, 1943. His first meeting with Schevchenko did not end in good chemistry.

The day had dawned hot and humid. By eleven that morning, Haas's classroom reached ninety-five degrees and he released his people—flight engineers, pilots, line supervisors—a few minutes early. The empty room already felt cooler.

Then the room filled again with Larry Bell and a half-dozen guests. One appeared to be a well-dressed businessman. The others were distinguished VVS officers in crisp, white Soviet Air Force uniforms decorated with enough medals to make a fruit salad jealous.

Bell introduced the two men, Mr. Andrei Ivanovich Schevchenko and Mr. Loren George Haas, with a formality probably meant to signal to Haas that this was very important. Bell placed his hand on the smartly dressed man's shoulder in a friendly manner, though Larry thought he saw a flicker of annoyance in the Russian's eyes.

Bell explained to the man that Mr. Haas was training Russian pilots and Bell maintenance engineers.

Schevchenko barely nodded and looked down at his watch.

Haas disliked him already and decided to test the man's mettle. He pointedly ignored the honorific and the usual courtesy of surnames.

"Andry, nice to meet you." He gave Schevchenko a big American smile and a hearty handshake, clasping the Russian's hand in both of his just a little longer than he reckoned a dapper European would appreciate.

Schevchenko replied with curt thanks in heavily accented English. He returned a reserved smile and gave Larry no more than glancing eye contact while turning to look at a cut-away model of an Allison V-1710-85 V-12 engine, the P-39's current power plant, on a stand beside Haas. He seemed to wonder if Haas's hands might have contaminated him with engine grease. Clearly, he considered Haas a technician of a lower order.

Bell knew Haas well and understood his impromptu calibration of Schevchenko's personal style. He looked away and tried not to smile, but he quickly re-stressed the *Mr.* in Schevchenko's name and explained that he was the Soviet Union's purchasing agent and inspector of P-39s. Mr. Stalin had assigned him to see that his purchases met all specifications, exactly, and on time.[2] Probably dreading Haas's reaction, Bell cleared his throat and added that Mr. Schevchenko, along with his assistant and two of the accompanying officers, would occupy the office right next to Haas's in the Technical Maintenance Department.

Haas decided it would be best at this point to fall in line, but he could not resist one more nudge. He had met a few other Soviet dignitaries and planned to enjoy disarming this one.

"You can relax, Mr. Schevchenko. After all, Mr. Bell and I know just how to build good airplanes. You needn't hardly get your hands dirty over the matter."

Schevchenko answered with a curt nod and wasted no more of his poor English on Haas. He turned dismissively back to Bell. "We should now retire to my office."

Haas, now brushed off, disposed of Schevchenko in his own mind as arrogant and unimportant. Calibration complete. Larry accepted it as mutual.

Schevchenko labelled Haas at best only a *poleznyi durak*—a useful idiot.

Schevchenko told Bell that Colonels Kostiuk and Guryev, indicating two of the young officers wearing the well-tailored, carefully pressed, medal-bedecked white uniforms, would accompany them to his office.[3] Their agenda would focus on adjustments Russia needed to Bell's airplane delivery systems, especially on the Iranian route.

Bell, as if with an afterthought, turned back to Haas. "I am sure," he said with a barely detectable wink of amusement, "that you will be delighted to know Mr. Schevchenko is working hard with an English coach to prepare himself for his partnership with you."

Haas's double-take asked his question before he could speak.

"It is for the Russian pilots, Mr. Haas. They need more detailed technical instruction. Mr. Schevchenko will help with that. He is an aeronautical engineer. He can translate your technical terms into Russian."

"Oh, fine." Larry's smile this time was more restrained.

Haas heard a paragraph inside Bell's explanation. His ground-school for Soviet pilots ferrying P-39s from Bell's plant to Russia usually relied on a few comrade-pilots who spoke some English, though often broken. The classroom babble that sometimes followed a sentence or two of instructions had become a common learning event. Haas had almost forgotten how annoying it had become. He was used to it and the outcome was always good. The run-up to production in Bell's new plant in October of 1942 had been so hectic that this language glitch was only now being addressed.

Andrei Schevchenko was the Soviet government's answer to Larry Haas's problem.

"I will send you my class schedule," Larry said, adjusting quickly to this new reality. Then, just because it amused him, he added, "Be punctual. Classes *will* start on time and the sorties *will* launch on time."

Schevchenko stiffened but agreed and added, "I have a letter from General Secretary Stalin. It creates all the urgency we needed."[4]

"Certainly. I have read that letter, too." He enjoyed the surprise on Schevchenko's face.

Stalin's letter, addressed to President Roosevelt, had been forwarded from Washington to Larry Bell in October 1942, just as the Bell assembly lines started to roll. A copy, quickly dubbed "The Letter," went to each of Bell's executive staff, the Military Contracts Department, the division chiefs in production, and the shipping expeditor. A copy even found its way to Leona Franey's bulletin board, where Haas found it on one of his late nighttime forays.

The copy looked like a neatly retyped excerpt of a longer communication.

Joseph Vissarionovich Stalin   October 7, 1942
General Secretary
Central Committee, Communist Party of the Soviet Union

Mr. Theodore Roosevelt
President, United States of America

[In part] the difficulties of delivery are reported to be due primarily to shortage of shipping. To remedy the shipping situation the Soviet Government would be prepared to agree to a certain curtailment of US arms deliveries to the Soviet Union. We should be prepared temporarily fully to renounce deliveries of tanks, guns, ammunition, pistols, etc.

At the same time, however, we are badly in need of increased deliveries of modern fighter aircraft—such as the [P-39] Airacobras—and certain other supplies. It should be borne in mind that the Kittyhawk is no match for the modern German fighter . . . War experience has shown that the bravest troops are helpless unless protected against air attack . . .

Joseph Stalin

Haas now reckoned that Schevchenko needed him more than he needed Schevchenko. He would not play up to Schevchenko's ego or his rank. Nevertheless, out of necessity the two men did start to develop a civil business relationship.[5] For all their talk about proletarian equality, though, Haas found that Schevchenko, like all the other high-ranking Soviet communists he had met, was far more status conscious than most Americans. Haas planned to enjoy bucking that mindset, though he did not yet fully understand the forces he would be bucking.

Over the next few months, Schevchenko confirmed Haas's hunch about who-needed-whom. Schevchenko frequently visited Haas in the Technical Maintenance Department to request improvements and modifications to the P-39s. The Russian government's purchase of the upgraded P-63s gave Schevchenko even more reasons to visit Haas.

———◆———

Before setting out from Russia to the United States, Schevchenko would have been trained, if only briefly, at the Second Moscow State Pedagogical Institute of Foreign Languages operated within the Foreign Countries Studies military school. Espionage and subversion would have been among skills he was to apply at Bell Aircraft.

Nothing in that training, however, prepared him for the changes that were coming.

CHAPTER FOUR

An Invisible Network

While Andrei was learning his way around Bell Aircraft, Larry was starting to sense the forces taking shape around him. Their worlds were growing more complex than either man yet knew. The US-Soviet alliance against Germany was becoming riddled with rivalries. Their still-unspoken enmity was fueled by incompatible ideologies and nascent jockeying for postwar supremacy. As allies, they made strange bedfellows.

In November 1941, less than a month before the United States entered World War II, a Yugoslav-American communist named Steve Nelson, deeply engaged in international Soviet espionage, offered his American communist comrades a prediction.

> Roosevelt and Churchill are fine men, but we cannot expect them to promote socialism. We know there will be quarrels, but now we must fight Hitlerism-Fascism. You may have to take guns against the United States and England later.[1]

The stage being set for that battle included Bell Aircraft. As an opening salvo, Andrei Schevchenko was placed at the point of a Soviet spear aimed at targets inside Bell.

Schevchenko, however, started his work as a flawed instrument. The US State Department routinely gathered intelligence, though mostly of a superficial nature, on all Soviet officials before they arrived. By the time *Myrmidon* sailed into New York Harbor, they knew from his entry documents that Schevchenko had a degree in aeronautical engineering from the Aviation Institute of Moscow and had served in the People's Commissariat of Aviation Industry. Before Andrei set sail, however, someone else was already looking over his shoulder.

Schevchenko's firstborn, a son named Arseniy,[2] was left in Moscow to receive a good "Leninist education." Soviet officials assigned anywhere overseas knew not to call this arrangement by its other name: hostage. Stalin called it loyalty insurance.

Within Andrei's first year in the United States, he was undermined by his own hierarchy. The suspicion-ridden nature of Soviet society under Stalin also tainted the culture of Soviet citizens living in the United States. On August 7, 1943, FBI director Hoover received an anonymous letter written in Russian on a Cyrillic-keyed typewriter. The letter warned that America's staunch ally, the Soviet Union, was engaged in military-industrial espionage against US interests. Among its many disclosures the letter writer identified Andrei Ivanovich Schevchenko as an NKVD agent stealing America's secret aircraft plans[3] and working as an assistant to Vasily Zarubin,[4] the Soviet intelligence *rezident* from 1941 to 1944 and Second Secretary at the Soviet Embassy.[5] Internal evidence in the letter was insufficient to conclusively identify its writer. Years later, though, he was identified as Vassili Mironov, a victim of schizophrenia who was eventually tried, convicted, and hospitalized in Moscow but later shot for ongoing attempts to contact the US Embassy.[6]

As Hoover saw the matter, though the letter matched his suspicions about the Soviets, it held little solid, actionable evidence against Schevchenko and the others at Amtorg. Nothing in the letter would stand up in court. Hoover could only pass the information to the War Department and wait for them to act. He did, however, quietly raise the alert level at Bell and started to strategize about catching Schevchenko in the act of military-industrial espionage.

The FBI field office in Buffalo, due to its proximity to the Bell plant, was assigned to find hard evidence. That office was new to such work. At this point, German and Japanese espionage had mainly occupied their time. Surveillance of an ally was different from watching enemies. The Buffalo agents quickly made up for their inexperience with diligence, enthusiasm, and surprisingly few slipups.

The US Congress had been warned only a few years earlier by US Naval Intelligence and the War Department that "there is a great deal of espionage going on in the US, particularly in obtaining secret information concerning our aircraft . . . It is time that both the Army and the Navy exerted themselves more to neutralize this condition . . . the joint chiefs report Soviet espionage networks are far-reaching, well organized, and the personnel well trained."[7] In 1941, the FBI's New York City office reported that "employees at the Amtorg Trading Corporation are active in stealing industrial plans, blueprints, and other critical data."[8]

As the FBI became more aware of Amtorg's role in fronting Soviet spies, they started to take action. In a 1944 "black bag job," for example, agents broke into Amtorg's offices and stole reams of messages written in Russian along with their encrypted equivalents. That started to open secret Soviet communications to successful FBI scrutiny.[9]

By the time Schevchenko had done what he could to befriend Leona Franey, he had already been under FBI observation for some time, though at first only in a cursory and episodic manner.[10] They did not yet know that Andrei's twice-a-week English lessons were helping him build a spy network that crisscrossed the American aviation industry. In spite of Andrei's inexperience in espionage, his administrative skills helped him extend deep and dangerous tendrils into at least a half-dozen strategically important aircraft plants across the Northeast.[11]

As early as February 1945, FBI agents assigned to follow suspected Soviet XY-line[12] operatives like Schevchenko credited him with ten intelligence sources.[13] Andrei's network had come to include 1917 Russian émigré, aeronautical engineering professor Alexander Nicolas Petroff[14] at Curtiss-Wright Aircraft in Williamsville, New York, and Michael K. Cham, previously at Douglas, where a number of other employees assisted Schevchenko. Another Curtiss-Wright aeronautical engineer named Bill Pinsly fed Schevchenko warplane intelligence through the end of 1944. Andrei also ran sub-agents at North American, Boeing, Grumman, and Republic Aircraft, where a rocket engineer codenamed B (identity unknown) gave Schevchenko information on the JB-2 Robot bomb, similar to the German V-1 flying buzz-bomb.[15]

Within Bell, Schevchenko wanted to cultivate two more sub-agents, Leona Franey and Larry Haas. They would join the head of Bell's Aircraft Service Department, A. L. Fornoff, Haas's immediate superior, a man of Russian parentage, who spent considerable time with Schevchenko professionally and personally.[16] William Plourde and another Bell engineer named Harold Smeltzer, a Bell division chief (referred to as "Armor" in New York-to-Moscow radio traffic decoded later), and a Bell plastics engineer named George Beiser[17] also provided intelligence to Schevchenko. Vladimir Markovin was a Bell research aerodynamicist who accepted Andrei's tried-and-true assurance that, "You will be helping America's best and strongest ally in its hour of greatest need. How can that be wrong?"[18]

Schevchenko also contacted a former Bell employee (whose name was redacted from records) and entertained him on several occasions. Schevchenko contacted him by letter on June 14, 1945, and asked him to conduct "an industrial survey of the Buffalo area." Schevchenko said he was "primarily interested in high temperature-resistant steels which could be used in the manufacture of turbine wheels on jet propulsion units." He promised to "pay all expenses incidental to the survey and pay a commission on products later purchased by Russia from manufacturers included in the survey."[19] Schevchenko was happy to tie his country to future financial obligations, and he portrayed himself as one man who could make those promises bear fruit.

Schevchenko often moved about Bell with a uniformed Soviet officer named Nicolai Pavlovich Ostrovsky, whom Leona Franey had met at her library. In addition, an engineer named Vladimir Nikolaevich Mazurin,[20] later known to be an undercover NKVD officer, was also employed at the Bell plant. His connection to Schevchenko was strengthened by the fact that he was a 1936 graduate of the Moscow Aviation Institute, Schevchenko's alma mater, and may have known him in Moscow before the war.

Schevchenko's intelligence network, therefore, was broad and highly organized for gathering military and industrial information. He carefully kept his sub-agents ignorant of each other. If one collaborator defected or was caught and interrogated, others could not be revealed. Schevchenko compartmentalized his assets.

Between Schevchenko's arrival in the United States in 1942 and the end of 1944, while he was developing his network, there is little evidence that "Subject Schevchenko" knew he was under FBI surveillance.

The FBI's surveillance, however, soon paid off. Schevchenko was sighted meeting socially with Larry Haas. Haas was immediately suspected as another Schevchenko sub-agent and targeted for investigation. If the FBI found Haas clean, he would be their candidate for a counterintelligence agent. If Haas was not clean, they planned to coerce him into the role anyway under threat of exposure.

Larry did not know he had already stepped into a trap.

CHAPTER FIVE

The Long Seduction

Within his first few months at Bell Aircraft, Schevchenko went to New York City at least three times. He met there with his mentor in spy craft, his control officer, Vasily Mikhailovich Zarubin.[1] Zarubin had served as Soviet intelligence *rezident*, chief of station in New York City, based in the Soviet Consulate since the autumn of 1941. Zarubin's wife, Elizabeth, served with him. Zarubin had already been an illegal for many years in a number of European countries. As an NKVD officer, he oversaw the infamous Katyn Forest massacre of twenty-two thousand Polish military officers and intelligentsia taken as Soviet prisoners of war. The anonymous letter to Hoover had also accused Zarubin of that atrocity.

Zarubin was by nature a crude, ill-mannered man who used obscenities and street language freely. He was unpopular with the other Soviet agents in New York City.[2] He was recalled to Moscow late in 1944 to face charges (later exonerated) of collaborating with the Germans. In his absence, Anatoly Gorsky, another experienced NKVD officer, took the reins. But he was also recalled to Moscow along with Iskhak Abdulovich Akhmerov,[3] a highly successful illegal. Stepan Zakharovich Apresyan, the next legal *rezident* (early 1944 to spring of 1945), then controlled Schevchenko. Apresyan, however, was very different. He was well educated and well liked for his easygoing temper and kindness, and for his skill as a linguist.

In 1942, when Schevchenko reached New York City, he would have reported to Zarubin, but it seems unlikely he met many illegals operating there. Zarubin reported directly to Stalin at Moscow Center on both the atomic bomb and jet-power intelligence. Schevchenko would be Zarubin's man for jets.[4] That placed Schevchenko only two steps away from Stalin. Failure would surely be fatal.

Schevchenko, who had not asked to be a spy, would have found Zarubin formidable and Zarubin would have thought Schevchenko unsuited to the role. Schevchenko would need a crash course in reality and a hard shock to drive his temperament in new and darker directions.

The old-fashioned morality he had learned from his parents, he discovered, was to be reframed as sabotage to the conduct of his job. He was now in a land of enemies disguised as allies. He must trust no one and use friendship only as a tool. He must never befriend an enemy, except in appearance. Anything else could cost him everything, including his life. Schevchenko soon found himself living a nightmare under two death sentences. He had to kill the man he was—or risk death by not doing so.

Schevchenko now had to assume all three of his real identities: NKVD officer, illegal spy, and legal employee of Amtorg—almost totally unlike the life path he had once planned. Among his new skills would be ruthless exploitation of an enemy's weaknesses. He now understood how to use a lesson learned in Moscow.

> Do not mistake American patriotism for ideology. Few Americans understand their own founding principles. Capitalism makes wealth their highest virtue. Use money freely to motivate cooperation. They will mistake it for a sign of friendship. It will override weak scruples and overpower suspicions.

Another lesson came from a message Akhmerov had once sent to Moscow Center.

> In the United States, the more you engage in all kinds of commercial and financial business, the more respect you command and the better your social position. Here a semi-literate businessman looks down on a professor.[5]

Andrei also now knew he would never design or build the aircraft he had dreamed of. His life had become a tool in someone else's hands.

One lesson in spy craft remained, but this one he already knew verbatim. It was the technique called "the long seduction." It was already ancient by the time twentieth-century Soviet spies adopted it. The method called for patience and flexibility, though the latter could be as risky as it was useful.

Andrei should have been a natural at seduction. In his teens he had fancied himself a poet and tried out the life of a wandering troubadour. He trekked through the Russian Caucasus for two years and lived at a *tsyganskiy lager*, a gypsy camp. With stars in his eyes, he wrote a torrid romance novel about gypsy life and dashed off reams of love poetry to one particular woman. Then he learned that a man who makes love to a gypsy woman must without fail marry her. He barely escaped with his diary and his balalaika. Thus, he thought the art of seduction was safely behind him. But not necessarily so for Soviet spies in the 1940s.

Schevchenko now saw seduction in a new light. Though it would have to be modified to succeed, it could be a tool of spy craft. It was akin to persuasion, but more powerful and possibly more dangerous. Seduction attracts its victim to new beliefs and daring acts to please the seducer. But if needed, coercion could lock it in. That corruption of the art, Schevchenko now knew, was one he might have to master. And Bell Aircraft was the place to find his targets.

Schevchenko reviewed the detailed steps he had been taught. They turned an experience he had once thought romantic into a cold, mechanical system.

1. First Meeting. Have a respected party introduce you to a target, or meet the target "accidentally" in a cordial setting. Create rapport. Make the "First Date" in this meeting. For all encounters, remember:

   a. *Vinum amicus facit.* (Wine makes friends.)
   b. *In vino veritas.* (Wine reveals truth.)

2. First Date. Social contact only. Include a nonthreatening third person known to the target. Observe your target's likes, dislikes, views, and any common interests you may find. Admire, don't flatter. Plan a second date.
3. Second Date. Include the third person again. Nourish common interests with your target or find a common enemy.
4. Third Date. No third person this time. Probe interests more deeply, be a confidant. Reveal that target has something you want. Repeat these meetings until a strong bond forms.
5. Disconnect. Pull away. Make the target sense a loss and come looking for you.
6. Accept rapprochement at target's request. Confirm a new, stronger friendship.
7. Make small asks that bend only some minor rules. Repeat until you can escalate to violations that can be easily justified or rationalized.

Appeal to adventure, higher values, and so on. Reward with money, sex, drugs, praise, and the like.

8. Make the "Big Ask." Promise bigger rewards.
9. Continue rewards if there are more events. Threaten withdrawal of rewards, blackmail, or deadly force if withdrawal or the possibility of betrayal are suspected.
10. Coercion can replace cooperation if necessary at this point. Make the threat credible and severe.

This corruption of seduction troubled Andrei. But he also saw a way out of this emotional quandary.

Andrei had come to the United States to fight for Russia, to defend his homeland from total destruction. That was the work of a soldier. In that, a spy was also a soldier as truly as anyone in his Red Army on a battlefield.

In that moment, Andrei saw the possibility of spy craft as a noble work. He could keep his morality and ethics intact, merely locked away until better days. Andrei was, just then, reborn as a Soviet spy. Whether his sincerity could make up for missing skills, however, remained to be seen.

CHAPTER SIX

Seducing Leona

Andrei Schevchenko focused his intentions on Leona Franey.[1] Just before Christmas of 1943, Schevchenko asked Leona Franey for a list of engineering textbooks appropriate to a technical aeronautical library. Leona drew up a list of one hundred books available to the general public. She believed that Captain Ostrovsky delivered that list to the Soviet Embassy in Washington. Andrei thanked her with a small box of chocolates.[2]

Seduction in the classical sense of romantic entanglement, however, was not part of Andrei's strategy. Leona had a husband who Andrei thought could also be of use, so his seduction had to be a package deal. He planned to seduce them through friendship and money as he understood their roles in American society.

Andrei ramped up his game in June of 1944 with lavish entertainments, big spending, and idyllic job prospects in the coming, postwar Soviet paradise. He asked for little in return at first, but a hint of escalation was soon to appear.

———◆———

On the evening of June 6, 1944, FBI agents of the Buffalo field office, while engaged in routine surveillance, saw Schevchenko dining with a man and woman at Lorenzo's Restaurant in Buffalo. That sighting interested the agents. At 9:05 p.m., after their dinner with Schevchenko, the agents followed the couple to a house on Niagara Road in Bergholtz (Wheatfield), New York. They noted that the house was near the Niagara Falls International Airport, perhaps a location with strategic interest to Schevchenko. The couple parked their car, a 1940 Buick coupe, New York license 1944, 4B 92-12, and entered their home. At that point, Joe and Leona Franey became people of interest to the FBI.

About a month later, on Monday, July 10, Andrei made a social call at the Bell technical library. He wanted to talk to Leona about a dream job he envisioned for her future—a wonderful technical librarian job he would create just for her in Russia—but after the war was over, naturally. In fact, he saw such bright prospects ahead for her that he asked to share his vision with her husband.

Two weeks later, on Wednesday, July 26, Schevchenko hosted the Franeys at another dinner at Lorenzo's. He treated them to a sumptuous meal and cocktails at an exorbitant cost of fifteen dollars. He avoided business talk throughout the evening, except for one peculiar request. He asked Leona if her library had a copy of the Manufacturers Catalog published by the Carborundum Company in Niagara Falls. He said Russia was unable to get contracts with Carborundum and asked whether Leona knew any employees there. If she would just help him in this simple matter, he would be most grateful.

Only five days later, Schevchenko hosted the Franeys for dinner again, this time at Louie's Restaurant in Niagara Falls. On this occasion the Buffalo FBI agents caught them on film.[3] Andrei laid out a more modest but still generous $7.50 for the evening's outing.

Feeling confident that he had now achieved something like a first and second date, a "getting to know you" kind of exercise, Schevchenko assumed he could now establish his value as a new friend. Andrei invited them for an after-dinner sunset stroll through scenic Niagara Falls Park.

Andrei wanted them to know all about his country and its glowing future. He explained that after the war Russia would have three main interests—synthetic chemistry, machinery of all kinds, and explosives. The last item, he admitted, might seem odd, but it would be needed to demolish war-damaged buildings before reconstruction could begin. Concerning airplanes, the focus of all his work at Bell so far, he again puzzled his friends by revealing that Russia would have no interest at all in building them. They would simply buy all they needed from the United States. Andrei's peculiar version of small talk eventually led him to offer his bait.

He revealed that he had been appointed to head a Russian government committee to recruit American citizens for postwar work in Russia. Good people would be needed in each of the three industrial categories he had described. And best of all, he would be able to, in fact he would love to, create ideal jobs tailored just to the Franeys' liking. They would come with good incomes and a high standard of living for life.

Leona, quite surprised, hardly knew what to say. She simply asked what Andrei would be doing back home.

Andrei thought for a moment as if reluctant to answer, then simply said, "I am not going home." With that odd announcement, he abruptly ended their visit. He looked at his watch and said he was to meet an unnamed Bell employee at his home quite soon.[4]

Later, in an FBI debriefing, speculating that Andrei was leading up to a request for more reports, Leona made it clear that she knew she could give Schevchenko only information from the library that was "not designated as secret."

But she added that Schevchenko was held in such high esteem by Bell plant personnel that he would have no difficulty obtaining any secret information he asked for and might not need her at all.

During this time, Larry Haas and Andrei Schevchenko's relationship remained professional, personally distant, and unremarkable. Schevchenko had not yet realized Haas's value, and Haas was naturally reticent concerning work matters that other people did not need to know. Haas was still not as interesting as Leona's library.

But by August, Andrei seemed less interested in Leona. Probably still reluctant and unsure how to ask the head librarian for restricted material, Andrei approached someone less daunting. Though he had worked himself up to this ask, he was apparently not yet fully confident he could manage it.

On Thursday, August 17, Andrei asked the assistant librarian on duty, at a time when Leona was not present, for "information concerning the qualitative analysis of an aluminum alloy designated XB 75 S." This strategically important metal was manufactured by Aluminum Company of America (Alcoa). Schevchenko carefully justified his request by saying that the information was necessary "for structural repairs of planes in Russia." The librarian, having been briefed by Leona on how to handle such requests, told him the information was not available. Schevchenko's second request a few days later received the same reply from a different librarian.

But rejection heightened Andrei's impatience. On Friday, September 8, he returned to the library, this time prepared to ask Leona again. He asked for a report titled "Preliminary Data on the Longitude Stability of the P-63A."[5] And—for at least the third time—he asked for "Jet Propulsion In-Flight," an advanced report designated "Confidential."

Leona was shocked the first time he asked. Nobody was supposed to know such files existed at Bell. How could this Russian know it? But she remained calm and kindly gave Andrei the first report. It was unclassified. The second one, however, she refused, but politely as before. She knew Bell had an agreement with the US Army Air Corps allowing Russian representatives any and all information on P-39 and P-63 aircraft, Bell helicopters, or other Bell planes destined for postwar civilian use. Schevchenko was not entitled to data or reports on jet propulsion or any other experiments conducted by Bell for any branch of the US government.[6] Leona knew that Schevchenko knew that but often tested his boundaries—though unsuccessfully so far.[7]

Andrei Schevchenko apparently came under increasing pressure for technical aircraft data from Bell during a visit to his embassy in Washington at that time.

On Friday, October 6, Schevchenko visited Leona Franey with a new idea. He invited Leona and all four of her librarians out to dinner and a show. But after talking it over with them, Leona told Schevchenko "the girls are not enthusiastic" about his hospitality and did not feel comfortable being entertained by him.

The following day, whether undaunted or pressured even harder from above, Andrei gave Leona the money he had planned to spend on the librarians. This was so that "Mr. and Mrs. Franey might go to the show and have a few drinks." Andrei handed her a plain white envelope, which she refused, having become uncomfortable receiving gifts she considered unmerited.

Andrei countered her reluctance by reminding her that she had kindly provided him with that "Preliminary Data" report four weeks ago. That report had prepared him well for something he called "critical technical consultations on" the P-63A at Wright Field in Dayton.

Leona reluctantly accepted the envelope and later found it to contain thirty dollars.

Andrei was satisfied. Leona had given him something legal and useful and he had rewarded her. He had completed another key step in his plans for her.

On Friday evening, November 10, Andrei Schevchenko took Leona to dinner at the Samovar Restaurant in Niagara Falls. They were accompanied by Andrei's two assistants, one of whom Leona knew. She had been giving Nicolai Pavlovich Ostrovsky English lessons for some time. The other guest was Vladimir Mazurin.

"I'm going to Moscow," Andrei said, "to meet with V. M. Molotov, Minister of Foreign Affairs. Among many important matters, we will discuss work you and Joseph may do. In my absence, Ostrovsky will assume my duties at Bell. Please give him the cooperation you would give me." After a cordial dinner, Andrei paid for the meal and gave Leona another plain white envelope "as a Thanksgiving gift." Unable to decline gracefully in public, she accepted it. Once again, she found three ten-dollar bills.

Only ten days later, Andrei's plans changed again. He cancelled his trip to Moscow, started teaching Russian to a group of Bell Aircraft Corporation executives, and told Leona neither Ostrovsky nor Mazurin would be coming to the library in his stead. Andrei appeared concerned. Matters at Bell needed his attention. Too much was in play to delegate to assistants whom he may not have trusted. At times, those working relationships looked strained to Leona.

Leona Franey was apparently the priority Andrei would not leave to others. He immediately presented her with candy and perfume for her and her assistants. He then made an appointment to take Leona and Joe to see the stage play *Rebecca*[8] at the Erlinger Theater in Buffalo on December 5.

By the end of that week, on Friday, November 24, Andrei apparently felt he had prepared the groundwork sufficiently to raise his ask. He had previously requested a jet-propulsion report titled "Study of Jet Propulsion System Comparing Blower Burner and Nozzle N. A. C. A., E4E06."[9] But he had not received it. Now he asked for it again. Leona, however, caught between Andrei's kind gestures and the regulations that she knew, did not openly refuse him. She simply said that particular report was charged out by an employee in the Flight Research Department. It was still not available. Sorry.

Then Andrei changed again. On Saturday, Leona called Ostrovsky to cancel his English lesson for that day. She was working alone and could not spare the time. Apparently immediately notified by Ostrovsky of Leona's presence, Andrei appeared at the library within minutes.

He repeated his request for the jet-propulsion report, but now he was demanding it. He told Leona that Russia would be done buying P-63s in January. They would start buying Bell's jet planes. So, it was urgent that she give him that jet report immediately.

Leona shook her head no with a smile. "I am so sorry. That is not available."

Andrei recalibrated. In a conspiratorial tone he let her know this was all confidential. "Only a few people know of Russia's plans in this—not even my boss knows about it. I am right now writing the contract to buy those jets. But if I do not succeed, my head will come off." He was almost pleading now. Could Leona please help him?[10]

Leona, though still offering a kind smile, remained unmoved. She did not give him the report.

By now, Andrei had known Leona for more than a year. Like a workman at a task, he had applied his lures, ploys, and sweeteners of seduction with no results yet to show for it. He had found no ideology or vice, pride, or greed by which to draw her into his schemes. If he mistook her acceptance of cash and entertainment for a sign of partnership, he confused effort with success. The right man for the job might have switched targets by now.

For Leona, whether by coincidence, providence, or someone else's watchful eye, help finally arrived.

On Friday, December 8, a Bell Corporation executive visited the library. He reassured Leona that neither she nor any of her assistants should give Mr. Schevchenko nor any of his people any reports classified as Secret, Confidential, or Restricted. If such a request were made, Bell's administration was to be told immediately. No was their safest answer to Mr. Schevchenko. There would be no repercussions from Bell's administrative offices for refusing his requests.

"That is my policy exactly," Leona said. "I've already told my assistants." But to herself, she breathed a sigh of relief to receive company backing.

"Mr. Schevchenko has already made and been denied such requests," Leona assured the man. "We have no further questions. Thank you."

CHAPTER SEVEN

Everybody's Enemy

The still unseen storms brewing around Larry Haas and Andrei Schevchenko were about to be complicated by real winter storms building over the eastern United States and Europe.[1]

Between December 11, 1944, and February 1, 1945, ninety inches of snow blanketed and paralyzed America's entire northeast. By December 29, thirty-six inches of snow had already fallen on Buffalo, compared to less than two inches the year before. Temperatures topped freezing only twice, and then barely, throughout fifty-two long, cold days of December and January.

The first thirteen inches of snow that fell on Monday and Tuesday, December 11 and 12, froze freight trains to hundreds of miles of tracks and switch yards. Movement of raw materials into Buffalo and finished war supplies back out were stopped cold. Bell Aircraft, Curtiss-Wright Aviation, Buffalo Arms, American Car & Foundry, and others were frozen out of operation. Five thousand men braved record cold and high winds to painfully shovel mountains of snow off the tracks by hand.

Buffalo was also starved for the food and fuel that ordinarily arrived on eighty-five trains pulling 5,200 railcars every day. Milk did not reach the city from nearby farms. Bakers received no flour and baked no bread.

On Christmas Day, another eight inches fell, a harder cold snap set in, and the next punishing blizzard struck just as the last big dig-out was finished and commerce began to inch back into action.

On Monday, January 22, forty-five-mile-an-hour wind-driven sleet and snow shut down Buffalo and the entire northeast again. By the twenty-ninth, soldiers and railroad workers had cleared the ice and snow once more, but only until January 31, when another winter blast engulfed the trains and tracks once more, this time building twenty-foot drifts.

Fortunately, on Tuesday, February 6, North American weather patterns finally stabilized, bringing more favorable skies. Cities, factories, and rail traffic slowly rolled back toward normal.

Among the fiercest combatants of World War II, it happened that none were more brutal and treacherous than the weather that year—nearly everywhere in the world. It fought everyone. On the battlefields of Europe, that winter had fallen hard, devastating both combatant and civilian. Winter's harshest blows seemed to fall on the Soviet Union that year, and especially on Andrei Schevchenko's homeland, Ukraine. Even Napoleon had fallen victim to Russia's most brutal general, General Winter, more than a century before.

Though the winter of 1944–1945 was nobody's soldier, it was everybody's enemy, and Larry Haas was about to become one of its victims.

CHAPTER EIGHT

A Man to Be Dealt With[1]

Sunday, 3:15 p.m., December 10, 1944, a pilots' preflight briefing at Bell Aircraft

Larry's mood was getting as bad as the weather. He hated watching the snow squalls blow in off Lake Erie and pelt his airplanes on the runway. The fourteen Russian pilots and the dozen Air Transport Command (ATC) ferry pilots in the conference room were waiting for a fly/no-fly sign from the tower. The takeoff window for their sortie was closing in dangerously fast.

The specially invited Russian Air Force officers and a select group of Bell engineers in the room, however, were waiting for something else, a special briefing by Larry on "something new" they would hear about in private after the mandatory preflight drill. Larry Bell was there, too.

"*Davayte letat'!*" one of the Russian pilots called out, his voice edged with impatience. Larry knew that phrase. "Let's fly!"

If the runway closed, their beautiful *Kobrushkas*[2]—their P-39 "Little Cobras"—would be stuck on the ground waiting for bluer skies by . . . who knew when. Every pilot in the room knew that wait would make their planes useless over the Russian battlefields for just that much longer. Every extra day of delay would cost more lives. All eyes fixed on Larry.

"Listen up," Larry said loud enough to be heard over another gust that rattled the windows. He nodded at Andrei to translate.

Andrei called out something in Russian that sounded to Larry like it could have been "Shut up and pay attention!" A Russian officer gave Andrei a scowl, but the room fell silent.

This briefing was not optional. All ears required. These pilots would fly their P-39s across the Northwest Staging Route to the Alaska-Siberia (ALSIB) air road and down into Siberian Russia. The flight, if made in winter, was known to be treacherous.[3] The first leg ended at Great Falls, Montana. From there, they would fly across Canada and on to Ladd Army Airfield in Fairbanks, Alaska. The Northwest Staging Route ended there. The final leg of the ALSIB route took them over the icy Bering Strait to Siberia and down into the heart of the Soviet Union, and at last into the air war on Russia's European and eastern fronts.

With everyone's attention now on him, Larry quickly ticked off the most recent revisions to the P-39's powerful Allison V-1710-85 V-12 engine, especially as they related to extreme weather conditions. Updates left unexplained could confound even the most seasoned pilots. Andrei translated as quickly as he could.

Larry finished and gave a readout of the worsening weather conditions. "Any questions?"

Andrei cut off any possible replies. "No more time!" He glared out the windows. "They fly now or not at all." But one Soviet pilot did have a question. He called it out in English before Larry could react.

"Why do you lie about the P-63s? I have to fly one."

Larry and Andrei both stared at him, speechless. That was to be the subject of the later briefing, not part of this preflight rundown. Larry Bell sat upright but managed a poker face.

The P-63 was superior to the P-39 in almost every way. It incorporated new features requested and designed by the Russian pilots themselves. Its promised speed, however, was the only promise that had never quite materialized. It was, Larry had to admit to himself, a sore spot for him, too.

"I will deliver my *Kobrushka*," the pilot continued, "but then I will be deployed to the east, toward Japan with one of your P-63s. Mr. Bell promised it would be faster than the P-39 and all of the German and Japanese fighters." Larry recognized the pilot's voice now. He was not one to be easily put off. The Soviet officials had also become especially attentive. They had the same concerns but had agreed to hold them until the private postbriefing meeting that Bell and Haas had called in order to discuss the matter.

"It is faster, Vadim. Check your specs." Larry looked at Andrei for help but saw a stony stare that worried him. Andrei obviously agreed with his comrade.

"Only by thirty miles, fifty kilometers, an hour," Vadim said. "That is nothing! Why is this so?"

"No time for that right now, Vadim." Larry tried to put him off.

Andrei translated for the non-English-speaking pilots and officers. That released a loud chorus repeating Vadim's question.

Taken off-guard, Larry almost answered more than he should. That answer was reserved for the men who had been invited to hear it.

The problem those men had come to discuss was that the P-63 was supposed to be the answer to the P-39's sluggish performance at any altitude above fifteen thousand feet.[4] But Bell's shiny, new P-63s only partially delivered on that. Larry was frustrated by that, too. In his lab, he had invented a solution of his own that he could prove would work. But Bell refused to accept it. Like the Russian pilots, Haas felt betrayed, but he knew his place. He defended the airplane.

"The P-63 can top forty thousand feet in minutes and do it with ease. That's five miles, a full eight kilometers, higher than the 39. That's what you asked for. And we all know that you know just what to do with it. From up there, you dive so fast that you blow those Nazis out of the air before they even know you're on them. Are you complaining about that?"

"But that does not work in a dogfight," Vadim complained, standing now, addressing the room more than Larry. "For that we need the speed you promised. Mr. Bell says you *cannot* make the P-63 faster. We think you *will not*."

Larry could not explain that to Vadim or to the other fliers. He dared not. This was a confidential matter that extended far beyond Bell Aircraft. Neither the Allied Joint Chiefs, the exiled French leaders, nor Churchill or Eisenhower, wanted Bell to solve that problem. Nobody wanted to see high-altitude, fast Bell-built VVS warplanes cruising the sky over Europe and the United Kingdom. Nobody but Roosevelt believed Stalin's promise to keep communism bottled up inside the Soviet Union. If Stalin wanted faster warplanes, he would have to build them himself. Even cobbled as they were, the Allies outlawed those P-63s on Russia's European front. Stalin's fliers were lethal enough over Europe in their *Kobrushkas*. The 63s would do their fighting in Asia.

But Stalin's fliers wanted more. And in his heart, Larry Haas sided with them.

So, on this particularly frigid winter afternoon, in spite of the howling wind and snow, and the layers of ice slowly encrusting the waiting airplanes, a brave young Russian flier goaded Haas until his patience failed.

"Okay, Vadim," Haas yelled in exasperation, suddenly beyond restraint, "I *can* fix it."

Andrei heard the words and translated them an instant before he realized what Haas had said. Andrei stared at him. Vadim and twenty-four comrades suddenly sat very still. The Russian officers and Bell engineers almost stopped breathing. Even the wind seemed to stop and listen.

"I can give this baby a lot more kick," Haas nearly shouted. His inner sensor had turned itself off. "How about eighty klicks more whenever you want it?"[5] He gave the P-63 demonstration engine on a display stand next to him a smack atop one of the Allison's 1,200 hp cylinder heads. "And I have ways to do more than that. And a *lot* more than even that!"

And "a lot more" is what Andrei heard like a gong in his head. It was the second thing Larry should not have said.

Then, with the more rational part of his mind waking up to hear himself, Larry stopped short. He caught his breath. The ironic truth was that Bell's original plan had promised the Russians what they wanted. It was a water-injection system designed for the P-63's Allison power plant. It did what the Russians wanted—but only on paper, not in the air. It was tried-and-true water-injection technology of the kind already used in race cars, trucks, and a few other planes. But in the Bell P-63, as designed, it simply did not work.

Andrei was now on full alert. Haas had just become much more interesting. Andrei now knew he had to force Bell to fix the 63s—and maybe a lot more. He could almost feel the Order-of-Lenin medal being pinned to his chest by Joseph Stalin himself. And if Andrei was right about something else that he *thought* he heard in Larry's words—something his intuition just barely dared to hope for—Andrei knew he could change the world.

Haas's world had already changed. Larry Bell had heard him.[6]

Bell addressed Haas with a firm and formal "Mister Haas!" His voice carried a sound of tight control that Haas heard even louder. Now that pre-flight was over, Bell declared, he had to interrupt. All eyes turned toward the man who had risen to be heard.

Haas bit his tongue and stood silent.

The flight schedule was slipping behind for this sortie, Bell warned, though everyone already knew it. It was time to get these pilots and their planes in the air. It was to be now or never, and now was better. Bell made a sweeping motion toward the door to say, "Gentlemen, after you."[7]

Andrei left with the pilots. But he made straight for his office, not the airstrip. He picked up his encrypted phone and asked the right people for approval on a decision he had already made. Superiors in the Soviet Consulate on East 61st Street in New York City, and more important, the NKVD in faraway Moscow Center, all agreed. Larry Haas was now a man to be dealt with.

Andrei's decision both thrilled him and scared him. He saw a chance to get vastly improved airplanes out of Bell's plant. The NKVD, on the other hand, might now watch him closer. Would capitalist wealth corrupt him? In addition, Andrei would now be expected to control Haas by any means possible. But internecine competition for control of valuable assets was rife throughout Soviet intelligence. Andrei could now expect new and unwelcome pressure to develop in his job.[8] And finally, there was always the FBI to worry about. Andrei knew they were lurking more and more watchfully around America's strategic industries. He did not think he was a target yet, but, unless he was careful, he knew his new interest in a key person like Haas might shift their eyes toward him. Being watched was not new to Andrei. He was, after all, a Soviet citizen in a foreign country, a condition that demanded a near-paranoid watchfulness at all times.

Andrei knew he needed a plan. The best one, he decided, was to befriend Larry Haas. He recalled advice he had been given before landing in America.

> You will meet people who are different from you: culturally, politically, and in personality. Welcome any initial awkwardness. It may create a desire in your target to overcome the unintended distance. Your new acquaintance's desire for rapprochement, if you use it correctly, can accelerate a bonding experience.

Andrei was sure of that initial awkwardness. He blamed himself now for the lack of foresight that had allowed it. He did not know of any desire on Haas's part for rapprochement. He knew, however, that he would now have to befriend Haas, though they had little in common except an affinity for aircraft. Andrei quickly decided to act on that slim connection to plan a first date.

———•———

Friday, 4:10 p.m., December 15, 1944, in Larry Haas's laboratory at Bell Aircraft

Andrei did not always see patience as a virtue. As a boy, he had hated his father's old saying, "*Tishe yedesh' dal'she budesh'*... Ride slower, get farther." As an adult, he was still impatient. He thought the long seduction was too slow, if it would work at all. What seduction had meant to him as an impulsive young man had nothing to do with the thing he was coming to see as its perversion in spy craft. His experience with Leona Franey suggested that improvising could do no worse. So, with Larry Haas, he would move *now*, preliminaries be damned.

Andrei smiled as he stepped into Larry's lab with a breezy wish for a pleasant afternoon. He had already sat himself down in a chair in front of Haas's desk before he finished asking permission to enter.

Larry welcomed him, belatedly motioning toward the seat. The slightly puzzled look on his face seemed to ask if there was something they needed to talk about.

Andrei returned a disarming smile. There was something he would *like* to talk about, he said, not something he *needed* to talk about. Why not consider this a social call?

Larry agreed, relaxed, and leaned back in his seat, though now even more curious.

An inveterate chain-smoker of American cigarettes, Andrei occasionally "forgot" Bell's rigidly enforced no smoking policy in the plant. When necessary, he deemed offices to be remote territory—far enough from the assembly line floor that a single match and a bit of smoke could be deemed harmless. And sometimes, he simply considered himself Russian and privileged. On this day, he fished out a disfigured Camel from a nearly empty pack. He tapped it on his thumbnail to repack the tobacco and lit it. After a long, slow drag to compose his thoughts, Andrei revealed his purpose for this late afternoon visit. A hint of tension in his voice, however, belied his casual demeanor. Just a "little word or two" about his Kingcobras is all he wanted.

Larry nodded and waited.

Andrei thought a moment and added that he reckoned there was just one small problem. Maybe they could solve it between themselves—engineer to engineer—no brass or bosses needed.

Here we go! Larry told himself, bracing for another conversation he did not want to have. Those 63s are complex machines, he reminded Andrei, and immediately knew that gambit would get him nothing. Andrei's smoke burned Larry's eyes, but he ignored it. If this went where he thought it would go, cigarette smoke would be the least of his irritants.

Speed, Andrei said, as he had said before, was the issue. The Soviets wanted faster airplanes and the P-63 was breaking Bell's promise to provide it. Larry, of course, knew all that. But Andrei continued before Larry could answer, and he twisted the conversation in a way Larry could not have anticipated.

The problem, Andrei said, was language, the language of the bookkeepers, bureaucrats, generals, and politicians—a language neither he nor Larry could speak. They spoke a different language; it was the language of scientists and engineers.

Larry never quite remembered Andrei's next words or novel arguments exactly, but when Larry told and retold the story years later to Kay and her family, his paraphrase made Andrei's shocking point clear. It made Larry's own snap decision seem almost logical. He recounted for Kay their later beer hall conversations with the same kind of clarity—the clarity that came from the trauma of a life-changing crisis met unawares.

"So to hell with them all!" Andrei said. "Let's solve our problems between ourselves, share all that we know, and create a new world without them! Why can't we just talk?"

"Okay," Larry said easily enough before he realized he had been drawn into something he should have thought about first.

"Perhaps after hours today?" Andrei suggested, pulling the trigger as he had practiced for just this moment. "I will buy you a beer for your time."

Larry's keen instinct for "something's up" came awake. But his insatiable, often intrepid, curiosity decided to go along. "Got a good place in mind?"

"Do you know the Kenmore Theater?" Andrei asked.[9] "Down the street a few doors there is a place called Homer's Tavern. It is an easier place to talk. Is six o'clock good?"

"Sure, fine. I know the place," Larry said. "I'll see you there."

"Excellent!" Andrei nodded and disappeared out Larry's door without another word. He walked toward his office and straightened his red silk tie, pleased with himself. He felt he could leave the building now. His work was done. He put on his coat and pushed his black mink *ushanka* down hard against the icy wind that stung his cheeks as he stepped out of the factory and into the night. He soon found a man-high drift piled against his car. Yet, it warmed him. He wondered if the same snow falling in deep blankets across Europe was teaching Hitler's *Fuszsoldaten* and his tank battalions the same terrible lesson it taught Napoleon's *Infanterie* and his starving mules 130 years ago. He smiled at the pleasant thought while he swept snow off his windshield.

Larry had driven by Homer's Tavern a thousand times but never stopped in. He reckoned it was just another old bar.

The heavy oak door opened on squeaking hinges as Larry stepped in. He found himself in a smoky, dark world. A few of Homer's denizens looked up from their ten-cent beers when he entered, but they showed no particular interest. He figured they'd need a better reason to look twice. It was a place where ordinary working men in battered work boots and frayed shirts could sort out their everyday cares. Some of the men looked like GIs home from the war, most able-bodied and a scattering who were not.

Andrei was waiting in the farthest booth with two foamy beer mugs in front of him. "Charming place," Larry said, sitting down. He raised his mug. "To your health."

"And to yours." Both downed a long swallow. "It is quiet here," Andrei said, "and the beer is good."

"Proletarian at heart, eh?"

"Working class," Andrei clarified. "Comfortable." *And anonymous*, he reminded himself, looking around once more as casually as he could. Vigilance must never be obvious.

Larry, on the other hand, had been looking around like a tourist. He smiled at Andrei and casually asked, "So what's up?"

"Airplanes, my friend," Andrei said. "Once in a while I would rather talk about them than inspect them or buy them. I am an engineer after all, and like you, a designer of airplanes. You should know I envy your job very much over mine. So, do you mind? I have had nobody to talk aviation with since I left Russia, and I think you think like I do."

Larry had not expected that. "Well, I guess I'll take that as a compliment. What interests you most?" Only later did Larry spot the lie. Andrei had Russian fliers and military men to talk to about aviation all day long.

"Performance!" Andrei said it with a gleam in his eye. "Speed and agility. I love such machines but I hate to build them for war. In any case, at least we learn new things while we do it. Is that not so?"

"Yes, we do." Larry hefted his mug again. "Here's to learning." He had decided to encourage Andrei in as neutral a way as possible. There would be more to this conversation and Larry was curious to follow its trail. Andrei might prove more interesting than he seemed at the plant.

"And for me, that means learning how to build better airplanes," Andrei said. "For instance, like me, I am sure it hurts you to send out your P-39s the way you must build them."

"As warplanes? Sure. They're made for killing. In a better world, we wouldn't need them."

"Of course, it's that," Andrei said, almost dismissively, "but I mean something else. That airplane is—" Andrei paused. He searched for a word, then spat it out in his own language, "*kastrirovan.*"

"Kast-ree . . . what?"

"Castrated!" Andrei almost shouted, having finally landed on the English word he wanted. Then, more calmly, "That airplane had its manhood cut off before you sold it to us." He tried to add a good-natured laugh but didn't quite pull it off. "We know you neutered that airplane.[10] Don't you see? I'm sure you do not like that either."

Larry merely tilted his head as if he wanted to hear more and waited. Instinctive caution held his tongue at this odd twist of the conversation.

"You—I mean Bell—pulled out that machine's supercharger. Your air forces wanted less weight and less drag, but by the time they were done making changes, they added sixteen hundred pounds and nearly crippled it.[11] They did not seem to care that made it slow and useless at any height over ten thousand or fifteen thousand feet. To give your Mr. Bell credit, though, I will admit that he blamed his air forces for meddling with his beautiful airplane. In truth, though, you sell us airplanes your own air forces will not fly."

Larry wondered how the conversation could have taken such a sharp turn. He now found himself strangely moved to defend the airplane as if it were his own. "But aren't your boys shooting down Nazis like—" fish in a barrel didn't make sense, "like clay pigeons at a skeet shoot? A couple of your pilots have already racked up fifty kills in their 39s, and they're still counting."

"It's their skill, not your airplanes." Now Andrei's eyes smoldered.

Larry feared the conversation was lost, but he gave it one more try. "That's why Bell built you the P-63s. You asked for it and we did it. They top out at forty- or forty-five-thousand feet. That's eight miles up! Any higher and it would be a spaceship for God's sake." Larry's face reddened. "You think that's not enough?"

Andrei answered smoothly, like a cat closing in for the kill. "But Bell forgot the speed. The 39's top speed is about 390, less than promised and far less than possible,[12] and the 63 adds barely thirty miles an hour to that. It is not only inadequate, it's an insult!" Andrei's right fist was clenched now. "Did Bell forget that, or . . .?" he let his voice trail off, leaving the implied alternative hanging in the air. Larry knew Andrei was right. One rumor circulating around the Bell establishment even hinted that Bell pulled out the supercharger and more just to save money. Haas refused to believe that one, but even in wartime, and maybe especially so, a capitalist profit motive could legitimately anger a good communist. Maybe Andrei had a point.

Nevertheless, Larry made one more try. "That's why the P-63 triples the altitude of a P-39. Dive from 45K and you're flying fast enough to almost rip the wings off. You're invincible. Your flyboys aren't complaining about that, are they?"

"Of course, they are invincible," Andrei nearly shouted. Then, remembering that rooms can have ears, and remembering that he wanted to make a new friend here, he leaned forward and lowered his voice. "But invincible is only half of it if you deliver the airplane you promised. That climb and dive eats fuel and time. German bombers drop their loads and run for home before we can engage more than a few of them. And worse, now Germany has rocket-propelled airplanes."

Larry sipped his beer. He did not counter.

"But just a few days ago, you said you could *fix* all that." Andrei sat back. "Maybe you shouldn't have, but you did. You broke the rules. You couldn't help yourself because you are on our side." His eyes glinted with the revelation. "Am I wrong?"

Larry passionately believed in the Russian pilots and their mission to save their motherland. He would be pleased to admit that and proud of his piece of it. It was the politics of their leaders he had no use for. Wrangling with Andrei over that distinction just now, though, was a rabbit trail he did not want to take.

Larry held his tongue except for a quizzical smile.

Andrei looked into Larry's eyes. "So, I went to Mr. Bell on your behalf, Larry, in support of your uhm . . . is *invention* the right word?"

"It's good enough." Larry already knew about that visit but did not say so. "Thanks. What did Bell say?" He already knew that answer, too.

"He promised an answer soon."

That, Larry knew, meant No! Washington and London considered Stalin a good ally to keep on a short leash. But he decided not to explain American "bureaucrat-speak" just then and merely said "Good" and tried to change the subject.

"So, let's talk about something more interesting." Larry took a long pull of beer and emptied his mug.

Andrei ignored Larry's bid. "You said you could fix the P-63's speed problem. Forgive me, Larry. I will be blunt. If you can give us a faster P-63, but will not do it, then more of our pilots will die." Andrei's fist rested on the checkered tablecloth between them clenched hard enough now to whiten his knuckles.

Larry sat quite still for a long moment sizing up Andrei's words. A lifetime of thought compressed itself into that moment. He realized his next words would not be a snap decision, no matter how much it might look that way.

"Okay, Andrei. Let's talk aircraft."

Andrei sat back slowly and relaxed, releasing his tension into the air. "Okay," he said, and waited.

"Sometime last year, somebody at Bell teamed up with Allison and installed a water-injection system on the P-63 engines. That should have made the airplane act like it was shot from a cannon. But the thing was absolutely useless."

"We know," Andrei said flatly. "Thank you for admitting it."

"So," Larry continued, "I did some experiments of my own. I love puzzles, and that one begged for my attention. That's one of the things they pay me for. I found a simple fix. All the system needed was a stronger spring on the water regulator and a fifty-cent check valve. It was a dollar's worth of fix for a million-dollar problem."[13]

"Did it really work?"

"Naturally!" Larry snapped his fingers. "Just like that! I installed it on one of our planes and an army test pilot flew it. It worked just fine—more power and more speed."[14]

"Thank you," Andrei said, not hesitant to show his satisfaction. But he had hoped for, even expected, something like that. Mostly, though, it readied him to spring the real question.

"So then what did you mean by 'and probably a lot more than even that'?"

Larry suddenly realized he had been trapped by his own words. Fortunately, in a tight spot, few things came more quickly to Larry's mind than plausible half-truths, and one immediately arrived. "That 'a-lot-more' involved the use of a turbo-supercharger and other parts already used on most airplanes. You can even salvage them in Russia from old, downed planes and build a nearly jet-propelled unit. I could suspend it from the belly of the P-63s and boost the whole works up to rocket-speed."

"How much?"

"At least a hundred miles an hour. Maybe more!"

Andrei laughed. "That's nice, but I meant how much money? How much do you want for your idea? For the technical details, I mean." Andrei did not care that he had just skipped a bunch of steps in the so-called long seduction. The word jet had jumped out of context into a mind eager to hear it. Now he was sure he was on to something.

"I'll have to think it over" was the best Larry could do by way of an answer to such a remarkable question.

"Thinking takes beer," Andrei said, suddenly jovial. "Take a few days to think it over. Maybe we can do some business—" He caught himself and added, "good business for our countries, of course." He waved at the bar girl, pointed at their empty mugs, and raised two fingers for refills.

Soon, they were just old boys daydreaming about adventures in the sky, about what might be in years to come, and finally about their families, and even the weather.

Before parting an hour later, they arranged to meet again outside the plant on Monday, December 18, this time in front of Shea's Kenmore Theater at 6:30 p.m. to discuss the price of Larry's thoughts.

———•——•———

Larry and Andrei met under Kenmore's marquee and strolled down the avenue, back to Homer's Tavern. Neither man spoke except for a greeting until they entered the beer hall.

Andrei motioned toward the far table where they had sat on Friday night. Larry brought the beer.

Andrei lit up, looked at the ceiling, and blew a perfect smoke ring at it. He smiled, hefted one of the mugs, and toasted to all things that fly.

Larry toasted back to magnificent flying machines and half-emptied his mug.

Andrei seemed satisfied, even pleased with Larry's toast. It let him set their course just where he wanted—on the newest of those magnificent machines. He was sure his friend Larry had brought its secrets with him tonight; secrets Andrei was ready to buy.

Only three months ago, Bell Aircraft had introduced it to the world. It seemed to him as a matter of fact, Andrei offered with a wink, that Larry had something to do with it, no?

Larry understood instantly. He named it reluctantly. The P-59 jet fighter.

Not just the P-59, Andrei corrected, the *Bell* P-59, America's first jet-powered warplane, the aptly named Airacomet.[15] Bell built it. So of course, Larry knew about it. Was Andrei not right?

That deduction was too obvious, but Larry had to deny it. He affected a look of agitation and complained that the thing had surprised him as much as it had surprised Andrei and the rest of the world. Bell, Larry objected, had him tied up in P-39s and P-63s, implying that was all Bell thought he was good for.

Andrei sympathized, but Larry read the opposite in his eyes. This would be an unannounced, unacknowledged sparring match. Larry tried again.

If Bell had rejected Haas's fuel injector system, he reasoned—that simple two-bit fix he'd cooked up for Andrei's 63s—he surely wouldn't let Haas play around in his jet program, would he?

Andrei gave Larry a noncommittal shrug, still unconvinced.

Larry gave him one small concession. He had heard a few rumors about a jet-power project, he admitted, but that thing had been locked down tight. Larry's voice rose. Andrei had to believe it made him mad.

Larry had, in fact, been on that team for months; collaborating with General Electric to reverse engineer the British Whittle jet engine and build a Bell airplane around it.[16] He also trained the technicians, service engineers, and pilots in its operation. The experimental version, the XP-59, had flown more than a hundred times at Muroc Lake, an ancient, dry desert lake bed in California, before the story leaked to the press. Paul Emmons, Bell's head of aeronautical engineering, brought Larry in under Ed Rhodes, assistant chief engineer for aerospace design and the XP-59 project engineer. They had handcrafted the first prototype around a modified P-63 airframe at a secret location—the disguised old Main Street Ford assembly plant in downtown Buffalo's industrial zone.

But Larry would have to deny it all.

He had a suspicion, though, that Andrei already knew too much because of one enormous snafu at Bell. Someone had assigned Andrei an office next to a conference room. But it was not an ordinary conference room. It was the one reserved for top secret briefings, including P-59 flight-film screenings. Only a plasterboard wall separated it from Andrei's office. He might have learned everything before somebody thought of soundproofing the conference room.[17]

To get off the hook, Larry turned the tables for a little jousting of his own. He admitted that Andrei was probably right. Bell must have been working on that airplane for a while for a finished product to show up suddenly in the news. But why, Larry challenged, did Andrei sound quite so sure of it all? What did he know that Larry didn't?

Andrei, caught up now in their give-and-take, lowered his voice and confided that he did have sources of his own—and he was sure Larry had his, too. So, when peace comes, Andrei knew that men like the two of them—and mysterious "others of like mind"—would bring aviation to the world in remarkable new ways. If war made it possible, they would make something better out of it. Secrecy—like whatever surrounded that jet project—only delayed a better future. Secrecy, Andrei complained, was the enemy of human progress.[18]

The salesman in Larry admired Andrei's pitch, delivered with passion. He had just been invited, in the craftiest way, into something that could be treasonous. He had never before met a spy but suddenly wondered if Andrei might be one, or something close to it.

Andrei looked into Larry's eyes. The Soviet Union, he said, respects men like him.[19] In a tone of sincere friendship, Andrei made the rest of his pitch. He wanted to hear the price Larry would accept—along with the gratitude of the Soviet Union, of course—for his invention, the one that would transform a P-63 into the truly lethal weapon it could be.

Larry was stunned, experiencing a rare loss of words. But Andrei continued before Larry could marshal a reply.

Andrei had a "down payment" to offer before Larry even mentioned a price. Andrei would bring Larry and Dorothy to Moscow for two years as a scientific consultant. Larry would live well and pay for nothing. Housing, travel, entertainment, fine foods, all would be his. All Larry would need to do in preparation would be to draw up any work plans and the specs on equipment and facilities that he wanted. Write any notes he might want to make, too, on the jet propulsion unit used on the P-59 airplane.

Larry stopped him to repeat that he had no detailed knowledge on that project, though he was beginning to see that Andrei would refuse to believe him.

Andrei waived it off. Larry could, after all, gain access to everything, could he not? He was a pilot trainer and he'd have to know all about that new airplane. He could simply place everything in any secure packaging he liked and seal it any way he wanted. Andrei would then send it ahead in a diplomatic packet. Andrei had no diplomatic immunity, but he did have his ways to promise secure passage.[20] Larry's materials would stay that way until he reached Russia and began his work.

The stakes in this chat had grown higher and stranger than Larry could have predicted. Andrei read the portent on Larry's face. He capitalized on the moment and asked his question.

"So, what's your price?"

Larry had to think that over fast. He stalled with steepled fingers and a furrowed brow. What had he created with a few unguarded words? He decided to make it Andrei's decision, and he'd make it obvious what that should be. He saw one last chance to escape from a suddenly insane situation. On the spur of the moment, he'd throw out an outrageous number, like ten times an average American's yearly take-home. It would reduce to an absurdity that could only mean, *I'm not taking this seriously.* He answered with a laugh and mock grandiosity.

"Then how about fifty thousand?"[21]

Andrei did not blink. He stood and stubbed out his last cigarette. "I will talk to my superiors in Washington and in Moscow. In the meantime, for both of our sakes, we did not have this conversation." He dropped a twenty-dollar bill on the table for Homer and walked out into the night alone. He thought, *In this land money rules all. It is impossible not to take Haas seriously. He proves all we say about the capitalist mind.*

Larry finished his beer and wondered what had just happened.

⸻

Wednesday, December 27, 1944, 5:15 p.m. in Larry Haas's office at Bell Aircraft
Once again, Andrei did not knock. He simply opened the door to Larry's office, stepped inside, and called out a hello.

The voice from behind stopped Larry in mid-reach for a hefty parts catalog atop a cabinet behind his desk. He turned toward the voice.

Andrei was lighting a Camel by the time Larry asked what he could do for him. His answer was a non sequitur. "Quitting time soon?"

"Not if I can help it," was Larry's standard answer for anyone mentioning quitting as if time had anything to do with it. Larry generally thought the idea silly. He didn't think clocks belonged at work. A paycheck entitled the company to forty-five hours every week, according to the bureaucrats who thought they ran things. Larry, on the other hand, thought a paycheck entitled him to spend all the time he wanted playing with all the company's interesting and expensive toys. Work was recreation for inventors. At the moment, though, Larry thought Andrei probably had an interesting reason for asking.

Larry glanced at his watch and looked at the paper snowstorm on his desk. He realized he had not eaten since breakfast and he thought he might have forgotten lunch. He guessed it was quitting time after all. What did Andrei have in mind?

All he wanted was a minute to talk.

By now, Larry had learned that would be an understatement. The rest of Andrei's request proved it. Andrei did not want to talk in Larry's office. He looked around as if there was something wrong with it. He wanted to meet in the car lot, in Andrei's car.

Larry agreed, bemused and too curious now not to go along. He checked his watch and promised to be there in fifteen minutes.

Andrei promised his car would be warm.

The parking lot that night had been carved into a maze of plowed paths between snow piles higher than the cars. Larry Bell had sent most of the snowplows to the line-workers' lots. "They do the real work around here," he was known to say. Bell was confident enough to take himself lightly and smart enough to respect his workers.[22]

Andrei's car, a dark blue 1939 Ford coupe, sat alone among drifts in an island of darkness between faraway light posts. Except for its billowing exhaust, Andrei's snow-covered car looked like an abandoned igloo.

The car felt warm with its motor purring softly when Larry got in.

Andrei immediately announced that he had little time. He had a plane to Washington to catch in . . . he checked his watch . . . twenty-seven minutes. But for just this moment he had wished to bring Larry and his wife . . . was her name Dolores?

Dorothy.

. . . a Christmas card. Appearing somewhat uncertain of himself, Andrei told Larry such customs were no longer permissible in Russia, but in America many kind people had made him feel welcome with it. He wished to return that kindness. He held out a white envelope with graceful Cyrillic characters handwritten across the front: *Счастливого Рождества, Ларри.*

Larry thanked him but turned the card sideways and back, puzzling at the script. He looked at Andrei.

Andrei spoke the words aloud. *Schastlivogo Rozhdestva, Larri*, Merry Christmas, Larry.

Larry was moved by the kindness and offered the same good wishes in return to Andrei and his family. On its face, this was a fine gesture from a man usually adept in social graces. But the secrecy puzzled Larry. Was Andrei afraid the Soviet thought-police were watching him? He could have offered his best regards for Christmas inside the plant.

As if understanding Larry's unspoken question, Andrei said Larry would find a small gift inside the card. He said he felt he owed it to Larry for his patience.

Once again, Larry did not understand.

With an apologetic smile, Andrei said his bureaucrats were as slow and frustrating as Larry's. Larry's offer had been heard, but an answer had not yet come back. The small gift in Andrei's card was, if not consolation, then a down payment.

Larry started to ask, then suddenly understood exactly what it was for.

Andrei told Larry he would soon be a wealthy man. Fifty thousand dollars, when it is approved, would even be too little to pay for the Russian lives Larry would save.

Larry started to object, but Andrei interrupted. He had to go. He shifted his car into reverse and gave Larry a sideways glance that said it was time to go.

Larry barely felt the wind and snow sandblasting his cheeks on the way to his car. A very strange corner had just been turned, one he had not seen coming. He realized he was heading down a road he did not know how to navigate.

Seated in his own warming car, Larry opened the envelope. He found a handwritten note folded inside an ornate and traditional Russian Orthodox Christmas card. Flowing Cyrillic lettering in gold leaf illuminated its message. This was clearly outside the realm of greetings sanctioned by Andrei's atheist, Leninist hierarchy. Larry found the gesture odd, yet strangely moving. Andrei had become a paradox, an enigmatic friend who might also be something else.

Larry,
Antonina and I had hoped to invite you and your wife for a social evening in our home. But it has become impossible. I must quickly go to New York City and Washington.

When I return, please join me and another friend I will invite at Casa Lorenzo on Pearl Street in Buffalo. You will be my guest for dinner and drinks. Tuesday, January 2, if you can, if 6 p.m. is good. I will expect you unless it is inconvenient.

Enclosed is a Christmas gift for your wife which I hope she will enjoy.

Happy New Year
Andrei Ivanovich

Larry unfolded a sheet of paper nestled inside the Christmas card. He had to catch his breath as five crisp twenty-dollar bills fell out.[23] Driving home, the icy slick roads demanded enough attention to distract his thoughts. He would have to give this new development the attention it needed later that night.

Andrei drove toward the airport, where a plane chartered by the Soviet Consulate waited on the icy tarmac. Once in the air and sure no eyes now lurked close to him, Andrei wrote in a small blue journal, the only confidant he could trust.

Proper sequence be damned. That was too important to wait. I apply the last advice first. Larry will respond to cash. Improvisation is risky but this will work. I have placed our "First Date" in second place, after Larry's cash reward, not before it.

CHAPTER NINE

First Date

Six days later. Tuesday, January 2, 1945, 5:45 p.m. at Casa Lorenzo Italian Restaurant, Buffalo, New York

Larry reached Casa Lorenzo at 5:45. Fifteen minutes early was on time in his book. Even better, it gave him a chance to take the catbird seat. Larry despised worry, but suspicion was a different thing. He did not know what to expect, but he planned to watch Andrei Schevchenko like a cat watches a canary. Among his suspicions was that Andrei would be watching him the same way. The evening might prove to be interesting, amusing, and revealing.

Three feet of snow had blanketed Buffalo by that afternoon. At sunset the temperature slipped into single digits. Larry was grateful for the warmth of Lorenzo's front lobby. He checked his hat, coat, and scarf with the hat-check girl, and rubbed his hands together to drive some warm blood into his fingers. He asked the maître d' for a table in a secluded alcove where he could wait for Andrei and his mystery guest.

Windblown snow off Lake Erie stung Andrei's face as he stepped from his car. He pushed his *ushanka* down hard against the wind, but as always not his earflaps. That would spoil the *ushanka*'s dignity.

Warm, golden light shown through the restaurant's front window and glistened on the sidewalk. As Andrei approached, a smartly dressed man stepped out and held the door for his companion. Her fur coat shimmered in the wind as she wrapped it closer around herself.

She called out a New Year greeting toward Andrei over the gusting wind. The couple smiled at him warmly.

Andrei returned the well-wishes and the smile. These people symbolized everything Andrei appreciated about Lorenzo's, aptly billed as "Buffalo's Rendezvous of Artists." Such pleasures, however, were sometimes guilty ones when Andrei recalled that his countrymen were being frozen into starvation five thousand miles away. An assignment such as Andrei's in America—a wonderland by any comparison—sometimes challenged his scruples.

The aromas that usually wafted down Pearl Street from Lorenzo's classic Italian kitchen, however, stilled his moral dilemma. He rationalized that service to Mother Russia need not be a hardship. The vintage 1934 Tuscana he had asked Lorenzo to set aside for the evening would further relieve any lingering qualms. Life in America was good. No need to deny himself.

Andrei did not notice the heavily bundled man who stepped out of a car up the street and crossed to stand in a dark, recessed doorway a half block farther on. The position let him look through Lorenzo's wide front windows with little chance of being seen.

On entering Lorenzo's lobby, Andrei stamped snow off his elkskin boots and dodged a clutch of limp party balloons dangling from a rafter, stragglers from the New Year's Eve party two nights before. A hand-scrawled cherub dubbed *Bambino 1945* decorated a nearby wall. Tonight, only quiet conversations drifted through the restaurant accompanied by soulful Italian folk tunes played by a roving violinist. This was the American version of Italy, Andrei realized. It paid no homage whatsoever to Mussolini's current, mad rendition of that storied land.

A slim, athletic young man waved in Andrei's direction. It was Larry Haas.

Andrei lifted his *ushanka* in greeting and a clump of wet snow slipped off onto the plush, red carpet. He smiled an apology at the hatcheck girl, an attractive young lady he knew as Margaret.

She accepted the apology from the kind "Mr. S." she saw here often, along with his hat. She wiped a soft cloth across its crown and sides.

He informed her that on this evening he would be dining with colleagues, and would she please ask Mr. Lorenzo to come by his table, if he should find a moment to do so.

"Sure thing," was Margaret's usual answer for all customer requests. She hung his coat on her rack with his *ushanka* above it. She caressed its soft fur a little more than she would another man's ordinary fedora.

A moment later, a tall man stepped through the door, letting in a blast of cold from the street. Colonel Milo Miller, the army air forces' representative at Bell,[1] looked comfortable in civilian dress. He greeted Mr. Schevchenko with a smile and a firm handshake and thanked him for the invite.

"Call me Andrei, please," was the necessary reply. Andrei ushered Milo toward Larry's table as graciously as a maître d' might, if he had waited for one. But Andrei was eager. As he approached the table, he silently rehearsed the roles he had assigned to his guests: target and foil.

Andrei looked from man to man, smiled warmly, and wished them both a Happy New Year, though he focused on Larry a moment longer. He sat down across from Larry with Milo on his left. Andrei assured himself this night's dance would be simple. He needed only two basic steps: small talk and listening.

Andrei assured his friends of Lorenzo's exceptionally good food as he picked up a menu.

Milo looked at the offerings and nodded agreement. Larry suspected his military mind was already at work wondering why he was here and what this was about.

So Larry asked. Was there some business to talk about? He saw a tiny flinch in Andrei's eye, but it quickly disappeared behind a smile.

They would toast the New Year and that would be enough, he assured Larry. He was, he explained, 7,500 kilometers from home and in a foreign land simply hoping for an evening in good company to start a new year. He called to a nearby waiter in Russian-accented Italian, "*Il vino, per favore.*" He told Larry that on the day before he had asked Lorenzo to select a special dry red from his excellent cellar.

The wine arrived moments later in Lorenzo's own hands.

Andrei introduced his guests. Each was welcomed with a gracious pour of Lorenzo's 1934 Tuscana. Watching each pour, Andrei reminded himself, *in vino veritas.*

Andrei raised his glass to Milo and proposed a toast to his commander in chief, Mr. Roosevelt. All three men drank to the president's good health.

Milo answered with his own toast to Joseph Vissarionovich Dzhugashvili.

Larry added "To Mr. Stalin," a clarification nobody needed.

Andrei answered "*Vashe zdorov'ye!*" To your health! They clinked glasses all around and drank again.

Larry offered his toast to Winston, a tough man on a little green island surrounded by giants.

And for a third time, all drank to another great man. Andrei, however, did not quite drain his glass this time, but he poured generous refills for the others.[2]

Their dinner had started exactly as Andrei had planned, with accolades to the three most important names among the three Great Allies. He reckoned it a good way to start his inventory of politics and biases. War talk colored just about every American conversation in 1945, and Andrei could use that to his advantage. But he did not yet know Larry Haas well enough. The always ready imp in Larry's brain spoke up.[3]

Politicians, he said, were just people, too, weren't they? But maybe just a little eccentric. Take Mr. Stalin, Larry said. He winked at Andrei, inviting him into the jest. Wouldn't you call him eccentric?

Andrei had to stifle a cringe. His Soviet comrades would call that heresy. But now he had to play along. He mused for a moment and suggested they say "*unikal'nyy*" "unique." He could take that as a compliment, as could Roosevelt and Churchill. No?

Milo did not know Larry well either, but he thought he was up to something. He said, "Hear, hear," and sat back ready to be amused.

Larry pressed on and posed a hypothetical. He wanted his friends to dream up a chance meeting between those three statesmen one evening in a bar, someday and someplace far away. Would they become friends if they had never met one another before? Then to add an exotic note, he said he'd bring them together in Timbuktu.

Andrei laughed and told Larry the joke was on him. They don't have bars in Timbuktu.

Larry waved a fork like a magic wand and declared a miracle. Now they do! Besides, they could use a few. So who, Larry asked, would buy the first round of drinks? He picked up the wine bottle to illustrate his story but looked at it in mock horror. It was empty.

That one worked in Andrei's favor. He uncorked another bottle and topped off his friends' glasses, even though they hardly needed it yet. Of course, he answered, it would have to be Roosevelt who bought the drinks. He paused to time his punch line. Roosevelt, after all, had all the money.

Milo, watching silently so far, now rose to the challenge and defended his commander in chief. Mr. Roosevelt, he corrected Andrei, had all the Soviet IOUs, but certainly not the money. Milo caught the slight wink in Larry's eye and proposed a new toast of his own—to the two men who would actually buy back all those IOUs. He raised his glass toward Andrei. To postwar riches for Winston and Uncle Joe and their paybacks to Uncle Sam.

And who, Andrei asked, would pay up first? Andrei seemed to be enjoying the impromptu joust.

That's easy, Milo said. It would be Churchill. Mr. Stalin does not mean to pay anything. *Ouch*, Larry thought. *But Andrei set himself up for that.*

Andrei laughed again, prompted by the always ready ideological twist communists in America often needed. Russians, he said, would say just the opposite. Capitalists are the ones who hang onto their money. So he raised his glass and they all drank "to better times." Privately, Andrei checked off a couple of boxes in his inventory. *Haas: Freethinker. Miller: AntiSoviet?*

After that, the table talk took many more turns. Some were unexpected and a few ended just short of heated, but most of it went where Andrei wanted—a good harvest of prejudices, likes, dislikes, and desires. He kept on probing and made sure to keep his friends' glasses comfortably full.

Andrei asked Larry if he agreed with Milo about those IOUs.

Larry surprised himself with a momentary sympathy for the Soviet leader's plight. He said Mr. Stalin *could not* pay the United States back. Britain was being battered, but Russia was being ruined. Bemused by his alliteration, he looked at his glass and found it empty again.

Andrei turned to Milo and told him that his friend had it right. He raised his glass again and they all drank to that.

Andrei had, so far, scored himself a few wins. Milo had shown himself distrustful, and Larry, sympathetic. Andrei could exploit that difference. He started by asking for Milo's opinion on a military matter on which he hoped for differing opinions.

Noting that Milo was an officer in the US Army Air Forces, Andrei asked for Milo's opinion on Russian pilots. Andrei asked because he already knew the answer. It would be useful.

Whether responding to the relaxed atmosphere of the place, the easy camaraderie that had developed around the table, or the wine, Milo smiled. For quite some time he had hoped a Russian would ask that question. Normally, diplomacy would have reserved his opinion for American ears only.

Larry braced himself. He knew Milo's thoughts on the subject, too. Milo answered with one word.

"Cowboys."

Andrei's eyes widened. It was all the encouragement Milo needed to elaborate.

Russian pilots, he allowed, were sharpshooters, good ones and fast on the trigger. Hell-bent for leather. That's what they had flying. But, Milo said, that was also a problem. Cowboys all ride to their own bugler. They were deadly in the air, nobody could take that away from them, but they were undisciplined in that, and so, dangerous to their own chain of command.

Andrei countered that the comradery of brave men might at times be more valuable than commands. Andrei reminded Milo of America's own revolution almost two hundred years ago, the battles of Lexington and Concord, the shot heard round the world. Americans, he said, had invented guerrilla warfare, individualistic, undisciplined, disorganized, but deadly. Russia was fighting a guerrilla war in the sky.

Andrei realized that Milo knew less about Soviet fliers than he thought. They were highly disciplined when needed, but Milo's opinion served Andrei's purpose just now. He turned to Larry and asked what he had to say.

It was not a matter Larry had given much thought, but he found himself agreeing with Andrei. Maybe there was a higher military discipline at work here. Larry knew those pilots man-to-man. Every one of them was his own commanding officer in the cockpit. They rewrote any rule they had to if it won them another kill. Their superior officers knew it and counted on it. That was not really a lack of discipline.

Milo looked like he was about to answer, but Andrei had what he wanted from that foray and spoke first to forestall the quarrel it could become. Brilliant, he declared, on both sides.

He settled the matter with a toast to both cowboys and commanders. Privately, he was pleased that a simple difference of opinion had helped in his ongoing calibration of Larry Haas. He refilled his friends' glasses and raised his. All drank to that.

Larry noticed, not for the first time, that Andrei only sipped. Larry was watching and learning, too.

As they set their glasses down, their food arrived, steaming, fragrant, and beautifully presented. Andrei kept the conversation lively asking questions and getting to know his two new friends better. His fascination with American life seemed endless and he listened more than he spoke. When dessert arrived, Andrei suggested they end with *Ruskaya voda*, an old tradition to "settle the stomach."

Larry had gradually realized he was losing to Tuscana's whiles and decided he'd rather end the evening on the right side of stupid. Russian vodka? he asked, trying to sound amused. In a good Italian restaurant? Thanks, but since he simply didn't have his Russian friend's ability to drink rocket fuel anyway, maybe a traditional Italian after-dinner dessert and *caffè* would be better.

Andrei set his fork down, wiped his lips once more on one of Lorenzo's fine linen napkins, turned to Milo and spoke as if to a confidant. Since our friend had gone dry, must he buy him a cup of coffee?

That would be good all around, Milo said. He had caught Larry's hint, though belatedly.

Espresso with dessert then, Andrei prescribed. Lorenzo himself took his order, *dolce dopo cena con caffè.*

Moments later, a cup of strong Italian *caffè* topped off with Lorenzo's honey-laced *cioccolato al mascarpone*—thick with dark chocolate cream nestled inside sweet milk-chocolate cups—helped Larry set himself back on course. Milo ordered a cup of American coffee, black, please.

Andrei, still watching his friends closely, was surprised to see a certain discipline in alcohol consumption. He decided to probe the sobering American mind on a topic where emotion alone might loosen lips without bottled help. His topic was dear to every real Soviet communist.

Andrei sat back, rested an elbow casually on the back of his chair, and spoke to Milo. He admitted that Milo's candor was interesting. The military mind seemed fascinating because it was so different from his.

Milo's smile seemed almost a smirk. Good thing, Milo said. It looked to him like Andrei had some pretty tough military colleagues.

Andrei agreed. And that was exactly what prompted his next question. It was about the men in the US Army Air Forces.

Milo looked skeptical now. But as long as Andrei asked nothing confidential, he said, then Andrei could ask away.

Not like that, Andrei promised, beginning to smile. What if, he began, your American men simply were not men?

Milo and Larry looked at each other and then back to Andrei with a single thought. What was this Russian talking about now?

Not men, Andrei said with a laugh—women. Russian women flew combat missions. This was known to American forces but little regarded in the press or official communiques. His question, however, challenged something deeper than the news. What did Milo think about trying that in the American air forces?

Milo was aghast. Girls in combat in *his* air force? Andrei had to be joking.

Andrei answered with a cold stare. Russian women are not girls. And they fly Russian airplanes.

Milo bridled, just as Andrei would have bet by now. In no uncertain terms, he informed Mr. Schevchenko that he would never see an American female in combat of any kind.

Andrei leaned in. Russian *women* had been flying night bombing raids over German battlefield positions since 1941. They were highly effective. Did Milo see a problem in that?

Before Milo could answer, Andrei extolled their prowess. The all-female 588th Night Bomber Regiment, the "Night Witches"—soon promoted to the elite 46th Guards Aviation Regiment—flew into enemy territory under cover of darkness on moonless nights, sometimes as low as two hundred meters. And they did it in old, open-cockpit U-2 crop-duster biplanes using old-fashioned stick-and-rudder, seat-of-the-pants grit. Near their targets they cut their engines, glided in like witches on broomsticks, and tossed 350 kilograms of bombs overboard by hand. Any one of them could light up a munitions shed or a fuel depot, fire up her engine again, and get away clean—while their enemy scurried around on the ground like rats in a burning barn. And if nothing more, they kept the enemy up all night just to ruin their days.

Andrei's voice was rising now. He told his dinner guests of one particular woman, Marina Raskova—he interrupted his rant to add emphasis, *Major* Marina Raskova, the "Mother of Witches," a graduate of the Leningrad Air Force Scientific Research Institute—one of whose fliers took a hundred men and twenty tanks off the battlefield in one single night. His eyes glowed now. That, he said, was what Soviet women did for the war.

For a second, Milo was taken aback by Andrei's outburst, but not Larry. Stung by Andrei's insinuation of American weakness, he stepped in before Milo could muster his next words.

That certainly was patriotism of the highest order, Larry admitted. That's what Russia's Great Patriotic war was all about, of course. But every day at Bell he challenged Andrei to see the same. It only looked different. American women built Russia's warplanes working alongside the men. They earned the same pay and they did the same jobs. They were just shooting rivets at the Nazis instead of bombs.

Andrei was fascinated by the contrast between Larry's response and Milo's. Did Larry really approve of the women's role?

Damn straight he did, Larry shot back. And when Bell rolls out those airplanes, it was American women who jockeyed a lot of them to Alaska, most of the way to Siberia. They even flew in formation with Russian pilots along that treacherous air route.

Andrei relaxed. He had heard enough and he had learned enough—just about all he had come for. Time to step away and let matters settle.

But Milo gave him one more piece of his mind after Andrei summarized the thoughts they had traded. Regardless of their differences, Andrei said, they still had the same enemy and that made them allies. As friends, these little differences were okay.

Milo agreed, then added—at least for now.

Andrei saw to well-wishes all around, offered New Year's good cheer to all and platitudes of friendship. He thanked his new friends for their generosity in sharing their time with a lonely foreigner.

Let's do this again, Larry said. He was glad Andrei had thought of it. To himself, though, Larry added *but not until I figure out what this was all about.*

They donned their hats and coats, tipped the hatcheck girl generously, wrapped their scarves tight, and stepped out into the night, where a light snow was falling again.

A cab pulled to the curb. Lorenzo's maître d' had called it for Milo. He stepped aboard and tipped his hat in farewell. Larry bid a good night to Andrei as they headed for their cars. Larry was amused to find himself feeling like he had just said good night to a nervous, first-date suitor.

The man with numbing fingers who stood in a darkened doorway half a block away scribbled license plate numbers on a small pad.

The next morning, SA (Special Agent) Vincent M. Quinn, at the FBI's Buffalo field office, carefully deciphered his agent's numb-fingered scribbles. He filed his first report to Director Hoover based on the heightened surveillance on subject Andrei Ivanovich Schevchenko and the events of January 2. Quinn's report began:[4]

> Subject: Information concerning contacts between Andrei Ivanovich Schevchenko and Loren George Haas.
>
> On January 2, 1945, surveillance revealed that Schevchenko met two men at the Casa Lorenzo Restaurant in Buffalo, New York, and that all three had dinner and drinks.
>
> One of the men with Schevchenko upon parting from the group entered a 1941 Chevrolet Coupe bearing 1945 New York license plate No. 7B-91-63 . . . issued to Loren G. Haas, employed as an engineer for the Bell Aircraft Corporation.

Larry Haas had turned a second corner on a road he did not yet know he had started down. It led to places he would never have planned to go.

CHAPTER TEN

Rethinking Flying

Friday, January 19, 1945, 5:15 p.m. in the Bell Aircraft parking lot

Larry Haas had gone to Bell's office to talk about a fabrication problem in the P-59 program, but afterward, he nearly forgot what they talked about. Without knowing it, Bell had set Haas's mind on a new course.

Haas had always felt drawn to ideas that were a little dangerous. That included anything different from what he already knew. On this particular evening, Bell made an accidental accord with Schevchenko that set Haas's mind in motion in a new and dangerous direction.

It started with a small, framed quotation hung on Bell's office wall.

> If I don't manage to fly,
> someone else will.
> The spirit wants only that there be flying.
> As for who happens to do it,
> in that he has only a passing interest.[1]

Haas, though never particularly attracted to aphorisms or maxims, knew he was one of those who had heard that call. And like Bell, he had heard it sooner than most Americans. Haas, in fact, had already built wonderfully designed jet engines in his lab by the time he joined the P-59 team. His lab, however, was the same one Einstein spent his life in, the lab of the *gedanken experiment*, the thought experiment. Haas's lab equipment was pure thought, and the sky where he flew his jet planes was his imagination. Though he did not know the word for it, Larry Haas had accomplished the rare scientific feat of parallel invention. That's where Schevchenko caught him.

Before Wilbur and Orville Wright flew *The Flyer* at Kitty Hawk in 1903, a century of would-be fliers had already invented and patented flying machines that nearly flew. The *Spirit of Flying* had bred a whole century of parallel almost-inventions before the real thing happened.

As soon as *flying* was established, the spirit of *flying faster* arrived. That was when parallel invention of jet engines began. Inventors in Russia and England, Germany, Japan, and Italy all heeded the spirit, but they did so in isolated, secret laboratories under the pressure of wars and rumors of war.

The isolationist United States stood aloof at first. Invention was honored as an individualistic pursuit in America, not driven by government. America's NACA, the National Advisory Council on Aeronautics, the predecessor to NASA, ignored the worldwide drive toward jet propulsion, convinced it could be of little value. America was the last to hear the *Spirit*'s call to flying faster, except for a few visionaries.

Those words on Bell's wall reframed Haas's thinking about himself, Schevchenko, and the war. The spirit of flight was clearly being subverted—yet still being propelled forward. The buying and selling of flight as a means of destruction, and the secrecy as if it belonged to anyone alone, suddenly made Andrei's arguments into a new kind of sense. That, Larry realized, like all other interesting ideas, could be a little bit dangerous. The social time he and Andrei had planned for the next evening at Cappellini's in Buffalo now promised to be more interesting.

After a few drinks and pleasantries, Andrei's conversation wandered as if something else in his mind was clamoring to be said. In time, he told Larry he had a more important matter to discuss but didn't think that they were in the right place for it. He looked around, suggested they go for a ride, and placed a twenty-dollar bill on the table.

Larry followed Andrei to his car. Andrei drove casually through nearby neighborhoods while they spoke of day-to-day matters. But after a few minutes, Andrei stopped himself in mid-sentence. His next words seemed a peculiar non sequitur.

Andrei said he wished he had blinked.

It sounded to Larry like the last sentence in a dialogue Andrei had been carrying on in his mind for a while. But Larry was stumped and said so.

Andrei simply answered with a number. Fifty thousand.

The entire conversation returned full-blown in Larry's mind. It was not one he had ever wanted to revisit, but Andrei continued. He told Larry the Soviet government had declined his request. Colonel Pisconoff[2] had called Andrei personally from Moscow. He had not stated his reasons, nor those of the bureaucrats, generals, and industrialists who, Andrei knew, had also had their say.

Larry had no idea how to reply, but Andrei continued and saved him from his indecision.

Andrei seemed both sorry and embarrassed to have broken what he had meant as a promise of wealth and a good life. However, he doubled down with a new promise that after the war Larry *would* be well paid. Russia would obtain billions of dollars of postwar credit in America. Larry would never have another financial concern when he did business with Andrei. Larry's talents, Andrei assured him again, would be more valued in the Soviet Union than in the United States. Such talents should not be bound and stifled by borders or laws. But since America's laws were so restrictive, Russia would gladly free Larry from such restraints.

Larry bit his tongue. He was stunned. He thanked Andrei but told himself, *The less said here, the better.* Andrei was talking as if he had read the same words Larry had seen on Bell's office wall.

Andrei said he would not bring up the subjects of his invention or the P-59 and jet propulsion again and handed Larry a white envelope that he said was to compensate Larry for his disappointment.[3]

Larry pocketed it with a simple thank you.

Andrei slowed and Larry saw they had pulled to a curb behind his own car.

Offering thanks for the lift, Larry stepped onto the snow-slick asphalt. Andrei's short ride now seemed like it had been much longer and had taken him in a new, even stranger direction.

Five new twenty-dollar bills fell onto his car seat when Larry opened the envelope. He folded them into his wallet with an uncomfortable thought.

Money is supposed to buy things. What does Andrei think he's buying?

On Wednesday, February 14, 1945, at 5:00 p.m., Andrei met Leona and Joe Franey at gate No. 2 of the Bell plant. He told them that he had to decide within five days whether or not to accept a new position. This one would be at a place called Amtorg in New York City. It was the Soviet Purchasing Commission he already worked for at Bell, but this would be a move up to the headquarters office. He explained that he was inclined to make the move because his son, now seven years old, would be obligated to attend a Russian school, something not available in Buffalo. The only one was at the Russian Consulate in Manhattan.

Andrei, however, said he was sad. The move would jeopardize "the education" he had been receiving at the Bell plant. So, to continue his education, he wanted to keep getting copies of reports from Bell if Leona could help him with that.

Leona, however, reminded Schevchenko again that he could not receive any secret, confidential, or restricted reports from the Bell Aircraft plant. The US Army Air Forces would not authorize him to receive such material. If she sent it to him, she would violate the espionage law and become liable for prosecution.[4]

Andrei, undaunted, tried again by another means. He asked for Leona's opinion. Could she help him get such reports if he had written authorization from Larry Bell? Sadly, Leona said that also could not be. Even Larry Bell could not override the army regulations.

Andrei changed his ask again. He proposed that someone else could obtain the reports for him, charged out under Andrei's library account. Leona said no again but added a sincere apology. No offense meant. Really.

Finally, Andrei was reduced to a simple plea. He did not want the army to hear of his requests. Leona only answered in the kindliest way possible that she understood. She was beginning to suspect, though, more than he would have liked.

Receiving no satisfaction at all, Andrei might have merely bid his soon-to-be-forgotten friends a fond goodbye. But he had a plan that did not permit defeat. A different tactic was needed.

With a smile, Andrei changed the subject. Wasn't it true that only a few days ago Leona had celebrated a birthday?

Not to embarrass the man who had, after all, been quite nice to them, Joe refrained from telling Andrei that this exact day, February 14, Valentine's Day in fact, was really Leona's birthday. So Joe just nodded yes and smiled.

Andrei offered congratulations, and he gave Joe fifty dollars to buy a birthday gift for Leona.[5] They parted with good wishes all around.

Andrei had apparently decided to trust his spy craft in regard to giving gifts, though continuing to pay the Franeys while getting nothing in return was probably not a good seduction technique.

On the way home, Joe showed Leona the fifty dollars. They reckoned it was meant to buy more than a birthday present.

CHAPTER ELEVEN

Second Date

One week later. Wednesday, February 21, 1945, 6:17 p.m., outside the Kenmore Theater

For this night, Andrei had planned something special—an appeal to pathos, a clash of ideologies, and a call to higher ideals. There's nothing like a night at the movies and a few bottles of fine, vintage wine for plying the fine art of seduction, he reasoned. It interested Andrei that improvisation in seducing his target was turning out to be effective. At least so far.

Larry pushed his hat down and tightened his scarf. The Buffalo airport weather station, KBUF, had predicted warmer westerlies, but the drizzly mist didn't feel warm. Cars hissed past on rain-soaked Delaware Avenue.

When Larry stepped beneath the Kenmore Theater marquee, his watch showed 6:17, thirteen minutes early. Street lights and storefronts were starting to light up along the avenue as the evening grayed toward sunset.

A moment later, Milo arrived, responding to the same invitation Andrei had made to Larry. Neither man, however, knew why he was there. Milo leaned out into the rain to see the marquis lights. "*Thrill of a Romance*," it read, "with Esther Williams." If Andrei wanted them to watch a potboiler like that, he told Larry, he would kick him all the way back to Russia.

At exactly 6:30, Andrei pulled up at the curb in front of the theater, parked squarely in the middle of the drop-off zone, and exited, smiling as if he owned the theater and cared nothing for such regulations. He answered Larry and Milo's puzzled questions with an even more puzzling statement.

They were there because the theater was closed. He pointed at a cardboard notice propped up in the box office window, hand-lettered, all in caps:

THEATER TEMPORARILY CLOSED
ONE NIGHT ONLY
WEDNESDAY, FEBRUARY 21
FIXING A LEAK. THANK YOU FOR YOUR PATIENCE.
SHEA'S KENMORE

Andrei rapped a half-dollar piece on the large glass door. Inside the dim lobby, a man in overalls rose slowly from a folding chair, crushed a cigarette under his boot, hobbled forward, and peered out.

Andrei unfolded a note from his pocket and held it at the man's eye level. He squinted for a moment and suddenly became a different person.

The disheveled character behind the glass suddenly snapped to military attention. His voice, though muffled by the door, came through with a clear statement that Andrei and his guests were expected and all was ready. He cranked a large key around twice in a lock at the top of the door and swung it open.

Andrei motioned Larry and Milo through and told the workman that he would give the projectionist a wave at the right time. Larry heard the man lock the door behind them.

Andrei led his guests down the dark middle aisle of the cavernous, empty, 1,500-seat theater. Larry heard switches click in a distant corner. Just enough lights came up to see the closest seats down front. The rest of the rows stretched back into darkness.

Andrei sat beside Larry, leaned forward to see Milo beyond him, and said something so surprising that Larry never forgot it.

"We are guests of General Secretary Stalin tonight."

He had Larry's attention now. Milo's, too. He glared at Andrei and demanded to know, as an officer of the US Air Forces, if this was in any way a diplomatic or military event. If so, it violated protocol and he would leave immediately.

Andrei's answer was not an answer but it arrested Milo's attention. Andrei explained that he had come into possession of a banned film, unfit for release according to American generals. Andrei's embassy, on the other hand, accepted this version for viewing by the Russian people. Andrei said he had invited Milo as Citizen Milo Miller, not as Colonel Miller.

Milo decided to stay. *I better stay*, he told himself.

Andrei was pleased. He had persuaded the theater owner to arrange this viewing especially for them.

Larry wondered whether the owner was an obedient, or even ardent, member of the Communist Party of the United States (CPUSA) sacrificing 1,500 seats worth of income for a night, or was he an owner responding to a threat. Either possibility was chilling.

Satisfied, Andrei introduced the movie he was about to screen. He recited the opening credits from memory. This was *The Battle of San Pietro*. Director and Screenplay: John Huston; Producers: John Huston, Frank Capra; Musical score: Dimitri Tiomkin; Cast: General Mark W. Clark and US Infantry, Ranger, and Parachute troops.

Milo knew all about San Pietro. He sat forward and snapped that it was a damn bloody battle—a damn bloody *stupid* battle.

Precisely, Andrei agreed. Huston had filmed almost the whole thing alongside the soldiers in battle in December of 1943; he had put all the blood, guts, and gun smoke right in front of the camera. That was what Americans were not allowed to see, Andrei told his guests, but it is what Russians saw every day in their own country.[1]

Milo's anger was rising now. He knew the numbers and he spat them out. The Nazis had killed 1,100 American troops almost instantly and blown up twelve of the sixteen Sherman tanks the United States had sent in along a road littered with mines and in plain sight of German artillery. Though the GIs eventually pushed the Germans out of San Pietro, Milo called it a Pyrrhic victory at best.

Almost smiling, Andrei wondered if the American tactics could be called "questionable." Milo let the sarcasm pass, but it set his mood on edge, exactly as Andrei had hoped.

Larry listened carefully but held his thoughts. The dynamic that Andrei was creating struck Larry as odd, worth noting. He asked if this screening was the "little leak" the box office sign was talking about.

Andrei answered only with a wink, waved to the projectionist, and sat back.

The American eagle rose across the screen, talons gripping battle arrows and an olive branch. Under that, War Department. Army Pictorial Service.

Heroic martial music by the Army Air Forces Orchestra filled the theater. The picturesque Liri Valley appeared, ringed by the Apennine mountains of central Italy. The camera followed a mountain pass and then dropped down into the heart of San Pietro. Capra's voiceover explained in measured tones that the last few months of war had destroyed what seven hundred Mediterranean summers had not. The founding cathedral's hand-wrought iron gates and its steeple now lay in ruins. Trees were blackened and the vineyards were leafless. The camera panned upward toward open sky where the bomb-splintered roof had once sheltered the cathedral's last altar. Capra's voice, cool with irony, said, "Notice the interesting treatment of the chancel."

In the flickering light, Larry saw Milo's knuckles turn white on his armrests.

Capra's camera jolted with explosions mere yards away, watched soldiers fall amid flying debris and gun smoke, then drifted among burning buildings and bomb-scarred countryside. Courtyards and streets lay strewn with pale-faced corpses staring into an eternity that had come for them too soon.

In the final scene, Italian peasants rebuilt their village out of rubble. Women toted salvage on their heads. Children smiled at the camera while GIs gave them candy. Angelic voices of a boys' choir and the Mormon Tabernacle Choir sang in praise of salvation, liberation, and eternal comfort. The screen faded to black behind one final word: *Victory*.

Andrei signaled the projectionist and the lights came up. His next words reframed everything they had just seen—this, he said, was only the prologue.[2]

Following the movie, Andrei stood and faced his friends as if to make a formal statement. "Comrade Stalin wished for me to make a point."

"That war is hell?" Milo said. "We know that."

"We, like you, are a peace-loving nation, yet we wage war. This is a paradox."

"Not at all," Milo said. "We have a common enemy to stop, the Nazis, and we have our people to protect. That's not news and it's not a paradox."

"That is where I will say you are wrong," Andrei answered. "And that is Mr. Stalin's message. Our enemy is not the Nazis. It never was. That is Capra and Huston's message in this film, too, though they claim it is not. Our enemy is neither people nor nations. Our common enemy is war itself."

The logic was so simple that it startled Larry. Such logic sidestepped politics, philosophy, and competing ideologies. Its simplicity felt elegant.

Andrei continued. "This war will end nothing." He turned to Milo. "When this war ends will your army end?"

"Not mine and not yours," Milo admitted, allowing himself a wry smile.

"So, I have a plan," Andrei said. "But it is better discussed over good food and good drink. Will you join me?"

Larry and Milo, having encountered the unexpected again, acceded to their curiosity and agreed. "Okay," Larry said. "Where to?"

"Oliver's. I have reservations for three at seven-thirty." Andrei turned away, strode up the aisle, and gave the projectionist one last wave. The lights went out behind them. Part two of the second date would be critical.

———•—•———

Less than two miles down Delaware Avenue from the theater, where addresses changed from Kenmore to Buffalo and neighborhoods grew more urban, Oliver's Restaurant stood on the east side of the thoroughfare. Its gracefully scripted name—Oliver's signature spelled out in red neon across a store-wide expanse of midnight blue glass above picture windows—created the restaurant's striking and famous art deco facade.

Frank Oliver had made his mark in Buffalo with fine food, drink, and his sweeping, one-of-a-kind, grand-circle bar of polished mahogany. Dignified men in white slacks and shirts, wearing tailored white jackets, stood behind it tending to the drinks.

Once seated, Andrei told his friends to order anything they liked, to which they readily agreed. Before the main course arrived, a 1935 Cheval Blanc bottle already stood empty in the center of their table. The wine, according to Andrei, was part of the last shipment to reach America from France before the war. During dinner, conversation turned to more serious matters. Andrei set the course.

Gentlemen, he addressed them somewhat formally, speech in Russia was not free. It could be ... he searched for a word ... it could be *treason* to say certain things. He looked at Milo. They were allies, he said, yet there was much they could not say to each other. Was that not so?

Milo admitted as much. There were laws about secrecy and security, and Americans respected them. There were prisons for people who did not.

Russia had firing squads for that, Andrei countered.[3]

Milo said then perhaps the conversation should be over. His skepticism had resurfaced. But then, trying not to seem confrontational to a generous host, he offered that if it was unsafe for Andrei, they would be glad to talk of other matters.

Andrei's reply surprised Milo. He said it all depended on his definition of certain words. Was it treason, for example, to save lives?

Of course not, Milo answered with his frown turning puzzled.

Larry sat back to watch Andrei and Milo. He decided to stay out of it for now and enjoy the show. Andrei was pleased to see Larry shift into the spectator role. Milo was turning out to be a useful foil.

Andrei posed a strange scenario for his friends. If a government or its officials did not protect the innocent in war, could that not be called treason?

Without waiting for a reply, he slanted his proposition in a slightly different direction. American politicians, generals, and civilians, he noted, had now wasted more than three years blaming one another for the Pearl Harbor attack. Had there been a failure of intelligence? He stared into Milo's eyes. Or had preventive action merely not seemed expedient for his generals? Had they actually wanted an excuse for war? Andrei saw Milo stiffen and reframed his original question before Milo could answer. Was it treason or patriotism to assign the blame in this, and would free speech allow for one but not the other?

Milo straightened in his seat, a flush rising in his cheeks. He told Andrei he got his point but warned that he was on thin ice. Some decisions looked bad to people who didn't see the whole picture. So, he challenged Andrei, he would have to answer the same charges. American soldiers took on the Germans at San Pietro to keep them away from the Russian front and save Russian skins. If Americans had stayed out of it, lots of Italian lives would have been saved, but the Nazis would have been freed up to violate Russian soil once again. American and Italian lives were sacrificed to save the lives of Andrei's people. So did they commit treason against the people of San Pietro? Milo's voice had risen above the conversational hum of the room and a few heads had turned. But unconcerned in the heat of the moment, he told Andrei that maybe all those deaths were Stalin's fault.

Andrei sat back, and to Larry's eyes, looked strangely pleased with Milo's challenge. Excellent question, he said. It was indeed the one that had to be asked. And Milo had asked it just as Andrei hoped he would. And in America this is freedom of speech, not so?

Naturally! Milo looked triumphant.

Not so for me, Andrei countered, and far from it. Some questions, and especially their answers, were too dangerous to speak of back home, but he could voice them all quite openly here. Considering Pearl Harbor, for example, he reminded Milo that Russia had its own. It was called Operation Barbarossa and Stalin had bungled it with utterly fatal consequences. Talking about that in Russia, however, would be a fatal error.

Milo did not answer, making his silence urge Andrei on.

Andrei said he would now speak a dangerous truth, and Milo was to judge for himself whether it was treason. Mr. Stalin ignored his own intelligence services when they told him—in more than eighty coded messages from his intelligence network stretched across Europe and Asia—that his friend Mr. Hitler would invade the Soviet Union in June of 1941. Stalin was told the day, the time, and the place. Yet Stalin ignored it all.[4] Is that Russian blood not on Stalin's hands? Andrei said he could ask that here, but he would be shot for asking back home.

He turned to Larry. Now it was his turn to hear a challenge, the one on which Andrei had based the entire conversation with Milo. While piercing Larry with his eyes, Andrei said Larry knew exactly what he was talking about.

Larry felt the prod like a knife. Andrei wanted him to speak his own grievances about lives he was not allowed to save with his invention for the P-63, and possible secrets he would not divulge about the P-59. Unsure what Milo knew of those matters, Larry merely looked down at his hands and did not respond.

But Andrei wanted the issue to stay on the table. Now speaking to both of his friends, he demanded to know if Bell was killing Russians, Ukrainians, and the people of a dozen other parts of the Soviet Union by withholding better aircraft, weapons that could save uncounted lives.

Larry had to answer now, though warily. He admitted that he did end up in hot water for admitting he could build faster planes. That information had not been cleared for release by Bell.

Or the army air forces, Milo said with a warning look at Larry.

Andrei turned his attention back to Milo. He explained that he had told Mr. Bell that if Larry could build faster airplanes, Russia would kill more Nazis. That, obviously, would save lives, maybe beyond counting. But Bell, and Andrei presumed the generals, refused. Andrei now addressed Milo directly. Did America's boast of freedom of speech allow Milo to explain?

"No!" Milo's face now set itself in stone. Behind Milo's single word Larry saw a volcano about to erupt.

Andrei leaned forward. Milo, you *can* help. You are a colonel in the army air forces of the United States. You are our ally, Andrei implored. He was not asking Milo to violate the espionage laws or to break security. He was simply asking for help in solving a problem. If this was asking too much, he asked Milo to forgive him, but war made desperate men like him ask desperate things. Stalin's message of friendship and an end to all wars, Andrei said, was real, yet Andrei had been willing to also speak treasonous truths at this table to prove his friendship, sincerity, and trust. Could they not help? The sooner this war ended, the better for all.

Milo's expression softened. Plainly, he conceded, Andrei was being squeezed in a vice. He assured the Russian that he could rely on American freedoms here that his leaders would not tolerate at home. Andrei's job, clearly, placed him in the middle of a dilemma, but then, that was the job he had taken. He had Milo's sympathy, but concerning substantive matters of policy and diplomacy, he could not hide behind the civilian role Andrei had previously assigned him for this evening. As an officer, he simply could not continue in this conversation.

Milo picked his napkin off his lap, folded it neatly in half and in half again, and tidily aligned its corners. He placed it beside his dinner plate. Milo said he was sorry and stood. Their common enemy might be war itself, but the terms "friend" and "foe" were not the only two alternatives to describe the relationship between the Soviet Union and the United States. He repeated his apology but stated that they would not have this discussion again. "Thanks for the drinks." Milo smiled in as friendly a manner as he could, pushed his chair in, turned, and made his way toward Oliver's front door. He said no more except for an occasional "Excuse me" to seated diners he disturbed on the way.

Andrei waited until Milo was beyond hearing distance before he spoke again.

Apparently undisturbed, perhaps even relieved at his departure, he turned to Larry to say Milo's dilemma was not theirs. Instead, they could do some good if they worked together. They had much in common, aviation science and principles on which he knew they did agree. He repeated a statement he had often made. "I am a Russian and you are an American, but we can't let nationalities interfere with progress. Scientists must be international."[5] Such matters are above politics and generals and need not lead to war. Larry knew that sentiment was common among many scientists and colleagues. But he was still ambivalent on the topic. He had, however, been moved to a middle-ground position between Andrei and Milo, just as Andrei had intended. Milo had served his purpose. Doubts had been planted concerning Bell, based on Bell's rejection of Haas's speed-boosting invention, and based on the negative light Milo had unwittingly helped him cast on militarism. Those were sentiments Andrei now planned to nurture.

Andrei looked around as if he might be overheard and confided in a softer voice that there was more he wanted to talk about.

Larry agreed, but on the spur of the moment decided it could be a good time to share a confidence of his own. He had something to say that nobody else at Bell yet knew.

Andrei looked puzzled. What kind of surprise could Larry possibly have?

"I am going to Philadelphia tomorrow," Larry said.

A fine city, no doubt. But why, Andrei wanted to know, was that important?

The issue was a job interview for a job at Westinghouse Electric and Manufacturing Company.

Andrei caught his breath. This was stunningly good luck. It was exactly what he had been planning to tell Larry to do—if he could get Larry alone, and if Larry would listen. Fortunately, Milo had reacted as Andrei hoped, and then he had left. Now Andrei had the privacy he needed. His informant network had uncovered secret jet aircraft operations under way at Westinghouse, including hints that it was even more advanced than Bell's P-59 project that Larry still refused to talk about. But he had expected an uphill battle to convince Larry to make such a switch.[6] Now Andrei was intrigued. Did Larry already know what he knew? It suddenly seemed that Larry would need no convincing at all. Making a snap decision, Andrei reached into his pocket for something he had prepared as an inducement. Now it would serve as a reward.

"Excellent!" Andrei said. He told Larry he had been wondering when he would realize that he could do better than Bell. Andrei was finding words as fast as he could. Do go to Westinghouse, he urged.[7] The pay was better there, for sure. Philadelphia was a bigger city and Dorothy would like it better there, too. He held out a small packet of folded bills. Take this and enjoy Philadelphia, he told Larry.

Surprised, Larry accepted, said thank you, and slid it into his shirt pocket without counting it.

<hr />

Less than one week after Pearl Harbor shocked the nation out of complacency, the Westinghouse Steam Turbine Division in Philadelphia had created its new Gas Turbine Division to study jet propulsion for the US Navy.[8] Westinghouse, by order of the Navy Bureau of Aeronautics, would develop its own jet and owe nothing to the Brits' Whittle jet engine, the Germans' Messerschmidt, or the GE-Bell collaboration under the US Army Air Forces. The navy's gas turbine/jet engine was to be strictly a "Yankee invention." In turn, GE and Bell were to know nothing of the navy's secret project at Westinghouse, where they were developing novel innovations and design advances of their own, including new metallurgy and control systems. Westinghouse was building an axial-flow jet unlike the centrifugal-flow design under development in the air forces-Bell-GE collaboration. Teams from both sides did not even meet until mid-1943, and only after both had crafted their own carefully developed, working jet engines.[9]

Andrei's spider web of sources had detected the invisible Westinghouse project in March 1943, after that first entirely US-designed and manufactured jet engine had been tested there. It had been developed on a fifteen-month fast track for the US Navy. Westinghouse was planning to develop an aircraft carrier–based jet fighter, eventually to be rolled out as the McDonnell F1H Phantom.[10]

Andrei's sources behind the scenes had brought him hints that the Westinghouse machine was promising, though overweight and underpowered. What he had, though, was little more than rumors pegged to cryptic names like J-30, TG-180, WE19-A, and 19-B. All were more tantalizing than informative. He clearly needed Larry Haas at Westinghouse.

Andrei told Larry he would be traveling for the next few days[11] and then return to Bell just long enough to finish up some details. Before they parted for the evening, though, Andrei made sure they set up an appointment to meet again. He had a clear purpose in mind now. He suggested they get together on March 18. Could he do that? They could meet at 12:30 in the Hotel Empire lobby in New York City.

Larry agreed before he knew why he said it. This instantly sounded like another idea that might be a little bit dangerous, and as usual, curiosity stepped in front of caution. Without realizing it, his interest had been piqued by the strange notion of a meeting in New York City. Larry would gladly take a train from Philly just to find out what Andrei had cooked up for them.

Andrei seemed pleased. Without another word, he left a twenty-dollar bill on the table and followed Larry out of Oliver's. With a handshake, a "Good day" and a "See you then," they parted ways toward their own cars, both minds swirling with new questions.

Larry had left his car parked in darkness between two distant street lights. He started his engine to power the dome light and pulled Andrei's gift from his shirt pocket. It unfolded into five new twenty-dollar bills.

When Andrei reached his car, he allowed himself a moment to savor the achievements of the night. His second date plans had paid off handsomely: Third person foil—check. Common interest nurtured with target—check. Common enemy found—check. Next date arranged—Andrei had a better idea. He'd work on Larry right away. Larry had much that Andrei wanted and Andrei had already paid for it. He was sure his little variation on the scheme would work. What could go wrong?

Unseen by the men leaving Oliver's Restaurant, Agent Quinn had watched from a coffee shop across the street. He drank the last sip from his four-times-refilled mug and wrote three New York State license plate numbers into his book. He had already noted the exact times when each of them left Oliver's. Detailed notes were important to the director.

Now, if only he knew where Schevchenko would go next.

CHAPTER TWELVE

Third Date and Goodbye

The day after their movie-and-dinner evening, Andrei came to Larry's lab with important news.

In the spirit of improvisation—Andrei was becoming quite comfortable with it by now—he had made another snap decision. He would play third date and takeaway together. This would take advantage of another brief one-on-one moment of privacy, a sharing of confidences, and then Andrei's calculated show of backing away. Larry had to feel a sense of loss, a sidelining of his importance to Andrei. Andrei could not yet have known with certainty if he had endeared himself to Larry sufficiently, but he was determined to proceed. The long seduction/sub-agent recruitment formula he was trying to follow was simply supposed to work, but he doubted it would in this case without a little tailor-made revision. Every circumstance, after all, had its own unique character.

Without any preface, Andrei simply told Larry he was leaving Bell.

Larry's surprise was real and obvious. Andrei was delighted.

Andrei drew an envelope from his vest pocket, extracted a letter, and unfolded it with ceremonial care. Larry noticed a US three-cent, first-class postage stamp on the envelope and an address typed in English. The letter itself, however, appeared to be typed in Cyrillic font. The Red Star emblem of the *CCCP* topped the page.[1]

Andrei had been promoted. He was now *vitse-predsedatel*, which meant—Larry watched him struggle for a moment with his English vocabulary—vice-chairman at Amtorg. So instead of the purchasing agent at Bell, Andrei said with obvious delight, he would now be the Soviet, Lend-Lease purchasing agent for all of the United States. He held the letter out in both hands like a holy relic. And the move would be fast. He would arrive at New

York City[2] two days from then, on Sunday morning, to find a temporary residence and begin looking for a new permanent home for his family.[3]

Larry congratulated him. This was indeed a very big deal. But of course, it posed a dozen questions for Larry. He started by asking if there were any particulars Andrei could talk about.

As far as aircraft were concerned, Andrei said, he would have full and final authority over all Soviet airplane and power plant purchases in the United States, not only from Bell. Beyond that, he would also be empowered to buy licenses to build American products of many other kinds in Russia.

That statement was hard for Larry to let pass, though for the moment he held his tongue. The openness of American society was a great asset to the Soviets in WWII, but Larry knew they used that liberty to America's detriment. Soviets had openly obtained more than a hundred thousand patents from the US Patent Office,[4] reverse engineered US military materiel, then violated US patent and industrial law by copying the processes and products in their own factories. According to the War Department's Military Intelligence Division (MID),[5] they neither admitted to it nor paid the debt they owed to the American inventors and the industries they pirated.

Larry knew all of that and hated it. He had his own way of fighting it. While at Bell he had spearheaded critical innovations through a number of design and engineering innovations and inventions. He had, however, refused to process the patent applications. Why bother, he had asked. That would only make it easier for the Russians to steal. When pressured to patent, he simply claimed that the work was still under development, unready to formalize.

Andrei saw things quite differently. Privately, he believed the Soviets took only what should be theirs anyway. He eventually complained of it to Larry, but not just now. The Soviets, he would later say, were victims of America's over-competitive, capitalistic system that had repeatedly sold them worthless or misrepresented products.[6]

Now Andrei answered a question Larry had not yet asked. At Amtorg, Andrei said, he would need to rely on new American friends. He would need a consultant, for instance, in diesels and turbines. That might have been Larry, he was sorry to say, but that could no longer be. Finding new consultants would simply be an interesting new challenge. A city like New York would make for good hunting.

Larry was surprised to hear his mind instantly translate Andrei's good news into something darker. He rejected the thought immediately, but it still echoed in his mind. It felt as if Andrei had said, "Sorry, Larry. You're out!"

Andrei played his "takeaway" carefully. Without Larry, he said, he would have to pay strangers for services he would have gladly paid Larry for. But New York was the greatest business capital in the world and Andrei was sure he would find a way to enjoy the new experience. This was the moment, Andrei had been instructed, when a lightly hooked fish could be coaxed to bite on the whole bait.

Larry, now even more bemused by his own reaction, realized he had heard a word that instantly appealed to him: consultant. He had never thought of himself as one, but the seed was planted. He also heard the words diesel and turbine.

Turbines, Larry said quickly, were right up his alley. Couldn't help with diesels, though. But if Andrei needed a turbine consultant, he assured Andrei he would not be far away.

Larry found himself searching for a word for the odd, unfamiliar feeling behind his impulsive reply to Andrei's sudden step away from their . . . was it friendship, comfortable collaboration, or shared concern for those brave young Russian fliers? With a jolt, he saw it clearly. He felt jilted. *Don't be absurd*, he told himself. He wanted to crawl out of his own skin, but he couldn't shake it. He instinctively wanted to regain control, but he managed only a mild question.

Had Andrei told Mr. Bell?

Andrei said he had done so immediately. But now, speaking in a confiding tone, he was telling Larry for a different reason. He warned that he would be leaving Larry in poor hands with his successor if Larry stayed at Bell. Andrei's successor would be an *apparatchik*, a petty bureaucrat, a man who did not understand aircraft—nor would he understand Larry. To count the P-63s he buys from Bell he would probably count the wheels and divide by three. You will miss me, Andrei said.[7]

Larry tried to shrug off the sense of loss. In the blink of an eye, he had been made to feel demoted from important to irrelevant. But Andrei had one more surprise, another improvisation of his own for which the timing and the opportunity now seemed perfect.

Andrei assured Larry that quitting Bell for Westinghouse really was his best move. Their work, Andrei said, would interest Larry far more.

That instantly startled Larry. *How could Andrei possibly know what was going on there?* He could almost hear Andrei's "connections" reporting in.

Larry congratulated him on his new job in New York City and said he would miss their talks, too.

Andrei, of course, knew very well they would stay in touch. The stage was now set.

Chapter Thirteen

Birth of a Counterspy

*Two weeks later. Wednesday morning, March 7, 1945, midmorning in
Larry Haas's office at Bell Aircraft*

The rap on Larry's door changed everything.[1] Not long ago, he had wondered about turning some mysterious corner when he accepted money from
Andrei. Now he would meet the monster that lurked around that bend.

Haas's phone had rung ten minutes earlier to warn him. He recognized
the caller's voice. It was Larry Bell.

Bell sounded tense. He wanted to know if Haas was alone.

Haas said he was. Why?

Bell was sending two men down to see him. Their IDs said War
Department and they wanted a face-to-face with Haas. Nobody else would
do. Bell didn't argue with government people these days, but something
about them seemed sketchy. "Any idea what it's about?" Bell's question did
not sound like casual curiosity.

"No idea," Haas said. Something, however, rang an alarm far back in his
mind.

One of the men, Bell said, called himself a War Department scientist.
He claimed there was a problem with the aluminum/magnesium sheet metal
stock and he wanted to start his investigation with Mr. Haas.

That did not make sense. Haas sat up straighter. He reminded Bell of
Fornoff, the top man in that department who should answer such questions.
Haas felt an inexplicable urge to sidestep whatever was coming.

"They want to talk to you," Bell continued. But for his own curiosity he
had shown the *scientist*—he said it as if he meant "so-called"—an Al-Mag
phase diagram for the alloy the plant was using. "He couldn't tell an alumi-
num/magnesium ratio diagram from a road map of Scotland," Bell scoffed.

Haas promised to look them over but added what he thought almost too obvious a question to ask—"why not just call the FBI if they look so questionable?"

Bell had opted for plant security instead, all of Department 28's day shift was now on alert, just in case, and he had detailed officer Byron to hand-deliver the men to Haas. Bell was being cautious. "Give Byron about ten minutes," he said, "and take a close look at those credentials." Bell didn't know how the gatehouse police even gave them a pass. He'd look into that right away.

"Okay," Haas said. But that little alarm bell was getting louder, though he still was not sure why. "I'll be here with bells on," he said, then bit his lip.

Bell let the pun pass without comment, except for an exasperated sigh. He hadn't thought it was funny the first hundred times he'd heard it around the plant either.

Nine minutes later, Haas heard the knock on his door.

"Open and enter," he called out but did not rise. Make them come to me, he reckoned, was a good opening gambit.

Byron Smyth, one of Bell's "old-timers," opened the door. Byron was an old soldier at the age of forty-one, a WWI vet who had been marched a little too close to the bombs and the mustard gas. He had survived, though just barely. Bell took on men like him whenever he could in respect for their service, and because the wartime man shortage made them the only men around for such work.

He ceremoniously presented the two gentlemen Mr. Bell wished for Mr. Haas to meet. Byron stepped aside for them to enter, braced, and gave a crisp salute—his signature courtesy for anyone above him in the company's food chain. He turned on his heel to leave but turned back with a self-deprecating smile to close Larry's door quietly behind him.

Haas, with equal gravity, asked how he could help the gentlemen.

The shorter man stated brusquely that Mr. Haas first must assure them that the room was secure.

"Pardon me?" Haas was too surprised to say more.

"Secure, sir," he repeated as if that explained everything, but added was there anyone else here, anyone else Haas was expecting, or was there a recording device active? He scanned the small room with probing eyes as if somebody might be hiding behind a bookcase or even a waste basket.

Yes and no, Haas guessed, still off-guard. Yes, the room was secure, and no, nobody else was coming. As for recording devices, his irreverent imp finally chipped in, "not unless you plan to sing for me."

"Maybe you will be the one singing for us," the taller visitor answered as fast as Haas had quipped. There was no humor in his voice. "But if so," he said, "we will be sure to record you."

Larry stood up now, fists on hips. "What the—"

"Please sit down, Mr. Haas," the shorter one interrupted. He reached for something inside his jacket and stepped forward.

Larry did not sit. He braced himself.

"I'm Wilcox, Mr. Haas," the man said, more like an announcement. He was the special agent in charge at the Buffalo Field Division office of the Federal Bureau of Investigation. His partner was Special Agent Vincent M. Quinn. Wilcox pulled out a leather card case and flipped it open. A gold badge shimmered beside an ID card. The letters FBI were embossed in bold, black letters. Quinn showed Haas the same. "May we have a seat," Quinn said with no hint of a question in his voice.

"Okay," Haas said warily and sat down himself. His mental alarms rang louder now. "Show me those badges again," he demanded, then added "please" to rescue a vestige of civility in case this was real.

The men pushed Larry's two straight-backed office chairs from their places beside the door toward his desk. They sat and reached forward to display their badges and ID wallets again. Both IDs looked quite real. Larry studied them for a long moment. They were there, Quinn now said in measured tones, to talk in confidence. Then he added an order Haas never forgot and often repeated in retelling the tale of this day.

"You will repeat nothing we say here. Is this understood?" This question was also clearly not a question.

"Not until you tell me why you are here." Haas glanced at the badges again. "Mr. Bell did not buy your story, and neither do I."

"Good," Quinn said. The agents put their IDs away. "Mr. Bell saw different IDs. He thinks we are metallurgical researchers from the War Department."

"No. As a matter of fact, he does not."

"Good again." Quinn seemed pleased for the first time. "He was not supposed to. I expected him to call and warn you about us. Did he?"

"He certainly did."

"Excellent. Mr. Bell cannot know who we are or why we are here. He saw these." Quinn tossed another ID onto Larry's desk. United States War Department was printed in bold letters a little askew on flimsy card stock above something that looked like official fine print and a couple of illegibly scrawled signatures.

"Fake," Larry said. "Wouldn't fool anybody. Least of all Bell." He sat back and folded his arms. "How did you even get past the gatehouse cops with those things?"

"They are law officers.[2] They saw the real IDs and they will say nothing, even to Mr. Bell."

Larry leaned forward, now fully intent on Quinn's answer. "Then what's going on?"

"We are watching you, Mr. Haas. We have been since January 2." Quinn said it like an accusation.

"Why?" Larry's hands tightened into fists. Larry Haas angry was not the Larry Haas most people knew. He looked ready to launch himself across the desk.

"Because, Mr. Haas, J. Edgar Hoover, director of the Federal Bureau of Investigation, told us to look at you. Heard of him? You have been seen hobnobbing with a foreign agent, a man we have watched for two years so far. He is a spy."

Larry's mind refocused itself with a jolt. "Schevchenko!"

"Exactly. Association with him makes us suspicious."

"But it's my job. I have to get along with him." Even as he said it, a chill ran down his spine. The words "fifty thousand dollars" finally echoed up from someplace deep in his memory.

"When it comes to national security, association is guilt." Quinn stated it like a truth. Hard-nosed dramatics had its uses in the FBI.

Their director, J. Edgar Hoover, condoned it,[3] and his choice of assistant director had confirmed it for any special agent who was paying attention. Special Agent Edward "E. A." Tamm, a fifteen-year veteran of the Bureau, had come up through the ranks in the gangster era. He was legendary among agents for his tales and written reports. His language reflected the law enforcement culture of those years. He publicly spoke of such tactics as "knocking off [Pretty Boy] Floyd," and he once wrote a well-circulated memo referring to "Ma" Barker and son, Fred, in which he told Hoover the case was closed "after we exterminated them."[4]

"Forget due process, Mr. Haas. That's for the press," Quinn said. "We do not catch innocent people. It's a waste of time. But your friend Schevchenko is a Ukrainian Soviet spy who calls himself Russian." Then he played a hunch. "We just want to know what he paid you for so far, and how much."

Larry stood up so fast he knocked his desk back against Quinn's knees. "What?"

"Sit down, Mr. Haas," Quinn ordered with a steely calm in his voice. "This is the conversation that will not leave this room. And neither will you until we say so." Vincent Quinn rose and stationed himself beside Larry's door. He folded his arms. His biceps stretched his sleeves more than his off-the-rack, ten-dollar suit was meant to accommodate.[5]

Larry sat down, deliberately calming himself. He reckoned he'd be better off just now trusting his brains more than his muscles. More composed, he said, "I am not a spy. As for Schevchenko, he's never bought me more than dinner and drinks."

Quinn's hunch had paid off. Larry's physical reaction had been instantaneous, but his denial had taken thought, so the denial had to be the lie. Wilcox pressed harder. "That will be your last lie, Mr. Haas," he said icily. "We have been watching. That is also why Mr. Bell will not know we are FBI."

Confused now, Larry could barely form a question, and confusion always angered him. "Why shouldn't Bell know? I'll call him myself, right now." He reached for his desk phone.

Wilcox moved faster and clamped his hand on the phone before Larry could reach it. "He will not hear that. He will hear only what we tell you he will hear. If we report even a suspicion that you are collaborating with a dangerous foreign agent, you will be fired instantly. Bell will be allowed no choice. We, on the other hand, want you right here." He stabbed his finger down on Haas's desk. "Plain enough? You have two choices. Cooperate or get fired. I can also blackball you for any one of a dozen security reasons. You'll be lucky to build Tinker Toy airplanes after that." He stared into Hass's eyes. "Still want to call Bell?" Quinn reached behind his back.

Larry heard the click of something being unhooked from a belt loop under Quinn's jacket. He drew out a glistening set of silver bracelets connected by a chain. It took Larry a moment to recognize it.

"Cuffs? Really?"

"That's not our preference either, Mr. Haas." Wilcox turned to Quinn. "Put them away, Vince. I think Mr. Haas is ready to cooperate."

"Maybe I am not," Larry said, teeth clenched. "So do not waste your gangster act on me. And do not accuse me of anything unless you can back it up with something better than a trained ape." He waved dismissively at Quinn. "You boys can back off right now or we will all get hurt when I throw you out of here."

Quinn laughed. "Last time somebody called me that, he got away with it because I'm a nice guy. But only once." He widened his stance and folded his arms. "That was your once."

The three men glared at one another across a battleground of stalemated wills. Larry did not know the technique by name, but he instinctively understood it—a request for cooperation backed by threats. It was a cooperate-or-else fork, one of law enforcement's oldest tricks. And they always rammed it home with whatever lies they needed to get the job done.

Larry pulled back, but just a notch. "Okay. Talk. And it better be good."

"You hung the sword over your own head by drinking with Schevchenko," Quinn answered. They all sat down. "That was not smart for a man in your position. You know what that looks like, don't you? We believe you are already in his pocket. So, start by telling us what's going on. We will listen. Then we will call the shots as we see them."

"First," Larry said, "get this. I am on your side—on *our* side. Andrei is quirky, but he's one very smart Russian, or Ukrainian, or whatever he is. I'm not sure I like him, but I find him interesting in a couple of ways. We work around airplanes and we talk about airplanes at the plant and sometimes someplace else over a beer or two. But I tell him no secrets."[6] Larry sat back and folded his arms. "And I have no lies to tell you. Sorry if that's confusing." He leaned back and laced his fingers together behind his head. "Now what's your first question?"

"Start when you first met the subject."

Larry explained that he had disliked Andrei from the beginning, as he did many Soviets working in the United States. On first meeting, Larry said, Andrei seemed arrogant. He saw nothing interesting about the man. They worked together when they had to, and that was that. Last Christmas, though, Andrei had made unexpected overtures of friendship, highlighting their shared interests. Bell had encouraged the connection.

Nearing noon, Larry had told Wilcox and Quinn everything he knew about the man they called Subject Schevchenko, everything from his extravagant dress to their discussions over mathematical insights on supersonic propeller tips; from his bookkeeper-like documenting of every drop of lubricant in Allison engine gearboxes; to his interest in Dorothy's hatred of wartime grocery rations, and Andrei's chain-smoking Camels; and from his interest in Larry Bell's P-59, its GE jet engines, and to anything else in top secret aeronautical research. The agents listened to every word so intently that Larry could have believed they themselves were tape recorders.

Finally, Larry took a deep breath, steeled himself, and told the story of his fifty-thouand-dollar[7] offer to sell his P-63 speed-enhancing invention to Andrei. He explained that Andrei had taken it seriously enough to bring Colonel Pisconoff from Washington to the Bell Aircraft plant to meet

Larry. He told them about Andrei's apologetic, big letdown when Pisconoff declined to buy whatever Schevchenko thought Larry had offered to sell. That story of contact with a highly placed Soviet military officer revived the agents' suspicions. A long conversational detour followed, but it eventually came out in Larry's favor. Candor proved to be his most persuasive argument in the end.

Then the agents asked Larry the question Larry had already asked himself more than once: What was Andrei's three hundred-dollar gifts supposed to buy? Larry assured them that he had not asked for the money. Andrei called it gratitude and justly deserved, though Larry left out the troubling words "down payment." Andrei had asked for nothing in return, at least not overtly.

"Nothing in return *yet*," Quinn said. "Do you think you owe the subject anything?"

"Nothing that can hurt us."

"Then, Mr. Haas, can we count on your help?" Now Wilcox wanted to close the deal he had come to make.

Larry nearly shouted his answer. "Of course not!" He had been waiting for that question.

"What?" Wilcox nearly choked. He thought they had finally reached a common understanding.

"Except for J. Edgar's panic over the Red Menace, do you actually have something, anything at all, on Andrei Schevchenko?"

"Of course, we do. It's obvious." But in spite of his words, Wilcox looked pained. "We just need the hard evidence. Nothing we have so far can hold up in court."

"I thought you said suspicion was guilt," Larry threw back at him.

"We say a lot of things and we always say we have proof. We connect the dots for people, and sometimes we have a lot of dots. Take our mysterious Soviet letter writer, for instance. Whoever wrote it included some insider stuff about people we can verify but nobody else outside the consulate would know. That writer named Schevchenko as a star player in their spook lineup. Your friend is definitely a hard-core spy. We are positive of it. But he tiptoes around us without leaving a trail of bread crumbs. That's where you come in."

"How, specifically?"

"It looks like Schevchenko has you in his crosshairs. He will try to seduce you. First, you'll cooperate, and then you'll collaborate. It's their way and it works. They like a long, slow seduction. Done right, people they do it to don't even notice—until it's too late. That's why we need you next to him, but as our eyes and ears, not his."

As Larry listened, little things started falling into place, quirky patterns in Andrei's behavior. Larry let the pieces assemble themselves, and scattered bits began to fit into a new shape. Eventually, logic and intuition came together and made his decision.

"So, can we count on you?" Quinn asked again.

"Okay, I'm in."

Together, the men had finally crossed a line. Suspicion and coercion had changed to trust and cooperation. But Larry's inner watcher now raised a new question. It had been just a tickle at the back of his mind at first, but over the months to come, it would grow stronger. For the first time he gave it words: *What will I have to become?*

Quinn's face relaxed into a tired smile. "Now that we understand each other, let's get to work." He rubbed his hands together like a handyman eager to tackle a long-overdue job.

"What's my game then?" Larry asked.

"Not much to it." Quinn shrugged. "Just keep working, cooperate with the subject where you can. Give us a good set of eyes. Get us a smoking gun. We'll take it from there."

"His name, by the way, is Andrei," Larry said. "I don't call him Subject. I've got to like the guy at least a little, don't I, if I'm going to get close enough to nail him?"

"Okay, it's Andrei, then," Quinn agreed. "So, let *Andrei* seduce you."

"Let him do what?"

"That's how you'll catch him. Then seduce him in return. There will be nothing more seductive to the subj— to Andrei, than making Andrei think he is the one doing the seducing. But be careful, he will be a slippery one. He has to keep his eyes sharp. For him, it comes down to 'kill or be killed.' If he slips up in any way, if he fails in his mission with you, or with anybody else in his network, a boat will take him back home for consultation—in front of a firing squad."

"Then why not just send them all home?" Larry thought it a simple remedy.

"We're not that brutal." Quinn laughed. "But be careful. They are that brutal. An American who collaborates with us against Soviet spies—as you will when you let Andrei talk you into being his sub-agent—just might die mysteriously or simply disappear. All it will take is his suspicion you are working with us. Counterspies are always in danger. Your job will be to commit counter-seduction. Make him trust you."

For Larry Haas, lessons in seduction—clearly a kissing cousin to salesmanship—were not needed. The idea and the act were intuitive for him. He would start by falling for Schevchenko's lures. Larry knew just as surely that he could catch Andrei. He would enjoy exposing Andrei's spy craft, and maybe his whole network.

"I never thought I'd be a cloak-and-dagger kind of guy. Isn't that your line of work?" Larry asked.

"Wrong. That is exactly what we would be bad at. We do not fit into his world. You do."

"Well, maybe I can draw something out of him by . . ."

"Don't." Quinn nearly jumped. "It's not what you can get him to say that matters, it is what he can get you to do. Doesn't he already ask for more than he should?"

"Sometimes." Larry thought it over. "He knows the limits of what he can get, but he can get a lot. After all, the Soviets are our allies. And they are whipping the Nazis like an old mule now by flying Bell's airplanes—*my* airplanes. I have a lot to do with that and Andrei is a legitimate part of it. We are saving civilian lives and the lives of Allied soldiers. I am proud of that, and so is Andrei, rightfully." He paused, remembering something Andrei had once said. "He likes the expression 'This is our final and decisive battle.' He says it a lot, like a motto."

"Naturally," Quinn said. "It is a motto. It's from their anthem, the *Internationale*. It says, *'This is our final and decisive battle; With the Internationale humanity will rise up!'* Want to hear a piece of the chorus? Hoover makes sure we all know it. It's part of our training. The thing is all about terrible people like you, your friend Mr. Bell, and the worst of all the creatures on Earth, our president. Sorry I don't know the tune, but listen to the words. This is what they have to say about you":

> *You've sucked enough of our blood, you vampires,*
> *With prison, taxes and poverty!*
> *You have all the power, all the blessings of the world,*
> *And our rights are but an empty sound!*
> *We'll make our own lives in a different way—*
> *And here is our battle cry:*
> *All the power to the people of labor!*
> *And away with all the parasites!*

"Lucky for you Schevchenko thinks you are a *smart* parasite, therefore a useful one," Quinn said. "The Soviets are our allies for now, but they are dangerous bedfellows. Their cooperation is only expedient and short-lived, not a true alliance. Off the battlefield, they are already adversaries. Remember this—they believe peace is only a name for the time between wars, a tool for planning the next one. That's from Machiavelli, not Hoover, and Stalin is counting on it. The Soviets are working hard for that kind of peace. Your friend Schevchenko is a top-level officer on that front. Prepare yourself."

"Then I should pick better friends," Larry said, quickly rethinking his connection to Schevchenko.

"Wrong again," Quinn said. "He's your new *best* friend and you'd better get to know his other ones. Do you know Mrs. Leona Franey?"

"Sure, but what does she have to do with anything? She's a librarian."

"Back in 1942, when Andrei first reported to the Bell plant," Quinn explained, "we contacted Leona and her husband, Joseph, in case Andrei started nosing around. Leona was managing Bell's new technical library. We were too late to warn her,[8] and we're not sure yet about Joseph. He works at Hooker Chemical, where there's something going on called—" He stopped in mid-sentence. "Let's just say something's going on we don't want the Soviets to get their hands on. Andrei had already been asking Leona for low-level, non-classified material. Those asks were meant to get Leona used to dealing with Andrei without raising her suspicions when he finally asked for more. That's a first step in his seduction routine."

"I'm not surprised," Larry said. "She's been helpful to me, too." He stopped himself there. Just how helpful wasn't anything Quinn needed to know.

"Too helpful in Andrei's case," Quinn continued. "He was already raising his asks by the time we met Leona. He wanted more sensitive materials, though not yet material classified as top secret. We let her give Schevchenko what he asked for, but only after we cleared every page with our experts. They would have cut us off if Schevchenko asked for anything more sensitive. We had experts doctor up a few things with misinformation, but they stopped doing it. They were afraid he might catch on."

"He is smart. You could have blown the whole deal," Larry said, already feeling protective of their plans. He liked the idea of conspiring with the FBI. The thrill of the chase promised to be exhilarating.

"You'll have to be careful, too," Quinn cautioned. "You have already seen some of Andrei's tactics."

"I guess I have," Larry said. He had a lifelong aversion to being manipulated. Andrei's gifts and friendship had tweaked that nerve, though not quite consciously. He would be embarrassed to admit it now. "But wait a minute," Larry said. "This all might be a gigantic waste of time."

"What are you talking about?"

"He's leaving Bell. We won't be working together anymore."

"He's what?" Quinn looked at Wilcox. "He's pulling that old stunt?"

Larry wondered if he would ever stop being confused by these agents.

"It's the takeaway trick," Wilcox explained. "He wants to find out how committed you are to your friendship and to his plan. Make a play to stay in touch. He wants you to commit."

Larry's head spun. "Sounds like I need spy school."

"No!" Quinn laughed. "You're a boy scout, Haas. I don't want your corruption on my conscience. All you need is safety school." Quinn knew that counterespionage work attempted by untrained civilians who were facing off against experienced Soviet spies was a risky thing. Quinn warned Larry, "After you commit to him, Andrei will come at you with his mice."

Wilcox winked at Quinn as if he had just told an inside joke that only they knew. Then he looked back at Larry. "Or has he already?"

"With mice?"

"Yes. M-I-C-E." Quinn pronounced each letter. "It's the ultimate tool of corruption. It goes by a lot of other names, too, but they all mean about the same."

Quinn gave Larry his primer on MICE, succinctly and to the point. "M is for Money, the ultimate lubricant for slippery deals. It's the temptress of the needy and the greedy. He's already testing it on you. Hundreds of dollars' worth and some high living, right?"

Larry could only smile back and nod an obvious yes.

"Next comes I for Ideology—whether it's the saint or the Satan in capitalism, or the savior or slayer in communism—every ideology can be ramped up to attract useful zealots. Apparently, he's testing you for an anti-war ideology convincing enough to make you betray your country."

Fine wine and dinners quickly came to mind. Larry saw he had been handled already, not just entertained.

"The C in MICE," the agent continued, "can stand for a couple of things. Compromise can lead to Coercion. You might swerve ever so slightly from legal and ethical to do even the smallest favor for a friend. But having done it once, the next ones come easier and a little closer to illegal. Properly managed, compromise can open you up for guilt, shame, and blackmail. That's the C for Coercion."

Larry got the whole picture now, all at once—a picture staring him in the face that he had not quite seen until now.

"So that's all one big banana peel on top of a slippery slope," Larry said. The first hint of anger rose in his voice. "It only looked like socializing over tech talk and beers. But taking money in return for little or nothing makes sense now, from Andrei's perspective. It started like an innocent stroll down the lane, but now I see that lane ends in Hell." Though it was clearly an evil scheme, the perverse logic of the thing fascinated Larry. Most of all, it surprised him with its familiarity. This was, after all, little more than the wicked cousin of his old friends, salesmanship and buymanship. More odd pieces fell into place, but Larry held his thought. He wanted to hear the rest of what Quinn had to say about his mice.

"Now watch out for the big E," Quinn said. "E is lots of things. It can mean Ego or Excitement. Egotists are easy prey to flattery. They love cloak-and-dagger stuff. They also love feeling powerful, superior, godlike—little people be damned. Superspies feel invincible. I don't think that role is tempting for you, but if it works, convince him he hooked you with it. Some egotists thrive on big risks. If you'll take a big risk for him, we'll catch him fast.⁹ The advantage of you taking big risks, though, is that E can also mean Extortion. Once you're guilty of something important, he will own you."

New ideas flooded Larry's thoughts. In his mind's eye a road map spread itself out and showed him a path to counter-seduction. He'd gladly guide Andrei down a slippery slope of his own. Andrei would learn buymanship, he'd think he was a master seducer able to buy anything with his charm, brilliance, and money. Larry and the FBI would then make Andrei pay the ruinous interest rate that always went with deals like that.

"Tell me where you are vulnerable." Quinn brought Larry back into the moment. "Andrei will befriend you, probe you for your soft spots. Even your strengths can be weaknesses. For instance, you are an American with ambition, aren't you?"

"Right." Larry immediately decoded that trap. "The money Andrei gave me was supposed to feed my ambitious, capitalist heart."

"Right. Next, he'll try ideology, any ideology," Quinn said. "Whether for or against any dogma, he will go along with it. Even if you're an anti-communist, he'll agree and suggest a higher calling to follow, like serving science or world peace. All you'd have to do is help him sabotage those warmongering politicians and generals."

"Right on target," Larry said. "He already tried that one on me and on . . ." Larry stopped himself.

"Milo? We know. Colonel Miller is one of the other reasons we are here. He reported Schevchenko's dinner and a movie plot. He suspects you bit on Andrei's bait. He thinks you bit hardest on the elitist part about the scientists who should rule the world over capitalists and dictators, presidents, generals, and the rest of the toads running planet Earth just now—after all, those parasites are beneath you."

"I did hear that from Andrei, though he put it a little more subtly. But you can tell Milo I'm too smart to be that stupid." Larry's jaw tightened.

"The colonel's business is none of yours," Quinn said. "Forget everything about what the colonel thinks. It will be mutual. He has also been advised your business is not his. You are not relevant to his command. Be assured he did not rise to his rank without understanding 'need-to-know' language. Drop it there. He already has." Quinn's tone was clearly a warning.

Larry understood. "What else?"

"We estimate Andrei's most dangerous hook will be compromise. That could make it your best tool. Andrei will ask you for something harmless at first. Then, with that in hand, he'll ask you for something just slightly risky, barely improper, nearly harmless. Once you get comfortable with that small game—and the money and ego-stroking that goes with it—he will play the big game. He'll go for the gold, the big things he really wants."

"I would spot that," Larry said.

"You better. That will be your sign to give in and give it to him. We want to catch him red-handed with things he should not have."

"I can get him the goods," Larry said. The whole counterplot now seemed obvious and simple, with only one catch. "I'll need permission to give him stuff, even small stuff."

"We'll work on that," Quinn said dismissively. "As long as it's even slightly restricted, he'll warn you you're already compromised. He can then make it a noose around your neck if he thinks he needs to. The friendship, if it existed at all, could evaporate in an instant. You would not even be a co-conspirator by then. You'd be ripe for the other E—Extortion. But, because he also knows that could make you dangerously unstable, he might prefer to enlist you as a respected fellow traveler, sympathetic enough to his cause to be a willing and earnest accomplice. Then, if he ever needs it, he still has coercion up his sleeve."

Larry laughed. "Coercion? Like what you guys tried on me? You said a few beers, a dinner or two, and a little cash was enough to send me jobless to the federal pen, unless I cooperated."

Quinn did not laugh. "We still can. But you learn fast, Larry, so let me be plain. You are between a rock and a hard place here. You can resent being turned into a tool, but you are an important one. You will be the gun we aim at our enemy. Are we clear on that before we continue?"

Larry took a deep breath. The imagery was too clear. "Yes. Don't ask again."

"Done," Quinn said.

"This is demonic," Larry said. "It is also ingenious. How do you know so much about their methods?"

"Their methods? You're not that naive, are you? They're our methods, too. Only sharks can swim with sharks, and the weakest ones get eaten. In the spy business, it starts with seduction and ends with control. Remember you are in Andrei's sights."

"Of course," Larry said. "And yours."

Quinn just nodded.

"By your yardstick," Larry said, "Andrei has me someplace between Money and Ideology, with a little Ego in the mix. He throws flattery around like New Year's confetti."

"Good. You are where we want you. Pick yourself a weakness and get yourself seduced. Let him start to run you, but vacillate a bit, just enough to make him work for it. That will convince him it's real. Based on what you've told us about his little takeaway game, now is the right time to chase him. Tell him you do want to stay in touch. Plan for another meeting."

"I guess I already did," Larry said a bit sheepishly. "Don't know why I did it, but I agreed to stay in touch. I guess that 'takeaway' tactic already worked on me."

"Only once," Quinn said. "After that, you'll see it coming. And this time it worked in our favor. What's the plan?"

"We set it up for a couple of weeks from now." Larry ticked off the particulars in quick succession. "Sunday. Noon-ish. March 18. The lobby of the Hotel Empire. New York City."

"And the purpose?"

"Education. He thinks he might be under surveillance and wants me to learn how not to be. He claims being watched is normal for every Russian, so it's easy to spot and easy to slip. Being seen with him, however, might be bad for me. When I get to the hotel, he wants me to watch for him but not appear to see him. I'm to take a cue from what he does. I'm not sure if it is cloak-n'-dagger-ish or a child's game, but I'll play along. I'll let you know how it goes."[10]

"No, Larry, you probably will not tell me or Agent Wilcox," Quinn said. "It will be somebody else. You will be in Philly by then."

Larry stopped Quinn, alarmed. "How do you know that? I just applied at Westinghouse. I don't know yet myself."

"Did you forget we've been keeping eyes on you? Get used to it. I am not confirming anything about your transfer out of Bell Aircraft. But I am counting on it as much as you are. You're our responsibility now," Quinn said. "We take care of our own. Your next move is as important to us as it is to you. By the way, it is important to Andrei, too."

"Got it." Larry swallowed hard. He looked at his watch. Nearly two hours had passed. It seemed much longer. Then he realized it was a mere blink of the eye compared to the life, his life, it had just turned upside down.

Quinn jotted a few short lines on a piece of paper. "Here's the address of the Philadelphia FBI field office. Report to Special Agent in Charge Fletcher from now on. Be there at 9:00 a.m. on Monday, March 19. Tell him what happened on the eighteenth. As far as Andrei is concerned, play along and stay alert. Nothing more."

"Okay then." Larry looked at the address and handed the paper back. "It's safer up here." Larry tapped his forehead.

Quinn laughed. "You do learn fast. Any more questions?"

"What do I tell Larry Bell about you two imposters?"

"I'll trust you for that. Think of something, make it good, and tell me some day. I'm betting you have a good sense of humor. As far as Bell should know, you can't even spell FBI."

Wilcox opened Larry's office door and motioned to Quinn while saying, "After you." They stepped out and closed it quietly behind them.

An hour later, the phone on Larry Bell's desk rang again. The green light flashed.

"You called it, Larry," Haas said. "Those two jokers were frauds."

"Thought so. Who are they?"

"Don't be too hard on them, they were trying to save me some embarrassment. They're private eyes out of Amherst. They figured I wouldn't want my boss to know my private business. This was the most anonymous place they could think of to ask me some personal questions. It seems there's a crazy woman in my neighborhood accusing my wife of having an affair with her husband."

"You're kidding!" Bell laughed. "How did it turn out?"

"I said if they knew my wife and that guy, they'd know better. Neither one of them would put up with the other long enough for an affair. Not even a one-nighter. They're both crazy. In the meantime, I heard much more neighborhood gossip than I want to know. Forget them. They're history. Sorry for the trouble."

"Make sure that thing stays settled, for your sake and mine. I don't want to see those boys here again."

"You won't. Neither will I."

"Good!" Click.

This was the second fact Larry Haas had withheld from his boss that day. This morning he had ducked mentioning Westinghouse to Bell when he could have said something. They had met in the company parking lot and Larry could have at least asked for a chat over coffee later.[11] He now had motives within motives and lies within lies on his mind. He wondered if he would turn into a puzzle even he could not solve.

On March 19, Fletcher sent a lengthy summary to the director. It began succinctly,

> As advised by Buffalo SAC Wilcox, informant Lauren G. Haas has agreed to cooperate with the Bureau and appears able to furnish considerable information concerning his contacts with Schevchenko.[12]

Chapter Fourteen

Moving There[1]

Thursday morning, March 15, 1945, at the Haas family breakfast table

"Are you crazy, Larry? Look at this." Dorothy Haas set down her orange juice glass, wiped a napkin across her tight lips, and slid a glossy flyer across the cluttered breakfast table toward her husband. "The government won't let you quit Bell. There's a war on. Nobody gets to change a job like yours, not these days. Look at this." She tapped her finger on the flyer. "They handed these out at work yesterday. Everybody got one."

Larry looked down at it. President Franklin Delano Roosevelt's face gazed benignly up at him beside his morning coffee mug.

He read the leaflet.[2]

Your President Says—"I call upon every American to stick to his post until the last battle is won. Until that day, let no man abandon his post or slacken his efforts." F. D. Roosevelt

Your US Employment Service Knows Where You're Needed.

"What is it, Daddy," Kay asked, wondering how a glossy sheet of brown and white paper could tell him something, anything at all, that he didn't know already.

"We'll see, Bunny," Larry said, using the nickname Kay loved. Haas was a surname derived from the German *der Hase*, which means the rabbit. So, Kay was Bunny. Her father stood and dropped his napkin atop his plate of watery scrambled eggs. He winked at Dorothy over one last gulp from his mug, ruffled Kay's hair, and headed for the kitchen door. Kay followed to watch him through the window and give her usual wave as he backed out of the garage. It was their special morning ritual. Early sun was already melting last night's dusting of snow. Larry's footsteps quickly changed into wet, black patches of driveway leading toward his car.

Before dinnertime that evening, Larry opened the day's mail and found something important enough to interrupt Dorothy's preparations.

"Better start packing, Dorothy. I won. Who says I can't get a better job?" He waved a single sheet of thin paper in front of her eyes. His smile was wide and his eyes bright. "Westinghouse *can* pay me what I'm worth."

Dorothy dropped a half-peeled potato into a pot of water and set her peeler on the kitchen counter. With a smile crossing her face and a quick swipe with a hand towel, she took the paper in wet fingers and read it aloud.

WAR MANPOWER COMMISSION
Region 2
Buffalo 3, New York

Mr. Loren G. Haas
417 Kinsey Ave.
Kenmore, New York

Issue: To determine if appellant is entitled to a statement of availability on the basis of underutilization of high skill and training and if appellant is entitled to out-of-area clearance to Westinghouse Electric & Manufacturing Co., Philadelphia, Pennsylvania.

NOTICE OF DECISION

Date: March 12, 1945
In the case of: Loren G. Haas (versus) Bell Aircraft Corporation
Decision by Area Labor Management Committee:

The facts disclose that the appellant's highest skill and training is not being utilized in his present position. The appellant is therefore entitled to a statement of availability. The facts further disclose that the job offer with the Westinghouse Electric & Manufacturing Co. at Philadelphia, Pa, would fully utilize his highest skill and training. On that basis the appellant is entitled to out-of-area clearance to this company. The action of the review unit in their denial of both issues is hereby reversed.

Joseph D. Canty
Area Director
War Manpower Commission[3]

"Well, Larry, you did convince them." Dorothy kissed him, holding his face for a long moment between her wet hands. "Now we can afford a better place."

"Bell Aircraft gets only three days to appeal this." Larry held out the paper in both hands like a judge at the county fair showing off a blue-ribbon chicken. "It won't do them any good, though." As pleased as he was that his next career move had worked out exactly as he planned it, his mood was a bit darkened when he realized that Andrei had apparently "pulled a few strings" with the War Department "just to help it along." Andrei was, after all, a valued and influential representative of America's increasingly powerful ally, the Soviet Union.

Within two weeks, Larry hoped to find a new home. He would move his family—including Kay's thirteen-month-old sister, Judy—from Kenmore, New York, to Chester, Pennsylvania. Chester, on the western bank of the Delaware River, the border between Pennsylvania and New Jersey, housed a permanent population of sixty thousand. It also hosted a mostly commuter, wartime workforce of one hundred thousand, and the Sun Shipyard, which by 1945 would grow to be the largest in the world. Chester was twenty miles southwest of the Philadelphia Westinghouse plant where Larry would start his new job signed on for his next big step into the sky as headquarters engineer, Service Department,[4] on Monday, March 26, 1945.

Kay was scheduled to start first grade at Chester Elementary that year. The changes of school, grade, and neighborhood were more traumatic for Kay than anyone expected. First, there was the matter of Kay's name. She did not like anyone, especially a stranger, a teacher, calling her Kay. Nobody she liked called her that. Her name was Bunny, and that was that. She had inherited her father's fierce self-determination and insisted on being called Bunny with a stamped foot and an evil eye whenever necessary.

Over the next six months, bigger changes would rock Kay's world even more drastically than being called Kay.

Chapter Fifteen

A First Collaboration

Sunday, March 18, 1945, 11:30 a.m., Penn Station, New York City[1]

Larry stepped from the train feeling rested and looking well groomed, a cosmopolitan man-about-town. He walked at a leisurely pace to the corner of 7th Avenue and 34th Street, where he stopped for a moment to look up at the Empire State Building only two blocks west. Then he hailed a cab.

"Hotel Empire, please," Larry told the cabbie.

The man pegged Larry as an out-of-towner as soon as he heard "Please" and decided this fare needed a correction. "You mean Empire Hotel, don't you, Mack?"

"That's the only one there is, pal. Want help finding it?"

The cabbie smirked but didn't answer, shifted into first gear, and headed toward 34th Street.

Larry ordered the cabbie to skip 34th and head straight up 8th, then take Columbus Circle to Broadway. It would be shorter than crosstown to 10th. He looked at Antonio DiDonato's ID tag attached to the meter. "Okay with you, Tony D?"

Tony D reckoned he might have miscalculated this guy.

Larry said Tony could drop him off at 63rd, and he'd be happy to find his way from there.

Tony D. got the dig. That was the Empire's exact location. At the posted rate of twenty cents for the first mile and a nickel for every additional quarter mile, the route Larry insisted on was cheaper and quicker. Larry had checked a Manhattan map at Penn Station. He liked knowing these things.

Tony D. looked into Larry's eyes in his rearview mirror. His "Sorry, buddy" sounded good enough to Larry.

Tony explained he was used to everybody thereabouts just calling it the Empire. The big red neon sign on the roof said Hotel Empire but the front door still said Empire Hotel. The new owner, in Tony's opinion, didn't even know what to call his own place. Trouble was, the guy was an out-of-towner.

"That bothers you?" Larry asked.

"Everything bothers me, but don't take it personal, okay, mista'? Try pushin' this thing around town all day"—he slapped his steering wheel— "and see how you like it."

"But it's a living, right?"

"It's a livin'," Tony D. agreed. Except for a few muttered curses and useful instructions for slow-footed pedestrians, Tony ferried Larry the rest of the way in silence. The 1.6 miles his meter ticked off tallied up fifteen minutes and a thirty-five-cent charge. Larry didn't complain about Tony's rounding up to the next quarter mile and flipped him a fifty-cent piece. Tony caught it like a shortstop under an easy pop fly.

Heading for his next pickup, Tony D. called out to Larry's receding back, "Welcome to N'yawk, pal."

* * *

The Empire Hotel's main lobby. 12:11 p.m.[2]

Larry arrived nineteen minutes early. He found a comfortable seat in a far corner of the lobby and idly thumbed through an abandoned copy of the *New York Times*. Almost nobody looked in his direction.

At exactly 12:30 Andrei Schevchenko stepped through the lobby's elaborately engraved glass doors. Seemingly uninterested in his surroundings and making no obvious attempt to look for Larry, he acted like a bored businessman passing the last few minutes of a lunch break. He strolled past the main desk, nodded the attendant a casual "Hi," offered a disinterested hello to the bellhop, and continued on a slow, ambling circuit of the lobby, eyes down, musing over nothing at all. After briefly admiring a few deep-green leaves on a potted palm, he found his way back to the front door and disappeared into the stream of passers-by on 63rd Street.[3]

Larry was intrigued. That little act had to be the message. A bizarre new game was afoot. Larry had to play. After two restless minutes, Larry strolled casually out to the street, just another bored New Yorker with nothing important to do. Only one tourist in the lobby had noticed him leave.

On the sidewalk, Larry mingled with the throngs of lunch-hour pedestrians. To the right, Broadway churned with cars and people, but no Andrei. He looked left.

The red light on Columbus Avenue turned green. As if a dam broke, a wave of pedestrians flooded onto the crosswalk from both sides. One lone figure, another lunchtime loafer enjoying one last smoke, remained at the curb leaning against a lamppost. For Larry, though, the pin-striped suit pegged him like a signature.

Larry walked past him and joined the crosswalk crowd. Andrei peeled himself off the lamppost and meandered alongside.

Andrei spoke something softly. He could have been a man musing aloud to himself. The words could have been meant for nobody or anybody.

Larry barely heard him above the traffic noise and did not look at him. He asked in the same offhanded fashion what this was all about.

Andrei was pleased. Larry did learn fast. Andrei said more plainly, it is *about* time for a beer. Pick a tavern. Stop in. Wait. Andrei would watch. He changed course and disappeared among the pedestrians crossing in the opposite direction, then walked south. At mid-block he stopped to admire the goods in a store window and, more importantly, the street scene it reflected behind him, which included Larry stepping into the Green Dragon Tavern. For another twenty minutes Andrei executed a dangerously abbreviated surveillance detection route. He saw no watchers watching anything and made his way to the Green Dragon. Thick smoke and loud talk all but guaranteed anonymity. Larry was sitting in a rear booth with a half-empty beer mug in front of him. He was reading a menu for the fifth or sixth time.

Andrei stopped at the bar, ordered a beer, and made his way to the booth, where he found Larry waiting with a mixture of curiosity and annoyance. He was playing along, but now he wanted to know what was going on.

Andrei raised his mug, smiled, and offered a toast to Larry's education. Larry looked promising. Andrei pulled a folded magazine from the inside pocket of his jacket and pressed it flat on the table.

On the cover of the February 1945 edition of *Aviation Magazine*, Larry saw an airplane he recognized. It was an Aeronca 11AC Chief, a single-engine, side-by-side two-seater that was just entering production in Dayton, Ohio. Larry knew it was big news for civilian fliers because it was one of the first American aircraft slated for the postwar consumer market. The artist's rendering showed off a flashy red and sunshine yellow plane banking high over summer-greened farm country.

Andrei slid the magazine in front of Larry and asked if he liked it.

Larry did. It was, after all, a civilian airplane for a change, a welcome switch from warplanes. "Buying one?" Larry wondered.

Andrei laughed. Why buy one, he asked, when he could build a better one? And then a thousand more!

Andrei's enthusiasm and an easy smile that Larry had rarely seen at Bell impressed him. Larry asked if Andrei was just daydreaming or already tired of his new job.

Andrei smiled and corrected himself. With apologies, he had not meant to say that *he* could build a better airplane. He meant *we*. Andrei's country, didn't Larry realize, would very soon need the kind of work they could do together. He could promise it would fix Larry's finances forever and free him to do any kind of research he wanted.

This was really something new from Andrei. Intrigued, Larry asked to hear more.[4]

Soviet industrialization was poised to create a new world, Andrei said, his chest swelling with pride. As true revolutionaries, Soviets were now like Americans once were. America became prosperous beyond its founders' dreams and the Soviet Union would go beyond that. Andrei's enthusiasm seemed real. When this war ended, they would revolutionize everything. Everything! The pursuit of happiness, to borrow the phrase, was going to arise from mechanizing all means of production, reducing a worker's hours of labor and giving everyone everything they needed. In time, work would be done only in pursuit of art and creativity. Larry, Andrei said, must be a part of that.

Larry's head spun with Andrei's rapid-fire description of the coming Soviet utopia. Soviet ideology was drawing many of America's intellectual elite toward this same mystique. All Larry could think of to say was that it all sounded perfect. But to himself, *to pull that off, you'll need somebody better than that bloodthirsty dictator of yours.* He knew the Soviet government was actually granting Soviet citizenship to American workers attracted to that vision. Hundreds of Bell's best people had already migrated to the Soviet Promised Land to build Soviet aircraft. Unfortunately, they had given up their US citizenship in the bargain and soon found themselves under virtual house arrest. Then they learned that complaints and independent thinking were considered subversive in their new paradise, and such behavior risked a transfer to Siberia.

Andrei, still enthusiastic—not sensing Larry's reservations—drew a neatly folded blank paper from his pocket. He set it down on the table in front of them, smoothed it carefully, and started sketching a picture in lines and curves and right angles. His gold-tipped fountain pen was now a compass needle pointing toward the future. His squares and rectangles connected in a pattern that started to look like a floor plan.

Andrei picked up his drawing and held it out like a masterpiece. This factory, he declared, would turn out a thousand neo-Aeroncas every month, each one faster and lighter than its American cousins.

Larry saw hints of Bell's groundbreaking assembly lines showing through Andrei's sketchy schematic. He was quite sure far more detailed drawings were already finding homes in the Soviet Union's rapidly reviving aircraft industry. The always-ready imp in Larry's mind asked him if imitation was flattery or really industrial espionage.

Andrei said the planes that would come out of this dream plant would be the ones Larry was already helping Andrei design. Larry assumed Andrei had been as much a student of American technology as he was an inspector and buyer of it during their many chats, collaborations, and quality inspections at Bell. Andrei's sketches now fascinated Larry.

Engrossed in the exercise, Larry helped Andrei tweak his figures and drawings while they finished off a third pitcher of beer. In the process, Andrei continued to mine Larry's knowledge of manufacturing methods in aircraft construction. He filled three more pages with scribbled notes and calculations. As an engineer himself, Andrei was deeply conversant with much they spoke of. That sharpened his ability to gain insights beyond the conversation.

After an hour of drawing and redrawing his plans, Andrei looked at his watch. He raised an eyebrow and stopped in mid-conversation about differential speeds of moving assembly lines.

He stood abruptly, declared he must go, gathered up his drawings, and stowed them in his pockets. He paused only long enough to thank Larry for his contribution to "the working masses of the world." He looked toward the distant front door of the Green Dragon and hurriedly added an instruction. Larry was to meet him at 254 West 54th. He said it was merely a short walk of eight blocks south. He was then to look for Wivel. Andrei would arrive not much later by cab. He tossed a twenty-dollar bill on the table so Larry could pay for the beers. A moment later, he dashed out the door, hailed a cab, and headed north.

Andrei's sudden departure in the opposite direction left Larry wary. A warning started tickling the hair on the back of his neck. And Wivel, whatever that was, would clearly be in the run-down heart of Hell's Kitchen. He started walking south a more cautious man than the one who had stepped off a train a mere two hours earlier.

Same afternoon, 2:00 p.m. at 254 West 54th Street in Hell's Kitchen, Manhattan

Wivel, Larry discovered, was a Swedish restaurant at 254 West 54th Street. In fact, it was one of the original inhabitants of the west-side region that later became Hell's Kitchen, a blighted neighborhood that stretched from 59th Street south to 34th Street and from 8th Avenue westward to the Hudson River. The locale was rich in gangsters, famous for mysterious disappearances and gruesome murders, and according to some, haunted by tormented spirits.

Larry stepped through Wivel's door and into a different world. He was met by a mélange of tantalizing aromas, luxuriously set tables, and a softly lit dance floor. The smorgasbord was set on an enormous circular table, laden with foods and soups, tureens, and platters of delicacies piled almost man-high. But something strangely disorienting was happening to the table. It took Larry a moment to realize it was turning. The farthest half was rotating slowly away through the wall as new offerings slid into view at the opposite end. It had to be the world's largest turntable ever devoted to a never-ending delivery of fine foods. Apparently, as guests depleted its specialties, kitchen staff behind the wall would replenish the offerings and let them slowly rotate back around. As Larry's eyes adjusted from the glare of the street and his mind absorbed the novelty of the place, he scanned the room for Andrei but did not see him.[5] Larry selected a booth in shadows at the far end of the room.

A blond Scandinavian goddess—obviously a sister to Thor himself—greeted Larry and escorted him to the booth. She wore a perfectly tailored tuxedo that she nicely improved on the customary fashion of a maître d'hôtel.

Larry told her he was waiting for a friend.

"*Det blir bra.*" Her smile was as bright as sunshine but Larry frowned.[6]

"I am sorry, sir," she apologized in charmingly accented English. "Most of our guests for lunch are Swedish. My words were, 'That will be fine.' When your friend comes, I will bring her to you." She added a wink to her smile.

"My friend is a he and this is business. But thank you."

"Oh. Sorry twice." She blushed. "My name is Maja. I will bring you coffee."

"Thank you," Larry said. "*Det blir bra.*"

Just then, the front door opened. Andrei stood silhouetted in the brilliance. "There he is," Larry told Maja. "Make that two coffees."

Andrei sat himself across the table from Larry without speaking and lit a Camel. He was perspiring.

"Okay," Larry said. "What's *this* episode about?"

Andrei took a long drag and blew a silver cloud toward the ceiling. "You are a good sport, Larry Haas, and you are learning. This luncheon repays your patience, but there is one thing you must know first. I am not here."

Larry blinked. "Is there a beginning to that story?"

"You and I have slipped the watchers. They follow me like fleas on a hound. You will attract them soon, too, if we are seen together now that I am at Amtorg."

"Why is that a problem?"

"You are not that naive, are you? Our countries are allies, but certain factions in Washington trust communists only slightly more than they trust Nazis. And when we encourage the sharing of intelligence to defeat our common enemy, Washington calls us spies. At Bell, I was a bean counter and of very little interest to your secret police."

"Our secret ... what?"

"Your FBI. Don't you know what they really are? Director Hoover thinks we are worse than the bank robbers his men like to shoot at. As vice president of Amtorg, only a couple of steps from Comrade Stalin, I am now of interest. If seen with me, you will come under suspicion, too. With the FBI, suspicion is the same as guilt."

"I've heard that before," Larry said before he remembered to measure his words.

"Do not worry. I will teach you to spot the watchers and how to lose them. I came here by a surveillance detection route to see if either of us was followed."

"Was I?"

"You were not and I lost my tail."

Larry was sure that was wrong and realized Andrei knew less than he thought. It was time to turn the tables. Larry started with flattery.

"That's shrewd." Larry raised his coffee cup in honor of the deed. "To becoming invisible!" To himself, he toasted the FBI agents who were apparently even better at invisibility than Andrei.

Andrei looked at the groaning tables. "We once assassinated a tzar for eating that way while his peasants froze. Someday, we will make it a sinless pleasure for all people."

"Sure of that?"

"Trust me!"

Larry shivered at the thought but answered, "I do, of course."

They approached the magical table and explored its delicacies. Imported *pâté de foie gras* in ornate crystal cups sat beside creamy wedges of *Svensk ost, Schweizer Käse,* and German *handkäse.* Roquefort *pâté de fromage* platters bedecked with crackers, breads, and caviar waited beside tureens of steaming soups and sauces. "We've come only a quarter of the way around," Andrei said, hefting a full plate. "Let's sit for a while and talk. We'll come back."

While assaying his own plate for a point of attack, Larry asked casually, "Do you miss Bell?"

"Actually, yes. I see aircraft now only from afar. That makes me sad."

"Then what do you do every day?" Larry had to ask.

"Last week I met with the presidents of five of America's biggest corporations to plan for postwar reconstruction. General Electric has already posted four hundred good men at construction projects all across Russia."

"Will Bell leave many of his men there?" Larry knew they had already lost that choice by exchanging their American citizenship for Soviet passports on the way. They had lost more freedoms than they could get back, and the harsh wastelands of Siberia waited for them if they complained.

"We will invite them to stay after the war," Andrei said. "They will build our planes, the ones you and I design."

Larry knew such planes were already in production on Soviet assembly lines where Andrei was no longer needed. The Yakovlev aircraft,[7] Larry knew, were proven in battle as robust, low-maintenance flying machines with excellent performance. Some Allied fliers even gave the Yak-3 higher marks than the Mustang and Spitfire.

"Ours will be better than your P-39s and 63s," Andrei said. "And best of all, you can build a better P-59." Andrei delivered that with a gleam in his eye, but Larry once again let it pass.

For the next hour they dined, and talked, and sketched out more paper dreams. Wine glasses had replaced their coffee cups.

Preparing to leave, Andrei handed Larry two more twenty-dollar bills. "Take these. Settle our account with Maja. The change is your consultant fee for today. Well earned."

Maja offered a traditional parting wish at the door, "*Tills nästa gång vi träffas.*"

"'Till next time we meet," Andrei answered in kind.

Apparently no longer concerned about surveillance, Andrei accompanied Larry on a leisurely stroll back to Penn Station. Reviewing the day on the long train ride home, Larry found himself left with new misgivings.

The next morning, Larry kept his appointment with SAC Fletcher in Philadelphia.[8] He learned that every meeting with Schevchenko from that date forward would be followed within a day by an FBI interview—a word Larry preferred over interrogation. These tell-all meetings were followed by a signing of a transcript of everything Larry said by all of the parties present. The agents were pleased at the close match between Larry's story and their physical surveillance reports.

Afterward, Fletcher fidgeted with a pencil next to his appointment book. He wanted to know what was next.

Larry said that Andrei had invited him and Dorothy, not the kids, to meet in New York City with him and his wife about a month from that date. It was to be a strictly social affair after Larry had settled in at Westinghouse. Andrei would have lots of questions by then, Larry was sure, but just to satisfy his scientific curiosity, of course.

Fletcher said he couldn't wait to hear what Andrei asks about—or for. When and where would that be? Surveillance would cover them from start to finish.

Larry was ready with the details: Sunday morning, April 29, about ten-thirty at Radio City Music Hall.

Fletcher scribbled the particulars in his book and congratulated Larry for doing so well. He had asked good questions, just enough to get started. Now Fletcher leaned in more concerned. How did Larry feel about all this now as a counterspy?

Larry looked down at his hands. It felt strange. Andrei was clearly not the ordinary man he made himself out to be, but he also knew less than he thought he knew. If a man was known by the company he keeps, Larry didn't like keeping company with Andrei, especially a man close to Stalin. Andrei would not be a man to cross.

Fletcher said he was glad Larry noticed. This could be a bumpy ride. The agents were not used to it either. Chasing bank robbers and drug pushers was not like chasing Soviets, who have an army of spies and thugs to back them up. Fletcher paused in thought for a moment and then asked, in light of that, if Larry was still on board.

Larry admitted that question had been at the back of his mind for a while. He had said yes a month before, but now he saw it deserved more thought.

Fletcher did not quite mention the two-edged sword his Buffalo colleagues had hung over Larry's head but simply added quietly that a lot was riding on this—especially for Larry. He was satisfied to let the innuendo do its work. He handed Larry his business card with a request for Larry to call him to say whether he decided to step away or stay in. They would keep an ever-closer eye on Andrei, but they knew it would be harder without Larry.

Larry reminded Fletcher that Andrei was already nervous.

Fletcher said that was natural. Andrei was living a dangerous life. Then he thought for a moment and asked a question Larry had not seen coming. Had Larry talked to Dorothy about this?

Not much, Larry admitted. Why did Fletcher ask?

"Do it," Fletcher said. "She has to know everything." The Bureau had checked her out, he said, and found her not a security risk. Fletcher saw Larry's surprise. Sorry, he said, they should have warned him first, but this is national security. They turn over every rock. But, Fletcher added with a warning tone in his voice, Dorothy would become a security risk if she refused to play along.

Larry shook his head. How many bizarre new twists could a single day hold? Then he laughed. The only risk, he told the agents, would be to his neck when he did tell her about the Schevchenko affair.

Fletcher smiled. He'd wait for the call.

Fletcher's next report to Director Hoover concerning Larry's contact with Schevchenko noted Larry's concerns and ended with one more detail. It would have convinced Larry that both he and Andrei were under day-and-night surveillance, if Larry still needed convincing.

After a friendly handshake between Haas and the subject at Penn Station, Schevchenko proceeded to a small rooming house located at 102 W. 32nd St., New York City, where he spent the night.[9]

FBI agents had mastered invisibility well enough to be anywhere either man might go.

Chapter Sixteen

The World Changes Again

Sunday morning, March 25, 1945, Larry Haas's home

The moment Larry walked in the front door of his home, Dorothy confronted him. She held out a crumpled telegram in a clenched fist that nearly connected with his nose. She demanded an explanation.

Larry was stunned. But he was no longer surprised to walk into another of her dark and short-fused moods.

Who is Hattie? Dorothy wanted to know. And what, for God's sake, was she doing in their kitchen?

Larry snatched the paper from Dorothy's hand and unwrinkled the flimsy sheet.

> WESTERN UNION
> 1945 MAR 24 AM 6 37
> Went back to house. Last inspect.
> Floor soft at kitchen sink. Stepped
> hard to test. Shoe in basement. Will
> fix. My expense. Or $200 back. Call or
> gram if other instruct.
> HATTIE

Larry gathered as much restraint as he could. He calmly explained that Hattie was the realtor in Chester, Pennsylvania, and the homeowner of the house he had just bought for Dorothy. Still trying to sound patient, he added that she would take care of whatever problem it was before they moved in. Anything else?

Dorothy was not done yet. She reminded Larry that he had gone to Chester to buy a house, not a shack. So what kind of deal did he make with this Hattie? Dorothy would bet she was a looker. Suckered him right in, didn't she? Sweet deal for her.

Such a conversation with Dorothy in one of her all-too-unpredictable moods ended as well as Larry could hope in a compromise. They would go to Chester and re-inspect the place together. Fortunately, Larry knew Hattie had seen these dynamics before and she would put on a well-honed spousal-soothing performance.

After the meeting with Hattie, Dorothy still had reservations. Dorothy stood on the front lawn of the house at 1200 Perkins Street and pointed north. There was no mistaking it. They could both plainly see the tank farm from there. That was a million gallons of something flammable right up the hill from their house, Dorothy insisted. She raised her nose to test the breeze and wrinkled it. The gas they were flaring off smelled bad, too.

I guess this is not over yet, Larry told himself.

It was still not resolved a month later on April 28, the day before Larry and Andrei had agreed to meet again. Larry phoned Andrei and blamed transportation problems for preventing him and Dorothy from making the trip up to New York City. Larry apologized and offered to reschedule.

In fact, Fletcher had already advised the reset while he and his superiors debated over their next move against Andrei.

That change in travel plans finally forced Larry to explain everything to Dorothy. He sat across the kitchen table from her with a coffeepot and their mugs standing between them like chess pieces aligned for attack and counterattack. At some length, Larry described the espionage angle that had surfaced in his work. He explained who Andrei really was, what the FBI wanted from Larry, and the urgent national security angle behind the whole story.

Dorothy's response, as Larry had feared, hardened from reluctant to fierce. But just then, staring angrily into Larry's eyes, she saw something that surprised her. It changed her mind. It was the flash of that reckless, adventurous free spirit that had long ago drawn her to him. And now it was back, steeled with his anger at Andrei and the Soviets. She turned away and held her words, silent for a long moment in thought. Her next words surprised Larry. They came quite naturally.

"Okay, I'm in." She smiled. "Really."

A few days later, Andrei wrote to suggest a new date to visit.

Come to my new home. We are across the avenue from Central Park. One can walk untroubled in this neighborhood. The address is 4 West 93rd Street. If midday Sunday, 20 May, is open, please come and be our guests.

Larry booked the date and waited.

———•——

In the meantime, Andrei turned his attention back to unfinished work with Leona Franey.

"Mr. Schevchenko wishes you to telephone him please tomorrow," Captain Ostrovsky told Leona at the Bell technical library on Monday, April 2. "He has returned from New York City to his home in Kenmore and wishes to make an appointment to see you."

Leona complied, motivated in part by the unaccustomed formality. Andrei, she discovered, wanted to invite Leona and Joe to New York City, all expenses paid, for something that sounded like a whirlwind day of entertainment on April 15.

Blandishments of many sorts continued to be part of Schevchenko's seduction efforts toward Leona and Joe. Some seemed so excessive they created suspicion. None so far had created results for Andrei.

Andrei's two carefully planned meetings, however, would take place in a very different world. The events of April 12, 1945, would intervene.

CHAPTER SEVENTEEN

New Priorities

Thursday afternoon, April 12, 1945, the Little White House, Warm Springs, Georgia

"I could feel a chill in my heart," Grace Tully said. When the telephone rang in her room in the early afternoon of April 12, 1945, her hand inexplicably shook as she lifted the receiver.

Grace had been Franklin Delano Roosevelt's private secretary for seventeen years. On this particular occasion, she had accompanied the exhausted and ailing president and his entourage to his "Little White House" in Warm Springs, Georgia.

Though paralyzed by polio from the waist down in 1921, FDR had experienced a degree of revival in his right leg while swimming at Warm Springs for the first time in 1924. Now, pale and spent, weakened and weary from wrangling with the Great Depression, enduring the duress of a world at war, beginning a precedent-breaking fourth term as president of the United States, and twelve years in a city where he said "everyone talks and nobody listens," FDR had retreated in April of 1945 for a short respite near his always-faithful Warm Springs waters.

The president's aides had seated him comfortably at his desk after a light lunch on Thursday afternoon. He reviewed papers of state, which he insisted his aides pile within reach. Though working, he tried to relax for a noted Russian-American portrait artist, Madame Elizabeth Shoumatoff, who was daubing her water paint on a fresh, gesso-primed canvas a few steps away. Even in repose, the president remained keenly aware of schedules. Duties of state were both his lifeblood and his nemesis. At exactly one o'clock, the president told the artist, "We have only fifteen minutes." Whether that moment revealed a mystical prescience granted to few men or merely another habitual bit of schedule-minding, no one with him that afternoon ever knew.

At 1:15 Roosevelt raised his hand to his head with a quizzical expression, complained of a terrific pain, and slumped backward in his seat as if asleep. But he never woke again.

His physicians found themselves powerless in the wake of a massive cerebral hemorrhage. The nation's thirty-second commander in chief died at 3:35. First, his attendants had called Grace. Then they called the president's wife, Eleanor, who had stayed in Washington to deliver a speech. Vice President Truman was immediately called to the White House. On arrival, he asked Eleanor what he could do for her. She returned his kindness with a question of her own. "Is there anything we can do for you? For you are the one in trouble now."

Roosevelt's death also created a problem for J. Edgar Hoover and his FBI. His president had been many things to him, assuring yet challenging, like-minded yet contradictory, manageable yet irksome. Overall, Hoover and Roosevelt had been useful to each other. On the afternoon of April 12, 1945, Hoover must have felt a chill in his heart, too.

J. Edgar Hoover had an empire to keep—his FBI. Its niche was that of a symbiont—it grew by feeding on its host while serving it, the United States of America and its president. FDR had been both a means of growth for and the benefactor of Hoover's nascent empire.

In building his empire, Hoover found himself on a playing field surrounded by political minefields. Great care was always needed. His Bureau provided a vital service, though at times Hoover was accused of commingling its work with self-serving agendas. His overriding goal, however, was unquestionably the security of the United States.

Detractors caricatured Roosevelt as a would-be dictator. His accusers cited his 1937 Supreme Court–packing scheme, his 1938 meddling in midterm elections to stamp out Democratic Party dissidents in the Deep South, and his tradition-breaking third and fourth terms as president in 1940 and 1944.

Not until the McCarthy era were many men more staunchly anti-communist in Washington than J. Edgar Hoover.[1] He was especially troubled by the subset of American intellectuals who held a fawning reverence for what they imagined were lofty Marxist-Leninist ideals. Among those men, Hoover suspected, was the president himself and many in his administration.

Harry Lloyd Hopkins, America's eighth Secretary of Commerce, brought both the social sensitivities of his social-work career and his communist sympathies into FDR's government in the New Deal and the Works Progress Administration, the WPA. Throughout World War II Hopkins served Roosevelt as chief diplomatic adviser and troubleshooter. He influenced the Cairo, Tehran, Casablanca, and Yalta Conferences.

Hopkins once said, "Russia ... must be given every assistance and every effort must be made to obtain her friendship,"[2] to which Roosevelt added, "I think that if I give Stalin everything I possibly can [through Lend-Lease] and ask for nothing from him in return, *noblesse oblige*, he won't try to annex anything and will work for world democracy and peace."[3] Many historians now argue that FDR's tolerance, even posthumously, allowed Russia to overrun Eastern Europe. He envisioned the United States and the Soviet Union as long-term, postwar allies.[4]

Hoover the anti-communist walked a tightrope with the US government penetrated by Soviet agents of every kind. FDR excused many of those the FBI director suspected as foreign agents. The president tolerated them as "innocent idealists." Hoover knew, however, that hardcore Soviet agents counted on these "fellow travelers" as valuable operatives, information sources, and agents of influence inside Roosevelt's left-of-center White House.

Elizabeth Bentley, who later famously defected from Soviet thrall, identified dozens of such infiltrators. The Venona decoding team confirmed much of her testimony. Venona, run by the US Army's Signal Intelligence Service, came to be known as the greatest code-breaking squad in world history, possibly even topping the Enigma code breakers in England. Venona routed out hundreds of Soviet agents in the Roosevelt administration.[5]

Hoover balanced himself on the tightrope by occasionally supplying Roosevelt with surveillance of his critics and political enemies. In return, Roosevelt promoted Hoover's domestic crime-control programs, and eventually, though grudgingly, accepted some of Hoover's anti-communist warnings. Overall, Hoover was learning that secrecy and misdirection, seemingly staple political tactics, could also be essential to his advancement.

By 1945, Roosevelt finally authorized wiretaps on Harry Hopkins and others Hoover distrusted in the White House brain trust. By then, the FBI had grown from a small, limited agency into a powerful and influential federal bureau.

President Roosevelt's death destabilized Hoover's domain. The new president, Harry Truman, wanted nothing to do with Hoover. Truman distanced himself by assigning his military aide, Brigadier General Harry Vaughan, to liaison duty with the FBI.

Not long after accepting the assignment, General Vaughan showed Truman a transcript of an FBI wiretap on Thomas "Corky" Corcoran, one of

FDR's former advisers under suspicion by Hoover. The "vital" wiretap intercept disclosed nothing more than that Mrs. Corcoran had an appointment with her hairdresser.

Truman fingered the document like something he would have to wash off his hands after touching the thing.

"Well, I don't give a goddamn whether Mrs. Corcoran gets her hair fixed or doesn't get her hair fixed," Truman spat out. "What the hell is that crap?"

"It's an FBI wiretap." General Vaughn smiled. He liked Truman's analysis of the thing.

"Cut them all off. Tell the FBI we haven't got any time for that kind of shit." Truman, more than ever, wanted nothing to do with Hoover.[6]

Truman did care about Soviet spies, though. His anti-communist views were eventually codified as the Truman Doctrine in which he pledged worldwide support for any nation threatened by Soviet communism. He soon reversed Roosevelt's position toward Stalin as expressed at the Potsdam Conference. Truman called Stalin an aggressive expansionist. He agreed with Churchill that Stalin was "a devil-like tyrant leading a vile system."[7]

After Roosevelt's death, the FBI and J. Edgar Hoover's work on the Schevchenko case gained urgency. Now Fletcher needed Larry to stay with their plan more than ever.

The world was about to change one more time, but this time both Haas and Schevchenko expected it. The only uncertainty was when. So Schevchenko carried on with the plans he had made less than two weeks before, though it soon seemed to have been in a different age.

Chapter Eighteen

Trying Again

Noon on Sunday, April 15, in front of the Radio City Music Hall

Andrei, his wife, and their son met Joe and Leona Franey as planned. Andrei paid their admission to the famous Radio City Music Hall and assured them that everything else that day, including the Franeys' travel expenses, would be on him.

They enjoyed a stage show together and walked to the Wivel Restaurant, where Andrei paid a lavish twenty-five dollars for their drinks and dinners. Afterward, they took a leisurely walk through Central Park. Andrei used the opportunity to tell his friends all about the beautiful new furniture he had just bought for his new apartment. In less than a week he would move in at 4 West 93rd Street, ceded to him by the previous head of Amtorg.[1] He invited the Franeys to visit sometime after May 1 at his cottage in Rye, a very nice town an hour's drive north of the city.[2]

Leona and Joe acted suitably impressed, though they took much of Andrei's talk as boasting, apparently meant to say wealth and luxury were mere facts of life for the ordinary Soviet citizen.

After strolling a little farther, Andrei arranged to walk with Joe ahead of their wives and the child. He spoke of receiving an award from his government along with "a lot of cash." He was presently "going around buying [manufacturing] plants," and beginning another new, important project in aviation.

With all that in mind, Andrei wanted Joe to know that he might be able to offer Leona a technical librarian job at Amtorg. But first, Joe would have to please "get Leona to help me out on my new project. Maybe she could take some information home, like on spring tabs,[3] for instance. My government sent me money. I am willing to pay any price[4] to get information to help me carry on my new project."

Joe made no promises but accepted Andrei's sixty dollars to cover their traveling expenses to New York City.

And by the way, Andrei wondered, since Joe just happened to work at the Hooker Electrochemical Company in Niagara Falls, could he give Andrei any plans of the plant? Andrei knew the engineers at Amtorg would so appreciate seeing them.

Having completed his business with Joe, Andrei once again rearranged the parties so he could walk alone with Leona. He told her that he had wanted to buy her a present but he didn't know what she liked or needed. To make up for that, he said, "so here is two hundred bucks to buy something for yourself." He handed her two new hundred-dollar bills and told her that he had received an honor and considerable money from his government.

"You never knew it," he continued, "but I am an aircraft design engineer. Now I am taking two months rest before starting on a new project around May 1. Leona, you can help me. I have to have a lot of information now, like on spring tabs. Maybe you can give me information on spring tabs used by other companies."

This bizarre strolling round-robin of conversations finally ended when Andrei walked his guests to 59th Street and 8th Avenue, where they watched a movie called *The Corn Is Green*.[5]

Before parting, Andrei arranged to visit the Franeys at their home in Lewiston, New York, hoping to come soon. He would be in the neighborhood to retrieve some personal items he had left in Buffalo, so what a pleasant opportunity he would have to stop by.

In hindsight, Andrei apparently thought the day well spent. He had entertained and impressed Leona and Joe, introduced them to some socially enlightened theater, and rounded it all off with an ask for something just a little bit less than ordinary in its availability. Andrei apparently expected the system to work this time.

For their part, the Franeys had found it a peculiar day. But they did plan to cooperate with Andrei. That, however, was not because they liked him, but because they didn't. Their FBI friends would help them give Andrei a tainted dose of just what he wanted.

Then the world changed again.

CHAPTER NINETEEN

A New Beginning

VE Day, May 8, 1945

The European end of WWII, the biggest and deadliest war in history, waged among more than thirty countries, was finally won. As with the Great War before it, its end was supposed to be the start of a lasting peace.

President Truman did not think it likely. He warned America, "We must finish the war. Our victory is only half over."[1] Though Truman was clearly referring to the unfinished war in Asia, he also knew the general public might not have fully grasped the meaning of this peace. The hard work of ending the Asian war and helping to rebuild the world would have to be accompanied by ongoing vigilance.

In the first century AD, Lucius Annaeus Seneca, a stoic philosopher of the Roman Imperial Period, wrote, "Every new beginning comes from some other beginning's end."[2] Over the next twenty centuries, uncountable hopeful repetitions simplified his wisdom down to, "Every ending is a new beginning." As such, VE Day—Victory in Europe Day—was supposed to herald something new.

At least three dates can lay claim to that distinction. April 30, 1945, was the day Adolf Hitler committed suicide during the Battle of Berlin. On May 7, his successor, German *Reichspräsident* Karl Dönitz, signed the preliminary act of military surrender to the Allies in Reims, France. One day later in Berlin, almost midnight on May 8—early morning on May 9 in Moscow's time zone—German Field Marshal Wilhelm Keitel signed the act of unconditional surrender of Germany's military forces. Various nations, each for its own historic reason, celebrated VE Day on May 7 or 8, or in republics of the Soviet Union, May 9, Victory Day.

In the United States, the victory coincided with President Truman's sixty-first birthday on May 8. Truman dedicated the victory to the memory of FDR, who had piloted the nation through the darkest days of the war and died less than a month before it ended.

On VE Day, Larry Haas remembered Quinn's words. "Peace is only a name for the time between wars, a tool for people planning the next one."

Also, on that day Andrei Ivanovich Schevchenko began to scheme about getting his hands on the spoils of that war—the German jets, rockets, and the research that built them. He recognized VE Day as neither an end nor a beginning. He simply continued his work.

By VE Day, the United States, United Kingdom, and USSR—the Allies—had consumed $650 billion and fifty million lives before the hot war started shading into a Cold War that they were now calling peace.

The European war had left the United States the wealthiest, most industrialized nation in the history of the world. By the spring of 1949 a British historian, Robert Payne, spoke of the postwar prominence of the United States: "She bestrides the world like a Colossus." The United States had built 360,000 aircraft, 90,000 ships, 200 submarines, 10,000,000 rifles, more than 650,000 trucks, 650,000 jeeps, 100,000 tank chassis, and 90,000 Harley-Davidson WLA motorcycles—all in a scant half-decade of war.[3] Though peace promised to release that great power for good, the United States had already started to gird itself for growing conflicts with its one-time ally, the USSR.

VE Day also raised hopes that Japan's Pacific Empire would soon fall. Seneca's maxim, however, would once again prove to be a nuanced thing.

Larry and Andrei's plan to meet on May 20, 1945, had also become a nuanced thing. Once again, in the wake of VE-Day, May 8, they found themselves in a new world with old plans.

CHAPTER TWENTY

Into the Spider's Lair

Saturday, May 19, 1945, late evening at Penn Station, New York City[1]
Larry stepped from the train onto the Penn Station platform on Saturday night. Hoping it was not prescient, a couple of lines of childhood poetry came to mind.

> "Will you walk into my parlour?" said the spider to the fly,
> "'Tis the prettiest little parlour that ever you did spy."[2]

He made his way to the Tenth Street Turkish Baths, a comfortable bunk for the night. Travelers like Larry, and many of New York's pleasure-seeking patricians since the mid-nineteenth century, had enjoyed its famous saunas, cold baths, and massages.

The 8:30 Sunday morning express from Philadelphia delivered Dorothy to Penn Station. She had stayed home with Kay and Judy on Saturday night because the sitter cancelled at the last moment. Now she joined Larry for breakfast followed by a leisurely stroll along the avenue.

"I promise you this will be a day to remember," Larry years later remembered saying to Dorothy. "Look around. There's only one New York City in the world. And what a time to be here. Everybody is celebrating."

Dorothy surveyed the scene, at first skeptically, but she finally let herself smile and admit she couldn't argue with that. She had fixed her eyes on a woman walking past in a dress that could only have come from the most fashionable clothier on Park Avenue. The dog tugging on the leash the woman held was just as impeccably groomed. Its collar was spangled to look like a queen's tiara had dribbled diamonds on it.

Good, Larry thought, following Dorothy's gaze. Larry had made up his mind to enjoy the day in his own way by Andrei-watching. Spy watching spy seemed an intriguing, if slightly chancy, game on this particular Sunday morning.

Larry hailed one of the few city cabs cruising by in the sparse Sunday morning traffic moving along Central Park West. After a few minutes driving north, something caught Dorothy's eye.

She ordered the cabbie to stop. With a sparkle in her eye, she told Larry to pay the man. She was getting out.

Larry looked at his watch. They were early enough, he conceded. The cab pulled to the curb on the Central Park side between 90th and 91st Streets. Larry handed the man a dollar bill with a breezy "Keep the change." *After all,* he told himself, *it's Andrei's money anyway.*[3]

"So, what's up?" Larry asked.

Dorothy had run across the sidewalk to peer over the old stone wall into Central Park. Larry couldn't help imagining her namesake doing the same the first time she saw Oz. She beckoned him with an easy smile and a wave to come and look. Springtime in the park. Wasn't it beautiful? Her spirit seemed lightened by this morning's golden sunshine.

Larry still thought of that smiling girl as the real Dorothy he first met and fell in love with, though in time he had discovered that her moods too often turned toward darker things.

"Certainly is," Larry agreed. Then, with a happy "watch this," he clambered over the old stone wall and dropped down into a blossoming bed of escapees from one of the park's cultivated flower gardens. Larry plucked off a bright blue blossom from a cluster beside his foot. He held it up toward Dorothy like a trophy and climbed back to the sidewalk. His feet landed just in time for a patrolman strolling by to spot him.

The officer saw Larry holding out his flower, smiled, winked at Dorothy, and said "Top o' the mornin' to you, ma'am." He doffed his cap and walked on, satisfied he had duly noted what he was supposed to.

Sunday morning, 10:30, May 20, 1945. The Schevchenko residence, New York City[4]

Larry knocked on the door of apartment 3-D. It was opened by a version of Andrei he had not seen before. He looked relaxed in an open-collared, green-and-white checkered sport shirt. Larry thought the jaunty look suited him better than pinstripes.

Andrei showed no sign of the pressure he was under to produce results that day. The marathon of social events he had planned was designed to find out whether Larry should be groomed as a cooperative agent or as a managed asset. After all, he assumed it had worked on Leona and Joe a few days ago, so why not now?

Andrei welcomed them to their new Casa Schevchenko, greeting them with a warm smile. He held out his hand to Larry with a glass of clinking ice bathed in amber liquid. Humble though it was, Andrei said, he bade them come in. Andrei swung the door wide and proudly proclaimed them their first guests.

Andrei and Antonina made themselves genial and engaging hosts, especially generous with Andrei's whiskey, selected with care from a side bar well stocked with the best of many sorts.[5] He touted the beverage as America's antidote to their recent Prohibition debacle, a strange historic interlude that he likened to a national sickness. Andrei had learned that Prohibition-era doctors could write prescriptions for hard liquor to treat everything from stomach aches to cancer. The three-dollar government fee on every script, netting six billion dollars so far, had thus paid for a lot of US Army bullets.

Larry was amazed at how deftly Andrei had turned whiskey into a screed on capitalist war-funding. Andrei continued to pour generously in spite of the early hour. Larry was glad he and Dorothy had agreed to stay sober and neutral on political topics.

At noon, after changing to more businesslike attire, a short drive took them to Wivel. Maja greeted all four like old friends and once again, the smorgasbord did not disappoint. Andrei steered the conversation toward politics, but he heard little from his guests beyond kind platitudes for the heroic Soviet foot soldiers and fliers. On the topic of culture, however, Andrei had a surprise. He invited his guests to a matinee at Radio City.

The movie was *Valley of Decision*,[6] a love story starring silver screen idols Greer Garson and Gregory Peck. In Andrei's mind, it was also Hollywood's latest version of a class struggle tale between a wealthy Pittsburgh steel mill owner and his poor-but-noble workers. The tale, naturally, featured a beautiful starlet dressed in work clothes.

After the show, Larry made his opinion clear in a way he thought might ruffle Andrei's feathers just a bit. Such matters, Larry said, would depend on a moviegoer's point of view. In matters of the heart, love conquers all. Besides, worker-boss disputes always had two sides, didn't they? Larry reckoned that might be just ambivalent enough to chafe. Andrei's reaction was subtle, but Larry was not disappointed.

Larry and Dorothy continued to appear immune to Andrei's agitprop. Was Larry being obtuse on purpose, Andrei wondered, or was American open-mindedness simply an infuriating way to look at all sides of everything?

This unfruitful method of ideological pulse-taking soon seemed to Andrei a poor scheme for developing a sub-agent. As the day progressed, he grew quietly frantic in wielding a technique of seduction that might have come naturally if it had not been forced.

Larry and Dorothy were growing increasingly wary.

The next stop on Andrei's agenda was an elevator ride fast enough to be thrilling. It took them to the top of the Empire State Building. After enjoying the spectacular views that stretched eighty miles in every direction and a little snack at the souvenir stand—Wivel had left them room for no thoughts of dinner—Andrei reached inside his jacket and pulled out a small packet.

The times we could spend together, he told his friends, may be too few in the coming days. But they did have this day. He intended to make the most of it.

Larry wanted to sound enthusiastic. What, he asked eagerly, did Andrei have in mind?

To the opera, my friends! Andrei held up four tickets. He proudly displayed his tickets for Verdi, *La Traviata* at eight o'clock at the Metropolitan. *The Fallen One* still entertains, he said, these hundred years later. Andrei knew Dorothy was an accomplished musician. She would appreciate this. Andrei planned to re-interpret *La Traviata* as a class-struggle parable that could be dressed in modern communist ideology. How it resonated with his American friends might finally answer some of Andrei's questions.

As the curtain rose Dorothy whispered softly in Larry's ear that this must be a litmus test. Andrei, of course, wanted to see if they would turn red, or at least a little pink. Larry smiled at her pun, delighted she was still enjoying their game.

After the final curtain fell, Larry remained naively uncommitted. He thought the music was inspiring, but wasn't the story a little old-fashioned? It did not seem terribly relevant in 1945, unless he had missed the message.

He had indeed missed it, Andrei thought. His explanations did little to fix things.

Strolling from the opera house to the car, Andrei spoke little, apparently deep in thought. He drove his guests to Penn Station, where they expected to board the 11:45 train back to Philadelphia.

After pulling his car to the curb in front of the station, Andrei turned in his seat to look at Dorothy. He had a proposition to make.[7] He begged her pardon, but in fact he had some business he should have asked her husband about much earlier that day, but it had slipped his mind. They had all been enjoying each other's company so well, didn't she know? He spoke more quickly now, eyes darting between Dorothy and Larry. Andrei simply had to ask her permission to borrow her husband a little while longer.

Dorothy, unsure how to field this unexpected twist, checked her watch. All she could think of in the moment was to simply ask if he could make it quick.

Andrei upped his ask. He meant to borrow Larry for the night. There was a matter of some delicacy between their governments, something unfinished at Bell. This was surely an imposition, Andrei admitted, but he was afraid it was a matter of some urgency.

Something he *must* do? Dorothy sounded indignant. Larry now saw Antonina watching her husband intently.

Andrei drew three twenty-dollar bills from his wallet and held them out to Larry. Please take this for Mrs. Haas's train fare, he said, and to maybe make up just a little for this terrible inconvenience. Then, before Larry could answer, he asked Larry to return to his apartment with him. He had papers Larry must see and a deadline to be met tomorrow. He acknowledged that while Larry no longer worked at Bell, he was the only man who knew this matter.

Larry looked at Dorothy hoping she would stay on board with their plans for the day, and said, almost as a plea, that maybe he had to. Larry knew her well enough to see the subtle signs of her deepening fear of the thing he had gotten himself into. Now, she'd have to trust that Larry would learn enough for the FBI to end the whole thing soon, and for good.

I guess you should, Dorothy agreed. She had more to say, but it would have to wait until Larry got home.

Larry now felt a sharp edge of the dangers he had been warned about by the agents who had once come to his office. But for now, he had to play this out.

Dorothy took the twenties from Andrei's hand and blew a kiss at Larry. She placed her hand on Antonina's folded in her lap and thanked her for a wonderful day. She assured her that they had enjoyed getting to know them both. They must do this again someday soon, but next time in Chester. It was a charming little town.

That was the night Dorothy arrived home alone, strode to her bedroom, and slammed the door without checking on the girls or paying the sitter.

———•———

Shortly after midnight in Andrei's apartment, after Antonina went to bed, Andrei admitted he had lied. He poured them two drinks and said he had done it to show Larry something important. But first, he had a question.

Larry's patience was exhausted. He decided to play his hunch. He told Andrei that he knew where he was going, so he'd ask his own question first. Larry picked up his glass and swirled it in thought. He asked if Andrei would insist Larry become a Marxist for them to work together.

Startled, Andrei nearly laughed. No! The whole day's apparently useless anxiety fell from his shoulders. The rest of Andrei's answer finished the day's work. Nor would he have to be a capitalist to work with Larry. He needed Larry's answer though, to be certain.

So why, he asked, *would* Larry work with him?

Because, Larry said with his best smile, he agreed that science rose above every ideology, above small minds, and even above war. But, he said, backing away by just one calculated bit, working together would be dangerous, maybe too dangerous, if they were wrong.

Wrong?

Larry trotted out a carefully practiced piece of anti-American cynicism. The people they would rise above were the ones who wrote all the rules. Then their puppets—the police and the courts—enforced them with a vengeance. He reminded Andrei that he might know that even better than Larry. So, in spite of agreeing with Andrei, he was sorry, but he had to decline. It would be just too dangerous.

Andrei was ready for that objection, a common one in sub-agent re-cruitment. Not working together, he told Larry, would violate a higher law. A law neither man could ignore if he had a conscience at all. Didn't Larry see that people would die if they didn't cooperate? They could not hold onto secret technology that can save lives. They would bend man-made laws to serve a higher one. Obsolete wartime laws that profited politicians would make them murderers as guilty as an enemy soldier with bullets and a bayo-net. The intensity of his delivery sounded quite sincere.

Larry backed off but left a troubled look on his face. He guessed he'd have to think about it.

That would be just fine, Andrei said. Larry still had the hook in his mouth, but this was a precarious moment. Time for Andrei to add some bait.

Andrei reached for a long cardboard roll leaning against the wall beside his easy chair. He held it out toward Larry and said he worked on this every night. Paper slid out and unfurled itself like a great scroll. It revealed a carefully drafted skeletal frame of an airplane. Larry recognized it.

It was a Yak. Larry ran his finger across the drawing, a Yak-3, he thought. Larry knew the Russian Yakovlev designs. But something, a couple of things, were odd about this drawing. He tapped his finger on the mid-fuselage line and looked up at Andrei.

"My modifications," Andrei said proudly.

Larry looked closer. He saw skills in the work he had not credited to Andrei.

The Yak-3 had problems,[8] Andrei said. Did Larry see what Andrei had done?

Larry saw changes around the cockpit that did not match photographs he had seen of a few downed Soviet aircraft. Andrei had deftly redesigned the cockpit canopy.

Larry was impressed. He asked if it worked.

Andrei laughed but this time his voice held no humor. He simply did not know! Clearly irked, he said he would never get to build it or even see it built by somebody else. The war was over. But, he said, reviving his smile, peace will call for even better airplanes. That's where he needed Larry.

But Larry knew better. The Soviets already had better designs. Yak-9s had already beaten the new Luftwaffe Focke-Wulf Fw 190 and Messerschmitt Bf 109G fighters in the 1943 air battle over Kursk. The Soviets had hundreds of engineers on new design work. But rather than argue, Larry played along.

Maybe peace could pay off, he said warily. What was Andrei's plan?

Andrei looked triumphant. Larry, he said, had already drawn up the plans himself. Didn't he remember the Green Dragon?[9] You are one of us. His words hit Larry like a noose tightening around his neck. Now, Andrei said, just get me what I want.

Larry instantly remembered the dream-factory plans they had drawn up two months ago. They had come back in Andrei's hands to frame him as an accomplice. Andrei probably believed he already had enough leverage to control him. The C in Andrei's mice was doing its work. A cold chill ran down Larry's back.

Andrei continued. As to his plan, it depended on what Larry knew, by which Larry understood, *That depends on what strategic secrets I will steal.*

The ground around Larry was shifting fast, but the agents' coaching had readied him to see at least one step ahead. Andrei had cleverly roped him in, but rather than object, he decided to relent. With a shrug and a wry smile, he gave in, maybe too easily, but Andrei's enthusiasm had clearly elbowed aside his own skepticism in favor of the answer he wanted.

Now was the moment, Larry had realized, when Andrei could incriminate himself by telling Larry exactly which secrets to deliver.

Larry simply answered by setting his own trap. "Try me," he said.

Andrei charged right in. He needed to learn more about certain kinds of chemistry, by which Larry heard, *Do you have an in at Hooker Chemical?*

Larry smirked. Chemists were just a bunch of pot-boilers. Not his cup of tea. What else?

How about diesel power? Andrei probed farther. It would be the power trend of the future.

Larry knew the Russians were still testing long-range, propeller-driven diesel bombers, but he wanted no part in that. Diesels? Really Andrei, did Larry look like a truck driver? *Why was Andrei probing around places he already knew that Larry cared nothing about? Was he trying to disguise his real target among decoys?*

Andrei tried again. If not a truck driver, how about an airplane driver? Jet propulsion was a most wonderful thing. It might even give way to rocket-propelled planes or super-turbines. Why couldn't they put their heads together on that? Civilian and commercial jet travel would be the world's future, so naturally it could be theirs, too.

Pay dirt! Andrei had finally landed where Larry wanted him.

"Maybe," Larry said slowly. "What precisely do you have in mind? Are there specific documents or plans you are thinking of?"

"Anything new on jet propulsion would be helpful." Andrei put his hand on Larry's shoulder and looked into his eyes. He would so much appreciate anything.

Larry now only needed something specific. He reminded Andrei there was already a lot on the jet story in the popular press these days.

Andrei said with disdain that he had already seen it all. Larry could, and must, dig deeper.

Larry inched closer to the specifics he wanted Andrei to demand. He admitted he did get in-house, technical reports and research journals at Westinghouse, so he could quickly get Andrei some of them without much risk. It might bend the rule about in-house use only, but he was pretty sure he could manage that much.

Andrei now grew more eager. He'd bet Larry could get even more advanced materials. Andrei urged him to do that and drop the "maybe." This was their future, wasn't it?

Growing ever more impatient now, Andrei spoke more boldly. He already knew the exact reports he wanted. He would give Larry a camera that would cost him three or four hundred dollars, tossing off the sums as if it were a trivial thing. He would even give it to Larry with a special lens for very small pictures and teach him to use it.[10]

Okay, Larry agreed, thinking as he said it, *now he is making me his accomplice.* That realization, as much as he had schemed to achieve it, suddenly chilled him. Andrei had stepped into his trap while thinking he had done the same to Larry. In this web, each spider was now the other's fly, but only Larry knew it. It wrenched at his gut.

Sensing that Larry's reservations were not yet all behind him, Andrei reminded him they had known each other for a long time. He would not ask him to do something dangerous. Bending a law for a good cause was surely not breaking it. Some man-made laws impeded progress. If Larry helped, Andrei promised him a secure financial future. Think about it, he said, and come see me again. Anything you bring me will be appreciated.

Larry, now satisfied he'd made Andrei plead his case, promised to think it over and answer next time they met. He also saw Andrei had deftly deployed both carrot and stick in the same kind of fork the FBI had used on him not so long ago.

Larry now knew that if he continued, he would one day betray this man who thought him a friend. Regardless of Andrei's politics, he was still a man and Larry would take a hand in his destruction. It might be in an American prison or take place before a Soviet firing squad, but Larry would be an assassin. He might have already lost control of an inexorable process.

Maybe even more frightening, if Andrei caught on, Larry might meet the world's most efficient assassins himself. All this passed through his mind in the briefest of moments. It carried a weight he had never felt before. Larry suddenly wanted to step back from a terrible fate he had not seen coming. If this was what he would have to become . . . he dropped the thought unwilling to see more. But now with no other option, he realized he could only carry on.

Andrei gazed at his ceiling for a moment and consulted a mental calendar. Saturday, June 23, he said. He wanted Larry to return to the city that day and let him know for sure that he could work with Andrei in the way they had talked about.

Larry nodded. That would be okay.

At 2:30 a.m., Andrei and Larry retired. Andrei's was the most expensive couch Larry had ever slept on. Just before sunrise, Andrei drove Larry to Penn Station.

Larry boarded, found himself a window seat, and started planning for tomorrow morning's meeting with Fletcher. Larry realized Andrei had asked for no single thing that was specifically illegal. The entire conversation, however, could have led nowhere else. Larry now saw that the path he would send Andrei down—a man no matter what else he might be—made Larry see his own danger. To conspire in Andrei's demise would change Larry in ways he did not want to imagine.

By the time Larry reached his home, he knew that everything about this Schevchenko case violated the man that Larry thought he was and all the plans he had made for himself. The job did have to be done. But not by Loren G. Haas.

Larry arrived hot to talk for his next post-contact debriefing at the Philadelphia office. He told the agents he felt trapped, as if he'd been abducted by both the FBI and Soviet Intelligence. He told them every detail of his strange visit with the Schevchenkos. In the end, he said the conspiracy that he and Andrei were ready to hatch took him closer to violating his core and most cherished principles than anything had before. How could patriotism turn him into a liar bent on killing a man?

A suddenly steely-eyed Agent Fletcher was not sympathetic. He told Larry that a man didn't need a uniform to be a soldier and Larry just got drafted. This was more important than his feelings. And as for principles, soldiers kill enemies who were trying to kill them. Welcome to the Army.

Larry listened, but he knew there were two kinds of soldiers, draftees and volunteers.

Fletcher heard Larry out. Then he planned one more meeting, one Larry would not see coming, especially after Larry's final words.

"I quit."

CHAPTER TWENTY-ONE

Final Doubts

Thursday, 4:55 p.m., May 31, 1945, in Larry Haas's office at Westinghouse[1]

The phone on Larry's desk rang an in-house double chime. He picked up ready to state the usual name-extension greeting, "Haas, 533. Can I help you?" But the caller cut him off with an imperious command after Larry had only said "Haas."

"Mr. Haas, come to my office. It's Bucher, young man." His boss. He wanted Larry in his office. Now. The line clicked off.

"Right away," Larry told the dead phone and hung up. Apprehension when called to the boss's office at the end of the day was not Larry's style. He simply thought, *This should be interesting.*

George H. Bucher, a man of slight build with probing, dark eyes behind rimless glasses, always looked studious. His face combined smile and frown in a way that made people strive for the smile. He had risen to the presidency of Westinghouse Electric and Manufacturing through the ranks, starting as an assembly worker in the East Pittsburgh plant on September 1, 1909. From there, he worked his way up through coil winder, transformer assembler, and monitor generator tester. By the 1920s his hard work earned him the assistant general manager slot. In the Great Depression, Bucher was called upon to captain Westinghouse International until 1935. He rose again to overall company vice president, and finally to president of Westinghouse Worldwide by 1938.[2]

Bucher knew and respected his men because he had always been one of them. Larry Haas felt at home at Westinghouse.

Larry found Bucher's office door open. At 5:06 he shook Bucher's outstretched hand. Bucher looked at his watch and said there was not much time. The plane was on the runway and Haas was not going home tonight.

Before Larry could answer with anything more than a startled blink, Bucher told Haas to call his wife and make an excuse, but first talk to these men.

"What . . .?" Larry's search for words was quickly cut off.

These boys, Bucher said, had invited Larry to come along, and that was fine with him. Bucher motioned for Larry to look to his left. Larry turned.

Agent Fletcher was sitting in a comfortable leather chair in the corner of Bucher's office. As if continuing a conversation interrupted only moments before, he told Larry that they thought his question had deserved a better answer. A man Larry did not recognize sat beside him. Fletcher noticed Haas's glance and introduced Special Agent Harvey Rath.[3] He would join them. He was from one of the FBI offices in New York City.

New York? Larry was puzzled. He looked from Fletcher to Bucher and back. What was going on?

Bucher informed Larry that he might meet Mr. Rath again in New York, since that was where Schevchenko lived now. Then he told Larry to take a seat, he had a few things to learn. Bucher sat himself behind his desk and turned off his desk lamp, as if to disappear from the conversation. But to Larry he looked even more watchful.

Larry had rarely felt more baffled, a feeling he disliked very much.

Fletcher started. Did Larry recall talking to him after returning home from his New York visit with the Schevchenkos?

Larry, tensing with the memory, said that he did. He asked if this meeting was really about that.

Fletcher continued as if his next question would answer Larry's. Fletcher reminded Larry he had quit the Schevchenko case. Any further thoughts on that?

"You bet!" Larry nearly yelled. He refused to be an assassin. It violated his principles and beyond that the risks to him and his family were too high. Schevchenko's boss, after all, was a homicidal madman. His spies were thugs and Schevchenko's pin-striped suits were no more than bad camouflage. Larry would rather let the FBI handle him. Larry would be happy to talk aviation with Andrei all day long, but it would be way too risky to help him do his spying just so the FBI could catch him at it. Larry was sure that would end him up in somebody's crosshairs himself. Larry shoved his hands in his pockets and glared at Fletcher. He guessed that about summed it up.

That was a mistake, Fletcher said flatly. He informed Larry that he knew exactly what Agent Quinn told him the first time they met in Buffalo and Fletcher could carry out the same threat Quinn made. Larry's hobnobbing with Schevchenko—it was on the record as Larry well knew—was enough to end his career. Did Larry remember that? Fletcher's question sounded like a threat.

Of course Larry remembered, but he remained resolute. He refused to become what the FBI would turn him into. He'd happily pump gas in Hoboken before he did that. He challenged Fletcher to do his worst. It would not change Larry's decision.

At that moment Bucher spoke from the darkness behind his desk. You do not know what is at stake, he told Larry, though he said it softly as if to a friend. Now it was time he found out. Give Mr. Fletcher sixty seconds, he asked. If Larry did not like his explanation, Bucher promised to persuade him to let Larry out of the scheme.

Larry eyed Fletcher. Okay, he challenged the agent, he was waiting.

Schevchenko knew that peace was only a pause to reload, Fletcher began. His leaders were already planning the next shootout and this time they would aim for the United States, not Germany. But, Fletcher said, he was not the man to prove it to Larry. That was why Larry would come with them. Larry could walk, or—he reached for the cuffs on his belt—they could walk him. Those were Larry's only two choices.

Butcher stood and looked at his watch. "Gently, please, Mr. Fletcher," Bucher said. He preferred Mr. Haas to come as his guest. Boarding was scheduled for 7:25 at Philly Municipal Airfield and Air Tech Services Command was holding four seats for them. Bucher's friend was waiting to meet Mr. Haas. He motioned toward the door. "Mr. Haas," he said, "after you, please."

"No" did not seem an answer either man would accept and he knew this situation would haunt him for a long time if he refused. Despite Larry's misgivings and refusing to be intimidated, he decided to let his curiosity win out. He motioned toward the office door and returned Bucher's courtesy. After you, then.

Bucher pointed toward his secretary's desk and invited Larry to use Miss Konin's phone to call home. He could make up any excuse he wanted, but he must not mention travel. In compensation, Bucher promised that for tonight Larry would have a nice room and a hot meal, just not at home and with no telephone. Better call now. Time was short.

With Dorothy's usual ill-grace when told about urgent work again and impossible deadlines at the plant, she interrupted Larry's makeshift pretext with a curt, "Okay" and hung up. *That mood again*, Larry told himself. He set the phone back down in its cradle.

The four men drove to the airport in silence. Within minutes, Larry and his boss had been hastily ushered to seats at the back of an idling Douglas C-47 Skytrain. Bucher finally spoke.

"Now, about your questions," Bucher said. He handed Larry two sheets of light blue paper that he called the guest list for a top secret party. "Read *all* the names."[4]

Larry saw an embossed White House logo at the top of each page. He read as the airplane started its rollout: *Presiding: Secretary of War Henry L. Stimson, Chairman, by special appointment of Mr. Harry S. Truman, President of the United States.*

Larry's heart was starting to beat as fast as the airplane's wheels pounding down the runway beneath him. He would attend an Interim Committee meeting slated to start the next morning, Friday, June 1, at 11:00 a.m. and end at 3:30 p.m. with a lunch break in the middle.

The rest of the page mesmerized him. Name after name read like a Who's Who of the smartest, most powerful men in the United States—probably in the world.

Members of the Committee
- Secretary Henry L. Stimson, Committee Chairman. Secretary of War
- Mr. George L. Harrison, *Special Assistant to Stimson for atomic bomb development*
- Hon. Ralph A. Bard, *Navy Undersecretary*
- Dr. Vannevar Bush, *Office of Scientific Research and Development (OSRD), Manhattan Project*
- Hon. James F. Byrnes, *Office of War Mobilization. Representing M. Truman*
- Hon. William L. Clayton, *Administrator, Surplus War Property (under Byrnes)*
- Dr. Karl T. Compton, *US Radar Mission to the United Kingdom, Manhattan Project, 1927 Nobel Prize winner in Physics*
- Dr. James B. Conant, *National Defense Research Committee, Manhattan Project*

Invited Industrialists
- Mr. George H. Bucher, President, Westinghouse *Equipment for electromagnetic uranium isotope separation process* [Attending *sub-rosa*: Haas—aviation]
- Mr. Walter S. Carpenter, President, Du Pont Company *Hanford Project*
- Mr. James Rafferty, Vice President, Union Carbide *Uranium hexafluoride gas diffusion plant*
- Mr. James White, President, Tennessee Eastman *TNT/RDX explosive plant, Tennessee*

By Invitation
- General George C. Marshall
- Major General Leslie H. Groves
- Mr. Harvey H. Bundy *special assistant to Stimson*
- Mr. Arthur Page *Public relations—AT&T*

Larry refolded the pages carefully and handed them back to Bucher with a simple response. All he could think of was "Quite a party."

Bucher said his friend (not yet revealing that to be Truman) had invited Larry. Say nothing unless spoken to, Bucher warned, but remember everything you hear, then forget you were ever there.

Larry sat back to think while he watched the dark landscape slide by ten thousand feet below.

After landing in Washington, two army MPs escorted Larry to the grand Mayflower Hotel. They stationed themselves outside his door, blocked delivery of Larry's dinner until they inspected the bellhop and his food, and did the same for breakfast. Larry got everything he wanted. Except a telephone and permission to leave the room.

At 11:00 a.m. Larry stood with everyone else when Secretary of War Stimson entered the White House conference room. At his nod, all sat. Stimson welcomed the attendees and asked the generals for tactical updates. Following that, the meeting would be his.[5]

"As you now know, the president has approved continuing the Manhattan Project. As you may not know, as vice president, he knew nothing about it. He has now been briefed. Today, we are asking how close the Russians are to catching up. Mr. Rafferty, can the Russians duplicate Union Carbide's process to purify bomb-grade uranium?"

"They are not close, Mr. Secretary. They cannot beat us to a bomb." Rafferty spoke confidently. "To mass-produce U-235 and plutonium they will need ten thousand qualified workers they do not have. They will need years to make precision tools and strategic materials—special ceramics, vacuum tubes, certain unusual stainless-steel alloys, and more."

"That only means *not yet*," Stimson said. "They are neither lazy nor stupid. How hard are they trying?"

Bill Clayton answered. "According to the Office of War Mobilization, the Soviets rounded up a bunch of the German atomic scientists and technicians. The Nazis worked on atomics for years and the Russians scooped up a whole lot of it with them.

"You are right about the people," Clayton told Rafferty, "but not the hardware. The Russians didn't get much of that. We blew it all up in the last months of the war. We made a special point of it at their heavy water plant in Norway."

Clayton turned to Stimson. "The Soviets are ramping up spy networks everywhere. They are after all of us." He looked around the table. "And they happen to be pretty good at it."

"What exactly are they sniffing at?" Stimson asked.

"Everything, Mr. Secretary. Rockets and planes, ships, and submarines. Hell, they're probably even after Davy Crockett's musket."

"I'll make sure the Smithsonian keeps it under lock and key for us, Bill," Stimson said with barely a smile.

"Bill is right, sir," Bucher broke in. "The Soviets managed to grab most of Siemens and I. G. Farbenindustrie. By our reckoning, she can put up a sample-sized electro-magnetic plant, one like our Y-12 uranium isotope separator, in as little as nine months. Full ops in three years."

"So, we're back to *not yet*," Stimson said. "What else?"

"Everybody has a piece of this, Mr. Secretary," Bucher said. "Germany developed a lot of atomic bomb basics during the war. If they still wanted to—if we let them—they could purify enough U-235 for a bomb in fifteen months, eighteen tops. In Italy, Fiat could do the same just as fast. England, maybe a year."

Larry was stunned. What he just heard told him planet Earth could be blasted into oblivion overnight by any one of a half-dozen countries with any delivery system that could drop atomic bombs. That told him everything else he wanted to know about why he was there. Long-range jets could rule the world. All they needed was a few years of peace to get the jump on everybody else.

Stimson looked from General Marshall to Major General Groves. Bucher had scooped both of them. "He is correct, sir," General Marshall said. "Intelligence confirms those estimates. The atomic genie is out of the bottle."

"We've all been warned by Mr. Hoover's FBI about Soviet spies," Bucher said. "He knows the drill because of the German and Japanese spies he mopped up so far. The Soviets are the most dangerous ones who could deliver the next bomb. They have already tried to infiltrate our turbine and jet research projects. Others around this table have had the same experience."

Many heads nodded.

Larry imagined these could be the plans for Armageddon.

"Thank you, gentlemen," the Secretary said.

After lunch, the Manhattan Project and America's race to build the world's deadliest bomb gave way to a discussion about peacetime plans for atomic energy.

On schedule, Secretary of War Stimson signaled adjournment. "Submit your reports, gentlemen. I will read them and report to the president." The conference room emptied, but one man entered. He looked at his watch.

"I only have a few minutes,"[6] President Truman said. "Nice to see you again, George." Truman extended a hand to Bucher. "I presume this is Mr. Haas." He shook Larry's hand. "Mr. Hoover and I have studied your case."

"Pleased to meet you, sir," Larry answered. "My case?"

"You have met the enemy, Mr. Haas. The stakes are higher than anybody outside today's meeting can guess. Now you know. Your Andrei Ivanovich Schevchenko and his cohorts are penetrating every one of the companies and the programs you heard from today. Do you understand?"

"Yes, sir. I think I do now."

"If Schevchenko wins, the Philadelphia mint will print rubles five years from now, not dollars. Whether you meant to get yourself into this thing or not, you are now at the point of a spear we must aim at Schevchenko."

Larry looked at Bucher. "Why did you hire me, if you knew I was connected to a spy?"

"Because you were. That way we can get our hands on him. For a spy, nothing's more dangerous than friendship, so yours with Schevchenko is our secret weapon," Bucher explained. "Your transfer to Westinghouse was not approved on merit alone. You are good at what you do. I'm glad you are with us. But the employment waiver you received had some help. And the best part is that Schevchenko wanted you with us, too. You are his asset."

"That's why you are the man for this job," the president said. "I have ordered Mr. Hoover to get us ironclad evidence. And that's what he wants you for."

Larry's mind spun. "I did not know how big this was, so I . . ."

"Good," President Truman said. "Can we count on you?" He looked at his watch and left the room clearly assuming, and by inference ordering, Larry's answer to be yes.

CHAPTER TWENTY-TWO

Losing His Grip

Andrei's overtures of friendship to Leona and Joe Franey seemed more contrived as time passed. His rationale for requests concerning technical reports appeared more forced and artificial, almost oblique.[1]

On Thursday, June 14, at 7:00 p.m. Schevchenko entertained the Franeys at the Samovar Restaurant at Niagara Falls, this time for a more modest seven dollars, including a tip. Afterward, he invited them for a stroll through a nearby park called Devil's Hole. After about twenty-five minutes, they drove to the Franeys' home.

While there, Schevchenko confided privately to Joe that he had become interested in chemistry. Based on that new interest, he said, "maybe sometime you can get me small plan."

Joe honestly told Andrei he had no access to any plans of the plant.

"Well maybe through a friend you get a small plan—I will pay any price for it."

Schevchenko appeared extremely nervous throughout the evening. Something was troubling him. Eventually, he confided to Joe and Leona that he recently requested his government to recall him to Russia. He was badly disappointed that his request was denied. He told them that instead he would probably be "requested"—a word he pronounced as if he knew the word meant "ordered"—to stay in the United States until at least 1949.

He hinted that his job dissatisfaction was based on discouragement. He could not obtain information that he needed to continue his work concerning a technical issue called the "design of S-type airfoil"[2] and its application to missiles. Then he added that he was "attempting to obtain a speed four miles faster than sound." By implication, his problem could have been Leona's fault because certain technical documents to which he thought she had access remained beyond his reach.

Andrei's temperament then took an odd and disturbing turn. "You lied to me, Leona," he said, agitated.

"About what?" Leona was mystified.

"About the report on Japanese aircraft that you have in your library—the one I asked you for that you said you do not have."

As tactfully as she could, Leona told Andrei that Bell had no reports of any kind on Japanese aircraft. She could not have offered to provide anything of the kind. She was sorry for any misunderstanding.[3]

The conversation then returned to small talk of a general nature, but soon Andrei made one more request. He asked the Franeys to drive him to the vicinity of Vladimir Mazurin's home at 97 Parkwood Avenue in Kenmore. Oddly, he did not want to be taken to the home, only near it.

On parting, Schevchenko offered no additional money to the Franeys. Leona told Joe that she reckoned Andrei was holding onto his cash until they got to Amtorg.

Chapter Twenty-three

Reading Matter to Die For

Less than a month after his secret trip to Washington, Larry Haas became a thief.

His hands shook as if all the strength in his body had shifted to his power of hearing. A distant footfall, a murmur, or a turning page would be enough to make him freeze. The library stacks were so quiet he thought the sound of his own breathing might betray him. If he had been there only to read, nothing would have troubled him.

He placed two magazines inside the false bottom of his briefcase. Before this, he had only stolen with his mind, taking knowledge wherever and whenever he found something worth knowing.

The deserted stacks in the Westinghouse library remained silent while Larry finished his work. He had a right to be there but he felt like an intruder. He was, on this day, a thief.

Larry sealed the false bottom, added two more magazines atop that, and snapped his briefcase shut. He adjusted his tie and his smile, walked up the stairs to the main floor, and prepared to get caught.

"Ahem, Mr. Haas." The librarian, Clairie McDermott, always pleasant, would not have said more. But she did have a way of making herself heard this day when Larry walked past her desk toward the door. Adding just the barest edge to her voice along with a prim smile, Clairie reminded Mr. Haas that he knew the rules. In fact, he had counted on it. Westinghouse security was at least as tight as Leona Franey's had been at Bell.

As if caught in an absent-minded moment, he thanked Clairie most kindly, apparently embarrassed for being just a little too preoccupied. He turned back, hefted his briefcase onto the circulation desk, and opened it.

Clairie's smile turned down as she lifted out the two clearly visible magazines. She handed Larry two check-out cards to fill out and sign, adding the usual reminder that they were due back the next morning, as usual.

Larry repeated the admonition with a wink and a smile and quipped that would give him just enough time to memorize everything he needed.

Larry could not have taken his secret cargo out without his briefcase, and he could not have taken an empty case out without risking suspicion. Getting himself caught by Clairie gave him proof, should he need it, that he had borrowed only two ordinary items. The elaborate subterfuge convinced him that real spying was not his game. The hidden copies locked in the false bottom made Larry's briefcase feel remarkably heavy as he walked to his car.

Rules were made to be broken, Larry reminded himself, *for a higher cause, no matter which one it is.*

Friday, June 22, 1945, 9:00 a.m. in the FBI Philadelphia field office

Three magazines[1] landed on Agent Fletcher's desk with a thud, a sound more than matched by the thunderclap that rattled the office windows. The light drizzle Larry ran through to get there was turning into a pelting thunderstorm on a dark Friday morning in Philadelphia.

Those magazines were what Larry had picked out for Schevchenko. Two were of a kind the company did not circulate and one was from a nearby newsstand. Larry explained that the company magazines were not secret or classified, just proprietary to Westinghouse. A little rule-bending, but not quite illegal. Just what Andrei wanted.

Fletcher looked relieved. The previous Monday, Larry had not yet come up with anything. All he had been able to find so far had been either so basic it would insult Andrei, or highly classified. Fletcher had been afraid they were dead in their tracks.

This morning, however, Larry had delivered three safe, but he hoped tempting, pieces of technical literature. One of Larry's three articles was a May 1944 edition of *Westinghouse Engineer* featuring an article titled "The Combustion Gas and Gas Turbine Cycle." The writers were an application engineer, Fred K. Fischer, and a thermodynamics engineer, Charles A. Meyer.

Fletcher turned a few pages and said the math looked impressive. It looked so impressive as a matter of fact that he asked Larry if he was really sure it was okay to give away.

The material was nothing new technologically, Larry assured him. It was standard engineering background stuff. Andrei already knew it, Larry said. But it had been written by Westinghouse engineers with in-house engineering data. Andrei should feel good about that. And Larry knew the authors, Fischer and Meyer. That would definitely impress Andrei.

Fletcher looked up from the magazine alarmed. He ordered Larry not to admit that. He was sure that would prompt Andrei to have Larry try to recruit them, a complication the FBI did not need. The document itself should be enough to get his attention. The article diagrammed a turbojet engine and compared various engine types, from propellers, to jets, to rockets. The final theoretical section focused on the future of jet propulsion. Larry reckoned that would be the most enticing part.

Fletcher read the second title aloud. "The Day Dawns for Jet Propulsion." It was in the March 1945 edition of *Westinghouse Engineer*, equally technical and mostly proprietary. "Looks good, too." Fletcher said.

The third item was a new copy of *Aviation Magazine* that Larry had picked off the newsstand that morning for fifty cents. Fletcher read the cover feature title, "The Prime Time for Gas Turbines in Aircraft of Tomorrow." Larry did not mention he knew these authors, too. They were Westinghouse colleagues, design engineer Charley Flagle, working in the Aviation Gas Turbine Division, and Frank Godsey, the New Products Division manager.

Fletcher was troubled again. The article claimed to present "The newest research on turbojets." Wasn't that supposed to be top secret?

Larry dismissed it with a wave of his hand. Old news. It was only the latest news *to the public*. That sold magazines. It was meant to make people forget that America let the Nazis build jet airplanes first. Americans, according to Larry, had short memories. He told Fletcher that pretty soon the average citizen would come to believe the United States had always been the leader in everything jet propelled.

Fletcher frowned and called Larry a cynic.

Hardly, Larry disagreed. That was just the kind of thing he had learned when he let people rent money from Household. They figured it was low interest, not high rent.

Fletcher looked at the magazines again, still skeptically, and asked if Larry really thought they would satisfy Andrei.

Larry admitted it was hard to say, but he reckoned it would show Andrei a certain willingness to play along. But maybe, he added, his next little twist on the theme would be more convincing. Larry showed Fletcher the false bottom he had crafted inside his briefcase. With that, he would show Andrei how he stole the first two magazines. He had at least bent, if not broken, a rule for Andrei.

Fletcher smiled for the first time that morning. Maybe there was hope for Larry in this business, after all. Fletcher loosened his tie. The day had already reached eighty degrees, stifling with 100 percent humidity.

Larry pulled up the only other chair in the office except the one Fletcher was sitting on.

Fletcher pointed at the magazines. He called it a candid inside look at Westinghouse. Andrei would love it. Spies were voyeurs and so were he, all the other agents, and even Larry. He welcomed Larry to the club.

If he was a Peeping Tom, Larry said, then he had better be told what he was looking for.

Nothing! Larry must not even try. He was to simply remember everything Andrei asks for. Proof would come later, after he asks for something entirely illegal. Fletcher then shifted the conversation to ask for Larry's slant on Andrei's best arguments for Larry's cooperation.

It had been the line about scientists over politicians, Larry said. He believed it himself, even though his intuition told him something was wrong with it.

With a patient smile, Fletcher explained that it was an old Marxist line—all politicians are corrupt no matter the country. They are by nature money hungry and power crazed, unlike scientists. Their laws let them pick over the powerless underclasses. America, Britain, and Europe were therefore exactly the same as Germany, Italy, and Japan. The United States and its friends were as evil as the Nazis and the fascists. Larry was supposed to wish a pox on all their houses. Scientists, on the other hand, are honest brokers of truth.

Larry was flustered he hadn't seen that sooner. Imagine the irony of a communist playing the elitist card.

Next, Fletcher continued, Andrei would introduce Larry to the "science" of dialectical materialism—a communist staple—which would make the evil blood brothers of war and politics obsolete. That's the logic that called Roosevelt—now Truman—and Hitler two different pots of the same old porridge. Churchill and Mussolini are kissing cousins, too.

The core of Andrei's tactic was now clear as Fletcher explained its workings. With that, Larry saw Fletcher in a new light. These agents knew their work as well as Larry knew his. The FBI finally passed Larry's sniff test.

So much for the moral dilemma, Larry said. But he had to admit Andrei was slick.

Slick enough to be dangerous, Fletcher warned. Larry should not argue with Andrei about any of that. He told Larry to just buy Andrei's stories. Let himself be seduced. If Larry would not do that convincingly, Andrei's next step would be blackmail. Or he might drop Larry altogether. That would put the FBI out of the game, especially bad because J. Edgar Hoover and Harry Truman had a special interest in the Schevchenko case.

That chilled Larry. He had a lifelong aversion to being manipulated, and everything he had heard so far had hardened his attitude toward both Andrei and his own government. To hear so casually that he was now under the microscope of two of the most powerful men in the United States opened a dark place in Larry's mind. And Fletcher saw that now in his face.

Fletcher understood. On impulse, he reached into the vest pocket of his jacket. He had to draw Larry back into the intrigue rather than the high-risk exposure he now regretted revealing. He handed Larry a note. It had been written to Hoover and copied to Fletcher by Agent Conroy in New York City. It concerned Schevchenko.

Think about the money, Fletcher told Larry. He should get something out of this, too.

United States Department of Justice
Federal Bureau of Investigation[2]

To: Director, FBI
File number ACS: JCD Re: Andrei Ivanovich Schevchenko
June 13, 1945 Internal Security
Comintern apparatus

Dear Sir:

Reference is made to the reports of Special Agent Vincent M. Quinn, dated March 15 and April 28, 1945, at Buffalo. In these reports information is set forth concerning Schevchenko's payment of sums up to $300 to informant (Lauren George Haas) for certain "cooperation" on his part and also with the explanation that such sums cover traveling expenses incurred visiting Schevchenko. It is indicated that the true purpose in giving these funds to the informant may be to secure his assistance in obtaining confidential and secret information of an espionage nature.

It is believed that the Philadelphia and New York field divisions, in whose territory the informant in this case is located, should make arrangements with the informant in order that the funds obtained from the subject would be turned over to the custody of the respective field divisions handling the informant. In turn, arrangements could be made for the informant to receive in compensation for his services a like sum, or a weekly or monthly stated sum, to be left to the discretion of the Bureau and the offices handling the informant.

If such a plan is approved, the offices receiving the money from the informant for possible future evidentiary use should take a signed statement from the informant at the time the money is received, which statement should include full particulars and circumstances as to its acquisition; furthermore, detailed records relative to the serial numbers of the bills and the time of acquisition should be obtained.

No action should be taken on this matter until authorization is received from the Bureau.

Very truly yours
E. E. Conroy, SAC

CC: New York City, Philadelphia

Larry read the letter, sat back, and read it again. "Real interesting," he said. He refolded it and handed it back to Fletcher, smiling at a thought that crossed his mind while he read. He hadn't thought he could make money at this.[3]

Relieved, Fletcher told Larry the payroll idea was best. The FBI's money was clean. Andrei's was blood money. The FBI should have it, not Larry. And besides, it might be traceable by the serial numbers.

Blood money? Another unexpected twist.

American communists, Fletcher said, rob banks to fund people like Schevchenko. They also extort money, plunder unions, hijack businesses, and things much worse he'd rather not talk about.[4]

Larry thanked him for finding such an interesting playmate for him.

And with that, Larry decided it was time to go. He gathered up his magazines, carefully placed them back into their secret compartment, wished Fletcher a better morning, and headed down the stairs.

Satisfied his plan for Haas was on course, Fletcher opened a blue folder marked *Subject Schevchenko: Signals Surveillance*. A newly decoded teletype memo dated 6-15-45 was stamped URGENT. The director's signature gave Fletcher authorization for microphone surveillance[5] at Schevchenko's summer residence in Rye, New York, on Long Island Sound. That would be a tough one for the tech boys to manage right under the Soviet *rezident*'s nose, but he knew they'd pull it off.

Within forty-eight hours, Agent Fletcher reported back to the director that two Rye Bureau of Public Utilities employees had completed a "routine inspection" of the electrical service at the indicated address.

Listeners could now join Schevchenko's watchers.

———•—•———

Saturday, 8:30 p.m., June 23, 1945, at Andrei's apartment in New York City[6]

Larry barely released the door-knocker before Andrei opened the door. Larry was late. Andrei scowled. An hour late. Why? Andrei peered anxiously behind Larry. His normally cautious nature had shifted toward unstable. Larry suspected it was survival-honed thinking for everyone in the arcane Stalinist system. Andrei's split identity in the United States must have been compounding it.

Larry said he had walked, not rising to Andrei's pique. It was, after all, a beautiful afternoon.

Larry had left his cab at 72nd Street, slipped into Central Park, and strolled slowly along the lakeside bridle path as far as the 79th Street exit. There he had stood for a long while before the majestic, columned entrance of the New York Museum of Natural History. Such stolid realities felt reassuring. He knew he was about to enter an alien unreality. The con he would play on Andrei was to be built on lies. To start with, Larry would again play hard to get, this time in a way that would make his seduction beyond Andrei's ability to doubt. For a while, he watched the evening shadows stretch out under the park's ancient trees. Only when he felt ready, did he walk the last fifteen blocks toward Andrei's home, sorting his thoughts one more time.

Andrei now stood in his doorway surrounded by a haze of cigarette smoke and tried to turn his scowl into something better. He held out a tumbler with melting orbs of ice floating in watery whiskey. A welcome gift, he said. Come in.

Larry sipped his drink and walked toward the nearest window. It overlooked West 93rd Street. The last crimson rays of sunset reflected off rows of apartment windows stretching toward the Hudson River like a string of sparkling rubies. "Beautiful evening," Larry said.

Andrei stepped forward, grasped the chord, and lowered the blind in front of Larry. Without a word he moved from window to window doing the same at each. Then he turned with a sigh and declared that better. He offered to refresh Larry's drink.

Larry emptied his glass in a gulp, grimaced at the little ice ball he swallowed, and said sure. A refresher would be good.

Andrei poured generously to make up for lost time. He was sorry, too, he said, attempting to right the mood. He worked too late, too many nights. His nerves were . . . well, Larry understood, didn't he? He did not add the words he had said to himself far too often lately. *Moya proklyataya rabota!* My damn job! He had not even said those words to Antonina. In his world, such words traveled in ways even he could only guess. Whether she might be troubled by them or report them deserved equal consideration.

Larry nodded at Andrei's glass and said he looked like he needed that drink.

Andrei only sipped enough to wet his lips, then set his glass down. He lit another Camel.[7]

"Why the window thing?" Larry wondered aloud.

Andrei blamed FDR's death. Truman's opinion of Andrei's Mr. Stalin was lower than Roosevelt's. Hard-working Russians like Andrei were now more closely watched.[8]

Larry quickly reassured him he had nothing to hide, pleased he could say the opposite of what he knew and still sound sincere.

Andrei said he was glad Larry trusted him. He knew Andrei. They were friends.

"Right on, pardner," Larry drawled, wondering how a few sips of whiskey could have brought out his inner John Wayne. He peered into his empty glass and realized for the first time that it tasted too good. He reminded himself that alcohol was an anesthetic agent that put a drinker's inhibitions to sleep before his tongue. This evening, he told himself, a tipsy misstep could be deadly. He set his glass down.

Friends for sure, Larry reassured him. That's why he had brought him a present.

Andrei held a finger to his lips and glanced around the room. This was such a pleasant evening, he said, that they should have some music to enjoy it with. Andrei snapped on a radio, twirled the dial, landed on WPAT, a Patterson, New Jersey, classical music station not far across the Hudson River, and turned up the volume.

Larry understood. Andrei had said more than once that walls can have ears and implied that those ears might be either his own countrymen's or "somebody else's." Listeners would now hear more Beethoven than talk. Andrei pointed at Larry's briefcase. A present?

Larry opened his case, removed the newsstand copy of *Aviation Magazine*, unfastened the false bottom, and invited Andrei to come see what he'd done.

Andrei, impressed, lifted the magazines and spread them on the table like a feast before a king. He riffled through the pages. Which were the articles of interest, he wondered. He would now see how well he had planted his interests in Larry's mind. Andrei set the *Aviation Magazine* aside and drew the two *Westinghouse Engineer* magazines closer. These two were interesting, he said, but he had read the *Aviation* piece. He was a subscriber. But thanks anyway. He stacked all three magazines on a bookshelf and promised to read them later, most carefully.

Resettled in their easy chairs, Larry allowed another refill. Keeping a clear head while pretending not to seemed a calculated risk he had to take.

Andrei changed the subject. Westinghouse, he said, could be useful for both of them.

Larry pointed toward the magazines and repeated the concern he had mentioned the last time they met. He could get in a lot of trouble if he was caught. Some of the best material simply could not even be borrowed. It was illegal to take out of the library.

It *was* illegal during the war, Andrei contradicted him, but that was over. Surely those regulations were defunct by now.

Larry didn't think that law had changed.

Andrei assured Larry he had only missed one word, "yet." Peacetime would change everything. If it had not happened yet, it would soon. With that, they would join the gold rush to capitalize on peace. So why not start now?

Larry said that was great optimism, but it was still risky.

"Bosh!" Andrei almost shouted the archaic expletive that he probably borrowed from a Brit among his contacts. Larry stifled a laugh. Andrei drove on. This would surely benefit Larry's family. He would make "big money." Larry did not get into trouble bringing those magazines. He had brought something private, not hush-hush. Andrei was sure he could do that again, but maybe a little more? But not to worry. Andrei said his camera was coming soon.

Larry looked into his glass and swirled it like a tea reader divining a mystery. He was ready to ask what more Andrei was looking for.

Andrei revealed that he was designing a new airplane more advanced than that modified Yak-3. It would weigh six thousand pounds, cruise at six hundred miles per hour, and, best of all, it would be jet propelled.[9] A great deal of money was allocated to this project.

Larry whistled. That was quite a bird but it did not sound civilian.

It already was, Andrei told him. Larry should really read his own newspapers. Vannevar Bush, President Truman's science adviser, had said that military research must be put to peacetime, civilian uses. It was the only way to justify the money spent and the lives lost in war. It also should not have escaped Larry's attention, Andrei noted, that Bush said peace was never permanent. Peaceful nations have to prepare for war in peacetime.

Larry said that sounded like bad news for everybody.

Then he and Andrei would help keep the peace, Andrei countered. When both sides had the same knowledge, they simply could not threaten each other. Take the Germans' rocket-plane, for instance, the Messerschmitt Komet. It could hit six hundred miles an hour, but it weighed too much and only carried fuel for thirteen minutes. He and Larry could counter a threat like that and guarantee such an aircraft could never again threaten anyone's air superiority. They might even prevent the next war.

So, precisely what, Larry asked, did Andrei want? Larry planned to remember Andrei's next words exactly.

Andrei took a deep breath and began. First, they would need the fastest jets they could build to make the longest flights possible.

Larry froze. Those words, peacetime and long-range jets, came together in Larry's memory with a vivid image of the atomic bombs he heard about at a conference table in Washington, DC. Larry now knew he was in the presence of the greatest threat the United States of America might ever face. And that future was being placed in his hands. He barely noticed that Andrei was still talking.

Andrei wanted the best data Larry could get on high pressure compressors and pumps, and the most powerful turbines Westinghouse was building.[10] Larry could photograph it all on special film Andrei would give him. Was that all clear?

"Crystal clear," Larry said, but in ways more stunning than Larry would say.

"Good," Andrei declared. Find it. He would have Larry's camera soon.

Larry conceded that what Andrei had ordered was higher-level material than he had brought that day. Privately, he knew he would need time to persuade the brass to let him shoot something illegal for Andrei.

For Andrei's expectations though, Larry blamed his inexperience and lingering fears, predicting it might take him some time. If he could do it though, count him in.

Andrei agreed, hiding his annoyance at more delay. He asked Larry to let him know "next time I see you if you can go along."[11] He wanted that to be Saturday, July 21. They would go to his dacha[12] near Rye Beach.

Andrei shifted to an easier topic. Did Larry like his job at Westinghouse?

Larry said he was very satisfied with his job. Privately Larry reminded himself that the FBI agents wanted him to have a need Andrei could be prompted to meet. If Andrei found a way to be indispensable, he could believe he had Larry on a leash. They decided to blame Dorothy for a discontent Andrei could fix.

Dorothy, Larry admitted, was unhappy with their new home. The house was not good enough, and the neighborhood was bad for their children. Larry was afraid that if he could not do something about that soon, Dorothy would divorce him. He tried to look as desperate as his words.

Andrei listened in great sincerity. Antonina and he were very fond of Dorothy and they surely would help any way they could. Andrei pulled out his wallet, withdrew five twenty-dollar bills one at a time, and offered them to Larry. He said maybe it would help Dorothy find a nicer place.[13]

When Larry seemed reluctant, Andrei told him to consider it a down payment on the money they would make revolutionizing aviation.

Larry took the money. If Andrei thought he had Larry hooked, Larry would have Andrei just where he wanted him.

In return, Larry offered to take a detailed list of exactly what Andrei wanted from Westinghouse next time they met. He'd study it and do what he could, even if he had to bend a few rules to get it. Andrei decided it had been a very good day.

At 11:05 Andrei called a cab to be sure Larry wouldn't have to wait for a later train.

The Philadelphia run pulled out of Penn Station at 11:30, leaving Larry enough time for a good night's sleep at home before his Monday morning debriefing.

After Larry wrapped up his report to SAC Fletcher at the Philadelphia office the next day, he suggested they tell the army about Andrei's six-thousand-pound airplane, though he doubted the thing would be big enough for a pilot to fly.

More to the point, the agents asked Larry if he could give Andrei any of the things that he wanted.

In a minute, Larry said. But he would need permission. Westinghouse had it all. They actually had two or three complete and already obsolete jet planes. They were entirely different and more advanced than Bell's P-59.

The details were still confidential even though the engines were just not good enough. Larry reckoned he could give Andrei the outdated specs. They would be convincing, but with a little doctoring, they would not do him any good.

Fletcher wondered about the danger of Andrei spotting the fix.

Larry explained that when he was at Bell, he had been re-assigned to GE in Lynn, Massachusetts, for a few months. He worked on the P-59 jet there, first as a test engineer, then returned to Bell as director of Engineering Training. Between that experience and his work at Westinghouse, he knew exactly what he could safely give Andrei.

Fletcher told Larry to give him the particulars. He would work on the clearances. The chain of authority, however, would be complicated. He would need an okay from the company, the FBI's own specialists, the Joint Chiefs, and of course their boss's boss, Attorney General Clark. Even one "no" along that line would cost time they did not have.

How likely was that, Larry wanted to know.

Fletcher had to admit he couldn't even count all the vested interests that fed into that food chain. He told Larry not to hold his breath no matter how important this was, but suggested they stay positive. They all had a bad guy to catch. So, when would Larry meet with Andrei again?

July 21. He'd have to assure Andrei he was in.

And if not?

It's all over.

———✦———

The FBI tightened their cage around Schevchenko. On June 27, Conroy in the New York office addressed another memo to the director.[14]

Dear Sir:

It is requested that the Bureau authorize expenditures from the confidential fund of the New York office to cover telephone service, electric light service, and other incidentals in connection with the operation of the plant located at 22 Purchase St., Rye, NY to cover the technical surveillance of Subject Schevchenko at Rye.

This request was approved. But his request of a month earlier, on June 13, concerning weekly pay for Larry remained unanswered.[15] Conroy addressed

a letter to the director[16] on July 9 that implied that Larry's continuing association with Andrei might be in jeopardy.[17]

> Concerning the desirability of Haas's continuing his association with
> Schevchenko, it is felt this association should definitely be continued in
> order that the Bureau might be kept informed of Schevchenko's activ-
> ities and to assist in proving any violations of the espionage statutes by
> Schevchenko.

The FBI's first civilian counterspy was not being managed well and Haas
felt it.

CHAPTER TWENTY-FOUR

A Profitable Vacation

Between July 7 and 12, Joe and Leona Franey vacationed in New York City.[1]
At 11:10 a.m. on Monday, July 9, 1945, they visited Schevchenko's Amtorg office at his invitation. Joe was to deliver something special. How special it would be in Andrei's eyes remained to be seen.

This event revealed Amtorg's internal skirmishes between operatives and agencies competing for control of valuable human intelligence assets within the Soviet system. Joe and Leona Franey were regarded as a prize to be won. Such internecine warfare undeniably complicated and impeded Andrei's spy craft. His leverage apparently varied with the tides. His unsuitability to a clandestine role once again became apparent. He was increasingly unable to disguise his misgivings, his suspicions, and his vacillation between fear and anger toward other Russians he worked with.

On arrival, Joe opened a brown paper bag and withdrew seven copies of a publication entitled *Hooker Gas* and placed them on Andrei's desk. The June 9 issue featured an article listing the many industries served by chemicals produced at Hooker Electrochemical. While Andrei looked them over, Joe added a bulletin entitled "General Products List: 1945–1946."

In return, Andrei gave Joe a book about the same size as the stack of *Hooker Gas* pamphlets. "Put them in your bag in case somebody is watching when you leave. That way it won't be obvious you left something here." Andrei then asked Leona for an update on matters at Bell.

Captain Listvin and Vladimir Mazurin, she said, had made many requests for aeronautical reports in Andrei's absence. Leona said it with a disapproving look. Everything they asked for was all of a classified nature. Were they for Andrei?

Andrei's eyes widened and he sat up straight, braced as if to explode from his seat. "That was baloney!" Andrei spoke through clenched teeth. He looked around as if someone might be listening and pointed to his phone as if it might be the culprit. He lowered his voice to say the conversation was over. Joe and Leona would please leave. Now.

They looked at each other and then back at Andrei, puzzled.

Speaking more as an order than an invitation, Andrei told them to come to his apartment at eight that night. He waved a dismissive hand and began shuffling papers, then looked up as if startled they were still there. He pressed a button and a uniformed man opened the office door behind them.

Andrei said something to him in Russian, then to the Franeys in English. This man would show them out.

On arriving at Andrei's apartment, Joe and Leona found him more relaxed and cordial. He poured them generous drinks. Soon afterward, leaving Antonina at home with their son, the three went to the Wivel Restaurant, where Andrei paid $8.00 for their dinner, equal to a well-paid American man's wage for a day, and left a generous $1.25 tip.

During dinner, Andrei complained he was not feeling well. Joe and Leona later told agents in a debriefing that at dinner Andrei had acted very nervous. On returning from dinner, Andrei surprised them by giving Joe the key to his apartment. He insisted they remain as his guests. He claimed to be fulfilling an earlier promise he had made concerning their New York City vacation plans. It was the least he could do in return for the valuable information they would bring to his office.[2]

Andrei would be heading up to Rye in preparation for business he would conduct the next day. He promised to return that night at eight, which he did.[3] The Franeys found the entire affair odd and, suspecting listening devices might be in use, they spoke little and of nothing important when they did.

On return, Andrei entertained the Franeys at Toots Shor's Restaurant[4] at 51 West 51st Street, spending an exorbitant seventeen dollars. Afterward, they walked and rested on a tree-covered bench in Central Park. On two occasions Andrei had them change benches when other people approached while strolling past.

At one point he spoke again of completing a major project and being awarded "a lot of money" accompanied by extravagant vouchers for goods and services in Russia. He had put aside a few thousand dollars to be used on his next "new project."

With this financial windfall in mind, he said he needed as much information as he could possibly get on high-speed airplanes. To reassure Leona that his requests were solely for his own personal use, he told her again that he had never requested Listvin or Masurin to obtain any reports for him.

Leona told him that as a matter of library policy she would honor only requests directly from him. His next request, however, jarred her.

He knew the numbers of the reports that he wanted, and he knew they were in the Bell technical library. Had she dared, Leona would have asked how he knew that, but the fact that he did was enough to confirm once again that something nefarious was afoot.

Andrei surprised her one more time. He would pay her twenty to thirty dollars for each report. But no one at Bell Aircraft will miss the reports, Andrei assured her, anticipating an objection. She could photograph them all. He was specifically interested in graphs because, in Russia they had no wind tunnels to conduct the tests for aeronautical research. He then revealed (boasted?) that his wife, Antonina, was also a graduate aircraft design engineer. She would be helping Andrei in this new project.[5]

He asked Leona then if she had a camera she could use for taking photographs of the reports he wanted.

A camera like that, she said, would cost at least three hundred dollars. She didn't have one. But even if she wanted one, she didn't think it was possible to buy such a camera on the open market these days.

Andrei said he could and he would. He'd give it to the Franeys and teach them how to take small pictures. He would take their exposed film, develop it himself, and enlarge them.

When he obtained such a camera, he would send a postcard with a picture of the Empire State Building on one side and a note on the other side: "Hope everything is well by you." That would be a signal for them to come back to New York City on the second Sunday after the postmark date.

He said that when he gave them the camera, they could experiment with it at his apartment. When they were ready, he'd give them his specific requests. He would pay what he promised for each one—twenty or thirty dollars each. To start things off, he suggested a General Electric report titled "Flow of Air Inducts.[6] He knew it was available at Bell and it was unclassified.[7]

Andrei handed Joe five twenty-dollar bills to cover at least part of their New York City vacation expenses. He hoped they would enjoy it.

Neither Joe nor Leona thought the word "enjoyed" was right for this peculiar Schevchenko episode in the middle of their vacation. The FBI agents, however, found it fascinating.

CHAPTER TWENTY-FIVE

Spy Craft in Execution

Saturday, July 21, 1945,[1] *Penn Station, New York City*

Larry's train rolled into Penn Station on time at 3:00 p.m. He did not reach Andrei's apartment until 5:55 p.m. He walked all the way this time. At twenty city blocks to a mile, the three-mile stroll helped him burn away a lot of his nervous energy. A few things had changed.

Andrei had written to shift their meeting place. He now suspected the Rye dacha was being watched. Larry knew the place to be off-limits to all but Soviet officials, so Andrei's original plan had seemed odd.

Something in Andrei's thinking had become erratic and he had grown ever more wary. Larry put it down to the effect of chronic paranoia on an otherwise healthy mind burdened with a clandestine Soviet agenda. Andrei's heightened vigilance would now add one more strain to Larry's plans.

On this date, as Larry learned later, surveillance recorded that Andrei arrived home only forty minutes before Larry reached his apartment. He had parked his blue, 1942 Dodge on the street in front of his apartment instead of in the garage down the street where he usually parked. He had carried a small, black package from the car to his home.

When Larry rapped the brass knocker on 3-D's door, it swung open after the first tap. Andrei stepped halfway out and looked up and down the hallway. Without speaking he reached out, pulled Larry in, and closed the door as fast as he could without slamming it.

Andrei told Larry he had expected him sooner. Was everything alright?

"I'm okay and I'm in," Larry said, looking back at the closed door. Then he repeated himself with the meaning Andrei was waiting for. "I mean, okay, I'm with you."

Andrei looked surprised and delighted. Larry would work with him then? Andrei was indeed pleased.

Larry assured him again. He had thought it over and he would gladly take that camera. He was in.

On his way to Andrei's apartment, Larry had wondered again what this "I'm in" would do to him—the him he thought he was—just as before while facing two FBI agents. He had once thought Steinbeck's maxim was clever. Now he knew it was true. "Man is the only kind of varmint sets his own trap, baits it, then steps in it."

Now, Larry watched Andrei closely. He looked like he was about to say more, but he stopped and took a deep breath. His face relaxed into a tired smile and he said business could wait. First, they would drink to their new partnership. He poured two drinks over crackling ice.

Larry took one and sat beside a window overlooking West 93rd Street to watch the sun set over the Hudson River three blocks away. That's when he saw something that almost stopped his heart.

A crimson flash of sunlight had glinted off something shiny behind a third-floor apartment window directly across the street. Larry instantly knew it was a camera lens. He wanted to yell at the men in that apartment, *Be careful!* He knew agents were there taking still shots and motion pictures of Andrei's apartment. The FBI had quietly rented that luxury apartment for an exorbitant sixty dollars per month.[2] Director Hoover had personally signed off on it. The cover story for the rental, for the sake of gossiping neighbors, vaguely mentioned a reclusive, retired professor.

Before this meeting with Andrei, Special Agent Rath from the New York City field office told Larry that the Bureau wanted enhanced surveillance on Schevchenko "on an extremely discreet basis."[3] He introduced Larry to the three agents, Malone, Gregg, and Plant,[4] now holed up there. They recorded everything Schevchenko and his wife did, day and night, including every guest, delivery boy, and mailman who showed up at the Schevchenkos' address. In that, they would also be learning the art of motion-picture surveillance, a new skill the FBI was starting to experiment with in selected cases. Some agents were skeptical of its future, but the Schevchenko case made a good trial run for the New York office. Eastman Kodak, using proprietary technology the FBI would not yet buy, developed each day's films overnight in a nearby lab. Every morning the agents searched the new footage for evidence. As yet, however, they had found nothing that could stand up in court.

Larry turned away from the window hoping Andrei had not seen the flash. From his seat Andrei could have easily caught the glint over Larry's shoulder. Larry sat back, crossed his legs, and shifted himself nonchalantly to block that line of sight. He sipped his drink and watched his host.

Andrei raised his glass to Larry and said he would be a rich man if he could find the things that Andrei needed—he stopped to correct himself—that *they* needed.

Larry said he would keep trying, but he had brought nothing that day. He wanted to set an expectation of slow returns.

Andrei said that was okay for now. He lit another Camel with a match that Larry thought shook a little. Andrei was sorry. He did not have Larry's camera, either. It might take a week or two. Maybe Larry could come back in a few weeks, another Saturday, perhaps August eleventh? Then, he would teach him how to use the special film and a close-up lens. He would need to carry nothing from Westinghouse but a small roll of exposed film.

That sounded perfect to Larry and the eleventh was fine. Looking forward to it.

Andrei raised his glass. To a good cause. To profits.

With the war behind them, Larry said, if Russia's economy recovered as fast as Andrei promised, fast enough to build their factory . . . well then, here's to profits. He raised his glass, but only for a sip he hoped would look like more.

Andrei had more to say. Larry would have called it "to sell." Andrei told Larry the Soviet system was built for resilience. When he left Russia, for instance, he had been earning 340,000 rubles a year, then earned an 18,000-ruble bonus for coming to the United States.[5] And since then he had been decorated for his work in America. Wartime had not stopped that, and peacetime would only make it better.

Larry assumed that Andrei boasted about his income to make their joint venture more tempting. Larry's quick mental sum based on the current seventy rubles to the dollar exchange rate reduced Andrei's salary to about five thousand dollars per year, just like an average US worker. In Russia, that probably did amount to top pay.

But, Andrei cautioned, that placed some pretty big expectations on him. That was where Larry came in. So, in three months he would arrange for Larry to visit Russia at no expense. Everything would be provided.

Larry looked surprised and asked if that was the price tag for his cooperation.

Andrei blinked. That question came too soon. He backed away. Price tag? Not at all. Larry would be an honored guest, a partner. He would merely be asked to share his expertise. That, however, was a conversation for another time.

Another time then, Larry conceded.

For the moment, Andrei said, he would just tell Larry his priorities. He handed Larry a typewritten list.

Larry realized he might now be holding Andrei's death sentence, or at least a prison sentence, in his hands. He read it and every new line stunned him more than the one above it.

Thirteen numbered lines listed nearly every top secret project, instrument, tool, and technology in all of America's most advanced aviation research programs. Some details were so explicit that Larry could almost tell which technicians and scientists had leaked top-echelon goods to him. It was all at the cutting edge of aviation, rocketry, and strategic planning for warfare of the future.

Larry looked up with admiration and told Andrei his list was pure genius. It was about time this kind of technology forced its way into civilian aviation.

Andrei said he was glad Larry understood that. But nothing would get itself released by the people who were keeping it secret. So, he and Larry would release it for everyone's good. Of course, he said with a smile, they would do well for themselves in the process, too.

In fact, Andrei knew it would never be released to anyone except a select group of specialists at the Moscow end of a diplomatic courier chain and his own encrypted, shortwave radio link to Moscow Center.

But, Larry said, this was major stuff, riskier for him than he expected and quite dangerous. And worse for Andrei, if he was caught with it, he'd be sent home persona non grata. Was Andrei really sure about this? Larry realized again that he was inviting Andrei to dig his own grave even deeper.

Andrei said he was only sure if his good friend Larry was, too. Anything Larry brought back would be appreciated.[6]

Larry started to fold the paper to put it in his shirt pocket. He'd see what he could do with Andrei's shopping list.

Andrei quickly, almost roughly, retrieved the paper from Larry's hand, finished folding it, and tucked it back into his own pocket. Just do what you can, he said. He was confident Larry knew what was right. The choice would be entirely Larry's. In reality, Andrei said, he was asking for nothing more than Larry wanted to bring him. He would appreciate whatever that might be.

Larry said he'd see what he could do. But to himself, he screamed *Damn! That was slippery. The FBI could never nail Andrei for gifts Larry chose to give him. He needed that list.*

Larry decided it was time to quit for the night. He looked at his watch. He wanted to be at the station by 10:30. He asked if Andrei could give him a lift.

Driving downtown, Andrei played the radio turned up loud. But when Billie Holiday started to sing, he turned it off. Larry hid a smile. He was sure Billie's new hit was not the tune a spy wanted to hear. "I'll Be Seeing You in All the Old Familiar Places."

Larry boarded the 10:30 train to Philadelphia and tried to refresh his memory about the evening's events while the moonlit farmlands of southern New Jersey serenely rolled by.

<hr />

Monday, July 23, 1945. FBI Philadelphia Field Office interview with Larry Haas

Larry demanded to know why Fletcher couldn't get permission for Larry to hand Andrei some doctored docs. Didn't Fletcher have that sorted out yet?[7]

Fletcher said there was a catch. First, some of the brass worried that doctored docs might not be considered real and confidential information. As a result, Schevchenko could not be touched if he had them. So, they said he could be given real material, but only on the condition that if Schevchenko was arrested, they would guarantee the army that the Soviets would never see the evidence—the papers would be properly stamped in big red letters: TOP SECRET. They would have to nab him right between gaining possession and passing the stuff off to a courier. Schevchenko would probably set up the handoff for someplace where he could do it fast. Those Russian couriers would then disappear even faster. They were slippery.

Fletcher told Larry that all sounded too risky.

"Not to me!" Larry said. Why couldn't the FBI blanket the place with agents?

No dice. They would be spotted right away. But even if they could pull that off and close the trap on Schevchenko, they could not prosecute. The Justice Department had to follow certain rules of evidence and disclose the incriminating material to the accused and his defense. And that would include the people who were not supposed to see it in the first place.[8]

That was stupid, Larry said. Fletcher couldn't be serious.

As serious as the US Constitution, the agent said. But even if they could bypass those rules under some kind of national security waiver, the diplomatic furor would make the evidence very hard to hide from Soviet eyes.

Larry's frustration level was rising. Couldn't they just lock down all the legal proceedings behind closed doors under national security regulations?

"Things have been known to leak,"⁹ Fletcher said with disgust, especially with an inquisitive press mixed up in the mess. The FBI, Fletcher had to admit, was caught in a fork, a stalemate between the Justice Department and the Joint Chiefs of Staff. That was a lot of brass to take on.

Well, Larry said he had to give Andrei something, some kind of juicy bait. They would meet again on August 11. Could he take something technical that was not confidential, doctor it up to ID Larry as its source, and stamp it TOP SECRET?

Fletcher looked doubtful, but curious. Doctor it up? How? If he changed the scientific data, Andrei or somebody higher up might spot it.

Larry laughed. He couldn't believe he was giving FBI agents a lesson in "Devious." Suppose, Larry continued, he picked a technical report of some kind, added a comma in line seventeen of page three, misspelled "control" with two ls on the second diagram out of five, and replaced an "and" with a comma on the last page. Those three tiny, invisible typos would make a document into a fingerprint. He could do one on every page and nobody would notice. Anything would work, the smaller the better. If the FBI wanted to dangle Larry in front of Andrei, they just had to give him some bait to put on the hook.

Fletcher was impressed, but, sorry Larry, not convinced. The brass still might not go along. He would shoot it up the line, though, and see what happens. They were learning as they went along, he admitted. This was, after all, their first civilian-based anti–Soviet counterspy operation. Nobody in the Bureau could teach it to them.

Didn't everybody want to catch this guy? Larry pressed, nearly pleading.

Not necessarily, Fletcher told Larry. Andrei was a chess piece now, and so was Larry. A lot of powerful people have different ideas about how to play this game. Publicly, the Ruskies are still supposed to be our friends. It's bad manners to embarrass them, even if they have their knife in our back.

Larry thought he had heard it all. But he hadn't.

Dorothy and Larry, dating.
Stars in their eyes and his
eyes on the stars.
CREDIT: KAY HAAS

Larry marries and
postpones his plans,
but not for long.
CREDIT: KAY HAAS

Top: Dorothy and Larry; bottom, left to right:
Judy and Kay, approximately 1944.
CREDIT: KAY HAAS

In Miami days before Dorothy's death. CREDIT: KAY HAAS

Larry and Kay, Spring 1940. CREDIT: KAY HAAS

Kay "Bunny" Haas about one year before her
nearly fatal abduction on the way to school.
CREDIT: KAY HAAS

The house Larry built on Van Buren Avenue overlooking Olean, New York. Kay's room—where the break-in occurred—is on the left, facing the garage roof.
CREDIT: KAY HAAS

Larry Haas. Casual work dress suited him as well as three-piece suits or lab coats. CREDIT: KAY HAAS

Kay and second husband, Jerry, a mismatched couple (by about two feet) who could not have been better matched.
CREDIT: KAY HAAS

Only known photograph of Larry Haas instructing Bell engineers and military representatives, approximately 1945. CREDIT: KAY HAAS

Bell senior management. Larry Haas is in the back row, second from right.
CREDIT: KAY HAAS

Larry Haas (front, second from left) with engineering research group at Bell Aircraft.
CREDIT: KAY HAAS

Larry brings an F6F to Westinghouse to study folding wing dynamics for the navy's jet program. Larry—wearing a white shirt and dark derby hat, the unofficial badge of service adopted by Bell's close-knit jet team and kept by Haas even after joining Westinghouse— is seen at bottom right overseeing the plane's movement through a razor-thin main gate clearance.
CREDIT: KAY HAAS

The Freeman Supply Company

PATTERN SHOP & FOUNDRY SUPPLIES & EQUIPMENT

MAHOGANY AND PINE PATTERN LUMBER

Toledo 5, Ohio

1152 EAST BROADWAY
PHONE TAYLOR 4624
BOX 67 STA. A

March 1, 1950

Frederick Flader, Incorporated
Laskey Road
Toledo, Ohio

Attention: Mr. L. G. Haas

Dear Mr. Haas:

Speaking for the American Foundryman's Society, and also a number of individuals who have contacted me, I would like to thank you for the talk and discussion which you so kindly made at our recent meeting. Toledo members were very much interested and a number of them have asked that I extend their thanks to you as a pricipal source of an interesting evening, discussion, on timely subjects.

I would certainly be pleased to hear from you anytime and perhaps you would like to avail yourself of an invitation also extended to you by a number of the members to visits 1 or 2 of the plants.

Meanwhile, we will look forward to hearing from you and thanks again for your participation.

Very truly yours,

THE FREEMAN SUPPLY COMPANY

G. R. Rusk

G. R. Rusk

GRR;mld

Larry Haas begins to create a public presence, capitalizing first on his work with Flader in Toledo.
CREDIT: KAY HAAS

Russian ace Alexander Pokryshkin, with fifty-five kills in a Bell P-39 against Luftwaffe aircraft, congratulated by comrades. CREDIT: *THE BELLRINGER*, BELL AIRCRAFT ARCHIVES, NIAGARA AEROSPACE MUSEUM

Colonel of the Guards, pilot Alexander Pokryshkin, of the Soviet Air Force—"Sky Boss." After the war he attained the rank of Marshal of Aviation, though as one of Stalin's Falcons he was only one of the many Soviet pilots who flew Bell P-39s to decimate Luftwaffe squadrons over Russia. CREDIT: *THE BELLRINGER*, BELL AIRCRAFT ARCHIVES, NIAGARA AEROSPACE MUSEUM

Pokryshkin, the Soviet ace who terrified Luftwaffe fighters in his Bell P-39.
CREDIT: *THE BELLRINGER*, BELL AIRCRAFT ARCHIVES, NIAGARA AEROSPACE MUSEUM

Bell P-39 Airacobra. The "Cannon on Wings" that Russian aces called their "Kobrushka" (Little Cobra). Soviet pilots made it one of the deadliest air weapons Luftwaffe pilots faced. CREDIT: KAY HAAS

Three generations of Larry Bell's WWII aircraft. Top to bottom: P-39 Airacobra, P-63 Kingcobra, and P-59 Airacomet. CREDIT: KAY HAAS

Bell P-59 Airacomet. Bell and GE's top secret project to launch America's first operational jet fighter. Larry Haas worked with both Bell and GE to build the jet power plant for this groundbreaking aircraft. CREDIT: KAY HAAS

Chief test pilot Bob Stanley and Brigadier General (then Colonel) Lawrence C. Craigie, at Muroc Lake. CREDIT: KAY HAAS

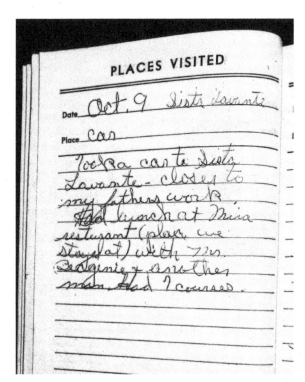

Judy Haas's European travel journal accidentally reveals "my father's work," a clandestine location in Sestri Levante on the Mediterranean coast ironically located on a promontory between the Bay of Fables and the Bay of Silence. CREDIT: KAY HAAS

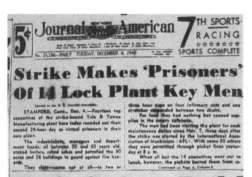

Red Spies Paid
For Jet Secrets

Push Law To Curb Strikes

WASHINGTON, Dec. 4.— The House Military Affairs Committee prepared today to give President Truman all he asked for—and more in the way of legislation to stop the wave of strikes and lockouts.

Speedy action was expected despite the opposition of labor to Mr. Truman's proposals.

Take Crippled Troopship In Tow

Bribed U. S. Engineers for Blueprints of Planes

By HOWARD RUSHMORE
Copyright, 1945, by New York Journal-American

Agents of the Communist International not only tried to steal secrets of the atomic bomb, but bribed technicians and engineers to furnish blueprints of military equipment including jet propelled airplanes the N. Y. Journal-American learned today.

Although these espionage activities are known to the State Department, no action has been taken to date against a Russian spy ring, which for two years has operated with unlimited funds and skilled personnel in an effort to steal confidential scientific developments.

The first of three successive (December 4, 5, and 6, 1945) front-page stories exposing Schevchenko and his entire Soviet spy network. CREDIT: UNIVERSITY OF TEXAS AT AUSTIN LIBRARIES

Byrnes Let Spy Flee, Jet Expert Tells Quiz

JAMES F. BYRNES
Associated Press Wirephoto.

Andrei Schevchenko who was identified as a Russian spy seeking wartime plant secrets. A witness testified that "Mr. Byrnes of the State Department" said the FBI they couldn't touch the Russian.

LOREN G. HAAS
International News soundphoto.

State Department Vetoed Arrest, Witness Says

WASHINGTON, June 6—(AP)—An elaborate plan to trap a Russian spy seeking wartime plane secrets, crumbled when "Mr. Byrnes of the State Department" vetoed his arrest, a jet engine expert testified today.

The witness, Loren G. Haas of Buffalo, N. Y., did not further identify "Mr. Byrnes" in his testimony before the House Un-American Activities Committee. But the period about which he was talking was 1945, and James F. Byrnes, former senator and Supreme Court justice, took over as Secretary of State in July of that year.

In 1949, House Un-American Activities Committee continues to investigate the enduring mystery of Schevchenko's escape from prosecution, with the public still blaming Byrnes. CREDIT: *THE WASHINGTON POST*

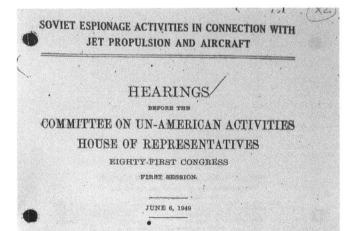

Again on October 1, 1945, this situation was called to the attention of the Attorney General by memorandum.

It is now my understanding that the State Department has granted this Bureau authorization to investigate further Schevchenko's espionage activities but that no prosecution can be contemplated until the State Department grants its approval.

ACTION: There is attached for the attention of the Attorney General a memorandum pointing out the reported attitude of the Department of State and advising him that all investigative activity possible to this point has been conducted and that an opinion regarding prosecution must be had.

Attachment

It is now up to the A. G. Our investigation is finished. No arrest can be made until we get specific clearance from the A. G.

- 6 -

Office memorandum. D. M. Ladd to Director. 10/1/45, 100-340996-96. Secretary of State Byrnes has been most commonly blamed for refusal to apprehend Schevchenko, but this Hoover "blue bomb" plainly states that responsibility rests with Attorney General Clark. CREDIT: FBI ARCHIVES

SOVIET ESPIONAGE ACTIVITIES IN CONNECTION WITH
JET PROPULSION AND AIRCRAFT

HEARINGS

BEFORE THE

COMMITTEE ON UN-AMERICAN ACTIVITIES

HOUSE OF REPRESENTATIVES

EIGHTY-FIRST CONGRESS

FIRST SESSION

JUNE 6, 1949

Printed for the use of the Committee on Un-American Activities

UNITED STATES
GOVERNMENT PRINTING OFFICE
WASHINGTON : 1949

Cover of 128-page transcript of HUAC investigation. CREDIT: US GOVERNMENT PRINTING OFFICE

The Haases and Franeys review evidence. *The Washington Evening Star*, Washington, DC, June 6, 1949. CREDIT: *THE WASHINGTON EVENING STAR*

WITNESSES AT SPY PROBE—The House Committee on Un-American Activities summoned three witnesses today for questioning about suspected Soviet agents at the Bell aircraft plant at Buffalo, N. Y. Shown waiting outside the committee room are (left to right) Loren G. Haas of Buffalo and his wife (not a witness) and Mr. and Mrs. Joseph J. Franey of Niagara Falls.

Franey exhibit 1

Class	Title	Source of report and report No.
To be classified.	Swept-Back Wings at High Velocities	German Bericht 127. Translated into English.
Do.	High-Speed Measurements on a Swept-back Wing (Swept-Back Angle, 35°).	German Report FB1813.
Secret.	Cabin Air Conditioning System of a Typical Jet-Propelled Fighter Airplane.	AiResearch Manu. Company Proposal Number B-12.
Confidential.	A Summary of Drag Results from Recent Langley Full-Scale-Tunnel Tests of Army and Navy Airplanes.	NACA ACR L5A30.
Restricted.	Landing Gear Design Considerations by James A. Hootman.	NACA 3D20.
Do.	Drag Determinations of the Forward Component Tricycle Landing Gear.	NACA T. N. 788.
Unclassified.	Thermal Requirements for Aircraft Cabins	Air Technical Service Command, Wright Field. TSEAL3-695-56.
Confidential.	Comparative Drag Measurements at Transonic Speeds of Rectangular and Swept-Back NACA 65I-009 Airfoils Mounted on a Freely Falling Body.	NACA L5G90.
Do.	The Characteristics of a Tapered and Twisted Wing with Sweep-Back.	British R & M 1226.
Do.	A General Solution of the Problem of the Glauert Loading of Wings with Discontinuities of Incidence.	Report 7629 Ae. 2005.
Do.	Wing Plan Forms for High-Speed Flight.	NACA L5G07.
Unclassified.	The Influence of Sweep on the Spanwise Lift Distribution of Wings.	Journal of Aero. Sci. March 1943, pp. 101-104.
Do.	Monoplane Wings with Sweep (Theoretical Calculation of the Spanwise Lift Distribution).	Aircraft Engineering, August 1938 issue, pp. 245-247.
Restricted.	Theoretical Distribution of Load Over a Swept-Back Wing.	NACA Report, dated October 1942.
Secret.	Athodyd Thrust.	General Electric Data Folder 29091.
Do.	Performance Comparison Between a Gas Turbine-Propeller Power Plant and a Gas Turbine-Jet Propulsion Unit Installed in a High Speed Fighter Airplane.	Curtiss-Wright Re. 911A.
Unclassified.	A Method for Estimating Gas Turbine-Jet Airplane Performance.	AAFTR 5193.
Secret.	Manufacture of Blades for Junkers Turbo-Jet Unit.	British Re. A.1.2 9.5.44 (Issued from Wright Field).
Unclassified.	The End Losses of Turbine Blades.	Brown Boveri Review, November 1941 Issue, pp. 336-361 (French).
Confidential.	A Metallurgical Investigation of a Large Forged Disc of 19-9 DL Alloy.	NACA 3C10.
Do.	Heat Resisting Metals for Gas Turbine Parts N-102.	Nat'l. Def. Res. Com., Office of Sci. Res. and Dev. M-16.
Unclassified.	Investigation of Blade Characteristics—Performance and Efficiency of Turbine and Axial-Flow Compressor Stages.	Trans. of A. S. M. E. July 1944 issue, pp. 413-430.
Confidential.	Compilation of Current Data on Selected Alloys Suitable for High Temperature Service in Gas Turbine and Supercharger Parts.	Nat'l. Def. Res. Com., Office of Sci. Res. and Dev. M-12.
Unclassified.	Vibration Studies on Turbine Blades.	From German Publication Motortechnische Zeitschrift.
Secret.	Cabin Pressurization and Conditioning Systems for Jet Propelled Aircraft.	Wright Field Eng. Data Report TSEPL-4-522-272.
Confidential.	Ram Jet Power Plants.	Manual No. 237.¹
Do.	Fuel Systems for Jet Propulsion.	Manual No. 218.¹
Restricted.	The Intermittent Jet Engine.	Manual No. 341.¹
Confidential.	Tests at Transonic Speeds of the Effectiveness of a Swept-Back Trailing-Edge Flap on an Airfoil Having Parallel Flat Surfaces, Extreme Sweepback and Low Aspect Ratio.	NACA L5HO1.
	The Calculation of Aerodynamic Loading on Surfaces of any Shape.	British R & M 1910.
Do.	An Interim Report on the Stability and Control of Tailless Airplanes.	NACA LAH19.

The following reports are prints of 35-millimeter microfile taken by either United States Army or Navy personnel.

Class	Title	Source of report and report No.
Top secret.	Performance of Ram Jets with Negligible Velocity in Combustion Chamber.	FW Rep 90-040.¹
	Design of Ram Jets.	FW Rep 09-041.¹
	Preliminary Reports on Tests of the FW Ram Jet in Wind Tunnel A9 of the LFA.	FW Rep 09-045.¹
	Stability Considerations for Swept-Back Wings.	UM3151.
	Extent of the Laminar Boundary Layer on a Swept-Back Wing.	FB 1626.
	Three Component Measurements on a Swept-Back Wing with a Split Flap.	FB 1913.
	Tests on a Partially Swept-Back Wing with Varying Dihedral.	FB 1458.
	Contributions to the Investigation of Swept-Back Wings.	FB 1501.
	Measurements of Pressure Distributions on Swept-Back Wings.	FB 1553.
	Lift Distributions on Swept-Back Wings.	

¹ Prepared for the commander in chief, United States fleet, by members of Jet Propelled Missiles Panel of Office of Scientific Research and Development. Reports forwarded to Bell Aircraft by AAF Air Technical Service Command (TSEFL-5), Wright Field, Dayton, Ohio.
² Focke-Wulf.

Exhibit 1. The list of documents at Bell Aircraft that Andrei Schevchenko requested from Leona Franey, as presented to HUAC on June 6, 1949. He also asked Larry Haas for many of these documents and comparable material later from Westinghouse. CREDIT: US GOVERNMENT PRINTING OFFICE

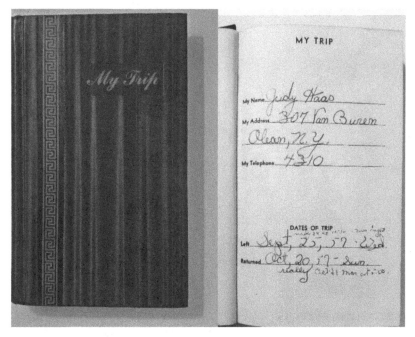

Judy's carefully documented "Family Trips," which trace clandestine meetings across Europe. CREDIT: JUDY HAAS

Dorothy Haas, Judy Haas, Larry Haas, and Mr. and Mrs. Bernie Williams meeting a second time on the other side of Europe. This table could still be found on the Ristorante Valle website until its pandemic closure in 2020.
CREDIT: KAY HAAS

At the Ctesiphon Arch in 1971, on the eastern bank of the Tigris River, and about twenty-two miles southeast of present-day Baghdad. On the far left is Sammy, Larry's driver, interpreter, and bodyguard. CREDIT: KAY HAAS

Larry Haas at Ctesiphon, good at joining in but not at blending in. CREDIT: KAY HAAS

CHAPTER TWENTY-SIX

Invisibility, Bombs, and Victors

Saturday, August 11, 1945, a coffee shop in midtown Manhattan[1]

All Andrei would tell Larry about why they had to meet in New York City on Saturday was that it could save both of their lives.

This would be an important weekend for Andrei. He had booked a meeting with Larry on Saturday and a meeting with Leona and Joe on Sunday.

So, my friend, Andrei began, you are here to gain a useful skill. Are you ready to take a walk?

A walk?

Walking to become invisible, Andrei explained. He wanted to frame this as a sport, not the lethal game it could be. Larry's government had a bad habit of watching its guests, according to Andrei. All foreigners had to be watched during the war, he admitted, that was understandable. But with the war over the sport remained, and that was not acceptable. People still followed and were followed. Many people had to learn the arts of evasion and invisibility.

Larry said that was just Hollywood cloak-and-dagger stuff, wasn't it?

Andrei leaned over the table almost far enough to dunk the tip of his silk tie in his coffee. He spoke in a hushed whisper. He was being watched by the FBI, he confided, but he knew how to evade them. Unfortunately, that made them even more suspicious. So, if he was watched, Larry would be, too. Andrei would now teach him how to spot the followers and how to dodge them.

To Larry, that sounded like more than a sport.

Andrei sat back, relaxed, and waved Larry's doubts away. The only danger would be if an undisciplined FBI agent gets too suspicious or too . . . He searched for a word, *"obozlennyy,"* or as Larry would say, *pissed off,* at being ditched. Some react beyond their authority. Andrei assured Larry he knew how American secret police worked. Larry might be of little interest to them right now, but they might someday take an interest. Andrei would show him how to become invisible. The art started with surveillance detection.

Andrei stood and left the shop without looking back. Larry followed him to the sidewalk. Andrei told Larry to look up at the windows above the coffee shop and suppose this was his neighborhood and he thought somebody was watching and following him. How would he know?

Larry reckoned he would look out his window or look behind himself while walking down the street. He tried to sound naive.

Andrei laughed. To spot a watcher you only do what you always do and only go where you always go, but you go a little more slowly and keep your eyes open. You do not look back or scan for watchers. That shows you think you're being watched, Andrei warned. Instead, you stay fifteen minutes here, twenty minutes there. Stop, browse, relax, and notice without seeming to look for who is close enough to see you. Be suspicious of anyone you see more than once, but do not evade them. Watch again another day. Make them think they remain unnoticed. Then, when you need to become unseen, you know who to shake.

They spent the next few hours getting on and off buses, going down into crowded subway stations, on and off trains, back up to the street, in front doors and out back doors. Andrei's coaching added a few interesting wrinkles to tricks the FBI agents had already taught him. Most amusing, though, was the FBI tails Larry spotted. Andrei missed them.

Eventually, still feigning naivete, Larry asked if Andrei was sure all of it worked.

He handed Larry a note with instructions to use it on the way to their meeting next week on August 18. It indicated the place they would meet. Be alone. Watch for watchers. Andrei was trained in this business and would know if Larry was tailed.

On parting, Andrei drew a handwritten paper from a jacket pocket and handed it to Larry, offering one word of instruction before he turned toward Central Park West and home.

"Practice."

⊷•⊷

A picture postcard of the Empire State Building had reached the Franeys' home.[2] They followed its instructions. On Sunday, August 12, at 7:30 a.m.,

Andrei greeted Leona and Joe at his apartment. His wife was not at home. Andrei and the Franeys breakfasted together at the Sterling Cafeteria, 85th and Broadway. Andrei paid for it all with two one-dollar bills.

Back at the apartment, Andrei asked Leona to retire to a bedroom for about an hour so he could speak with Joe. He then produced the camera he had promised. It was a Zeiss Icon for which he had paid $325. Andrei carefully handed it to Joe with six film cartridges, sufficient for a total of 180 exposures. He turned on the radio with the volume turned up and spent the next hour teaching Joe how to use the camera. Later, he did it all over again for Leona.[3]

Andrei handed Leona ten twenty-dollar bills to cover their traveling expenses (which totaled $78.84). He asked Joe to return with exposed film on September 9 and then gave Leona two more twenty-dollar bills toward the expense of that trip.[4]

Andrei told Leona to decide for herself which reports to photograph. He did not specify any particular reports, though he made his interests known. "I like NACA reports. I have some of them, but not all, but you often find important information and reports of other companies, such as General Electric."

With their business finished, Andrei enthusiastically gave his guests the same history lesson he had given Larry the day before. He insisted the Soviets deserved credit for hastening the end of the Pacific war. They had, after all, flooded Japanese-held Manchuria with 1.6 million Soviet troops. Defeating the million-man Japanese army in three days surely topped anything America could do.

They rounded out the morning at Caruso's Restaurant for a lavish $10.90 lunch, paid for as always by Andrei.

Apparently, Andrei was unaware that their morning was not spent alone. Harvey Rath and another agent had taken still photos of Leona and Joe coming and going at Andrei's address and captured it all on film.[5]

On return to Buffalo, Leona prepared a list of reports under all four standard designations—unclassified, restricted, confidential, and secret. She focused her selections on Andrei's areas of interest. They dealt with airfoils, athodyd thrust,[6] gas turbine–jet propulsion units, the newest data on special alloys for gas turbine and supercharger parts, cabin pressurization for jet-propelled aircraft, and a few other general technical matters.

Leona knew Andrei had interest in all of it, and the FBI was interested in anything that interested Andrei.[7]

The next Monday and Thursday, August 6 and August 9, changed the world again for Andrei and Larry. Andrei now reckoned a history lesson was more important than another spy lesson.

One could blame Dr. Einstein's famous equation, $E = mc^2$, for it. Einstein's formula dictated that radioactive material weighing no more than a dollar bill—hardly more than a gram inside each of two bombs—had killed more than 100,000 people and destroyed 60,000 buildings in Hiroshima, Japan, on Monday, August 6, 1945, and 80,000 people and 20,000 buildings in Nagasaki on Thursday, August 9.

After nearly four years of war, more than 100,000 US military casualties, hundreds of billions of dollars in battlefield costs, and two billion dollars invested in two atomic bombs, a paltry two or three grams of uranium and plutonium might have driven Japan to the brink of surrender. But it would surely surrender to Russia, even if America still had another A-bomb ready to drop on them, as Andrei saw the matter. He claimed that Einstein's American bombs could little more than soften up Japan for the big "storm" that Russia had started on Thursday. It was Russia's mighty August Storm, a promise to America kept by Stalin, just in case the Americans could not finish the job themselves.

"Do you people really think you already won the war? It's not over yet!" Andrei nearly spit the words at Larry. A mad Russian had finally shown up where Larry had only suspected one before. This could be interesting.

"Yeah," Larry said, smiling, idly swirling the coffee in his mug. "I think we'll have something to do with it."

"We just annihilated Japan's million-man army in Manchuria overnight. That was only two nights ago. The Red Army just mopped them all up. We can practically wade across the sea from China to Japan right now. That's why the Japanese will surrender to us. Just give them a couple of days, you'll see." Andrei's face was red. "They will surrender to our million and a half troops. That was our Yalta promise," Andrei said, "we promised to show up just ninety days after Hitler fell. We show up and Japan gives up."

"We took two entire cities off the planet with two bombs in two seconds," Larry countered, "and they better believe we would do it again. They'll surrender, all right, but they will surrender to us." Larry sat back, satisfied. He did not add his own speculation that, given the choice of conquerors, Japan would gamble that the United States would be the more humane victor.

Andrei added one more challenge. "When we got ready to attack Japan from the west, we scared Truman into dropping his bombs. He was afraid that after all his hard work, we would take the credit—and the prize."

Larry couldn't see solving this one short of fighting the whole war all over again right here in the coffee shop. Besides, he was pretty sure that a final surrender, whenever it happened, would not go Andrei's way. But Larry chose a diplomatic cease-fire on the topic.

"Here's to the fog of war, then." Larry lifted his coffee mug. "Only the emperor in Tokyo knows the whole truth, so why don't we just wait and see."

Also unwilling to either concede or keep fencing, Andrei nodded, raised his mug to Larry's, and accepted the cue.

——•◦•——

Two days later, the question of who won the war was settled.

At 7:03 on Tuesday evening, August 14, the fifteen thousand light bulbs on Times Tower's famous zipper sign high over the sidewalks of Times Square lit up for all to see. Five words crawled slowly around their track over and over again: "Official . . . Truman announces Japanese surrender." 7:03 p.m. in New York City corresponded with three minutes after high noon Japan Standard Time. Emperor Hirohito's voice had been heard on Japanese radio stations making one of history's most remarkable understatements: "the war situation has developed not necessarily to Japan's advantage."

The emperor continued, "Moreover, the enemy has begun to employ a new and most cruel bomb, the power of which to do damage is, indeed, incalculable, taking the toll of many innocent lives. Should we continue to fight, not only would it result in an ultimate collapse and obliteration of the Japanese nation, but also it would lead to the total extinction of human civilization." Hirohito's statement made no mention of his nation's disastrous Manchurian encounter with Soviet forces in China.

It was a rare moment in history. The vanquished had chosen the victor.

——•◦•——

Saturday afternoon, August 18, 1945, Central Park[8]
Andrei had asked Larry to practice what he had learned about surveillance detection a week earlier by arriving at his apartment by a special, prescribed route through Central Park.

Larry was to proceed from Penn Station by cab to the 79th Street Transverse across the park. From there, he was to walk along the footpath under the Greywacke Arch, across the Great Lawn, and then walk north on the Bridal Path to the 93rd Street exit on Central Park West. He was to follow Andrei's map with his newly trained attention to the faces and movements around him, near and far, and then report anything suspicious to Andrei when they met at the end of the tour.

Following his trek, on the park side of the exit onto the Avenue, Larry was to find a specific tree-shaded bench, sit there, and inspect his surroundings without appearing to do so. By the end of his long stroll, Larry could report that all seemed uneventful. Larry rested his arms on the back of the bench for a few minutes and then headed for Andrei's apartment.

Nicely done, Andrei complimented Larry. Andrei had watched him the entire way. Larry thanked him but neglected to mention that somebody else had watched them both.

Larry arrived at Andrei's apartment around 4:30 and left with him for Casino Russe on 56th Street around six o'clock for further conversation.[9]

Larry tried to remember everything. The other watchers would have a lot of questions.

———•—•———

Thursday afternoon, August 23, 1945. Post-contact interview. The lobby of the Ben Franklin Hotel in downtown Philadelphia[10]

Watchers were everywhere, or so it seemed to Larry now that he was watching for people trying not to look like they were watching him. As he strolled toward the Benjamin Franklin Hotel to meet with the agents, he began to understand how selective perception could shade toward delusion and, if unchecked, could slide all the way to paranoia. It must have been hard on a man like Andrei. Then he wondered if he was starting that slide himself.

Larry brushed off the thought and stepped into Ben Franklin's elaborately decorated lobby. He casually strolled to the reception desk and thumbed through a complimentary copy of *Life Magazine* for August 20.[11] The cover featured a man he admired, General "Tooey" Spaatz. He was a taciturn man of few but direct words. Larry's favorite was "I never learned anything while I was talking."[12] He had earned his place on this week's cover by overseeing the atomic bombing of Japan two weeks ago. But mostly, Larry knew Spaatz championed a strong and independent air force. Larry, however, became so engrossed in the article that he almost missed a man he was not supposed to notice.

The man walked to the desk and browsed through a newspaper paying no attention to Larry. He spoke softly without looking up and moved his lips no more than a ventriloquist.

Room 412. Do not follow me. He turned away, strolled to the elevator bank, and punched the Up button. Within a minute he disappeared through the yawning, golden doors.

Larry turned a few more pages, scanned a couple of ads as if they interested him, then folded the magazine, tucked it under his arm, and crossed the lobby toward the hotel bar. He ordered the hotel's finest old scotch and sipped it while idly surveying the room for faces he had seen before. Seeing none, he carried his drink down the ornate stairway to the lower lobby, called an elevator, and rode it up seven floors. He stepped out of the elevator into an empty hallway and took the stairway down to the fourth floor.

The door to room 412 opened on Larry's first knock. He entered, unbuttoned his collar, pulled the knot down on his tie, and smiled at Special Agents Ward Ervin and Howard Fletcher. "Hot day, gentlemen," Larry said. Nobody needed the reminder. He swirled his drink to make the ice cubes clink as he lifted his glass. This meeting had to start with a toast!

Fletcher blinked and almost snarled in his impatience. To what?

Larry only laughed and named their two new best friends, Little Boy and Fat Man. It had only been two weeks. Had the agents forgotten already?

Larry won chagrined smiles from both men.

Oh, yes! Those guys, Fletcher agreed. Good thing their side had dropped them before anybody else figured it out. He picked up his coffee cup, raised it toward Larry's glass, and toasted to Yankee ingenuity and two beautiful A-bombs.

"To VJ-Day, boys," Larry returned. He gave himself a long, slow sip, savoring the tart, smoky bite on his tongue. The taste reminded him again, however, that this particular enjoyment grew dangerously stronger the more he hung out with Andrei.[13]

The August heat made the room oppressive. The Franklin had not yet joined the air-conditioning trend. A sluggish southwest breeze barely ruffled the window curtains. The thermometer stood at ninety and the humidity made it feel like a hundred. The agents were eager to get this episode in the books and end another long day on the hot, downtown Philly sidewalks. Agent Fletcher took out his notepad and pen and asked when Larry had met with Schevchenko this time.

It had been as promised, Larry said, on Saturdays, the eleventh and eighteenth. The eleventh, however, had been a waste of time. But on the eighteenth they had met at Andrei's apartment at about 4:30.

Ervin was suspicious. He wanted to know how any meeting with Schevchenko could be useless. What really happened on the eleventh?

Larry laughed. He had taken an abbreviated lesson in how to evade FBI tails. Larry thought that part entertaining. He asked how he and Andrei had done.

Fletcher said not so good. They had pictures of Haas with Schevchenko looking suspiciously furtive. He offered to show them to Larry, enjoying his "gotcha" moment.

Larry got him back. He had spotted them, too. Larry smirked and told him exactly where. But not to worry, he reassured the agents, Andrei had not seen them.

Fletcher congratulated the new guy and then settled into business mode. So, what happened on the eighteenth, he wanted to know. Any business he and Agent Ervin should know about?

Larry said he had learned that day that the United States did not really win the war against Japan. The Ruskies did it first. Any questions?

Ervin laughed, said it figured, and brushed it off. He wanted to get down to business.

Larry agreed. Andrei had finally gotten his hands on a good German camera. But he had lent it to a girl at the office and she had broken it. To make up for it, he said he was getting a Leica camera that would cost him $340. He couldn't say when Larry would get it, though. Andrei would be taking extra cautions in delivering it. Instead of calling or sending Larry a note to pick up the camera, he asked Larry to write a note to himself. Andrei would send it to Larry when he thought it was safe to have him come back. It was odd, Larry said, but he played along.

Fletcher thought it strange, too. What did Andrei mean by when it would be safe to come back?

Andrei was getting worried, Larry said, more worried about surveillance every day.

Ervin knew why. He was sure Andrei was aware that a few major Soviet agents and American sympathizers had defected to the United States within the last few weeks. People like Schevchenko knew they were being watched closer than ever. In Ervin's opinion, Schevchenko was too smart not to be getting edgy. So, he wanted to know, what did Larry do?

He wrote himself the note and addressed it to his home in Chester.

Dear Larry,

Well how are you old boy? Just stopping off to see the town for a few days.
Will drop down to see you the later part of the week.

Julia and Larry Jones & family

Andrei liked it and promised to send it to Larry when he had the camera in hand. He would include a secret code only Larry could understand in the event it was intercepted. Andrei would write two numbers beside the date on the letter. Larry was to add the first number to the date and that would indicate the date they should meet. The second number would indicate the hour.

As soon as Andrei was satisfied that Larry understood his instructions, he relaxed and changed the subject. He asked if the Westinghouse technical library was like the one at Bell. Larry had merely shrugged. More or less had seemed a satisfactory answer.

Ervin was just about out of questions. He loosened his tie a little more, as close to a rebellious act against the FBI's strict uniform code as any agent was likely to go, no matter how hot the day, and simply asked if there was anything else Larry could offer.

Just one more thing, Larry said, but it was an odd one. He felt like he was being watched closely, too, but by the other side. Andrei had asked if he knew anything about a new aircraft power plant, a turbine engine—he thought it might be a jet—made by General Electric. He said he thought it was called a TG 200. Larry said he knew nothing of it but that the number hinted that it could be a very powerful engine. Andrei would not reveal how he heard about it. Larry thought it was just one more fishing expedition to see if he would admit to working on GE's jet for Bell's P-59. So he played dumb. After that, they went to Caruso's down on East 59th Street, had a nice dinner—paid by Andrei as usual—and Larry was on the train back to Philly by 8:10 p.m.

Once again, soothed by the southern New Jersey scenery as it rolled silently by, Larry tried to guess what Andrei would do next.

Two days later, Saturday, August 25, a letter from Andrei arrived and it was all wrong. He had apparently discarded Larry's *Well how are you old boy* letter and written something far more cryptic in his own hand.[14]

Dear Larry:

In reply to your letter I wish to inform you that I would be glad to ask Volter whether he can give you the house, but he is not in New York. He left the factory for Washington but not for New York and as far as I know boarded the ship last week.

With regard,
Andry [*sic*]

Larry decoded the strange message, more by intuition than by Andrei's arcane rules, and called the Philadelphia field office on Monday, August 27, to say he was on the way back to New York City to see Andrei. The scheme for indicating the date to meet, written on the bottom of the note, did not compute properly, but Larry remembered Andrei mentioning the number four frequently the last time they met. Larry added four to the postmark date and decided Andrei wanted to see him on the twenty-seventh.

On arrival at Schevchenko's home at 9:35 p.m., Larry was relieved to find that his guesses about the date and time had been right.

Andrei then said without further conversation, "Well I've got it." He pulled a Leica camera from under the cushion of a chaise lounge in his bedroom. Andrei instructed Larry in its use, attached a document photography lens, and gave him five rolls of 35mm Super XX Eastman Kodak film.[15]

Andrei explained that in the work he was doing, it was essential that he start from the beginning. Then, ignoring Larry's previous non-committal answer, he said that if Westinghouse had a decent library—something he was sure must exist—it would have the theoretical information concerning compressors, combustors, turbines, and so on that Andrei wanted. But he said he was more interested in theories concerning designs than in actual turbine tests and blueprints. But he was pressed for time, he needed that jet propulsion work as soon as possible. His colleagues in Europe had the advantage of access to captured German documents. They might be able to give the answer to jet propulsion to the Soviet government before Andrei could. He told Larry that if he could be first, he would be in line for an important decoration, a big reward.

He asked Larry to return with exposed film, but not with the camera, on September 22.

Unknown to Larry, Andrei's plan for their next meeting was constrained by rising paranoia and in-fighting for control of human assets at Amtorg.

The tense situation that Joe and Leona Franey had experienced in Andrei's office in July had not abated. Andrei wanted Larry Haas for himself and he wanted privacy to work with him.[16] People at that time were returning from their vacations and maybe Larry and Andrei should not be seen together too much. Next time, Andrei said, they should meet at Broadway and 93rd Street in front of Western Union at 9:00 p.m.

Larry felt sure the internal intrigue at Amtorg was placing Andrei under stresses beyond his abilities. He thought it was even possible that Andrei's position and authority might be in question. FBI surveillance alone did not seem a good enough explanation.

Andrei drove Larry back to Penn Station at midnight. This time, Andrei gave Larry no money. But the next day, Larry gave the FBI Andrei's camera.[17] They dusted it and identified Andrei's fingerprints.

Larry's new camera had some important work to do, if it would ever be allowed to do it.

Chapter Twenty-seven

The All-Important *If*

On Saturday morning, August 25, Leona and Joe Franey were certain they were doing the right thing, except they didn't know exactly what that would be.

In the company of two special agents of the Buffalo FBI field office, they photographed three unclassified reports and four classified reports from the Bell Aircraft library.[1] The classified reports were for Schevchenko, but only if permission was finally granted to catch him while guaranteeing that his superiors would never see the reports.

The handoff was planned for Sunday, September 9, at Schevchenko's apartment in New York City. Unfortunately, it appeared unlikely that by September 8 the FBI would have the authority to nab Schevchenko in the act. That was why they also photographed the unclassified reports.

When authorization to prosecute had not been obtained by their deadline, the agents advised Joe Franey to cancel his September 9 meeting. Joe blamed an unspecified illness Leona had suddenly contracted. Then it was up to Andrei to contact him with a new appointment date.

Leona had been opposed to the cancellation. She feared Schevchenko's disapproval. At times he voiced it in a particularly demeaning way and acted suspicious toward her. Either bringing no classified documents to him or arriving empty-handed seemed equally dangerous to her.

Coded letters between Schevchenko and the Franeys soon set a new meeting date for Sunday, September 30.

Throughout September, Andrei's suspicions about Larry and the Franeys had grown stronger. The heightened awareness forced on him by his work may have made him unusually sensitive to unconscious hints conveyed by his contacts. For example, on August 27, SAC N. J. L. Pieper in the San Francisco FBI office was following up leads the Franeys had supplied based on remarks made to them by Schevchenko. Those leads led agents to other Soviet operatives on the West Coast. With that, Pieper messaged back to Buffalo that Schevchenko is "familiar with microphone installations" in his home in New York City.

Pieper notes Schevchenko's common practice of "leaving them [Haases and Franeys] alone together in his apartment." Pieper then suggests to the Philadelphia and New York agents "that they stress the possibilities of his contacts being overheard in intimate discussions in Schevchenko's absence." It was imperative to maintain absolute secrecy as confidential informants in this case whenever in Schevchenko's home, office, or car.[2]

Such caution, unconsciously shown by his friends, might have been noticed by Schevchenko.

Larry Haas, in parallel to the Franeys, was also certain he was doing the right thing. But he didn't know what that was, either.

Improvising, Larry had borrowed another copy of *Westinghouse Engineer* for Andrei from the library. An article titled "Improvements Made in Turbine Alloy Strength by Altering Molybdenum/Vanadium Ratios" had caught Larry's attention. Though highly technical, nothing in it was classified, though it looked like it could have been. Since nothing else, especially nothing of a more sensitive nature, had yet been approved for him to give to Andrei, Larry hoped this goodwill gesture would allay his suspicions, at least for a while longer.

The Philadelphia field office had set up a photo lab with special lighting to use with Andrei's exposure settings and camera. They photographed the article and then used the same camera to make their own record of the material. Their copy would not be evidence of espionage, only evidence that Larry tried to cooperate with Andrei while the top brass continued to wrangle among themselves over arresting the Russian.

Larry had delivered the exposed film to Andrei and Andrei had developed it.

Andrei's thank you, however, seemed to be edged with annoyance. He said he appreciated anything Larry could get, but that, really, was not enough. Andrei nearly snapped at Larry to now work on that list! Andrei was not skilled at being both appreciative and demanding at the same time. He demanded to know why Larry had wasted time and film on nonessential matters.

Unable to say he was still restricted in the material he could deliver, he simply said that he wanted to try it out first. He didn't want to ruin anything important if he did it wrong. Larry worried that if Andrei was in any way wary, he would spot this as a delaying tactic. But arriving empty-handed would have been worse.

Larry told Fletcher at his next post-contact interview that he could not hand Andrei off-target material again. And he could not excuse putting off meetings much longer, either, or going empty-handed. Larry absolutely had to give Andrei something real and it had to be soon.

Fletcher was exasperated, too. Leona and Joe Franey had said the same thing. The brass, Fletcher said, not hiding his own annoyance, just could not decide whether to doctor the documents or release them whole. And if they did give him the real goods, they could not agree on how to collar him. Some others in Washington, he explained to Larry, actually didn't want to nab him at all. They wanted to just give him faked reports and send him on his way. They hoped that would be good enough to set the Ruskies back by a year or two.

Larry was angrier than Fletcher. While everybody was trying to cook something up for him and Leona to give Andrei, they had Larry and Leona way out on a dangerous limb. Andrei was getting uneasy. Were they sure Andrei would not do something to them?

Fletcher challenged Larry for a better idea.

Larry had one. How about something real *and* useless? Larry had confidential material that was way out of date, obsolete. Utterly useless now. But it was still stamped CONFIDENTIAL and SECRET.

Fletcher looked skeptical, but it did sound interesting.

Larry's paper came straight from Westinghouse—"Aviation Gas Turbine Engineering: Gas Turbine Lectures, March 26, 1945." He had the whole set of printed lecture notes on it from a jet-power research conference he had attended back in March.

Fletcher admitted it sounded like safe bait, but he could not make that decision.

Larry pressed him. The papers could be rolled out one at a time. They would interest Andrei but do him no good and take Moscow a while to figure out. Larry would convince Andrei it was stolen gold.

Fletcher frowned. Was it really both secret and useless?

Of course, Larry said, though he knew he was edging close to a cliff they could all fall off. But to a frustrated Larry Haas, inaction was worse than wrong action. He wanted something done.

Fletcher sent it up the chain of command. He wanted a noose around Schevchenko's neck, too.

Meanwhile, Schevchenko's plans were starting to crumble. Frustration and suspicion at no results were eroding Andrei's stability. His legal work at Amtorg, an organization rife with internal tensions, was also growing more difficult. He needed a new plan.

While Leona had access to information, Larry was an information creator in the technology that Andrei needed. He decided Larry was a far more valuable target. Andrei would raise the stakes. He might keep friendship and greed as motivators, but the time had come for coercion and maybe even deadly force.

Andrei knew such tactics were basic to his masters in Moscow. His firstborn son, after all, still lived in Russia as a guarantee against Schevchenko's failure in America. Birth order was important in the ancient traditions of such a culture, even if it was now called a "workers' utopia."

As Larry's firstborn, his daughter Kay would fit Andrei's scheme perfectly. Andrei devised a desperate plan alien to anything seductive and unlike anything he had tried before.

Chapter Twenty-eight

The Wrong Ride to School[1]

Monday morning, 7:30, September 3, 1945, on a suburban sidewalk near the elementary school in Chester, Pennsylvania. Kay Haas remembers in her own words:

As the first day of first grade drew closer, my mother took more interest than usual in what I was wearing. I hated the dress she bought me for the Big Day. It had a stiff white collar and tight, white sleeves that made my arms look skinny. It was gray and yellow and white and checkered and altogether ugly. I told her so. But as usual, she didn't think much of my opinion.

On Monday morning, after a gray and rainy weekend, the sun rose in a clear sky. Dew sparkled on the grass in front of my home at 1200 Perkins Street, a block and a half from my new school. This would be my first day in first grade. I was a big girl now.

Yet, there I was, ready to start school and very angry. It was that dress. Even a tantrum had not changed my mother's mind. It was on me and that was that. But I wasn't done bargaining.

"Then can I take my doll?"

"Okay." She sighed. "You can take it. Here." She thrust it into my hands like a bag of socks.

"She's a *she*. She's not an *it*." I started a new pout and turned away. But my doll's golden-brown hair, her pretty blue dress, and the painted-on smile that I really believed was just for me softened my mood. I was so proud of her. My new schoolmates would love her, too, and surely me as well.

"Now take my hand," Mom commanded as she opened our front door.

Naturally, I marched past her into the morning sun. I cradled my doll as if that was far more important. I heard the "Hmmmph" behind me just in time to stiffen my arm for the grasp I knew was coming.

"Oww! You're choking my wrist. Lemme go, Mom."

"You know what the men said. Your father said so, too. Now behave. I'll let you go when we get to school." We started marching down the sidewalk.

I looked over my shoulder, back down the street. There it was again. It, or another black car just like it, was always parked someplace nearby.[2] Two still figures—I imagined them store dummies—always occupied the front seats. I never saw their faces and I never saw them move. Staring straight ahead seemed to be their only job.

"Leave me alone. I'm not a baby anymore." Mom gripped my wrist even tighter.

"You are still choking my wrist!" I was an independent handful of a girl and I had dreamed that on this special day my mother would let me walk to school alone. I was, after all, a big girl now.

"Mom," I wailed, squirming in her iron grip in a way she had learned would soon become a full-fledged tantrum, "let me walk. I can walk by myself!"

"Okay," she said, though her voice dripped with exasperation. She released my wrist with a movement that felt like she'd really rather throw it away. "I will walk behind you. And don't you dare run."

"Way behind me, Mom." I pressed my advantage. Mom, to my delight, dropped back a couple of steps and fell back maybe a full six paces. Her tight-lipped smile said, "Go ahead and complain now." She never let me completely win anything.

It was a compromise I could accept. But neither she nor I knew what I had just set myself up for.

Street traffic was of no interest to me as I strode along. I was enjoying my independence. When a black car rolled to a stop beside me, I didn't really notice it. If I had, I would not have been surprised or alarmed. It could have been the same black car I usually saw down the street.

The doors on the sidewalk side flew open and three men in dark suits stepped out onto the sidewalk. One said, "Hullo leettle gurl. I heff car for you." His words sounded funny but he tried to smile. Then he swept me up with one arm and tossed me onto the back seat. Before I could sit up—and before my mother could even start to react—the other two men piled back in, one in front, the other in the back with me and the man who put me there. The doors slammed and we sped away.

I wondered if this was some kind of game. After all, men in black cars were a permanent part of our neighborhood. I was told such cars belonged to friends of my father. Besides, I was not only an independent-minded child, but fearless. It seems strange today, but I do not remember being frightened then. I did not know this black car was different from the others.

As soon as I was in the car, I stood myself up on the seat to look out the back window. I was horrified. I saw my beautiful doll—a gift from my mother to keep me occupied on the long drive from Kenmore, New York, two weeks ago. Now she lay sprawled on the street where I had dropped her when the man grabbed me. *Oh! I hope I can find her again*, I thought. Her beautiful blue dress was fluttering in the breeze. I saw the hand-painted, auburn hair on her finely featured wooden head and remembered the feel of the supple cloth on her body and legs, and then I watched her disappear in the distance under a cloud of black exhaust that billowed up behind our car as it began speeding away.

I wanted to tell her *I'll see you again*, or *Wait, I'll come back for you*, or *Goodbye*. But I didn't. I had not even given her a name yet. I didn't know what to call out to her.

Looking out the window, I thought, *Wow! I've never gone this fast! This must be some kind of new adventure, like one of those scary amusement park rides.* I had no idea—and could not have understood—the scheming that had gone into this carefully planned incident. It was, however, exactly the catastrophe my parents and the men in the other black cars—I later learned they were FBI agents—had hoped to prevent.

The driver, hunched over the steering wheel as if he could will this car to go faster, spoke to the three other men in a language I did not know. I noticed the one on my right—though I never knew why such trivial things would lodge themselves in a little girl's mind for a lifetime—was unshaven and wore a wrinkled white shirt with its sweaty collar rumpled under his blue, pin-striped suit jacket. He turned to look through the back window and said something that must have meant "They're behind us." The driver glanced in his mirror, made a bad face, and forced one more surge out of the car's roaring engine.

The moment I was grabbed, my father explained years later—I was fourteen when he finally decided it was a story I should hear—those two men who were always watching in their black car sped to the curb where my mother stood horrified. The door opened, Mom jumped into the back, and they raced off in hot pursuit.

"That little stinker," my mother muttered under her breath, though just loud enough for the agents to hear. "I am going to spank her like she has never been spanked before." Then she shuddered, struck by the awful reality. "If I ever get her back home."

My captors, with the chase car beginning to gain on us, sped westward out of town toward the hills, leaving Chester far behind. Years later, I re-traced the ride as well as I could from leftover fragments of memory and hurried snatches of road signs my mother recalled. After speeding past the great, silver refinery tanks and the smelly, flaming towers that I could see from my new backyard, we rumbled over unimproved country roads and jagged rocks. Any one of them could have ended in disaster. We skirted Garnet Valley, fled into the forest beyond Concordville, and flew down the valley, racing south along the old Baltimore pike.

Though skilled drivers were at the wheel in both cars, the pursuing FBI agents were trained for a car chase. They started to gain some ground.

In spite of the chaotic ride, I held my balance standing backward on the bouncing back seat to see the car behind us. The other car had just about caught up to us. I saw my mother and waved, edging toward frantic now in the chaos of this ride. A jolt bounced me high enough to bump my head and fall on the lap of the man beside me. He tossed me on the seat, pushed me down hard, and wagged his finger in my face. "Sit! Looking no more."

My mind fled to something I could understand and my eyes fell on my dress. It seems strange today remembering how incongruous it was, but I clearly remember thinking, *Now I have to sit here and look at this ugly dress.* I hated every bit of it, its plaid pattern of gray, white, and yellow, and its plain white collar. *Ugly! Who puts a cute little girl in such a weird dress?* I was sure my mother had done it just to be mean. Unfortunately, that is still the way I remember her.

The dark-suited man in the front passenger seat turned around and barked something that must have been an order.

"You," the man beside me yelled over the road noise, "come sit here. Now!" He grabbed my arm, pulled me out from where I was squeezed between the two men, and slammed me down beside the left rear door. He reached over me and began to work the latch. The angry voices and chaos had me confused.

"What are you going to . . .?" I had not formed all my words when the car door flew open. The man pushed me hard—out into the rushing air.

I felt only a moment of pain, then everything went black.

Chapter Twenty-nine

Accusations and Renewed Alliance[1]

Tuesday morning, 7:30, September 4, 1945, at the Roadside Waffle Wagon in Chester, Pennsylvania

"Damn, bumbling idiots!" Larry said through gritted teeth. What he had to say was for nobody else's ears except the man sitting across the table from him, though he wanted to shout. Chester's popular diner was packed with its usual breakfast crowd. But Larry wanted Agent Fletcher to hear him clearly, and deep in his gut. "My daughter is unconscious, cut, bleeding, bruised, and scraped to the bone. *No* thanks to your guys that she's still alive."

"Easy, Larry." Fletcher leaned forward. "They did their best."

"Don't hand me that bull. It stinks. Those guys were hanging too far back. From where they were, they could not have stopped that snatch. They gave those guys a big head start and when they finally made up the distance and got close enough, they didn't get the license number. And worse, from what Dorothy told me, they almost ran Kay over when those goons tossed her out of their car."

Fletcher could not deny a word of Larry's tirade. All he could offer was a weak, "We're very sorry, Larry. It shouldn't have happened, but those guys are smart. They'll learn from the experience."

"The only smart thing they did was fetch one of your doctors to my house. I can only imagine the questions a hospital would have asked. The story would have brought in the local police, reporters, and a bunch of worse complications you guys don't want. We're taking care of Kay at home. If what they say about commies behind every tree is even half-right, Andrei could have somebody in every emergency room in the county watching for us to turn up." Larry glared at Fletcher.

"And you say 'they did their best'? Not good enough, pal. That's not the deal we made." Larry sat back, red-faced and breathing hard, but he'd said his piece. His silence dared Fletcher to answer him.

"Okay. I can't blame you." Fletcher shook his head. "I know it wasn't good enough. We will tighten up our coverage. But you know Dorothy won't like it. She hates us being so close as it is. We tried giving her a little distance. But it backfired. It won't happen again. I promise."

"Some people learn their lessons hard. After this, Dorothy won't object," Larry said. "But don't worry, it's out of your hands now."

"What do you mean?" Fletcher sat up straight, eyes wide.

"You don't have to tighten up anything. I'm going after Schevchenko myself. You're out of this deal."

Fletcher almost dropped his coffee. "Bad idea, Larry. Really bad. Look, I get it. I'm a father, too. But you can't pull out. You have to leave this to us. Kay needs her father right here in Chester, not locked up doing hard time. And if anything happens to Schevchenko it will open up a big, nasty international incident that won't help any of us. In the end, we'll have no choice but to pull you in. Between you and me, we know he is behind this."

"So what's stopping you from arresting him?"

"Same as before. We have zero hard evidence. Your best bet is to help us nab him at what he's doing. We can give him a twenty-five-year ticket to Leavenworth. Who knows? Maybe forty years. And you are the one, the *only* one, who can make that happen."

"You mean you want me to ignore this whole catastrophe?" Larry stared into Fletcher's eyes.

"No! Exactly the opposite. I want you to remember it and work with us. We have the whole US government on our side. Together, we will nail his hide to a prison wall. Wouldn't that feel good?"

Larry weighed Fletcher's words for a long moment in silence. He sipped his coffee and watched the passing traffic a moment longer before he answered. "Okay. Let's get the bastard. Now it's personal. Anybody who threatens my family will get more than he bargained for. Uncle Sam's not a bad side-man in a fight like this, but now it's my fight."

"Right," Fletcher said. "Let's go get him. It looks like we have a new deal." But Larry stopped him.

"Not so fast," Larry said. "Do you remember me saying Andrei was stupid?"

Fletcher blinked. "Never!"

"Exactly. Not stupid enough that he won't wonder who chased his goons and who was following Kay close enough to give chase. I'll need a good enough story to convince him that I don't suspect him. I'm also supposed to see him again on the twenty-second with some secret goods."

"I cannot authorize anything yet for you to deliver." Fletcher was clearly frustrated.

"How about the lecture notes I gave you?"[2]

"I'll try again. The navy is playing this pretty tight, but Hoover wants action. I'll let you know."

"Now, about my story," Larry said. "And it better be good."

"Well." Fletcher thought for a moment. "I'll leave that to your silver tongue. I thought I'd laugh myself stupid at the fairy tale you handed Bell after those agents left your office in March. Did Bell buy it?"

"Yeah, I guess he did." Larry couldn't help laughing. "So, you got my number. I've always been able to tell a little fib when I need to. I always tell the very best truth I can make up." With that, a flash of inspiration with an entire story line showed up in Larry's imagination. The pleasure of creating a new, more devious strategy assured him he could deal with Andrei. In just a few weeks he was sure they could slam the lid on Andrei's case.

"The truth," Larry told Fletcher in great earnestly, "is that Kay's school principal had actually received a warning from the local police about a gang of kidnappers in the area. It seems that a traveling circus train was about to pass through Chester. The cops heard a rumor that some of the circus people were going to abduct a kid on the first day of school. Their sideshows were missing a freak, so they were going to put her in a monkey suit, strap antlers on her head, and throw her in a cage."

"Really?" Fletcher was shocked. Then, "Okay. You got me already. You're good."

"It was just good luck, my friend," Larry said, now in an imaginary conversation with Andrei, "that an unmarked police cruiser happened to be nearby when those goons tried to swipe my kid. Believe it or not, they tried it on another kid the next day. The local Hillbilly Cops are still looking for them. It's tragic. An outrage." Larry frowned. "And by the way, Andrei, I thought you and your guys were keeping an eye on me." He slammed his fist on the table, turning heads in the next booth. "I thought you were my friend, Andrei. Who the hell slipped up?"

"You're dangerous, Larry," Fletcher said, shaking his head. "If I didn't know better, I'd believe you myself. You'd make quite a con man, if you half tried."

"Who says I haven't?"

CHAPTER THIRTY

The Washington Hot Potato

Summer to Fall, 1945. Washington, DC. A Capitol Hill correspondence fiasco[1]
Andrei's misgivings about Haas and the Franeys in late summer and early fall of 1945 echoed their efforts to trap him, though he continued to try to use them as sub-agents. He did not know how those efforts made him a hot potato shunned all across Washington. Responsibility was being passed from hand to hand among the nation's highest officials, but nobody wanted to be seen making the necessary decisions.

Larry was learning in a most excruciating way that risk and bureaucracy have a powerful aversion to each other.

Hoover had begun reporting on Schevchenko to his superior, US Attorney General (AG) Thomas Clark, who headed the Department of Justice. Updates had reached President Truman. In addition, the Joint Chiefs of Staff, in particular the top brass of the navy and the army air forces, knew that Schevchenko's sights were trained on their most secret projects. Secretary of State James Byrnes dreaded the political uproar that would be unleashed if Schevchenko were prosecuted during negotiations over the postwar fate of the Soviet Union, the United States, Germany, all of Europe, and Japan. Dean Acheson, Under Secretary of State to Byrnes, complicated the matter further by evading his boss's requests for assistance in the matter.

In contrast, Hoover's FBI and the US War Department had developed ever more wary views of the Soviet Union, but the State Department still clung to its wartime alliances with the Soviets, though probably out of expediency rather than naivete.

As a result, Hoover grew more impatient. Inaction in Washington maddened him when he was confronting a threat to his country, especially from communists.

Hoover was a true Washington man. He had climbed the ladder to power step by step. Born in the city in 1895, he was admitted to the bar at age twenty-two in 1917 and appointed to head the Enemy Aliens Registration Section at the US Department of Justice only two years later in 1919. That same year, during the First Red Scare, he spearheaded the anti-alien Palmer Raids against anyone suspected of promoting radical, leftist views, especially anarchists and communists.

At age twenty-six, Hoover joined the Bureau of Investigation. Within three years, he rose to director. By 1935, when Hoover was forty, he reinvented his division as the Federal Bureau of Investigation, emerging as its first director. A year later, in 1936, President Roosevelt made the FBI the country's top watchdog over espionage, sabotage, and domestic intelligence. Few Washington men had ever climbed as far and as fast as John Edgar Hoover.

During World War II, the FBI's counterespionage and antisabotage operations derailed many dangerous German and Japanese spy operations. Hoover had always held strong anti-communist views, but he became an anti-communist zealot after the war. He led a string of forays aimed at snuffing out anything he considered to be communist subversion within the government and the private sector.

The Schevchenko case was Hoover's first, all-out anti-communist crusade, and it happened to be waged against a high, internationally prominent Soviet official. It became a hot-button case for him. It was burning a hole in his desk.

The prominence of the case was its downfall. It spattered across the nation's headlines at the exact time some of the world's most delicate negotiations were dividing up the planet along new and potentially unstable lines of power and influence.

Andrei Schevchenko became one of the worst hot potatoes Washington had seen in years. That put Larry Haas in the hot water with Schevchenko.

By December of 1945, Hoover had become exasperated by a cascade of frustrations in his quest to prosecute Schevchenko.[2] Hoover directed D. M. Ladd to compile a complete dossier on Schevchenko's activities starting in 1942 when he legally entered the United States. Ladd was to summarize the case against "Subject Andrei Ivanovich Schevchenko" and do it so conclusively that no official in Washington, including President Truman, could escape their sworn duty to nail the lid on Schevchenko's coffin.

The memorandum to Hoover began,[3]

You will recall that subject Schevchenko has been soliciting classified government documents relating to jet propelled aircraft from informants of this Bureau . . . [one of whom is] Loren George Haas, formerly of Buffalo, New York, where he was employed at the Bell Aircraft Corporation, and is now residing in Philadelphia, Pennsylvania, employed by Westinghouse . . . Mr. Haas was identified by agents of the Buffalo office as a contact of Schevchenko . . . Haas has acted under Bureau direction . . . since March of 1945.

Ladd's compilation opened with memoranda that had begun circulating in Washington late in August.

Friday, August 31, 1945. In a memorandum summarizing the case and referring to his five previous memos to AG Clark,[4] Director Hoover suggested that Clark discuss the Schevchenko problem with Secretary of State Byrnes or with President Truman directly. This was urgent before any decision could be made regarding prosecution, because Schevchenko was a Soviet official residing in the United States conducting legitimate government business.

Hoover requested the opinion from AG Clark before September 9, when Schevchenko had arranged his next meeting with Joseph Franey. Joseph was supposed to deliver photographs of secret documents his wife, Leona, was to have taken from the Bell library. Schevchenko had been supplying round-trip plane tickets to Mr. Franey for these courier services.

Saturday, September 8. AG Clark had not replied to Hoover regarding prosecution of Schevchenko. Hoover directed the Buffalo office to have Joe Franey delay his next meeting with Schevchenko. Franey complied, sending a letter to Schevchenko pleading inability to come because Leona was sick and he would be staying home to care for her.

Wednesday, September 12. Director Hoover again requested a decision from the AG. The AG referred it to Dean Acheson, Under Secretary of State. Acheson did not reply to Hoover.

The next meeting between Schevchenko and Haas was slated for September 22. This called for the navy and the Joint Chiefs of Staff to authorize Haas to give Schevchenko documents of an elementary nature concerning jet propulsion. The navy refused clearance to photograph them. The Joint Chiefs of Staff refused authorization that would permit the Soviets access to any such plans, no matter how basic.

Tuesday, September 18. Director Hoover once again urged AG Clark to make a decision on Schevchenko's prosecution. Fletcher had relayed Haas's concern that further delays would place the investigation in danger of collapse.

Fletcher updated Larry about the ongoing indecision. By then, Larry knew of Andrei's suspicions toward him and the Franeys. He had pleaded again for permission to deliver credible, secret documents to Schevchenko to catch him red-handed with contraband material. Schevchenko's rising suspicions now mediated against giving him falsified documents. Haas advised Agent Fletcher:

> [Fooling Schevchenko] is not an easy task. Schevchenko is an aeronautical engineer—one of the world's top scientists in the field of high-speed aircraft—not a man to be easily misled. He is extremely qualified for his job. He has a tremendous academic background. He was once one of the top men in the Russian Aircraft Institute. His knowledge is virtually unlimited in all the various aspects of high-speed aircraft.

Friday, September 21. In the continued and maddening silence from AG Clark, Hoover sent him a review of the entire situation. Hoover said that Clark's failure to authorize prosecution had now jeopardized the Bureau's informants. Without such authorization, the Bureau could no longer maintain even partial coverage of Schevchenko's espionage activities. He added that the Bureau could not be blamed for any further espionage activities by Schevchenko. Under the circumstances, Haas was instructed to cancel the Schevchenko meeting for September 22 with a suitable excuse.

The Joint Chiefs and their technical experts refused to approve giving Schevchenko the documents Larry had prepared for the meeting. He had given the Philadelphia field agents a complete transcript of "Aviation Gas Turbine Engineering—Gas Turbine Lectures, March 26, 1945." The transcripts were numbered and signed by each recipient and classified confidential.[5]

Tuesday, September 25. Clark's secretary called Hoover and advised that the AG had talked with Dean Acheson [known to have originally favored a conciliatory approach toward Stalin] on "a couple of occasions" about the Schevchenko case. Acheson's secretary told AG Clark that he was so busy that he hadn't been able to call the AG back about the matter. Authorization was still out of the question.

AG Clark did finally say, "If the FBI thinks it is all right to go ahead, it is okay." Hoover knew, however, that action would violate the government's entire chain of authority and accountability. It was the most offensive refusal of his superiors to act that Hoover had yet seen.

Hoover felt forced to conclude that the FBI would have to wait for clearance from the State Department because "if his Bureau went ahead [with apprehension of Schevchenko] and there was any repercussion from the Soviets, then the State Department would disclaim all responsibility and blame Hoover for creating an international incident."[6]

On September 22, 1945, Larry Haas had received permission from the FBI to visit with Schevchenko in New York City later that day,[7] in spite of orders to the contrary from Director Hoover.[8] But by now, in Larry's mind, "reckless adventure" was becoming a more attractive plan than waiting for permission. He was going empty-handed.

Larry reached the planned meeting place, 93rd Street and Broadway, at about 8:45 p.m., where Andrei and his wife and son were already waiting. Andrei took everybody for a ride.

The route he took turned out to be a meandering tour of big-city sights that ended up at the corner of Central Park West and 93rd Street only a few doors from his home. Larry could see something else was going on. Andrei constantly watched his rear-view mirror, almost as much as he watched the street ahead. He was clearly alert to the possibility that they might be seen or followed. Perhaps to alter the car's appearance to watchers who knew him, he placed Larry in the back seat with Antonina and his son in the front seat beside him.

When Andrei finally reached 93rd Street, he stopped beside the footpath entrance to Central Park. He let everyone out but looked in all directions before selecting a bench in the park where they could sit together. He placed himself so he could watch the park entrance.

Larry, prepared with a story he and the agents in Philadelphia had debated over and concocted for this occasion, told Andrei in an apologetic tone that he hated to disappoint Andrei, but he had been sick for several days. He had, however, finally located what he thought Andrei wanted.

Larry altered his previous description of the Westinghouse engineering library resources by revealing that he had found the personal library of the manager in charge of development engineering.[9] During the last week,

Larry said that he had taken this individual out to dinner on two occasions and was attempting to gain his confidence. Larry also said he told the manager of his interest in the theoretical aspects of their work and in improving his knowledge along those lines.

Andrei said this was fine and asked what kind of information was in his library. He had apparently accepted Larry's tale without questioning any further.

Larry said it concerned the theories of compressor, turbine, and combustor design, the exact interests Andrei had mentioned.

Andrei, eager to hear more, told his wife and son to go for a walk, which they did in spite of the fact that the sun had set more than two hours earlier.[10]

Andrei again reassured Larry that was fine and not to feel bad about not having brought it this time. He understood the conditions. Larry should go slow on that. Such things took plenty of time. Don't hurry. Then he asked if Larry had used the camera yet.

He had not. He wanted to wait until he could photograph the material Andrei wanted.

Andrei disagreed. He should use it on other information in his possession, service information, notes, or any other material he had around. If Larry would do that, he wouldn't spoil any of the good stuff when he got to it.

Later, Andrei and Larry ate dinner at Ship Ahoy near 66th and Broadway and talked about aircraft in general, a conversation that surprised Larry. He later told the agents, "It became apparent to me that there are a lot of things Andrei does *not* [emphasis added] know about airplanes." After dinner Andrei asked Larry how long he needed to get the information. Andrei hoped it would be no more than two or three weeks.

Bidding for more time, worried the Joint Chiefs and other Washington officials in the chain of authority might remain undecided, Larry settled on three weeks.

That would be October 13, Andrei said. Next time, how about meeting at Central Park and 93rd Street—the same place where they were talking that night—at 9:00 p.m.? He told Larry to keep a record of his expenses. He'd take care of it next time. He gave Larry no money that night. Larry had delivered nothing.

Andrei drove Larry to Penn Station for the 12:30 train back to Philadelphia.

As always, the long train ride across the moonlit farmlands of central New Jersey helped Larry sort his thoughts. This night, it came easily.

He'd crawled out on a limb and the guys who talked him out there were about to saw that limb off between him and the tree.

That was not okay.

—•—

Joe Franey reached Schevchenko's apartment on Sunday, September 30. Andrei greeted him in a friendly manner but did not introduce two other guests already there.[11] Joe assumed they were Amtorg employees. Andrei looked nervous. He arranged for Joe to transfer his exposed film canisters to him out of sight of his guests, his wife, and his son.

With the film canisters in his pocket, Andrei claimed there was a minor matter of Amtorg business he needed to attend to and left briefly. A few minutes later he returned and showed Joe a detailed list of reports from the Bell library that he wanted photographed. He would not give Joe that list but told him to copy it in his own handwriting.

Joe was astonished. He did not know much about airplanes, but he knew enough to see that Andrei was asking for something that looked top-echelon. He copied Andrei's list word-for-word.

1. Everything on swept-back wings for airplanes.
2. Everything on athodyd jet propulsion without compressor and (with) turbines.[12]
3. Everything on cabin pressure and temperature regulator.
4. Everything on landing gears.
5. Everything on aluminum alloys after March 1945.[13]
6. Everything on special steels for parts of turbines on engines.
7. New reports after March 1945.

When Andrei was satisfied that Joe had everything down right, he gave Joe eleven more rolls of film and two twenty-dollar bills for travel expenses.

Andrei had left his guests to talk among themselves but appeared suspicious of them throughout Joe's visit. Joe felt like he was being watched, too.

For their next meeting, Andrei explained a new way to meet. He took care that his other guests could not hear him and Joe. Joe was to stand on a certain street corner at nine, ten, and eleven o'clock in the morning. Someone would drive by on one of those hours and pick him up.

Later, Joe confided to Andrei that he had bought a new house and fallen into considerable debt (actually, the debt was tolerable but he wanted Andrei

209

to believe he was desperate). Understanding the hint, Andrei promised to pay well next time they met, even though the last films had not turned out properly. Andrei and Joe had now established the mutual dependence that played into the FBI's hands.

Monday, October 1. Hoover, in growing frustration, once again called this situation to AG Clark's attention. Hoover said the State Department had authorized deeper investigation into Schevchenko's spying, but he still refused to let the Bureau prosecute without Byrnes's approval at the State Department.

Tuesday, October 2. Hoover sent one more memorandum to the AG summarizing all communications to date. He pointed out the attitude of the Department of State and advised the AG that all investigative activity possible to this point had been conducted and that an opinion regarding prosecution must be forthcoming.

That final memorandum to AG Clark stated:[14]

TOP SECRET

October 2, 1945
To: The Attorney General [Thomas Clark]
From: John Edgar Hoover, Director, Federal Bureau of Investigation
Subject: Andrei Ivanovich Schevchenko

Reference is made to my memoranda of August 31, September 12, 18 and 21, and October 1, 1945, urging that an opinion regarding prosecution of Schevchenko, because of his espionage activity, be furnished.

It is my understanding that the Department of State has now granted authorization for further investigation of Schevchenko but desires that no prosecutive steps be taken until clearance is obtained from them.

You will recall that since July 1944 Schevchenko has been under investigation. Three confidential informants have been developed by this Bureau [Larry Haas, Leona and Joseph Franey] to whom Schevchenko paid money for the purpose of obtaining from them classified government information regarding jet propelled aircraft, which information has not been released to the Soviets by the United States government.

Further, you will recall that Schevchenko has furnished to two of these confidential informants with Leica cameras and film for the purpose of taking photographs of classified government documents and blueprints relating to jet propulsion.

You will recall further that clearance has been obtained from the United States Army to furnish photographs of such classified information on undeveloped film to Schevchenko by our informants only in the event prosecution is authorized and that the rolls of film can be seized incident to Schevchenko's arrest in order to prevent this vital information from reaching the Soviet Union.

Under the circumstances, our informants have been able to "stall" and make excuses to Schevchenko for their failure to meet with him at times and places specified when they were expected to turn over to him according to his request photographs of classified government material regarding jet propulsion.

As you have been advised by this Bureau, the Soviet government through its diplomatic and other representatives abroad is engaged in extensive military espionage activities against the United States. If the facts furnished by this Bureau relative to Schevchenko would warrant prosecutive action, possibly some decrease in their activities in this country might result.

John Edgar Hoover
Director, Federal Bureau of Investigation

A copy of that summary went to the Buffalo, New York City, and Philadelphia FBI offices—all which had worked the Schevchenko case to date. But in spite of Hoover, the US government's anti-espionage law enforcement machinery remained stolidly and infuriatingly inert.

Hoover, however, refused to give up.

Schevchenko was becoming increasingly suspicious while the FBI grew increasingly impatient to nab him.

On Saturday, October 6, Andrei met the Franeys in the lobby of the Hotel Lafayette in Buffalo. He arrived empty-handed, with neither bags or parcels. He asked for a favor. He wanted a ride to Niagara Falls in the Franeys' car, a trip of about twenty miles. Setting out, he skipped small talk and made a peculiar request.

"I want to see that crazy little box," he told Joe in a demanding tone. Joe realized that Andrei was speaking in impromptu codewords in case the Franeys' car was bugged. Andrei was talking about the camera. Joe asked Leona to hand it to Andrei.

211

Andrei took it from her and minutely inspected the settings. Apparently upset enough now to forget his suspicions about bugging, he spoke openly. "Some of the films you gave me were incorrectly exposed," he said testily. He reinstructed Joe in the camera's operation. "We must meet again."

They set a date for Saturday, October 27, in New York City. "Bring me new exposures," Andrei said and then stressed in very strong terms that he wanted the "athodyd thrust report" that he had asked for previously. Apropos of nothing else, except perhaps to prop up his standing in the Franeys' impression, he then told them that in September he had received another decoration from his government.

Before stopping, he advised Joe to use the "three separate times waiting on a street corner to be picked up" method of meeting that he had described before. Once that appeared understood and they arrived at Niagara Falls, Andrei's demeanor lightened.

He asked Joe to park near the Roslyn Restaurant on Buffalo Avenue for drinks and dinner. He gave the Franeys no cash on this occasion, but he did cover the dinner at nine dollars and a dollar tip. He ended their evening with a request to be dropped off at the Kenmore Theater. They parted with no indication that Andrei had a car anywhere nearby and no one to pick him up.

Joe Franey's spoiled film had made Andrei nervous. The poor quality might have revealed tampering to Andrei. He had apparently "bugged" the 35mm Kodak Super-XX film in a way that spoiled film would result from any mishandling. He had done the same with the film he gave to Larry.

On October 12, Larry and the agents in the Philadelphia field office had photographed an "Official United States Navy Installation Manual" of the Westinghouse Company that Larry had taken from the plant without permission. It was not, however, classified and not deemed a security risk for transmission to Schevchenko, so photography was authorized.[15]

They used the film Andrei had given Larry for the purpose and used the settings and lighting Andrei had prescribed—one second at f-9. The agents then took an identical set of pictures for their records using 36mm Kodak Super-XX film of their own.

Unfortunately, after finishing their work, the agents noticed that the Kodak Super-XX highspeed film canister from Schevchenko actually contained Agfa Minipan Film. That meant that the FBI's Kodak film was badly overexposed and useless as evidence. If Larry had substituted a real Kodak canister (possibly in order to have Andrei's film analyzed), the Agfa settings that Andrei instructed Larry to use would have also spoiled the Kodak film.[16] Andrei had attempted to create a tamperproof, telltale system with mislabeled film.[17]

On the night of October 13, a New York City policeman raised Andrei's paranoia level at least one notch higher. Larry had met Andrei at 8:55 p.m. on Central Park West near 93rd Street. Within minutes, the police officer stopped the two men, saying they were acting suspiciously and demanding to see their draft cards for identification.[18]

Badly spooked, Andrei suggested they retreat to his home less than a block away. Larry then delivered his exposed film in exchange for a new twenty-dollar bill. But Andrei said it was for "his dinner," once again distancing himself from payment for goods. Trying not to show his extreme care, Larry carefully folded the bill with his fingertips and placed it into his wallet. He delivered it to Agent Ring two days later for fingerprinting.[19]

They agreed to meet again on October 31, but Andrei had neither shown any interest in what Larry had photographed nor asked for anything new. Andrei had complained of feeling ill and seemed to want Larry to be gone as quickly as possible. This erratic behavior had become increasingly common. Then the hot potato got hotter.

———•◆•———

On Monday, October 22, Joe got a letter from Andrei. He wanted to meet on Saturday night, October 27, 7:00 p.m., at Andrei's apartment. But forget the street-corner waiting scheme. Just show up. Hearing that, Wilcox shot an urgent teletype to Hoover and SAC New York that night:

> Bureau requests to expedite clearance of aeronautical reports through military authorities in order that photographs may be taken for meeting of informant Joseph Franey with Schevchenko next Saturday. Request eleven rolls of film of the type Schevchenko used, thirty-six exposures each. Expedite. Film not easily available commercially.[20]

Unfortunately, by Thursday the Buffalo agents still had no permission for a document transfer of any kind. They told Joe to mail a letter to Andrei and cancel the Saturday meetup, but not to arouse Andrei's suspicion.

Joe laughed at that. No excuse could do that now, no matter how good it was. But he did it anyway. The Saturday night meeting was off.

———

Urgent Teletype: Hoover replies to SAC Buffalo.

"Film not available Washington. Schevchenko's film resembles Eastman Kodak Microfile, 35 mm, 36 exposures. Ask Eastman in Rochester or prepare locally from supply of Microfile available your office."[21]

———

Thursday, October 25. The Schevchenko case became the subject of a meeting in the offices of the Attorney General. It was attended by Acheson and other representatives of the State and Justice Departments. Acheson noted that an additional complication had arisen only weeks before with the defection of Igor Goushenko, a member of Russian military intelligence and a cipher clerk at the Soviet Embassy in Ottawa, Canada. Acheson said that "the president and the Secretary of State at that time held the opinion that no arrest should be made except to protect the security of the United States."[22] Assistant AG Caudle then told Hoover that AG Clark had sent the president a memo "recommending that affirmative action be taken."[23] The wording sounded mild, but "The-buck-stops-here" president could not ignore it.[24]

By noon, Ladd sent an urgent memo to Special Agent Tamm, saying that SAC Fletcher in Philadelphia was complaining about Haas's side of the Schevchenko case that still had to be dealt with. Fletcher insisted there was no time left. Haas must not be sent empty-handed to see Schevchenko. Approve the photography![25]

By Friday morning, in spite of urgent messages reaching as high as Truman's desk, no one had yet granted authorization for anything that either Joe Franey or Haas could pass to Schevchenko.

Finally, at 7:55 on Friday night, approval for photography found its way back down that day's serpentine chain of command. It had bounced from Truman to the Joint Chiefs, via Westinghouse Research and the US Navy Bureau of Aeronautics, and finally down to Army Captain S. B. Spangler, head of the Power Plant Design Branch, Bureau of Aeronautics in Washington. Spangler was apparently the man whose desk had been chosen for blame to land in case something backfired. He was, nevertheless, trusted to make such decisions wisely, as he had done before in other situations.

So, by 7:55, Agent Whitson in Washington called Fletcher with Spangler's okay. At nearly every step in the Schevchenko case, the agents had to scramble against shrinking time and obstinate bureaucracy to carry on.

Hoover had little patience left for these conditions.

Friday night, October 26. Photographs on Schevchenko's film were taken for Larry to give Schevchenko the next morning. The approved document was "Design, Study of Control, and Regulating System, Model X-9.5 Engine. Report A-176."

This document included recently rejected turbo-jet designs, plans, and specs.[26] Research in this field moved so fast that reports only a few weeks old were already obsolete, though CONFIDENTIAL and TOP SECRET stamps stayed in place. Larry hoped the bait would keep Schevchenko interested.

Then Hoover stopped everything.

While Haas and the agents set up the Saturday film handoff, matters in Washington took another direction. Clark, Acheson, and the State Department met with Hoover and refused to allow anything concerning jet propulsion to be given to Schevchenko. That overrode Spangler's decision. Washington was "not ready to handle any reaction the Russians might take to the prosecution of Schevchenko; and that the Army, of course, will give no authorization whatsoever on any of the Ram-Jet material, or related subjects under these conditions."[27]

"Tell Haas to cancel. And then cancel his plane reservations to New York," Hoover demanded.

A reaction came quickly

At 5:30 the next afternoon, a strange man knocked at Leona Franey's door. By his features, Leona assumed the man to be Russian. He introduced himself in halting English as Zhukov and handed her a letter that appeared to be in Schevchenko's handwriting:[28]

dear [*sic*] Joe and Leona.

I wish to ask you to return me that junk which I gave. I urgently need it now for one week at least. I tried to buy one more for myself but couldn't.

No such a things [sic] on the market but I cannot wait. That is why please hand in everything to him, rolls to [sic] even if they are not used.

With best wishes, Andre [sic] and Antonina.

Leona flatly refused. She neither knew nor trusted this odd man and realized that the case against Schevchenko would be jeopardized if the photographic equipment was returned or lost.

Zhukov denied knowledge of the sealed letter's content. Mrs. Franey returned a letter of her own to the man and told him to take it to Mr. Schevchenko. Her letter stated that "your reference to junk isn't clear." It also stated that she had obtained some of the material that Schevchenko requested but she was waiting for more material on the most important subjects.[29]

———◆———

On November 1, only four days after Zhukov's visit, Leona received a very friendly letter from Andrei. She deduced that he had been made suspicious, as Joe had predicted, by the repeated meeting postponements. Schevchenko had apparently wanted to end their use as informants. Leona's savvy reply through Zhukov, however, had allayed his fears.

———◆———

Still unwilling to drop the Schevchenko case, Hoover dictated another letter on Friday, November 2, to Under Secretary of State Acheson requesting that he revisit the matter they had discussed the previous Friday when they blocked Haas from giving Schevchenko the photographs.

Hoover made sure his letter was delivered directly to Acheson's office by special messenger on Monday. He told Acheson that the entire case now balanced on the knife edge of Schevchenko's suspicions about Haas and the Franeys. Though couched in diplomatic tact, Hoover was clearly telling Acheson that if Schevchenko drops the FBI's informants because of Schevchenko's suspicions, he will find new ones the FBI knows nothing about and the investigation of a dangerous spy will then fail in disgrace. And the whole disaster would land on Acheson's doorstep.[30]

On Thursday, November 1, Agent Ring, in Larry's presence, had already taken pictures of a specially prepared version of the "Model X-9.5 Engine Report." They had marked the title page with their "fingerprint" evidence, a comma after "item 2, (f)" and on page 3 added a comma after the next-to-last line on the page. They had taken the October 26 "permission to photograph" as their justification to proceed and allowed themselves to go deaf to other communications, should they arrive.

Larry Haas delivered that photographic film to Andrei Schevchenko's apartment at 8:15 p.m. on November 3.

Antonina had prepared a dinner for three, and they shared it in pleasant conversation. But as their time together progressed, Larry thought that Andrei appeared less organized in his thinking than he had been and, though he denied it, more suspicious and reclusive.

Larry asked how the two rolls of film turned out that he had delivered before.

Andrei said, clearly chagrined, that he had spoiled them both. He had developed them for three minutes and it should have been a minute and a half. They came out completely black. He did not blame Larry for taking the pictures badly. He did, however, admit that he had loaded the rolls with Agfa film. He told Larry to buy real Kodak Super-XX and ignore any other rolls Andrei had given him.

Larry asked about the exposure times and lighting.

Inexplicably, Andrei told him to use what he had told Larry before. That made no sense to Larry, minipan settings wouldn't work on Super-XX, but Andrei was insistent. He reached into his pocket, drew out five new twenty-dollar bills, and handed them to Larry without comment. They went on to talk about matters of aviation. In particular, Andrei critiqued Bell's current experiments with swept-wing designs and a specific rocket project, matters about which he should have known nothing, indicating he still had at least one active source at Bell.

As the hour grew later, Larry prepared to leave. Andrei then suggested that Dorothy join Antonina for a day of Christmas shopping later in December. That way, Dorothy could also deliver Larry's next shipment of exposed films. All of Dorothy's travel and shopping expenses would be on the Schevchenkos. Finally, Andrei suggested "We must be very careful in our dealings" until they could meet again in the latter part of January. He suggested seven o'clock on Saturday evening, January 26, at the Schevchenkos' apartment.[31]

Larry had stayed until 12:45 a.m. on the assumption that Andrei would, as he always did, drive him to Penn Station. But Andrei made no such offer this time. Larry walked to the subway station at 96th Street and 8th Avenue and barely arrived in time for the 3:15 a.m. train to Philadelphia.[32]

⋆—⋆—⋆

A telegram from Andrei reached Joe Franey at home on Saturday night, November 24.[33] It stated:

> Come in there is a vacancy.
> [signed] Antonina Schevchenko

In reply, Joe arrived at New York City on American Airlines just minutes before sunrise on Sunday morning. He reached Andrei's apartment by eleven o'clock.

Within minutes of landing, however, whether or not he meant to, Joe slipped his FBI tail. This meeting with Schevchenko was not covered by surveillance.[34] Joe, however, returned to Buffalo at 2:30 p.m. on American Airlines flight 123 and reported on the meeting at a post-contact interview shortly afterward.[35]

Joe had delivered two black envelopes to Andrei. One contained five rolls of film and the other six, all exposed on unclassified reports from the Bell Aircraft library.

Andrei, in return, gave Joe two twenty-dollar bills for travel expenses and ten more twenty-dollar bills for the film rolls. He set their next meeting for 10:30 a.m. on December 1 or December 8 back in Buffalo. Andrei, however, said he would not make the trip. Instead, he would send his representative, Zhukov, whom he now identified as an Amtorg employee. They would meet in front of Kleinhans Clothing Company at the corner of Main and Clinton Streets in Buffalo. Zhukov would give Joe new, unexposed film and instruct him on the nature of photographs to be taken next.

Andrei then told Joe he would no longer meet with him or Leona in person. They were also never again to communicate with him by letter or by wire. If either of the Franeys should ever want to see him again, however, they could come in person to his apartment in New York City.

Joe suspected this might be the takeaway that was supposed to test his friendship or allegiance to Andrei. If Joe or Leona showed up at his door, Andrei would know the hook was well set. On the other hand, they speculated that if Andrei knew FBI surveillance had become too intense, he could not be caught with evidence on his person.

Zhukov did not show up on December 1 or 8. The failure to appear on the first day was in keeping with recognized Soviet espionage tactics.

Zhukov's failure to appear on December 8, however, was undoubtedly the result of Larry Haas's disgust over how the Schevchenko case was being mismanaged. His new co-conspirator in Washington knew very well how to deal with such things.

On December 17, 1945, agent Ladd finished compiling his dossier titled *Subject: Andrei Ivanovich Schevchenko, vice-chairman of Amtorg in New York City*, covering all of Schevchenko's activities in the United States since 1942. But it was all too late.[36]

Ladd's document, probably to assure deniability, failed to note that Schevchenko had already been brought to justice, though by irregular yet time-tested means.

Larry had become frustrated with a Washington bureaucracy that seemed to have more layers than a Dagwood Sandwich and either refused to make decisions or was afraid to. But if nobody else would break the stalemate, Larry decided that he would. A powerful ally had come forward, though Ladd would deny it, long before his report was finished.

J. Edgar Hoover had his own complaints with Washington bureaucracy, some of which matched Hass's. Hoover, however, had a few interesting techniques to deal with those matters. One was called "the unauthorized leak," many instances of which used journalists[37] as disseminators of FBI information.[38]

If—in Hoover's never-to-be-humble opinion—a politician had bungled something and tried to cover it up, Hoover would discreetly leak it to a sympathetic journalist. He could then publicly decry the leak, defend the public servant as a friend if expedient, and keep that alliance alive. Hoover did not do it often, but when he did, it was devastating.

In the Schevchenko case, Hoover appears to have wielded that tactic with exacting skill. The reluctance of the attorney general, the secretary of state, the under secretary of state, and the president to prosecute Schevchenko had grown intolerable to Hoover and dangerous to Haas and the Franeys. Hoover was determined that something would get done about Schevchenko before the new year.

Back-channel discussions with Larry started on November 12 with an FBI agent sent from Washington by Hoover, the Franeys having chosen to remain in the background. Buffalo, Philadelphia, and New York agents were kept in the dark about the meeting to provide credible deniability for them in case of repercussions. Larry would set a trap to squeeze Schevchenko so hard he would have to pop like a squeezed grape into the FBI's hands. Hoover and Haas chose the first days of December 1945 for action—if nothing else had been accomplished by then.

Code-named "Operation Mount Rushmore," Larry's piece of the plan was about to debut in dramatic fashion.

Chapter Thirty-one

Trial, Prosecution, and Threat

Tuesday evening, December 4, 1945, at a newsstand on the corner of Columbus Circle and Central Park West, New York City

Andrei cursed the nickel he had just spent—as if un-spending it could change what he saw.

"Red Spies Paid for Jet Secrets!" screamed the bold, black headline on the front page of the *New York Journal-American*, a paper that quite accurately boasted: "The largest circulation of any newspaper in New York City." Nobody who mattered could miss it. Making matters worse, the subhead declared, "Bribed U.S. Engineers for Blueprints of Planes."

Andrei's hand shook. His heart pounded. His mind screamed in a hundred voices: *Betrayed! Danger!*

He had planned to enjoy a leisurely walk north on Central Park West before the bone-chilling blizzard hit, forecast to break over the East Coast the next day. Now he nearly ran. Antonina must be warned. A block on, he started to hail a cab, then stopped. *The cabbie could already know I'm a spy!* Then he thought he and Antonina should run empty-handed to the Hudson River docks, hop on any banana boat in port, and disappear from the civilized world. But a moment later, his rational mind cut through the panic enough to hail a cab.

"Ninety-third Street," Andrei yelled at the cabbie before he hit the seat. He tossed a dollar bill beside the driver. "Make it fast!"

Andrei forced himself to sit back and steady his hands. He unfolded the paper crushed in his grip and re-read Howard Rushmore's exposé in disjointed jumps from paragraph to paragraph.

Agents of the Communist International not only tried to steal secrets of the atomic bomb, but bribed technicians and engineers to furnish blueprints of military equipment including jet-propelled airplanes, the N.Y. Journal-American learned today.

How did they learn that?[1] Andrei's mind spun.

Although these espionage activities are known to the State Department, no action has been taken to date against a Russian spy ring, which for two years has operated with unlimited funds and skilled personnel in an effort to steal confidential scientific developments.

Two years ago? Who slipped up?

This Russian, now in the United States allegedly as a member of a Soviet trading company, spent several months in one of America's largest airplane manufacturing plants as an "observer" of a "friendly" nation.

This plant was working on highly confidential details of jet-propulsion for military aircraft.

A year ago, the Russian contacted technicians employed on jet-propulsion and left large sums of money with them pending delivery of secret blueprints and data.

Was it Franey? Colonel Miller, the man he had played as a foil in seducing Haas? Or was it Haas himself, the man he had counted as a friend? That last possibility made him clench the paper even tighter. He read on.

Ironically, the spy probably will fare better under Democratic justice here than if deported to Russia.

If found guilty of espionage, he probably would receive a long prison sentence.

But deportation to Russia would be the spy's death. The Communist International makes short work of its agents who are caught in espionage work and exposed publicly.

Andrei fumed. He muttered old Cossack profanities and new Russian obscenities. He searched his memory for contacts, informants, and sub-agents in a fierce, now frantic, hunt for the most likely sources of these damning tales that "the *New York Journal-American* learned today."[2] He knew it was not just today and the *Journal* must have heard it somewhere.

Andrei also noticed the article never mentioned his name but indicted him with inuendo and unmistakable inference. In addition, the thing was riddled with inaccuracies and mis-directions, including Rushmore's invention of a pseudonym for a different spy Rushmore also exposed, calling him Alfred Adamson, conflating him with one or more of the illegals operating in parallel with Schevchenko out of Amtorg.[3] Andrei recognized the pseudonym as a thinly disguised variant of Arthur Adams, another "legal" of Andrei's own ilk, also under deep cover running sub-agents imbedded within America's top secret atom bomb research.

A dozen tiny hints stood out to Andrei as if they were intentional mis-directions. Taken together with tidbits known to few but himself, everything finally boiled down to the one, most dreaded name. He spat it out syllable by syllable—"Lau-ren Gee-orge Haasss."

On arriving home, Andrei said nothing. Before he even removed his coat and *ushanka*, he poured himself a generous vodka, neat, and another for Antonina. He handed the glass to her along with the newspaper.

"*Ya pokoynik!* I am a dead man! Read this." He turned away, sank heavily into his easy chair, downed his vodka in a gulp, and sought what composure he could from another Camel, watching Antonina read.

Antonina closed the paper and walked slowly toward the bedroom, leaving only seven angry words in her wake. "You are not the man I married." A moment later, the door opened again. "And do you have a plan for Arseniy and little Andreika?" The question proved itself merely rhetorical by the door slam that followed it. Hearing his name and sensing the tension, the boy raised his head from the adventure book he was trying to hide behind.

"Is something wrong, Father?"

Andrei smiled at him, trying to deny the terrible trouble that had broken through the barriers he had tried to build between his lives. He answered in Russian, the comforting language of home. "Only something we will fix, Andreika. Go back to your book. It will be okay." He wondered how long such false hopes would work. A child's intuition could not be outwitted for long.

One hour later, at eight o'clock, the voice coming through Andre's telephone was loud, clear, and commanding. It did not introduce itself, nor did it need to. "You have twenty-four hours to identify your traitor, deal with him, and report to me. Is this clear?"

"Yes, Comrade Akhmerov."

Akhmerov responded with a chilling three seconds of silence followed by a soft click and the hiss of a dead line.

Andrei did not sleep well that night. On retiring, he had told Antonina he would explain everything to her soon, but so far too many unanswered questions left him too uncertain. He still did not know the whole story himself. He assured her the *Journal-American* knew even less.

Fear and paranoia played on Andrei's mind and swung him from revenge to despair and back again. Unable to sleep by 3:00 a.m., he got up quietly so as not to arouse Antonina. He rummaged deep inside a steamer trunk at the back of his closet for something he had hoped never to use for any purpose, yet now it seemed the answer to the worst of his problems. He withdrew the *Tokarev* from its old burlap bag. It was a Soviet Army–issue pistol he had bought before leaving Moscow. Its eight-round magazine was full. *Maybe . . .* he mused, feeling its heft in his hand. After a few moments he re-wrapped it, reburied it at the bottom of the trunk, and pushed it back into the closet. *It would only cause more problems*, he told himself and went back to an unrestful sleep.

— • —

Wednesday, December 5, 9:00 a.m., Amtorg offices, 210 Madison Avenue, New York City

Andrei had to be certain about Haas before he could carry out the order to deal with him. He entered his office at Amtorg that morning to averted eyes of staff and coworkers. He knew too well the deathwatch look that followed Soviet workers who were being groomed for discipline or for recall to Russia. Both were euphemisms with terminal implications.

His work that day was desultory, distracted, and inefficient. His normally busy desk phone did not ring once. No coworkers or staff entered his office to deliver reports, ask advice, or offer counsel. He left his office at the end of the day with papers scattered around the room. Lists of names, contacts, and informants marked and diagrammed in intricate networks lay strewn across his desktop and conference table. Names of recent defectors from American communist causes were scrawled on many of the scraps, such as *Daily Worker* editor Louis Budenz[4] and Elizabeth Bentley, who only a month before had renounced her allegiance to the Soviet cause and met with the FBI to implicate nearly 150 people. Most notably, she had rebelled against reporting to Akhmerov. Crumpled wads littered the floor. Torn papers overflowed the wastebasket. His conclusion had become irrefutable, and worse, infuriating.

The only name that fit the puzzle remained Larry Haas. He recalled the comforting heft of his *Tokarev* but dismissed the thought once more.

No one bid Andrei a good evening when he left the building. All remained unaware of his passing in the most carefully studied of ways.

On Wednesday evening, December 5, Andrei stood before a newsstand near the Amtorg office. Unwilling to do it, but incapable of not, he spent another nickel to buy that day's *Journal-American* and its second day of battering. He hailed a cab and settled in for another damning read. On first glance the headline looked smaller, but it extended in a single column from the top of page 1, over the fold, and on to the bottom. The headline over Howard Rushmore's byline this time declared, Soviet Ring Uncovered in Spy Hunt.

The story exposed detail after detail of the Soviets' international courier system operated by people the FBI called "messenger boys." They were said to ferry secret messages and packages from international capital to capital, from airport to airport, and from seaport to seaport. Everything was attributed to the same Abraham Adamson, but nothing, this time, pointed directly at Andrei. Then he turned to the jump page for the rest of the story and a new chill ran down his spine.

In further development of still another espionage division of Russian "boring-from-within" methods the New York Journal-American has learned that jet propulsion plans for secret American airplanes were seized in the possession of a Russian trading official a few months ago.

"Lies!" Andrei screamed and jumped from his seat, smashing his head against the cab's roof.

The startled cabbie hit his brakes and swerved toward the curb. "You okay, buddy?"

"Yes, yes. Never mind," Andrei shot back, rubbing his bruised scalp. "Just drive!"

Contrary to Rushmore's story, the FBI had never confronted him and they had never seized anything in his possession. This lie had plainly been planted to cause him more trouble. If Andrei had been caught as stated, damning questions would be asked at Amtorg: Why had he not reported this to his superiors? If he had kept it secret, his own government would now have to accuse him of covert dealings and traitorous collaboration with the FBI. He forced himself to read on.

Yesterday this newspaper revealed that the Russian "visitor" had been attached to a leading aircraft manufacturing plant in upstate New York as an
"observer" for three years.

Andrei was clearly the target in this exposé. It had the appearance of
news, but its real purpose had been to trap him between the teeth of a
terrible vise. Rushmore had connected him to a July rooming house raid
on 32nd Street and a seizure involving a different Soviet agent on a different matter. Rushmore went on to report that the FBI and the State
Department refused to prosecute a suspect fitting Schevchenko's description. And finally, the *Journal-American* reporter, on asking the FBI why
the spy was not prosecuted, reported their terse reply, "No comment." They
did, however, verify that the Soviet agent continued to work at the Russian
trading corporation and,

[T]he FBI has set up a special squad to break up this espionage ring. Their
code words were "Comintern Apparatus."

Andrei was now a caged animal with no exit in sight.

That night the Schevchenkos' telephone did not ring. The silence fell
ominously on Andrei's and Antonina's ears. Morning, however, brought
something even stranger than anything else Andrei could have imagined.

———⋅•⋅———

Thursday morning, December 6, 1945, the Schevchenko residence,
West 93rd Street, New York City

"Andrei Ivanovich." A mellow, friendly voice greeted Andrei as he lifted his
telephone on its first ring. Andrei's name and patronym were spoken with
such native Russian richness and good nature that Andrei answered quite
naturally, "*Da, slushyu,*"—"Yes, it is I." In that instant, however, the caller's
face appeared in Andrei's mind. Boris! An NKVD officer at the Soviet consulate. The friendly Boris was the most terrifying one.[5]

"We have learned that there will be a third installment of that Judas
Rushmore's lies in tonight's paper," the voice said, offering a note of reassur-
ance. "Buy a copy and bring it to the consulate office tomorrow. Can you do
that, comrade?"

"Of course, Comrade Boris." Andrei could not find breath for a longer
answer.

"Excellent!" The voice and tone now came over the line as warm as America's Jolly Old Saint Nick. "We have some detective work to do. Your help will be very much appreciated."

Fortunately, that invitation told Andrei more than he thought the NKVD wanted him to know, and it was the first ray of hope Andrei had seen since the ordeal began. They had laid out a chessboard. Andrei instinctively saw the weakness in that move. They did not yet know enough, and now Andrei knew it. They planned to play a strategic game of attack and retreat, probe and watch, dispute and listen, and leave no stone unturned in search of anything Andrei might reveal. That was where Andrei saw his opportunity. If he played skillfully, he might yet redeem his failure. He was good at chess, especially when the stakes were as high as life and death.

"Good, comrade." Andrei put as much sincerity in his voice as he could. "We will have to use all of our resources to solve this crime. Until tomorrow, then." They each signed off in agreement, "*Do zavtra*—Until tomorrow."

With the beginning of hope, Andrei was able to devise a plan. He mapped out the details of settling his score with Larry Haas. The pretext he settled on would be a dangerous one. Fortunately, he knew the right number to call to set it up.

All he needed for the purpose this morning was a twenty-four-block stroll south along Central Park West, though he knew it would really take him on a more circuitous three-mile surveillance detection route through a building blizzard to get there. He knew about a telephone booth off the lobby of the American Museum of Natural History. It would be free of phone taps, and if he was careful, unwatched.

At fifteen minutes after eleven o'clock, Andrei stood in front of a phone booth in a sparsely traveled hallway near the museum's grand lobby. Echoing footsteps of morning visitors made Andrei uneasy as he closed the booth door. He slipped a dime into the slot atop the phone and dialed the number. A male voice answered after one ring. Andrei made a logical guess about the name.

"Mr. Conroy?"

"Yes."

"Andrei Schevchenko."

Conroy jerked the receiver away from his ear as if it had bitten him on the cheek. He stared at it.

"Mr. Conroy? Can you hear me?"

"Yes!" Conroy pulled the phone back. "Mr. Schevchenko. From Amtorg?" Conroy was as close as he had ever come to speechless. He had no idea what to say. "What can I do for you, sir?"

"I think you know, Mr. Conroy. We should talk. It appears I have been given a choice, which is no choice at all, concerning whom I will work for. You seem to hold all the cards. You and Mr. Haas have stacked the deck."

Conroy barely regained control. This call was a surprise he had to capitalize on. He thought fast. "Well, I think you may have a point, Mr. Schevchenko. And I promise I can deal you a better hand than your superiors can."

"Good. The price of my cooperation is simple."

"And that would be?"

"Make me and my family disappear in a way that does not look like my choice. If I am seen to defect, I will pay a price you cannot imagine."

"Yes, I can. His name is Arseniy. He lives at a boarding school near Moscow."

It was Andrei's turn to be surprised. "You know?"

"Naturally. Now let's meet."

Before Andrei could answer, his dime dropped. The line went dead. He cursed himself for not having extra coins ready. A frantic pocket search found one more dime. He punched it into the slot, heard the click, and spoke fast.

"I am sorry, I must go. Matters are developing. I will call again to set a time when we can meet. Please do not contact me. Is this agreeable?"

"Yes, of course." Conroy had no other option. "When can you—?"

"Wait for my call," Andrei interrupted. "That is all." He hung up before Conroy could reply. *Good*, he told himself, *that is in place.*

Conroy did not know about the next call Andrei received on returning home.

Thursday, 3:00 p.m., December 5, 1945, the Schevchenko residence[6]

Operation Mount Rushmore had abruptly ended Andrei Schevchenko's career as a spy and as an Amtorg official. But as so many others have hoped over the millennia, he hoped desperately that endings made way for new beginnings. The only alternative was unthinkable.

Not long after Andrei returned home from the Museum of Natural History, his phone rang. The caller was the office manager who worked for Pavel Ivanovich Fedosimov, acting chief following a quick succession of interim chiefs and now calling himself the first secretary of the Russian consulate in New York City. Andrei had met Fedosimov in March when he replaced the previous New York *rezident*, Stepan Apresyan, who had been reassigned to San Francisco. Pavel and Stepan were rumored within the New York apparatus to be running more than two hundred spies, more than half of them US citizens.

"Mr. Fedosimov would like you to visit him at his office tomorrow, please, at half twelve. Can you do that?" The voice spoke in English with courtesy, precision, and the old-world style of telling time. Andrei became instantly alert.

"Yes. Of course." After a moment's hesitation, he added, "And the reason?" He bit his tongue.

"Mr. Fedosimov did not state. Good day."

Andrei heard the click of a disconnect while he was still saying, "And good day to—"

Friday, December 7, 12:25 p.m., Soviet Consulate, 7–9 East 61st Street, New York City[7]

Andrei arrived with all three of the damning *Journal-American* issues tucked under his arm. First Secretary Pavel Ivanovich Fedosimov and his wife, Vera Sergeyevna, stood at the entrance waiting, bundled warmly, and smiling.

"Come in out of the cold, Andrei Ivanovich," Vera said, taking his arm. Andrei heard "out of the cold" both literally and figuratively. Curiosity quickly followed relief. *What has changed?*

"Come to my office, Andrei Ivanovich," Pavel said, shaking Andrei's hand. "We have much to discuss."

Much indeed, Andrei learned. His world once again tumbled into new shapes and patterns. Seated comfortably in the old-world Russian decor of Pavel's office, warmed with fragrant, spiced tea and delicate Russian tea cakes dusted in sugar, Andrei felt disoriented by the comforts.

"See what I have on my desk," Pavel said. Andrei looked. He saw a thin, blue, hard-covered book and a sheaf of papers. He rose to see more clearly, and almost fell back.

The book's title stood out in flowing Cyrillic cursive, white on a midnight-blue cloth cover. It was a copy of Andrei's long-forgotten *Tsyganskiy Romans* (*A Gypsy Romance*). The other was a sheaf of typed, white papers titled *Traktat po Turbinnoy Mekhanike* (*A Treatise on Turbine Mechanics*). It was Andrei's graduation thesis from the Moscow Aviation Institute. Andrei looked up, amazed.

"You see, I know who you are, Andrei Ivanovich. I also know what has been done to you by the FBI and that Rushmore criminal."

Andrei could not answer at first. Pavel's pause lengthened into a waiting silence. Andrei finally asked, "What should I do?"

"You should build airplanes, young man. Your country needs you doing what you do best." Andrei also heard the implication that the work he was currently doing was not his best. Pavel's next words finished the job of turning Andrei's life upside down.

"In fact, we owe you an apology for placing you in a position unsuited to your talents."[8]

"Oh?" Andrei could hardly speak.

"Nevertheless," Pavel went on, "you are an intelligent man. You have undoubtedly learned much from this experience. Maybe you have learned more than you realize. I have asked Comrade Boris to make some time in his schedule to talk with you, or maybe, if he is too busy, write down a few questions for you to think about. We would like to see what you have learned of American tactics and businesses. Your work, we are sure, has been valuable in many ways. You have received awards for your work in America, have you not?"

"Yes, I have. Thank you. I will help if I can."

"We are sure of that. You will return to Russia soon," Pavel said. That sentence, no matter what else had preceded it, evoked fear. The messages now appeared to be mixed. Andrei's heart raced.

Pavel smiled. "For a three-month vacation. Then, on to the work you do best."

Pavel wanted Andrei to believe this. He sealed the conversation with the remainder of an hour of easy conversation, joined by Vera Sergeyevna. They spoke about family, home, and a new future for themselves and their nation. One last surprise waited for Andrei.

"Your intelligence operation here will be closed," Pavel said. "We no longer believe it is needed in the form it has taken. Your operational funds may be liquidated." He paused, then added, "At your discretion, of course. The Soviet Union will need years to rebuild from the war. The most efficient way for us to provision your future home will be with the obsolete funding assigned to your group. We will declare it surplus, at your disposal."

"Thank you," Andrei said. "I know what to do." He knew agents assigned to the United States who had amassed small fortunes. They purchased common household goods in America with "company funds" and sold them on returning home. The profit could be remarkable. It was officially frowned upon yet almost universally practiced. Then he cautioned himself. *It all depends on what "back home" really means.* Deeply conditioned paranoia could not be entirely lost during one conversation over sugared cookies and spiced tea.

Andrei and his hosts parted with suitable well-wishes all around. The fourth—and unseen—party to the conversation simply removed his head-phones. He walked the few steps from his post next door to Fedosimov's office.

"Nicely done, Pavel Ivanovich."

"Thank you, comrade. I think we will learn something."

"I know we will," the NKVD officer said.

Andrei walked the short distance to Park Avenue, south to the Grand Army circle, and west along Central Park South, where he stopped to watch carefree ice skaters on The Pond. He envied their freedom. He needed the cold wind to sharpen his mind while he sorted out the most unusual conver-sation he had experienced since arriving in America. He sifted every word yet still found himself hanging between hope and fear. He turned his mind to his personal bank accounts. The numbers were uncomplicated and all in memory.

On reporting to New York in April, Andrei had opened an account at the 34th Street branch of Chase National Bank, with about $500 in cash and a transfer of more than $1,200 from the State Bank of Kenmore, New York. He always kept a balance of $1,500 to $2,000, equal to about half of an American man's yearly income, proud it was a high multiple of the average in Russia. It paid for a few perks, all the $20 bills for Larry and the Franeys, and two $350 cameras. His banking was tidy and simple. With a current balance of about, $1,600, he was ready for some shopping.

On his return from the consulate, Andrei explained everything that he knew or surmised to Antonina. Suspicions and hopes, recriminations, ex-cuses, and justifications finally merged and settled into a simple plan.

Andrei withdrew $300 and they went Christmas shopping, determined to do it like capitalist consumers. On December 11, he withdrew $140 more, on December 12, another $850, and on December 13, $20 for dinner on the town.

On December 14, Andrei returned to the Soviet Consulate to deliver a lengthy and carefully crafted document. It contained answers to a long, written interrogatory the NKVD officer had given him. Though he waited for thirty-five minutes, he saw neither Pavel nor Boris. Ultimately, he merely left it with the desk attendant on duty.

That day, Antonina told a friend that Andrei had been awarded a new assignment out of the country.[9] "We are all going," she said, "quite soon." The friend, a neighbor in 2-D, later told FBI agents that Antonina did not seem as happy as her words suggested.

On December 15, an Amtorg maintenance worker helped Andrei hoist a pre-addressed, empty trunk into Andrei's car at Amtorg and accompanied him home. Later in the day, they lugged the now heavier trunk into a truck, which took it back to Amtorg. The next day, Andrei took the last of his cardboard cartons to the Amtorg offices.[10]

On December 17, at 11:00 p.m., Andrei posted a Christmas card to Larry.[11]

Larry and Dorothy,

Sorry that we missed our chance to see you on Christmas since we are leaving New York City today for three months' vacation in Europe. Hope to see you when we come back sometime near April.

With best wishes, Andre [*sic*].[12]

In the lower right-hand corner of the page, Andrei wrote 10-9. Larry would know to add ten days to the postmark date, which would be December 27, and to meet at nine in the morning. Andrei also knew that if he was right that Haas had collaborated with the FBI, Quinn would tell Larry where to meet and what it was all about. Andrei had set a complicated trap of his own.

On December 21, Andrei notified the Alien Tax Division of the US Treasury Department that he would soon leave the United States by boat.

While Andrei prepared for his move, the carefully worded document he had left for Akhmerov, and the cartons of files from his home that were now at Amtorg for shipping, were undergoing careful inspection analysis by two NKVD officers. A more detailed and focused discussion between Andrei and those NKVD men was postponed until they had a more conducive environment—aboard the ship. They had many more interesting questions in store for Andrei.

Thursday morning, 8:00 a.m., December 27, 1945, an abandoned warehouse in Hell's Kitchen, Manhattan—forethoughts

Larry Haas knew he had to come face-to-face with Andrei Schevchenko this morning, but worse, he now knew he had to come face-to-face with himself. This morning would force him to confront the lies he had lived. For most of his life his lies were promises he always found a way to keep. Except now, for the first time in his life, Larry was a real liar. His lie of friendship was still a promise, but a promise that would end in destruction.

Larry had befriended Andrei Ivanovich Schevchenko. The relationship was complicated, much like a real one, with liking and disliking, admiring and despising, laughing, cursing, and a lot of heavy drinking. Larry had accepted Andrei's trust and feigned his own for Andrei.

This morning, maybe illogically, Larry hoped for exoneration. Andrei might have been turned. Otherwise, Larry would feel guilty of murder by betrayal. Andrei was indeed an enemy of the people of the United States. As such he deserved betrayal, but Larry now knew that the righteous did not always feel guiltless.

CHAPTER THIRTY-TWO

The Threat Delivered

The threat is stronger than the execution.
—Aron Nimzowitsch, Russian Chess Master[1]

*Thursday morning, December 27, 1945, an abandoned warehouse in
Hell's Kitchen, Manhattan—consequences*

Larry Haas was nervous. By now, Andrei was on the way.[2]

"Good work, Larry. You brought him in," Conroy said, clapping him on the back. Special Agent in Charge (SAC) Edward E. Conroy was working on the Schevchenko case out of the FBI's New York City field office.[3] He knew Larry had put himself and his family through hell and exposed them to serious dangers to make this day happen. The FBI had never before mounted a sting like this, and Haas was a kind of tool they had not used before. Conroy knew why Larry was sweating in spite of the wintry chill in this old, midtown warehouse.

"I'm not sure I believe it yet," Larry said. "That man is what you told me he is, only worse." Larry was not a man accustomed to self-doubt, but his intuition was shouting a warning. For more than a year he and Andrei had traded lies and plotted each other's destruction while feigning friendship and loyalty to a higher cause. That, Larry had learned, is how the spy/counterspy game must be played.

A few days before Christmas, Larry had received a letter from Andrei.[4] Anyone who read it would have seen a friendly holiday greeting. Embedded within it, though, Larry found a message in secret code that Andrei had taught him. Andrei wanted to meet. He also named another man he wanted present, a man who would tell Larry where and when to meet.

Larry was shocked that Andrei knew Conroy. Earlier in December, a series of three front-page stories in the *New York Journal-American*—a Hearst Publication[5]—had publicly exposed Andrei's entire Soviet spy network. The stories dubbed Andrei Schevchenko "the most dangerous Soviet agent ever sent to the United States." Larry knew Andrei would blame him for that damning exposé. Worse yet, the stories had caught him in a trap from which only one escape remained—into American hands for protection from his masters in Moscow, who would be enraged by what they read.[6]

The plan now was to play Andrei like one who has come in from a storm, a celebrity defector to the American cause.

Larry looked at his watch. "Almost time, gentlemen. Get ready. Andrei is never late."

In a few minutes, Larry would greet Andrei with a smile and a handshake. The other four men in the room would offer him a safe haven guaranteed by the government of the United States of America. Larry wondered what kind of stealthy, surveillance detection route Andrei might be taking even now to keep this meeting.

———◆———

A light snow was falling across Central Park at seven thirty with the temperature holding at twenty-nine degrees. The morning felt cold enough when Andrei stepped from his car that he was glad for his fur hat—the *ushanka* that was his only style concession to Mother Russia. His hands, however, shook more from anger than cold. He left his official car and driver behind and traced a circuitous and meandering ninety-minute route. His walk would be only half the length prescribed for spotting watchers, but he thought he was good enough to beat them. He would walk four or five miles to reach the rendezvous point only a few blocks east. None of his people must know where he was going. Soviets in America watched each other even more closely than the FBI watched them. No position in the Soviet hierarchy was too high for paranoia.

Andrei arrived precisely on time. He stood in front of a nondescript door halfway down a decaying 10th Avenue block in Manhattan's Hell's Kitchen. He knocked hard enough for flakes of ancient gray paint to stick to the knuckles of his fine kid glove. The door was marked in a crude stencil: "Transfer Supply Co.—Annex E. No Solicitation."

Larry heard the knock. "Better make it official, Ed," Larry said. "You open the door. He's turning himself in to you boys, not to me."

Conroy walked slowly down the darkened corridor toward the door, rehearsing his greeting one more time.

Andrei had grown impatient by the time the door creaked open by a crack. An eye and a sliver of a man's face peered out at him.

"I am here. Do not make me wait." Andrei spat the words in angry, staccato syllables. "I must not be seen." His eyes darted up and down the street.

The door opened a foot wider. The tall, well-dressed man stepped aside for Andrei to enter the dimly lit, musty-smelling hallway. The door closed behind him with a thud. Andrei now confronted the first man he had met face-to-face since his arrival in the United States who willingly announced himself as an agent of the Federal Bureau of Investigation.

"We appreciate your cooperation, Mr. Schevchenko. I am Agent Conroy." He held out his hand to shake Andrei's.

"*Nyet!*" Andrei snarled. He peered past Conroy and squinted into the darkness beyond. Ignoring Conroy's hand, he pushed past him and strode toward a distant door where the only light in the building cast a yellow wedge into the hallway. Halfway along, he stopped and turned as Conroy caught up with him.

"I know you think you have turned me," Andrei said, "and now you think you can coerce me into cooperating with your government." He lifted his chin to glare angrily into the eyes of the taller man. "I lied. I will not cooperate. I came here for only one reason and that reason is mine, not yours."

"But . . ." Conroy began.

"No! It is I who will speak. Where is he?" Andrei demanded.

"Haas?"

"Yes. You said he would be here. Show me."

Conroy motioned toward the lighted doorway farther down the hall. "But why . . ."

Andrei cut him off with a wave of his hand, turned his back, and strode toward the light. He stopped at the door, his countenance lit as if by a spotlight. He shielded his eyes, already adapted to the darkened hall, and scanned the small room from left to right.

He saw four men in dark suits standing in the middle. They were talking in a friendly manner beside an office-worn desk with a semicircle of six straight-backed chairs facing it. A single, naked light bulb glared overhead. One man lounged comfortably in a chair behind the desk. It was Larry Haas. When he saw Andrei, he stood up and smiled. Neither he nor the other men had heard Andrei's outburst in the hallway.

"Hi, Andrei. Nice to see you." Larry greeted him with the ease of meeting a friend on a sunny day in the park. "I was surprised that you called a meeting like this, but here we are."

Andrei did not return Larry's greeting or his smile. His fists were clenched and his face was red. He took two steps into the room and stopped.

"Sorry for the troubles, Andrei." Larry sensed a tension he had hoped not to see.

Andrei approached a few more steps, roughly pushing chairs aside, his eyes fiercely boring into Larry's. Conroy reached the door behind Andrei, sensed the tension, and did not move. The other four men suddenly stood quite still, transfixed by the infuriated Russian. One of the men reacted before the others. He slid his hand slowly behind his back and wrapped his fingers around the handle of a holstered revolver under his jacket.

Andrei, blind to everyone else, glared at Larry. "You made me look like a fool in the eyes of my country," he said, "and I will get even with you in the worst way!" He drove a finger toward Larry's chest. "When a Russian makes a threat, Larry Haas, that threat will be carried out, no matter how long it takes!"

He pulled a roll of newspapers from his pocket and threw it on the desk in front of Larry. It fell open to the frontpage. The headline on the December 4, 1945, issue of the *New York Journal-American* blared: *Red Spy Paid for Jet Secrets: Bribed US Engineers for Blueprints of Planes.* The trap they had set for Andrei had clearly backfired.

Adding to the offense, Larry suspected the byline must have nettled Andrei as much as the headline. Journalist Howard Rushmore, once an outspoken American communist, had recently and famously turned himself into a fire-breathing anti-communist. Rushmore's next two exposés, dated December 5 and 6, painted an even darker picture of Andrei and his spy network, publicly stripping him naked of all pretense and artifice.[7] Andrei had surely read Rushmore's stories as a death sentence.[8] The penalty for security breaches in Stalin's intelligence service was exile to Siberia, or death.[9] His chiefs in the directorate, the Moscow Center, did not tolerate exposure and failure.[10] The newspaper stories were contrived to make the FBI seem like the only safe haven to Andrei.

Andrei glared at Larry one moment longer, turned on the toe of his wing-tip Oxford, and left the room without another sound except for the fading echo of footsteps and a distant, slamming door. Larry wiped beads of perspiration from his forehead, turned toward the five men, and offered a shrug and an innocent smile. "I didn't do it. Honest."

"Of course not," Conroy said with a wink. He knew how such things were done. He also knew the right outcome from such tactics was never guaranteed.

Andrei returned to his car by an even more devious route than he had come. What his driver saw in Andrei's eyes made him ask, "Is there a problem, Comrade Schevchenko?"

Andrei growled, "*Zatknis tovarishchu! Vesti mashinu!*" Shut up, comrade! Drive the car. He spoke no more.

PART II

Lethal Consequences

CHAPTER THIRTY-THREE

Another Name for Justice

Saturday morning, 8:45, December 29, 1945, the White House basement[1]
Larry stepped off the train from New York at Washington Union Station. The fog was thick and a cold mist was falling. Larry pulled his coat tighter around his neck and headed for the rendezvous point to wait.

A white, windowless van pulled to the curb two blocks north of the station. "Just get in, pal," said a rough-looking laborer behind the wheel. "It's just another workday, okay?" The van's side panel was stenciled "Capital City Heating and Renovation."

Larry opened the passenger door and climbed aboard. He looked at the driver's name-patch. "Hi, Bob. My name's Larry."

Bob scowled. "No, it's not, Malcolm. Look at your shirt." Bob handed over a garment bag. "Hop in the back and change, Malcolm."

Larry found a work-stained, denim-blue uniform in the bag. It fit poorly, the material was scratchy, and until he looked down at the patch on his left breast pocket, he could not even remember the name of the company. Beneath "Capital City Heating and Renovation," the name "Malcolm" was embroidered in red stitching.

Malcolm had been born yesterday in Agent Quinn's mind and he would cease to exist tomorrow. But for today, Malcolm would have to fool anybody he met in Washington except the president of the United States, in whose home he was about to impersonate a furnace repairman.

When Harry Truman moved into his new home at 1600 Pennsylvania, he discovered the place in shambles, drafty, decrepit, and in places nearly unfit for habitation. That, however, was perfect when the president wanted to talk to people like Larry Haas. Anonymous entry to the White House was all but impossible because reporters and capitol-watchers never slept and never strayed far from the official entrances. The parade of handymen, plumbers, and electricians continually moving in and out of the work entrances went largely unnoticed. A furnace repair in December was not a novel event at the White House in 1945. The 100-year-old heating system barely warmed the more than 150-year-old building. It wheezed and clanked enough on cold winter nights to make the place sound haunted by the thirty-two presidents who had preceded Truman.

At the security checkpoint, the White House officer laughed when he saw Bob roll down his window. "Back again?"

"You bet, Charles. I love the steady work." He motioned toward the other seat. "New helper. Name's Malcolm, okay?"

"Good enough," the guard said. He looked at Malcolm with a friendly smile. "Welcome to the family." He waved the van through and made a cursory entry in his log. He didn't usually record the names of Bob's helpers. They were always different and never came back a second time.

"Don't bother telling me why you're here," Bob told Larry. "And I don't want to know who you are. I get paid to get you in the door. That's good enough." He pulled his van to a non-descript service door in the west wing. "I'm going in and down one flight. Follow me down but turn right when I turn left." He glanced at his watch. "We're right on time, so whichever grand-high-potentate you're supposed to meet here today will be around the corner. As for me, I have a real furnace to fix. When you're ready to go, just get back in the van. I'll be back when I get back. Any questions?"

"No," Larry said. He liked this guy.

"Good. Me neither. Follow me."

Larry turned right where Bob turned left. On turning, Larry almost bumped into a small, bespectacled man standing in the hall beside an open doorway.

The good-natured chuckle surprised Larry. "Good of you to come, Mr. Haas," the man said. Larry backed up a quick step. He had nearly knocked over President Harry Truman and stammered, "Mr. President, sir."

Truman, smiling as if this was the first event of the day that really amused him, stepped aside and motioned Larry toward an open doorway.

"Good to see you again. Please take a seat." Two chairs on opposite sides of a small, knicked-up wooden table were waiting for them.

Larry composed himself. "I understand you have a job for me, sir."

"There is something I cannot do," Truman said. "But I must." He smiled. "Sound like politics to you?"

"So I've heard," Larry said, appreciating the droll humor.

"I understand that in the case of Mr. Schevchenko, you and Mr. Hoover achieved a trial-by-press along with something that amounts to a conviction, and maybe a death sentence when he gets back home. I assume your beef was with a couple of branches of our government that were being indecisive. Does that about sum it up?"

"Yes, sir." Larry watched the president's faint smile turn serious.

"As you know, we are negotiating with the Soviets right now over the fate of Europe, Japan, and China. The wrangling is now at a critical state."

Larry was about to say he understood, but the president continued. "We must also negotiate over Romania and Bulgaria, brutal police states controlled by the Soviets. They want US diplomatic recognition. Were you aware of that?"

"Not quite, sir." Not at all was closer to the truth. Larry was beginning to sense they were about to venture in where angels and aviation engineers should fear to tread.

"Then there's Potsdam. We were practically forced to agree to Russian occupation of Eastern Poland and the occupation of Germany east of the Oder River. That demand was high-handed and outrageous. And that was *before* you publicly rubbed their nose in the Schevchenko affair. Are you starting to see the shape of things you stirred up?"

"Yes, sir. But I didn't know." Larry was now completely defenseless.

"No, you did not. But your accomplice did."

"My accomp—? Oh, you mean Mr. Hoover."

"Now you're catching on. You see . . ." The president unfolded a few sheets of paper on which he had handwritten something quite lengthy. "Here are some notes for a message I'm preparing to send Secretary of State Byrnes.[2] There are portions I want you to hear. They also apply to you and to Mr. Hoover." He started reading.

It is absolutely necessary that the President should be kept fully informed on what is taking place. This is vitally necessary when negotiations are taking place in a foreign capital, or even in another city than Washington. This procedure is necessary in domestic affairs and it is vital in foreign affairs.

He looked up at Larry. "Do you understand?"

"Of course, Mr. President. I . . ."

". . . didn't act like it," the president finished his sentence for him. "Now, concerning the Soviets," the president continued, "I wrote . . ."

245

At first we were anxious for Russian entry into the Japanese War. Of course, we found later that we didn't need Russia there and the Russians have been a headache to us ever since. Unless Russia is faced with an iron fist and strong language another war is in the making. Only one language do they understand—"How many divisions have you?" I do not think we should play compromise any longer.

Truman put the paper down. "Now this is where you come in."

"Me, sir?"

"Listen carefully."

We should maintain complete control of Japan and the Pacific. We should rehabilitate China and create a strong central government there. We should do the same for Korea. Then we should insist on the return of our ships from Russia and force a settlement of the Lend-Lease debt of Russia. I'm tired of babying the Soviets.

Truman had finished reading. He refolded the paper, slid it into his shirt pocket, and looked into Larry's eyes searching for comprehension.

"Where do I come in, sir?"

"You will do the single thing I must do yet *not* do. As I said, I am tired of babying the Soviets."

A hint of Truman's meaning began to play at the back of Larry's mind, but he could not yet put the pieces together. "And my part, Mr. President?"

"I *cannot* punish Schevchenko publicly, not here in the United States. If I take that pawn, the entire international chessboard will change, all negotiations will become orders of magnitude more complicated. But I also *must* punish Schevchenko. If I do not, I stick my thumb in Hoover's eye, and I want him on my side. I will also offend all the other good people who know the Soviets for what they are. I want Schevchenko gone, but by my hand, not by his Moscow handlers. It must be known that I do this, but known only by the right people in Washington whose support I need, the people—and that uniquely includes you—who deserve that satisfaction and that justice. On the other hand, if Schevchenko is still alive when he reaches Russia, I will be seen as a weak leader who let the devils do my dirty work. But I also need clean hands in this, believable deniability with the Soviets concerning his end." He paused and looked into Larry's eyes. "Now do you see your part?"

"I think so." Larry took a deep breath. This was a terrifying answer to the question he had asked himself so many times before. The man he was about to become was not the man he had set out to be, yet at every turn he had done what he thought was right. How could this be?

The president handed Larry a large manila envelope. "Open it."

The envelope was not sealed. As Larry lifted it, the contents fell on the table between them. Larry separated the jumbled pile.

The first item was a US passport in the name of John L. Bergstrom. Beside it he saw a Minnesota driver's license, various membership cards, a photograph of an attractive young woman flanked by a small boy and girl posed beside a big, green tractor, money that looked like fifteen or twenty dollars in small bills, and a wear-worn leather billfold. There was also a typed page headed, *John "Jack" Lars Bergstrom: Legend—Read and destroy.*

"That's your second new identity for the day, Malcolm," President Truman said, reading the name tag on Larry's uniform. "But I think you missed something."

Larry picked up the envelope again. He gave it a shake and another paper fell out. It was a steamship ticket granting him passage for one on the SS *Stalinabad* for January 3, 1946.

"Bon voyage, Mr. Jack Bergstrom. You have a free hand."

"Yes, sir." Larry was stunned.

"Do what you have to do," President Truman said. He rose, shook Larry's hand, and left him standing before fragments of another history grafted unbidden into his.

Back in the white van, the security guard waved them on their way without checking anything. Malcolm's identity soon disappeared back into its garment bag and Larry Haas's identity reemerged. A man named Bob who worked for Capital City Heating and Renovation drove Larry back to Washington Union Station.

Jack Bergstrom now had a few days to get ready to catch a boat.

CHAPTER THIRTY-FOUR

Lost at Sea

Thursday, January 3, 1946, 10:45 a.m. The Claremont Terminal, Greenville, New Jersey, port of New York, boarding the SS Stalinabad

On December 20, 1945, Director Hoover had dispatched an urgent memo to the New York City office. *"Subject Schevchenko leaving US soonest. Search advised of luggage and trunks."*

On December 29, Hoover sent a similar message to Attorney General Clark. Heightened physical surveillance by New York agents had revealed that most of Schevchenko's belongings and records had been sequestered by his superiors. His financial dealings, however, remained available for investigation.

On Monday, December 31, 1945, the FBI confirmed that Andrei and Antonina Schevchenko had cleaned out—but not closed—their joint Chase National Bank account. Only $2.04 remained. If the Schevchenkos planned any New Year's Eve partying, they already had the cash. The Bureau placed a stop with the bank to begin on January 1 in case they received any further correspondence relative to the remaining balance. Surveillance on the Schevchenko apartment continued through the holidays.

On January 2, an Amtorg chauffeur drove the Schevchenkos' 1940 blue Dodge sedan from a garage on West 93rd Street and parked it at Amtorg.

On January 3, at 9:15 a.m., a truck owned by the Port Commercial Moving and Storage Company loaded wooden cases from the Schevchenkos' apartment. Shortly after that, the Schevchenko family entered a Soviet Consulate Buick driven by a consulate chauffeur. That car, followed by two others, drove to the Russian consulate at 7 East 61st Street. The moving truck arrived shortly afterward.

At 10:45 a.m., the truck, the Soviet Consulate car, and the two others departed the consulate in single file and proceeded to the Claremont Shipping

Terminal just across the New York Harbor from the Statue of Liberty. Upon arrival, the Schevchenko family immediately boarded the SS *Stalinabad*, a Russian-operated, Lend-Lease Liberty Ship that had been christened the *Willis C. Hawley* when it launched eighteen months earlier from the Oregon Ship Building Corporation.

Two men known to the Bureau as Red Army Intelligence inspectors, presumably NKVD, boarded directly behind Andrei Schevchenko.

At the time of boarding, the FBI's surveilling agents identified themselves at the dock and examined the passenger list. They confirmed that all three Schevchenkos, two adults and a young boy, were listed as passengers. The Red Army Intelligence officers were identified as escorts conveying a Soviet diplomatic pouch.

Such diplomatic communications always traveled under a triple seal, each accessible to progressively deeper levels of the intelligence apparatus. The agents were permitted to confirm the top level only, marked for a general government address in Moscow.

Diplomatic pouches were always accompanied by two well-armed couriers. The fact that on this occasion they were Red Army Intelligence officers suggested an additional assignment.

Together with US Customs Department agents, the FBI men examined the Schevchenkos' luggage.[1] The head of shipping for the Amtorg Trading Corporation was also present. The only possessions available for searching by then were two pieces of hand luggage—a suitcase and a small duffle bag. The search failed to detect any materials of a scientific or military nature pertinent to the FBI investigation. The rest of the Schevchenkos' belongings, a large trunk wrapped in burlap and seven hefty packing cases, were declared off-limits by the Amtorg representative, as they had been declared under diplomatic seal.[2]

Andrei Schevchenko, however, was not present for the inspection. Pavel Fedosimov, apparently accompanying the Schevchenko party, had disembarked only long enough to inform the US officials that he would represent Mr. Schevchenko. He apologized that Mr. Schevchenko was too ill to leave the ship.

At 6:50 p.m. the SS *Stalinabad* slipped out of the Claremont Terminal on the New Jersey side of the port of New York. Flying its Soviet flag, the ship was bound for Murmansk, Russia, via England.[3] This forced deportation, however, did not end the Schevchenko case.

The SS *Stalinabad* eventually arrived in Murmansk on schedule. Andrei Ivanovich Schevchenko did not—though Antonina and Andreika did.

—◆—

Wednesday, 7:30 a.m., an hour before sunrise on January 9, 1946, six days at sea out of the port of New York, somewhere over the Jutland Bank between the North Sea and Skagerrak, Denmark[4]

Andrei stopped cold in mid-step. He stared, eyes wide, straining to see through the pre-dawn gloom. A terrifying sight had just appeared before him on the rain-soaked deck. Andrei spoke to the specter in Russian. "*Kakoy novyy ad eto?*" Then in English, hoarsely, as if his throat had already screamed for a week, "What new hell is this?" He stepped back, stumbled, and grasped the rail.

By reflex Larry Haas reached out to steady him. "You look like hell."

Andrei recoiled, flicking Larry's hand away as if a bat had landed on his shoulder. He stumbled back two more paces. "What are you doing here?" His croak was hardly audible above the pounding North Atlantic swells forty feet below, where they rose and fell against *Stalinabad*'s hull.

"I'm here to save you."

"Save me? You have already killed me!"

"That's what I tried to stop." Larry pounded the rail with his fist. "You should be in an American prison right now. With luck, that's as bad as it would have gotten for you. Have your comrades offered you something better?"

"For a smart man," Andrei choked, "that is a stupid question. They have given me a choice. One of my family will pay for my failure. The other three will live long in the worker's paradise." The last phrase caught in his throat. "I have been given the privilege of choosing who pays."

The light beside the door Andrei had stepped from moments ago cast a wan glow through the fog, just enough that Larry saw the pain in his eyes. "What have they done to you?"

"Interviews and histories." Andrei glared at Larry. He raised his left hand. It was swathed in a crude bandage, darkly stained.

Larry caught his breath.

"My other hand is useful for writing confessions. They thank me with fresh air and enough time to smoke one cigarette twice every night."

"I know. We've been watching. That's how we knew where to find you, and when."

"We?" Andrei filled his one-word question with indignation.

"Me and two FBI men. This tub is a floating zoo full of deported agents, informants, CPUSA zealots, and the like. The two agents are here on legit

US government business by agreement with the Soviets. They are guests assigned to verify the right people get delivered where they belong. We don't want them accidentally misplaced back to where we shipped them from. Larry Haas, on the other hand, is not here."

"Then how did you get aboard? This is a Soviet ship."

"Easy. I'm Jack Bergstrom, a Minnesota dairy farmer. Nobody you would know. I am planning an agricultural exchange to help Russia rebuild with American plows and tractors. Want to see my passport? It's a work of art. I think you know how that is done."

Andrei laughed. It made him cough. "When did you know?"

"The FBI put eyes on you the day you sailed into the port of New York back in '42. They didn't get serious about watching you soon enough, though. But when they saw us together, they brought me in." Larry's voice grew harder. "But it took quite a while before you really got me mad."

"What did I . . .?" Andrei's voice trailed off.

"You offered a little girl a ride to school, didn't you?"

"But Larry . . ." Andrei's shoulders sagged. "She wasn't supposed to get hurt. They . . ." He stopped and looked out across the sea. A gray line now hugged the horizon below the clouds. Sunrise was only a half hour off. Andrei turned to Larry. "You said you came aboard to save me."

"So I did." This was one more lie Larry would make true.

Larry placed his arm across Andrei's shoulders, drew him close, and pointed down toward the water. "Look." A small boat had drawn near out of the mist. It bobbed forty feet below, keeping pace with *Stalinabad*'s heaving side. A crewman stood at the bow shining a flashlight at the water some distance ahead, as if to point out something that might be floating there.

The prearranged signal was clear. Larry moved his arm fast. A powerful, openhanded chop shattered the vertebrae at the back of Andrei's neck. A spasm shuddered down his spine. Andrei's eyes flashed at Larry for an instant then faded to a cold, vacant stare that Larry never forgot. Andrei slumped against the rail. A moment later the sailor's beam found its target rising and falling in the waves. A makeshift, blood-stained bandage slowly floated away from it. The war that had made this sea a vast graveyard to thousands of souls now took one more.

Larry leaned over the rail. "I did save you, my friend . . ." he said softly. He looked back at the door Andrei had left only moments before and added, ". . . from them." Larry knew that moment would return to haunt him someday, but this could not be that day.

Sixty seconds later, standing on the bobbing deck of the small but sturdy Danish fishing launch, Larry gave a hard jerk on the release that disconnected the escape line Larry had just hand-over-handed down from *Stalinabad*'s railing. He looked behind him and saw a freshly stenciled name above the small boat's wheelhouse window, "*Klar Havn,*" Clear Harbor.

"*Lad os gå!*" Larry yelled to the crewman. He knew the Danish phrase because it sounded almost exactly like the English words it meant, "Let's go!"

Klar Havn parted silently from *Stalinabad*'s flank and drifted away on the swells. Soon, enveloped in mists and darkness, she fired up her small motor and navigated away on a low-power purr, inaudible amid waves and wind. The *Stalinabad* disappeared in the graying sunrise. The only remaining evidence of its passing was a fading wake that barely rocked the fishing boat as it began to speed south toward Skagen Fyr, the century-old Skagen Lighthouse. Denmark's northernmost beacon was once again guiding a skipper home safe from the seas.

The seaman glanced at Larry and kept coiling his ropes, dour and unmoved. Men like him had battled Nazi invaders for the last five years. He—like uncounted others in the Danish underground—had grown too hardened to death to react to Larry's deed this night. From what he had been told, Larry was also a war-made man. After a few moments the seaman straightened from his task and spoke.

"*Gå rapport Kaptajn Lund.*" A thumb jab over his shoulder toward the pilothouse told Larry all he needed to know.

"Captain Lund, I assume," Larry said when he stepped into the wheelhouse. The man's stance was steady and as wide as his arm span across the wheel. His eyes held fast on Skagen's beacon while he spoke. "Welcome aboard, Mr. Haas." Lund spoke in an accent melded of his native Danish and his British finishing-school English.

"Glad you were here." Larry could think of nothing more to say. He turned to watch the every-four-second sweep of the distant beacon. The broken mist rising across Kattegat Bay made the lighthouse beam flash erratically a few points off the starboard bow. It wavered from bright to a hazy glow, to lost, and back again across the dark water.

"To come here for you is only a small favor, an easy repayment for a debt we owe your soldiers." Lund's stern face softened into a smile. "This boat is now home from our flotilla, once exiled in Sweden. Now you are welcome to use it. We are used to jobs like this after a hundred nighttime runs across the Kattegat from Sweden to harass the Germans occupying our country." A yelled call from the deck interrupted Lund.

"*Eksplosiv. Pas på!*" A loud thud to starboard and a scraping sound unnatural to open waters echoed through the boat. Lund's head snapped forward, eyes straining into the predawn gloom. He reached for the throttle and pulled back hard. The deckhand stumbled and nearly fell overboard.

"A sighting!" Lund called out to Larry. "Hold on to something." Larry grasped a railing on the back wall. Lund turned hard to port. "The Germans left thousands of mines in these waters."

As he spoke, an earsplitting boom lifted *Klar Havn*'s stern. A hard lurch threw Lund into the wheel and Larry sprawling across the wheelhouse. Lund righted himself so swiftly Larry could believe nothing had moved him. He struggled against a sluggish rudder to right his vessel and dragged it back on course toward the far-off beacon. Within moments the steady thrum-thrum of the motor returned in Larry's ringing ears. Shouts and pounding boots told him of a crew trained for action. Reports came to Lund in rapid succession. Larry made himself disappear against the wheelhouse wall.

Five minutes later, Larry's heart was slowing toward normal and his breathing was calmer. "Still afloat," he said aloud to no one in particular, though the slanting deck was clearly not normal.

"*Takket være Gud! Det var en dud,*" Lund said. Then for Larry, "Thanks be to God! A dud. We should be splinters on a Skagen beach by now. Part of that charge did not detonate. Those German mines are powerful. Kattegatt still has many floating about. The Nazis even sunk one of their own U-boats, number 235, with one of their own mines, right here. A seven-hundred-ton vessel with full crew, all with one charge. That is how I know this one was for sure a dud."

Lund continued to fight his balky rudder, a starboard list heading for twenty degrees, and a hiccupping motor. "We will make it into Skagen Harbor," he told Larry. Then to himself, *I hope.*

"Don't be surprised, Mr. Haas," an American-accented voice said behind Larry. "If the captain says we'll make it, we will. He's done it before."

Larry turned. A man in soiled, threadbare fisherman's garb held out his hand. Something about his bearing told Larry he was military. He asked Lund, "*Er vi okay?*"

"*Ja. Naturligt!*" Lund grunted.

"During the war," the stranger said, "men like Lund made a thousand secret night runs over to Sweden. They took nearly every Danish Jew there in secret so the Nazis never got their hands on any of them. So you see? Your little jaunt was nothing for the captain. Until you almost got us blown up, that is."

"I got them . . .?"

"Like I said," the man cut him off, "just another day at the office for these guys. My name's Voss, Desmond Voss. Corporal, US Army. Medic."

"Thought so," Larry said. "Or something like that."

"Right. I was attached to the Danish resistance. After the war I volunteered to stay for the cleanup. I'm taking you home from here, Mr. Haas, at least as far as London. Your embassy has your ticket from there."

Larry whistled. "Man, that's service." He clapped Voss on the shoulder. "I understood some arrangements had been made. But not a first-class escort."

"I have been briefed, sir. My orders come from the top."

"Eisenhower?"

"No sir. His boss calls the shots." Larry remembered that meeting that "never happened" only two weeks ago in Washington. In that short time, Larry had gained a fake identity, crossed the Atlantic in hiding, murdered a friend, and nearly got blown up. Definitely *not* just another day at the office.

"Okay, Voss, what's next?"

"The rest of the story, sir. Let's go belowdecks. This will take some time and a pot of good coffee. Your long night is about to get longer."

Voss wanted everything about Larry's time at sea, especially the tactical details—the timing and logic of every decision.

Having set sail on the evening of January 3, the *Stalinabad*, a destroyer-size ship of about 7,200 tons, had made a respectable eleven-knot crossing of the Atlantic and reached the United Kingdom eleven days out from New York. After a two-day layover, she crossed the English Channel and sailed up the North Sea past Belgian, Dutch, and German ports, then paralleled the western shores of Denmark. That took them to the place Larry had chosen. His logic was simple.

Ending the Schevchenko saga in or near US territorial waters could have allowed him to wash ashore on a US beach—unacceptable. Schevchenko's end could not come in international waters—Larry's extraction there would have been impractical. As a result, fourteen days had to pass with Larry mostly in hiding until his window of opportunity opened. By sunset on January 16, the *Stalinabad* had sailed far enough north. A burial at sea there would leave Andrei unlikely to wash up soon on any European shore. Yet the deed had to be done close enough to land for Larry to escape from the ship. Larry chose the waters west of the Skagerrak Strait between Denmark and Norway—the only place that satisfied all criteria.

The audacious fishermen of Skagen Port on Denmark's northernmost spit of land could not have been better suited for the task. They hailed from Vikings who sailed these waters a thousand years before. Skagen offered safe harbor on Kattegatt Bay on the eastern shore of Denmark. From there, a railway could take Larry all the way south to the port of Esbjerg on Denmark's west coast, and a boat back to England.

"And what about Schevchenko's disappearance?" Corporal Voss asked. "We guaranteed his delivery to Russia. How will we answer for that?"

"The Soviets will have to answer to us, not the other way around. They will assume he jumped overboard, sacrificed himself to save his family, but publicly they'll probably say he got drunk and fell overboard. Everybody knew he was a heavy drinker. His family will honor his sacrifice, though it's a better tribute than he deserves."

While Larry and the corporal spoke, the struggling *Klar Havn* finally reached Skagen Point and turned south. She hugged the coast in case she had to scuttle before reaching port. The sun rose over the bay in a clearing, blue sky. The neat, yellow houses and red-tiled roofs of Skagen Port came into view as Captain Lund limped his broken boat to the dock. Larry was tired, weary in a way he had not known before. He wondered if he could ever again sleep the sleep of an innocent man. Doing the right thing still did not feel like it.

He knew he'd have time to think it all over someday, but he wished that time would never come. For now, time was short. George Bucher expected him back at Westinghouse the first Monday in February. Settling the events of the last few weeks in his mind would take much longer.

Back home, Larry tried to forget Andrei Schevchenko and everything that proceeded from that debacle. He occupied himself with the challenges of jet propulsion, the projects underway for Westinghouse and the US Navy, their quest for air superiority over the seas of the world, and planned more advanced projects to come. It was a rewarding time, peaceful, and almost forgetful enough.

But Larry Haas did not completely forget the FBI. Nor did they forget him.[5]

CHAPTER THIRTY-FIVE

Metamorphosis

In spite of the Schevchenko affair, Larry Haas stayed the same man he always was—the way a caterpillar stays the same species when it turns into a butterfly. Opportunities always did that for Larry. It took only a few small matters of unfinished business with the FBI to restart that process in early 1946.

First, there was the matter of some money Larry wanted. He went to see an agent he already knew, ASAC [Assistant SAC, second line supervisor] William C. Hinze Jr., at the Philadelphia field office. Larry still had the high-quality camera and lens that Andrei had given him, and he knew the Bureau wanted it for evidence. The opportunity was obvious. He told Hinze that he had already turned down two private offers for $300 and $315. But, as he told Hinze friend-to-friend, he thought the FBI deserved a fair chance to make their own bid.

To sweeten the deal, Larry also told Hinze that he was willing to re-establish contact with the Russians if asked.[1] After all, Larry had his own score to settle with those people. Larry reckoned the FBI could help him get some payback. The reason he wanted it came from an odd discovery about himself. It had come in his last moment with Andrei—he discovered empathy. He hated what the Soviets had done to both of them. In an odd way, Andrei deserved justice of his own for what his Soviet handlers had done to him. Larry wanted that, too.

The FBI had already bought the Franeys' camera from them, setting a precedent for Haas.[2] In the Haas case, on November 13, the Philadelphia office was advised by Hoover to immediately block Haas from disposing of his camera in any other way. The Bureau was still not sure it held evidentiary value, so it had to be saved by Haas, not by the Philadelphia office. The Haas side of the Schevchenko case evidently still held Hoover's attention, but not yet quite enough to pay him.[3]

Hinze's second request carried more portent of things to come. Though he presumed it was unlikely that Schevchenko would return to the United States "the possibility still exists that Schevchenko's confederates might attempt to recontact Loren Haas to obtain his services as a sub-agent."

This did not account for the possibility that Andrei, under ship-board interrogation, would have disclosed Haas as his betrayer.

Haas's actions aboard the *Stalinabad* are not recorded in any known official documents in the United States or Russia. They are, instead, taken from his accounts and historical deductions consistent with that event. But because secrets, no matter how well buried, have a way of coming to light, Haas apparently crafted a plan to protect himself and the agents.

In the spring of 1946, Haas created a new public record. He reported that while driving alone one sunny Monday afternoon—May 6, 1946, at about 4:30 p.m.—he was traveling north on US Route 13 through Chester, Pennsylvania. He reported that he had passed a large, black sedan—a 1941 Buick or Cadillac—driving in the opposite direction. It was carrying three passengers and a driver who looked like Andrei Schevchenko. Unfortunately, the driver wore a hat or had lowered the car's sun visor. Haas could not see the top of his head or forehead. The facial expression Haas could see only in part looked like one he had often seen on Schevchenko. Larry did not record a license number or state, so follow-up was impossible. But the sighting was a definite enough "maybe" to cast doubt on Schevchenko's demise, should any later suspicions arise.

As a result of this "sighting," agents familiar with Schevchenko were advised to make "spot checks" at Washington, Philadelphia, and New York. No record of further sightings is documented. Larry did, however, promise to call the FBI if he was contacted in any way by any Soviet person in the future.[4]

On November 20, 1946, Ladd contacted Hoover to revisit the unresolved issue of buying Haas's camera. Hoover passed it on the next day to Assistant AG Caudle in the Criminal Division. The issue was finally resolved and Larry got his money.[5]

By March of 1947 Larry had not notified the Bureau of contacts from any Soviet citizen. On April 7, however, Hoover directed Conroy to set Larry in motion toward Amtorg. Hoover said, "His contact with Amtorg should be on the basis that he is attempting to re-establish his personal friendship with Schevchenko." Hoover asked to be "promptly advised" of Haas's progress.[6]

This would cast doubt on coerced accusations Schevchenko might have made against Haas to hide his own failures. Such an attempt, however, could once again place Haas and his family in danger.

In light of that possibility, Larry wanted protection for his family against physical violence from any Soviet agent. The answer was "Maybe." Haas just might be "on his own." He also wanted protection for security clearances he hoped to need in future work.[7]

The opportunity of this renewed contact did come with danger, but it also came with intrigue and new possibilities. And as always, Haas would bet he could make the opportunity outweigh the risks.

Accepting that opportunity, however, haunted the next twenty years of Larry's life.

CHAPTER THIRTY-SIX

The Power Nexus

Larry's ambition was renewed and new power came with it. He knew he would be measured by how he used it, and he determined to use it well.

As a young man, milk and bread delivery had not been enough for Larry, so he learned money-lending. When that wasn't enough, he dreamed of flight. Aircraft work with Chevy and Curtiss Wright soon paled, so he had lied his way into Larry Bell's warplane plant, where prop-driven planes soon seemed not fast enough for him. He moved up to jets, and then from Bell to Westinghouse, where they chased higher speeds even faster. While there, Haas delivered a Grumman F6F to the Westinghouse plant as a template for wing-folding and onboard maneuverability for carrier-based jet fighters, another groundbreaking innovation.[1] Larry Haas's ambition always drove him toward the next cutting edge of progress wherever he could find it.

By 1948 Larry had decided jet fuel was only weak tea. Atomic fuel burned so much hotter and the tank just about never ran dry. Fortunately for this new interest, Larry remembered the friends he had made on the way up.

Frederick E. Flader[2] had been one of those friends at Curtiss-Wright. When they met, Larry was building and testing reciprocating engines for the production line. Fred was designing them in the Research Division. Fred had already put his name on six Curtiss-Wright patents—from amphibian landing gear to aircraft wing designs—before he set off on his own. He established the Frederick Flader Division of Eaton Manufacturing Co. and set up in the Buffalo suburb of North Tonawanda.

When Larry achieved all he wanted to at Westinghouse, he went to see Fred.[3] By then, Fred was working with the US Department of Defense (DOD). Flader's work included nuclear power research. His company prospectus said he "provided consulting services and supported the development of auxiliary equipment related to nuclear power." Fred told Larry that was only the beginning.[4]

Larry discovered that one of Fred's friends, a fellow Carnegie alumnus named Charles Wilson, was the CEO of General Motors, and he had strong WWII ties to General Eisenhower. Larry saw that such a connection could bring him within steps of the new, vast, and powerful American military-industrial complex that the war had created—a treasure trove for anyone with ambition and a willingness to work hard. Such connections were becoming the bread and butter of the worldwide nexus Larry was building around himself. Soon there would be little on which he could not consult on an international scale with credibility and authority.

One of Flader's contracts with the DOD especially intrigued Larry. It called for "development of unconventional aircraft power plants." Larry agreed that an atom-powered airplane could fly for years and never need to land—ever-ready, ever on-guard. Its super-hot reactor could drive powerful jet turbines that would need only the rarest refueling. He reasoned that such a plane could also reach astonishing speeds and altitudes. Larry knew he was not the first to think of such aircraft, but he reckoned that he and Fred could take on the challenge. Together, they had a unique combination of experience in jets, atomics, and business.

On May 28, 1946, the US Army Air Forces kicked off its project, Nuclear Energy for the Propulsion of Aircraft, Project NEPA. The aim was to build nuclear-powered, military jet aircraft. The program received ten million dollars in funding and launched in 1947.

The air force chose GE to develop one of two competing prototypes for an atomic-powered jet engine. GE's version, the DAC—Direct Air Cycle—system forced air directly through the core of a hot, onboard nuclear reactor to power its jet engine. Simultaneously, Pratt & Whitney was tapped to compete with GE by developing an IAC—Indirect Air Cycle—heat-transfer system to power its jet.

On November 6, 1946, Larry left Westinghouse. On November 15 he signed on as Flader's chief development and test engineer in Toledo, earning what Larry called "a fairly substantial salary." That was less than six months after NEPA's air force funding was approved. Larry's previous work on the P-59 for GE and the US Air Force, and his work on the Westinghouse jet project for the US Navy, were right on target for Flader's NEPA contracts.[5] Several additional military and industrial Flader contracts for jet engines and gas turbines were also about to launch. Flader's plant was considered one of the most modern in the United States for building and testing advanced jet aircraft engine prototypes.

Flader was not the only contractor close to the NEPA project. In addition to placing Larry at a nexus between General Electric, the air force, army, navy, and the DOD, it connected him with a constellation of other top-echelon researchers in nuclear and aerospace sciences. Flader was also collaborating with the University of Toledo, its School of Engineering, and its Laskey Research Center, where Larry reconnected with Westinghouse through its Toledo Division.

By 1952, Larry had moved again. He was now manager of the Turbo-Machinery Research and Development Department at Clark Brothers in Olean, New York, about seventy-five miles south of Buffalo. Clark Brothers was a world leader in industrial gas turbine research, development, and production. Clark was a unit of the multinational Dresser Industries, a pacesetter in oil and gas transmission and technology since 1880, and maybe, most important for Larry Haas, a new network of connections and a platform with international reach.

Haas's work for Clark also made him a colonel—an authentic, bemedaled, string-bean-tied and mint julip sippin' Kentucky colonel—appointed by Kentucky governor Lawrence W. Weatherby in 1954. The statement proclaiming the Honorable Loren George Hass to be a true Kentucky colonel cites both his work to bring power to the rural Kentucky community of Morehead, and "Mr. Haas' counterespionage work during World War II."[6]

Larry no longer thought much about the fact that less than three years earlier his rise within Bell had attracted the attention of three of the world's most powerful leaders—Roosevelt, Truman, and Stalin—and their intelligence services, but he remained in direct contact with the FBI in investigation of Soviet espionage.[7] His profile was now exponentially higher, but such dark memories, when they arose, did not temper his ambition.

With the jet age and the atomic age advancing at a fevered pace around the world, the Soviets naturally thought *"Atomnyy reaktivnyy samolet"* made as much sense as "Nuclear powered jet airplane" did in the United States.

The burgeoning Soviet spy network that succeeded Schevchenko in the United States had never lost interest in Larry. Operatives quickly realized that few men in the United States carried a dossier as uniquely and broadly suited to the subject of atomic jets as Haas. He had become a unique, one-man nexus within his own vast network of strategic connections.

Many American engineers and scientists like Larry also engaged in work important to national security. In that respect, Larry was only one of thousands of such key personnel to benefit from some level of FBI interest during those years. Larry, however, plied his craft best under the radar. Confidential connections had become a rare and increasingly valuable commodity as the Cold War restructured world commerce.

The Soviets watching Larry by now may have been uncertain about whether Larry was a trustworthy intelligence source. In 1944 and 1945, they had trusted him based on Andrei's approval. But Andrei himself had eventually been judged untrustworthy. The Soviets apparently settled on a compromise judgment—Haas was unpredictable but he might not be unusable. As a result, Andrei's successors kept an eye on Andrei's old friend.

The watchers, however, were also being watched. The FBI was not about to let any more spies slip through their fingers. The Schevchenko case still smoldered in J. Edgar Hoover's memory. Although he knew the matter had been "handled," public interest in the Schevchenko case had not died. Somebody had bungled that case, and certain factions in Washington meant for somebody to pay.

When the press and Congress asked the question again in 1949, FBI director Hoover, US Attorney General Thomas Clark, Secretary of State James Byrnes, and President Harry Truman all replied, in one politically crafty way or another, "Not me. It was him."

The truth, though seventy-five years late, is finally out.

Chapter Thirty-seven

HUAC and the Blame Game

Monday morning at 10:30, June 6, 1949. At the Old House Office Building,
Washington, DC, Room 226. HUAC: Session 1

The war was over and won, but even in victory people remembered the battles that had been lost. Fortunately, there was enough blame to be placed that pundits and politicians could keep themselves busy with it for years to come. The bungled case of Andrei Ivanovich Schevchenko, in particular, remained a perfect target for after-the-fact fault finding. Soviet spies represented a convenient link from past failures to new and present dangers. Many years later, Hubert H. Humphrey, thirty-eighth vice president of the United States, said it most succinctly. "To err is human. To blame someone else is politics."[1]

Three-and-a-half years had passed and HUAC decided it was high time to investigate. They called on Haas, Franey, and the Schevchenko case for an encore. A Russian spy had slipped through everybody's fingers and by 1949 it mattered again. A new Red Menace was rising.

On June 6, 1949, during the first session of the eighty-first Congress, HUAC convened a hearing, open to the public, titled "Soviet Espionage Activities in Connection with Jet Propulsion and Aircraft."[2] This hearing promised to fix weak spots in the national defense. Schevchenko's shadowy accomplices—if any remained at large—and new spy networks growing out of those connections had become priority targets.

HUAC's purpose, since its creation in 1938, had been to probe charges of disloyalty to the United States. It focused on subversive actions by private citizens, public employees, and groups that collaborated with foreign enemies, especially the Soviet communists.

In the minds of Loren G. Haas and Leona and Joseph Franey, this investigation would come too late—except as an opportunity to finally be heard. They had risked much and been acknowledged little. Worse, they were denied the public satisfaction of seeing Schevchenko caught, publicly tried, and punished before the American people. Schevchenko had tried to sabotage the American way of life. For Larry, however, the rest of the story had to remain buried at sea.

On arriving home Wednesday evening, May 4, 1949, Larry was mystified by an odd story Dorothy told him. He immediately called Agent Dooley at the FBI's Buffalo field office to report it. Special Agent Edwin F. Dooley answered the phone, but after listening carefully, he said he could not answer a single one of Larry's questions.

A man Dorothy did not know had telephoned her at home alone that afternoon. He said he and another man would be at her house at seven o'clock. They wanted to see Larry but would not say why. He did, however, claim to represent a congressional investigating committee.

Dooley was as mystified as Haas. Teletype messages immediately flew up the chain of command to land on the director's desk. Word returned within the hour that the Bureau simply knew nothing of the matter. And worse, they had no advice for Larry. He was on his own.

When the committee men arrived, first they made sure they had their man. This Loren Haas, they confirmed, was the one who had worked at Bell and Westinghouse, so this was the man who had known Andrei Ivanovich Schevchenko. When Larry asked who gave them his name, they simply named the person as "a source" but assured him it was neither the FBI nor anyone he knew.

Larry decided to stonewall them. He objected to their intrusion and refused to say anything they thought they were entitled to know about Schevchenko.

They spoke of other people—names withheld, but people who could only have been the Franeys—people they said had been eager to talk. Nevertheless, if Larry refused, he would soon receive a subpoena summoning him to appear at Washington, DC, before HUAC, scheduled to convene on June 6, 1949.[3]

In a final bid for Larry's cooperation, one of the men explained "they felt that the FBI was doing a good job in the espionage investigations, but that there were limitations placed on the FBI. The Schevchenko case should have been prosecuted, but the hands of the FBI were tied. The Un-American

Activities Committee was attempting to bring before the public the limitations placed on the Bureau by other government agencies."[4]

Nothing they said surprised Larry, but he operated on a simpler principle—everything in its place. He would respond to a subpoena and answer to the committee in Washington if subpoenaed. His living room was not that place.

The committee operated as a bipartisan body under its chairman, a Democrat from Georgia, John Wood, along with four additional Democrats and four Republicans. For this meeting the lineup was selectively pared down to include only its ex-military, ex-FBI, and elected anti-communist members.

Two Republicans and two Democrats were absent, including Chairman Wood. Francis Walter, a Pennsylvania Democrat, would preside. Walter was a seasoned US naval warrior who would offer no quarter to a vanquished foe. In 1944, he infamously presented President Roosevelt with a hand-carved letter opener crafted from an arm bone of a dead Japanese soldier. Roosevelt did not thank Walter. He had the odious thing buried.

Frank Tavenner, HUAC's lawyer and chief interrogator, had served as acting chief of counsel at the Tokyo War Crimes Tribunal against Japan's leaders. In rough terms, he was the Pacific counterpart to Justice Robert H. Jackson, who led the prosecution of Nazi war criminals at Nuremburg. Tavenner knew how to prosecute enemies.

Louis Russell, a ten-year veteran of the FBI, was HUAC's senior investigator. A colleague, Harold Velde, Republican from Illinois, had served as a special agent for the FBI's sabotage and counterespionage division until three years before this hearing.

The committee's director of research, Benjamin Mandel, was an outspoken ex-communist who had once been the business manager of the CPUSA newspaper, the *Daily Worker*. He had turned and now had no tolerance for the government's failure to prosecute any Soviet communist, especially Schevchenko.

Also present was HUAC member Morgan Moulder, an attorney, judge, and U.S. Representative from Missouri (D) respected for fair and balanced deliberations. His later career revealed a strong commitment to racial and social justice.

Richard M. Nixon, the other Republican on the committee, was a thirty-six-year-old California lawyer-turned-congressman known for his strong anti-communist views. He listened to the first witness with an intensity she could almost feel.

Attorney Tavenner handed Leona Franey a picture. "Whose photograph is that?"

"Andrei Schevchenko."

"His date of departure from the United States was on January 3, 1946," Tavenner said, "and his present whereabouts and occupational assignment are unknown. Will you tell the committee, in your own way, what occurred in the course of your various meetings with Mr. Schevchenko?"

Leona told the committee that Schevchenko had not raised much suspicion until he began asking for classified documents on jet propulsion. "That had nothing to do with the airplanes the Russians were buying," Leona said indignantly. "That made me suspicious."

"That was when the FBI contacted me," she added. "I was at the point where I was wondering why he was asking for that material. I asked the other girls in the library not to issue material on jet propulsion to him, that if he asked for it to just walk to the files and pretend the material was out, whether it was or not." Leona thought for a moment and added, "I have a typewritten list of the secret information he wanted. I turned it over to the FBI."

Tavenner made it Exhibit 1.

"Sometimes he asked on a daily basis. He knew the confidential code numbers assigned by NACA as much as two weeks to two months before we received the reports. He wanted 35-millimeter microfilm of classified reports. My husband was to photograph them for twenty-five to thirty dollars each. All of it was done under FBI supervision, but only of unclassified material. Mr. Schevchenko was always very, very nervous. He smoked one cigarette after another and seldom listened to what you had to say. He liked to issue the orders and have you move as he said."

"Did he ever complain that the information you were furnishing to him was of no value?" Walter asked.

"Yes, he did, in no uncertain terms. Then he asked my husband to get data from Hooker Electro-Chemical Company. Under the supervision of the FBI, the officials of the company had given him a brochure of the products they manufactured, and we carried that package into the Amtorg Corporation in New York."

Nixon shifted impatiently in his seat, eager to pose questions of his own, but Walter signaled him to wait. Mr. Moulder asked only four questions to confirm testimony Leona had already given. Walter then nodded to Nixon.

"You said Schevchenko had confidential code numbers," Nixon said, "for confidential documents? Did he get them from anybody at Bell?"

"No, Mr. Schevchenko got them from NACA in Washington. They were stamped 'Restricted.' And he got some from his cohort, Nicolai Ostrovsky, a Russian military man who often went to Wright Field at Dayton, Ohio."

"So," Nixon said, "whether someone got the confidential code numbers at Wright Field or in Washington, it was *not* some individual at Bell who gave him the illegal material?"

"That is correct," Leona said with certainty.

"That is all." Nixon appeared particularly satisfied with her last answer and sat back, yielding back to Tavenner.[5]

Tavenner turned to Larry Haas. He began by reconfirming Schevchenko's identity with the same photo he showed Leona. He addressed Mr. Haas in a formal, courtroom tone.[6] "Will you state to the committee what proposals were made by Mr. Schevchenko to you regarding information concerning the aircraft business?"

"Maybe I shouldn't say so, but the Russian was an excessive drinker. Maybe he had some doubts in his mind as to my sincerity. When we drank together, on number of occasions, he put it this way, 'You should make no bones about helping me. I am a Russian, that is true, and you are an American; but we can't let nationalities interfere with progress. Scientists must be international.' And I do know that viewpoint does exist with many American scientists.

"Once while we were drinking, Mr. Schevchenko bragged that he knew presidents of leading organizations in our country, and he named several. He had dinner with them and they told him about their projects. He knew secrets only those involved in the development game would know. He knew of a jet engine manufactured by the General Electric Company before it was released for any source of publication. In fact, it was in the secret stage." Larry gathered his thoughts, recalling more ominous possibilities.

"If Mr. Schevchenko had been able to gather the information he wanted, and had the help to do it, four years ago the Russians could have had the aircraft we have today. That is why this information on Mrs. Franey's list was so important to him, and why he gave me the same list."

"Did he offer you payments for the information?" Tavenner asked.

"He did pay in values of a hundred or two hundred dollars, but often I had no information for him. Truly secret information had to be screened through proper channels. I tried to stall him so information could be cleared and doctored and prepared; and in some cases, it was impossible to obtain the information. I hedged by saying if he was patient, something much better was coming."

Harold Velde took up the questioning. "Do you feel he committed any active espionage, or was engaged in a conspiracy to commit an active espionage?"

"Definitely!"

"He never was arrested?" Velde asked, appearing astonished, though his dramatics seemed a bit hammy to Larry.

"No. And I am glad you brought that up. My wife and I and the Franeys became involved for at least a year during which we were subject to dealing with a character who was a potential murderer and a thief. The Amtorg Corporation was headquarters for the NKVD and Mr. Schevchenko was supposedly in charge of Amtorg. Anyone could put two and two together and be restless.

"I feel, and I am sure the Franeys feel, that Schevchenko was not merely a Russian, but a potential murderer and thief. He tried to give the Russian government weapons with which to murder us. And if they won out, they would take everything away from us.

"Frankly, if I had known Schevchenko would be let go, I wouldn't have done it. If, in good faith you help this government of ours, doing a good deed to restrain an individual such as Schevchenko, and the FBI says they have an airtight case, but you are passed off with such answers as, 'Well, Mr. Burns of the State Department says we can't touch him ...'"

"Who told you that?" Walter interrupted.

"Members of the Federal Bureau of Investigation."

"Who were they?"

"That was so long ago I can't remember their names just now. Maybe I can."

At this point Wood interrupted and closed the open session to be reconvened in closed session. He wanted to dig deeper into Larry's statement behind closed doors to guard against inadvertent public disclosures of more sensitive information.[7]

Following the closed session, Larry was surprised that Congressman Nixon asked for a private conversation.

"I looked into your background to prepare for this session," Nixon said. "I liked what I saw and decided to give you some protection."

"Thank you, but I didn't know I needed any."

"There was a suggestion that you could have been an accomplice. This committee has to place some blame, if it can. Then somebody can take credit for doling out punishment. I asked the questions I needed to ask to show Schevchenko didn't need you. He had a direct channel from Washington and Wright Field to the Bell library, long before you could have had access to the information he wanted."

Larry was stunned. "Thank you," was all he could manage. He saw that Nixon had oversimplified the entire affair for his benefit. This was a legal mind that could straighten crooked lines and probably twist straight lines crooked, if he thought he had to.

"Let me buy you a cup of coffee," Nixon said.[8]

The next day the committee initiated a new series of interviews—some called them an inquisition—of Robert Oppenheimer and his alleged contacts with Soviet spies hunting A-bomb secrets. Oppenheimer had spearheaded the Manhattan Project to create the atomic bombs. The June 7 HUAC meeting stretched into twelve volumes of transcript. Larry Haas and Robert Oppenheimer had been hosted by the committee at the same hotel and met there, beginning another friendship based on much in common in intellect, temperament, and outlook.[9]

By 1951, recriminations and repercussions of the government's failure to prosecute Schevchenko had still not entirely disappeared. HUAC published a report titled, "The Shameful Years—Thirty Years of Soviet Espionage in the United States."[10] It reported, in part:

> The policy of appeasement then in existence prohibited the arrest of Andrei Schevchenko, as he was allowed to return to Russia. However, in his case there is a strong possibility that his Soviet superiors have not looked too kindly upon the miserable manner in which he carried out his assignments, and it is improbable that Schevchenko is enjoying the glorious benefits of the Soviet life he so glowingly depicted to the Franeys.

Haas's name was omitted from that statement. The description of Andrei Schevchenko's operations relies only on the Franeys' activities and testimony. The strategy in play for Larry's protection was to remove his name as far as possible from Schevchenko's work and disappearance. As early as March 1946, Larry had offered the FBI his continuing services against Soviet intelligence, a relationship best maintained without Larry's name in any official commentary or publication.[11]

CHAPTER THIRTY-EIGHT

A Cover-up Exposed

Only one day after the HUAC hearings, newspapers across the country carried sensational stories, some bannered on page one, built on detailed accounts of Haas's and the Franeys' testimony. Along with those came strong, bombastic denials from Washington concerning blame for the failure, tantamount to refusal, to prosecute Schevchenko. The officials most often accused included FBI director John Edgar Hoover, US Attorney General Thomas Clark, Secretary of State James Byrnes, and President Harry Truman. Undersecretary of State Acheson, however, seemed to dodge most of the bullets.

Reporters of the day and later historians frequently refer to the United States' reluctance to embarrass the Soviets—the US ally against the Germans and the Japanese—by prosecuting a Soviet official for spying against the United States. Nevertheless, to many people who were less concerned with diplomacy, that was a wrong decision, even cowardly. It was not an easy matter to dodge in 1945, and the issue, continuing to simmer even after the war, came back to a boil in 1949. Blame simply had to be placed.

Though no statistical analysis is made, one individual appears to have been most prominently blamed and to have answered with the most full-throated protests and denials. That person was Secretary of State James Byrnes. The *New York Journal-American* exposés had directly blamed him. The FBI agents involved in the case at that time told Larry Haas and the Franeys that they blamed Byrnes, but they could not or would not cite their source. Byrne's denials, however, abounded in the press. So, for the public's assignment of blame, many might have relied on Shakespeare.[1] To paraphrase, "The culprit doth protest too much." But that was populist folly, at best.

First-person accounts by participants in an event can sometimes provide the most telling testimony, especially if recorded in real time in that person's own hand. In this case, that person was J. Edgar Hoover. He was known for adding notes to memos, teletype messages, and reports sent to him, and then returning them to the sender with comments handwritten in his unique blue ink. Those infamous messages came to be known throughout the Bureau as blue bombs, often signed with his distinctive "*H.*"

As an example, on June 8, 1949, concerning the testimony taken two days earlier at the HUAC hearing, Hoover reacted to flaws he saw in the various agents' management of the entire Schevchenko case. He responded on page five of Ladd's account with penned-in notes about mishandled information. He did not like agents telling informants that their hands were tied and it was Byrnes's fault. The final note is a typical Hoover blue bomb. He wrote:

> There was just too much talking in the field. The staff here must learn it is to convey instructions and must not elaborate on reasons, etc. H.[2]

During the "Hot Potato" runaround, Hoover penned another "blue bomb" at the end of Ladd's 10/1/45 memo. If refusing to act when action is needed is the same as an order to *not* act, then Hoover unequivocally placed the blame for Schevchenko's escape squarely on the shoulders of US Attorney General Thomas Clark. The blue bomb said,

> It is now up to the A. G. Our investigation is finished. No arrest can be made until we get specific clearance from the A. G. H.[3]

Clark knew the diplomatic dangers of arresting Schevchenko and he knew the laws Schevchenko had broken. Clark's choice of diplomacy over justice was the one-compromise-too-far that finally infuriated Hoover and Haas.

Hoover had placed the blame squarely at Clark's doorstep,[4] and then he didn't.

In a letter to AG Clark just before the HUAC hearing of June 6, 1949, Hoover shifted the buck to Acheson "inasmuch as there may be publicity as a result [of the hearings]."[5]

So, whether Hoover blamed Clark or Acheson, the Bureau's work had been blocked. Schevchenko was made free to go home to Russia. But loathe to be thwarted, Hoover apparently prepared his own version of justice. He was ready to deploy it in December of 1945. Howard Rushmore, the *New York Journal-American*, and the American people would serve as prosecutor, judge, and jury.

If Hoover pulled that trigger, he could make sure Schevchenko would pay.

CHAPTER THIRTY-NINE

Killing Me Seven Times

An unintended consequence of Schevchenko's 1945 trial and conviction by the press, if not by the courts, was the seismic shift it caused in Larry Haas's life. That change was both immediate and deadly, but its aftershocks continued for years with even more lethal aftereffects.

By 1953, the Schevchenko case had finally receded behind new geopolitical storms taking shape around the world. In that environment, the Soviet spy network inside the United States had to grow. With heavy reliance on human intelligence (humint), the Soviet spy apparatus searched tirelessly for people whose knowledge intersected their interests.

As Larry Haas expanded his connections in the booming, postwar military-industrial and scientific complex, his work often converged with the interests of international powers vying for supremacy, most notably, the USSR and the United States. Renewed Soviet interest in Larry Haas was, naturally, an unintended consequence of Larry's ongoing successes.

Humint is gained either by cooperation or by control of a target source. If Larry would not cooperate, intimidation and coercion could be considered if the intelligence value seemed high enough. Many such cases checkered Cold War history.

Larry Haas's case is not unique, but it is among the strangest. Some of the worst events in Kay Haas's life coincided with some of the highest points in her father's career and the world events he was connected with. Such a recurring pattern could not have been coincidental. Kay's experiences and conviction remains that Soviet agents used her as the fulcrum by which to force her father to open his network of influence and intelligence to them.

Seven of those events spanning twenty years of Kay's memory stand out vividly. The first one was the botched abduction that nearly killed her in

September 1945. The next one came eight years later in the summer of 1953, late at night in Kay's bedroom in Olean, New York.[1]

———•———

In Kay's words . . .

This, I believe, was the second attempt on my life.

The fact that my father worked for Fred Flader was not a secret. Anyone with some knowledge of Flader's work would have known he had access to the newest research on atomic-powered aircraft. Soviet research on the subject was also underway, but it was not limited to their own laboratories. Spies were among their best "lab assistants." That method of information gathering, however, was not unique to them. Just about every other major world power used similar methods.

Soviet agents in the years after Schevchenko must have studied his detailed and extensive files. Andrei would have revealed that Larry Haas never simply did his job. He absorbed it. He mastered its depths, added to it, and innovated. He worked that way for his own satisfaction as much as for his employer's profit. He had never felt a desire for advanced degrees, but he developed every job as if it would produce a PhD thesis. A paycheck never kept him in a job for long after he learned all he could, though he always gave his employer a fair return for the opportunities he enjoyed.

In the spring of 1953, my father reported that somebody had rifled his desk and inspected his lab late one night at the Clark Brother's plant. The snooper had tripped an alarm on entry but made a quick, professional job of it before he left and the security detail showed up.

Regardless of security measures wherever he worked, my father had his own, quirky habits to back them up. He always booby-trapped his desk drawers, office doors, and file cabinets with simple, harmless telltales. A single hair weakly glued on a cabinet drawer or door jamb, or a desk drawer left ajar by exactly three millimeters, would reveal tampering without alerting the one doing the tampering.

In this case, he discovered that his intruder had looked through every drawer of his desk but taken nothing. He had simply left a note beside the desk phone. "Larry! Make your mark."

My father understood. Someone was inviting him to leave a chalk mark on any lamppost near the plant. It would tell whoever that person was that he was willing to make contact. It was a dead-drop signal Andrei had taught him in 1945 in case he wanted my father to drop a secret message or parcel at a location not under surveillance. Andrei had never activated the dead-drop protocol, but my father never forgot it.

He told Fred Flader and his FBI contacts what he surmised about the break-in that had called out plant security only to find nothing missing. My father did not leave his mark. That apparently left only one option open for the intruder—control over collaboration.

Our new house presented an opportunity for intrusion we were not prepared for.

We had lived in my grandmother Florence Saylor's house on Third Street in Olean, New York, for three and a half years after my abduction. That would have been from about the end of 1945 until mid-1948 when I was finally allowed to return to school, in fourth grade. I was totally unprepared for it, having not been allowed out of my grandmother's house all that time. It had also been a time when my father was almost never home. From there, we moved to the nearby Linwood Apartments, where we stayed for about four or five years.

We had come to feel secure in Olean. It was a prosperous city of twenty-five thousand built on an older legacy of timber and newer oil wealth and, back in Prohibition days, a brief flirtation with rum-running.

By the summer of 1953, when I was about thirteen, between my eighth- and ninth-grade years, Dad finished building us a new home. It was high up on Van Buren Avenue, a sparsely populated, wooded hillside overlooking the city. Our new home was beautiful, built on three levels. The garage on the left side of the house was the lowest section. My bedroom was on the level that overlooked its roof. The hillside we were on sloped just enough that the back end of that roof was no more than man-height from the ground. It was tarred and had gravel loosely spread across its surface. A higher, wooded area stood about 150 feet behind the house beyond a wide backyard.

I remember the day we moved in. We were in a hurry. My dad had to leave for Saudi Arabia in just three days. He had been hired by the Arabian-American Oil Company, Aramco, to engineer the installation of a vast, new pipeline network across the desert. I learned years later that the company had pumped more than three hundred million barrels of crude from 130 wells just the year before and then discovered their three separate oil fields were really all part of one vast superfield. They expected soon to pump more oil than ever before, so they needed new and better pipelines to pump it all to their refineries and seaports.

About a week after moving into our new house, almost the only one high up on the heavily wooded hillside overlooking the city, my sister told me that for a couple of days when she was outside playing in the yard, she thought she saw someone watching our house from the woods way out behind the back yard. She was only about nine years old and used to construction workers around the property, so she paid little attention to it. However, after a few more days seeing the same figure in the shadows, she came to my room with something new.

"I think there's somebody in the garage, Bunny," she said, "come and look."

"It's probably just Mom."

"He has a hat on."

We walked out to the garage hand in hand and peered around the corner. A dark, unrecognizable shadow lurked in the back of the garage. Our sudden appearance apparently alarmed whoever it was. The figure turned quickly to the open back door, ran from the garage, and disappeared into the woods. We ran into the house, locked the doors, and shut the windows.

Night had nearly fallen and our house had become a very lonely and eerie place up on that hill. At the time there were no other houses nearby and no streetlights anywhere along the road.

We told our mom quite excitedly. She told us we were just imagining things, calm down, stop the nonsense, and get ready for bed. Something told me, though, that she wasn't too convinced of that imagination stuff, herself, and her annoyance might not have been entirely with us. On the way back to my room, I saw her pull the curtain aside and look out the kitchen window toward the woods.

Later that same night, I was awakened by a crunching sound coming from the gravel on the garage roof. It had happened every night for about a week after we were in bed. Judy had her own room, but both of us had heard the sounds. At first, we thought it was just a raccoon or a squirrel, but before long our imaginations had delivered a bear creeping from the deep woods behind our house.

I had left my window open, naively hoping the screen would keep out whatever it was, just in case it came back. My room had twin beds and I slept in the one farther from the window. This night, I heard the crunching again, looked up, and saw something pass in front of the stars.

In the light of a full moon, the silhouette of a man appeared. He was kneeling down just outside the window. As I lay very still and watched, he cut the screen with a knife, first from one corner diagonally to the other and then in the other direction, slicing a huge X. I was so horrified that I was paralyzed. I couldn't move. I couldn't even scream. He slowly and silently lowered himself down onto the spare bed under the window.

Fortunately, my bed was closer to the door. As his feet touched the other bed, I came to my senses, rolled off the bed, and ran to my mom's room. I heard sounds from my room but the man did not chase me.

Mom rummaged frantically in her bedside table. I could hardly believe I saw a gun in her hand as she ran out of the room toward the garage. I don't know which frightened me more, but I decided I was safer following her.

At the open garage door she flashed the inside lights on and off a couple of times. She told me it was a signal to the FBI men who were always on watch not far from the house. Apparently, the intruder realized his bird had flown. He had climbed back through the window, jumped from the porch roof, and run into the woods. The lawn wasn't seeded yet so his tracks were clear but he was gone.

Mom stood in the garage for a while talking with the two men who had come running to her signal. I couldn't sleep and stood listening behind her.

"What happened, Mom?" I asked. "Did those men find the guy?"

"Oh! You startled me," she said, turning to see me. "I didn't expect you to stay up. Go to bed. Now."

"But, Mom . . ."

"Ask your father!" She told the men good night, went into her bedroom, and slammed the door.

One morning a few days later, my mom told me to get some lunch money from her purse. But instead of lose change, I discovered a pistol.

"Be careful, Bunny," she said. "It's loaded."

———◦•◦———

The peacefulness of Olean's streets proved deceptive again.

By the spring of 1954, I was on the varsity cheerleading squad. After-school practice required a long walk home every day. I knew a shortcut across a long, high viaduct just outside the back door of the school. It shortened my walk by a mile and bypassed Olean's run-down Boardmanville district. Whenever my schedule called for me to walked home, one of the agents would wait at the far end of the viaduct.

One day after practice, about five o'clock, I started out along the viaduct. When I was about a third of the way across, a man, who I thought was a lo-cal resident saving himself a few steps like I was, suddenly ran at me. Before I could react, he grabbed me. One strong hand circled my throat. My books went flying. I gave him as good a fight as I could, but I was small, off-guard, and no match for him. He pressed me against the side rail to hold me still. I could see that if I tried to jump, I would drop onto the busy railroad tracks far below at the outskirts of the city's factory district.

Seeing the sudden tussle, the agent ran toward us as fast as he could and landed a solid punch in the middle of the man's face. I ran for home as fast as I could. The man ran the other way.

Later that night my dad and the agent talked for a long time.

"You okay, Bunny?" Dad looked into my eyes.

"Sure, Dad." I rubbed the red marks on my neck.

"I work for people who can pay for what I can do," Dad said, trying to explain what he thought had happened. "But some people I say no to don't like that answer."

"Schev's old friends?"

"Naturally!" Dad was surprised I had put that together. "The people I used to work for want to scare me into giving them a different answer." He looked at the agent and muttered two words. "Damn Russians."

The next year, my sophomore year at Olean High School, I started dating. We had no idea how dangerous that could be.

———◆———

In the autumn of 1954, the visitor returned, or someone very much like him. And, once again, it coincided with highly guarded military and defense projects my father was working on.

During that year, I had heard my father mention corporations he was doing business with. They included not only Flader, but Westinghouse, Dresser-Rand Gas Turbine, General Dynamics, and many other names I didn't know. I asked him if he worked for all of them all at once. That's when he explained what consultant meant. He said he was the kind called a project management consultant. He had connected everything and everyone he knew into one grand design. Money had never seemed his prime motivator, but this arrangement paid him much more than any of the companies could have alone.

The work my father was doing commonly paralleled similar work being done in a number of fields around the world. As dissimilar as atomic power, jet airplanes, and enormous, desert-crossing oil pipelines might seem, they all needed high-speed turbines. By the early 1950s, my father had quietly become one of the foremost turbine research, development, and application specialists in the field. Whenever possible, however, he "flew under the radar." He avoided fame so he could more easily work across geopolitical and military-industrial lines.

Some of those geopolitical lines, however, separated competing world interests in which his knowledge and influence made him a target.

In 1952, for example, the Soviet navy initiated Project 627 to build their first nuclear submarine, an attack-class boat called the *K-3 Leninsky Komsomol*, designed to launch atomic torpedoes at enemy harbors and coastal cities. In June 1954, they finally laid down the keel for their first boat, the *K-3* Кит (*Keet*, meaning Whale). *K-3* was destined for the Soviet navy's Northern Fleet and an expedition to the North Pole *under* the ice, the holy grail for both sides. The Soviet Union set a high priority on catching up with the United States in nuclear-powered submarines. From the outset, their Soviet nuclear submarine fleet suffered from hurried production. One price it paid was poor workmanship. Crew safety engineering, for example, lagged significantly behind the rest of the work. Testing and sea trial timetables were also too tight. Many Soviet naval officers believed the ships, when launched, would be unfit for active duty and combat. The Soviet Union was too late to catch up with the United States.

On January 21, 1954, the United States had launched the world's first nuclear submarine, the Nautilus, SSN-571, built by General Dynamics. It was powered by a Westinghouse Electric Corporation nuclear reactor and a specially designed steam turbine on which my father had worked, reprising both Westinghouse turbines and Flader atomics connections by shifting his focus from air to sea.

Soviet espionage, naturally, targeted the Nautilus program. My father was not the only American approached, cajoled, or suborned by Soviet intelligence, but the agents assigned to watch me stepped up to high alert.

The Soviet Project 627 reactor was designed by a brilliant Soviet academician, Anatoly Alexandrov. Nevertheless, whatever else they could learn from the US playbook could only accelerate that work. Once again, my father was an American engineer with something the Soviets wanted. All they needed, they apparently reckoned, was the right leverage to get his cooperation.

Though warned, my father did not, at first, seem to fear repeated Soviet interference in our lives. As a matter of fact, the Nautilus project was one of the few times he went out of his way to do a little showing off, at least for his family.

My father and his brother, my uncle Bob, had been lifelong friends. Bob's daughters—my cousins Betty and Carolyn—recall receiving occasional postcards their uncle Larry sent bearing exotic postmarks from around the world. Their dad generally would not explain why their uncle traveled so much. "It's best not to know" was his usual answer. But once, tired of the questions, he divulged just enough to make the mystery even deeper.

"Washington sent him there," their father told them. "He's a kind of spy, I think. But don't ask me for anything more."

Late in 1954, another of those cryptic postcards arrived at Uncle Bob's house. This time it was postmarked from Groton, Connecticut. My dad said he was on a consulting project for the General Dynamics Electric Boat Company. He invited Uncle Bob, Aunt Carol, Betty, and Carolyn to all come see something "like the world has never seen." When they arrived, my father greeted them from the deck of the USS *Nautilus*. The world's first atomic submarine was certainly something few people would ever get to see. My father just called it a little "project" he had been involved with for a while. After all, he pointed out, high-speed turbines powered by a nuclear reactor are not really that different from jet engines.

That magnificent boat sat high in the water beside its dock, a midnight-black vessel 320 feet long. The atomic reactor in its belly was close kin to the bombs that had incinerated two great Japanese cities and 200,000 people only nine years before. My father had helped turn that terrible force into something more measured. Now it could drive this sea monster and its crew of 105 beneath the deepest of seas at unheard-of speeds.

That was probably my dad's way of answering Betty and Carol's questions and giving his brother more insight into his work than he had before or ever would again. What my father did not figure on, however, was the interest of other watchful eyes.

Shortly after that time, Dad came home for another short stay. I couldn't wait to tell him my own good news. In September of that year, 1954, my sophomore year at Olean High School, I had been elected vice president of my class.

Sometimes the class officers met at each other's homes, which were scattered all around the school district. That, like any activity that kept me out after schooltime, especially after dark, was an obstacle, but we solved this one with an arrangement that called for either my dad or the principal to drive me home. I do not remember his full name anymore, but we called him Prof Smith.

One night after the meeting, it was Prof Smith's turn to bring me home. The sun was long past setting and our unlighted street was as dark as a long country road. Prof Smith's headlights shone like searchlights up Van Buren Avenue as we neared my home. The stillness of the night was broken only by cricket sounds and a soft breeze in the treetops when Prof drove into my driveway. I thanked him for the ride and stepped out of the car.

I turned to walk toward my house and was surprised by seeing a deeper darkness where the garage door should have been. Someone must have left it open. The blackness looked like a cave mouth waiting to swallow me. It was a little eerie and I tried not to notice it.

As I started walking up the driveway slope, Prof Smith beeped his horn once. It was a signal to my parents saying I was home. He waved goodbye and turned his car around to head back down the hill. As he did so, his headlights slewed across the open garage door. For the briefest of instants light flooded the space. Prof's attention must have been already turned to the street or he would have seen the man.

I was startled. The man wore a trench coat and hat like the one Dad always wore and stood a couple of feet from our front steps, where they turned right and toward our front door. I called out.

"Dad, what are you doing out here in the dark?" At exactly that moment the front door of my house opened and my father stepped out.

The figure in the garage braced himself to run, shoved something shiny into his pocket, ducked behind our car, and fled out the back door of the garage. He easily outran the agent who just made it to the curb in front of our house in time to see the man disappear into the woods.

I raced up the steps, past my father, and into the house. From his position, he could not have seen the man in the garage.

"Dad, you're here," I gasped.

"Where else, Bunny? Somebody had to watch this TV."

"But Dad," I said. "I thought that was you!" I pointed back toward the open garage door.

Seconds later, the man who had started giving chase returned empty-handed and was joined on our doorstep by a second man. I told them and my father what I had seen.

"It's time for some explaining, Larry," one of them told my father. "She needs the same warnings you get." Dad invited them into our living room for the chat.

One of the men spoke directly to me. "The more you travel outside your home, the easier it will be for them to get to you. But be careful. If a direct assault does not work, they might try something more friendly looking. That could be even more dangerous."

They were obviously assuming I knew much more than I did. I told them I was mystified and wouldn't they please start over at the beginning? I glared at my father. He had told me nothing about something I obviously should have known.

That was when I finally learned the whole story about FBI protection, Soviet spies, and my father's dangerous work. After that long-overdue history lesson, he told me about something else that had happened quite recently. They had intercepted something they called "new radio traffic" that hinted at bad people with renewed interest in my father's work. I soon realized that life as I knew it had probably changed forever. It was time for me to get used to it.

Before long, a confluence of events in the United States and around the world—unrelated except for threads of each woven into my father's network—reached me again.

⸻ ◆ ⸻

Soon, Dad left on business once more. A few long, uneventful months passed before he returned. Naturally, as always, Judy and I greeted him with a thousand questions. This time he was happy to explain. He had been to the Middle East, consulting with Aramco in Dhahran. It was a place on the Persian Gulf coast of Arabia's Eastern Province. Judy and I loved his new look, bald and tanned as a brown hen's egg. He explained that in Arabia, the desert sun, the sand, and the heat were simply easier to take without hair.

"So, Dad," I couldn't wait to ask, "what were you doing in a weird place like that?"

"I lived at the place called Main Camp," he said, as if I'd know what that was. "The oil company built it for all us foreigners. We were pumping oil out of the desert. My group worked on the Trans-Arabian Pipeline, the Tapline. It is a good 750 miles long. They hired me for two reasons, to help stabilize the pipeline over stretches of unstable sand and because I am a turbine pump expert. That pipe delivers a couple hundred thousand barrels of crude every day for a thousand tankers that show up thirsty in Sidon Harbor every year. My job was to fine-tune the flow."

"Sounds like a really big job," I said. "I bet you had a good team."

"Not really. Not much hustle in those guys. Triple-digit temperatures, no shade, and a million miles of sand will slow men down. But their king wanted his oil to flow."

"So, what did you do?"

"It only took a trip to the motor pool and the camp hardware store." Dad winked at me.

"Oh, no. You didn't!" I knew Dad's tricks.

"Naturally. I built them a still."

"What did you brew this time?" I couldn't help laughing.

"Whatever I could get. They have a lovely dish over there, it's called *kabsah*, spiced rice and meat. Fifty-pound bags of rice for food was easy to buy without any questions. I liked it. It's cheap and it ferments."

"Sounds tricky," I said, meaning dangerous. "Isn't alcohol against their religion?"

"They call it *khamr*—all intoxicants in general, alcohol in particular. But I found the average man there was only a little more devout than the average American. That rule is strict, but it is mostly enforced by making alcohol hard to find. So, if they do drink something, they have no tolerance at all. A four-ounce snifter is relaxation enough at the end of a long, hot day. Anybody who met his work quota could ask for a sundown-sip from my well. Nobody got hurt and a lot more got done."

"So, how about your Russian friends?" I asked. "Any of them over there?"

"Russians, I mean Soviets, are never far away if there is money around. But the Saudis and the Soviets absolutely will not talk to each other. There is bad blood out there. I had no such problems, though. Through the people I work for I met the king of Arabia, King Saud, the son of Abdulaziz. He enjoys giving hospitality and he treated me well. In August of 1945, Abdulaziz needed some help drilling for more of the black gold under his desert. He's got the biggest oil deposit in the world. All he needed to do was pump it up faster and get even richer. He picked an American company, Standard Oil out of California, SOCAL, to do the drilling. Abdulaziz felt safer because America had no imperial designs that he knew of, and California is just too far away to worry about."

"But we are not from California."

"I didn't need to be. My bit was only to help keep the oil moving once it came up from the ground."

"Wasn't 1945 when we moved to Philadelphia?"

"Chester, not Philly, but close enough. Do you remember that?"

"I sure do! I got thrown out of a car there, remember?"

"Look at me and smile," he said. "See? All your teeth are still there. Couldn't have been that bad." He had always refused to talk to me about that incident in any detail. I knew I'd get the whole story out of him someday, though.

"So, why Chester?"

"Westinghouse. They made excellent turbines besides the kind in jet engines. You see, jets, nuclear subs, gas pipeline pumps, and electric generators are all pretty much the same, but some people make them bigger and they have very interesting customers."

"It does sound interesting."

Dad scowled. "Not always. It depends who's interested."

⸻◆⸻

In 1956, long after my father had come home from Arabia, the Mideast exploded. He still had friends there and he had left a lot of his own sweat invested in that pipeline. The troubles there went by several names, including the Suez Crisis and the Second Arab–Israeli War. The Arab world branded it the Tripartite Aggression because of its three invaders, Israel, France, and the United Kingdom. The Israelis called it Operation Kadesh or the Sinai War. The war had as many names as it had sides.

In 1956, the Tripartite Aggressors invaded the Egyptian Sinai because they and the rest of the world had been "inconvenienced" by Egyptian president Nasser. In 1950, he had blocked Israeli shipping through the Straits of Tiran, and in 1956 he nationalized the Suez Canal. That jeopardized those hundreds of thousands of barrels a day of crude that my father had helped feed to the thousand tankers in Sidon Harbor. Oil-hungry United Kingdom and France were among the most enraged.

The Western world decided it was time to restore control of the canal. That re-created the old, odd wartime alliance between the United States and the Soviet Union. Along with the United Nations, they set out to force Egypt's three invaders to go back home. As a parting shot, though, the United Kingdom, France, and Israel inflicted enough bomb damage on the Suez to block it to all shipping. It took a half-year to clear up the mess they left behind.

The Mideast was then crisscrossed by a complicated reshuffling of alliances and pacts. America's closest ally in the region was Saudi Arabia, who saw a chance to build its influence in the area. Saudi King Saud decided to punish Britain and France. He stopped all oil exports to them. That's when things got even worse.

Syria blew up its section of the Iraqi pipeline to punish Iraq for support-ing the invasion of Egypt. That starved the Mediterranean tankers buying Iraqi oil and slashed Iraq's income.

That bomb blast highlighted one of Mideast oil's greatest weaknesses: vulnerable pipelines. That got my father's attention.

Rebuilding, revising, and securing such a massive and vulnerable infra-structure would need proven experts. That also roughly coincided with the beginning of Russia's own vast natural gas and oil resource development. Self-sufficiency, they would have reasoned, would be better than depen-dence, and beyond that, oil was money for any country that could deliver it. This, too, would need the help of proven experts.

Taken together, the events of 1956 raised the stakes for my father. His knowledge, worldwide connections, and influence would be a valuable asset for any regional power with oil to sell the world.

The Soviet Union was now into its third year of post-Stalin reconstruc-tion. Only months before, Nikita Khrushchev, the new Soviet leader, had de-livered his famous closed-session anti-Stalin speech, "The Personality Cult and its Consequences." Overt or discoverable acts of brutality were going out of vogue, at least in public.

As a result, the next attempt to gain my father's collaboration in this arena did come in a gentler form as the FBI agents had predicted. The result would have been the same—control by coercion—but the method this time was far more subtle. It almost worked.

One day, a new boy turned up in my English class at Olean High School. His name was Jarek Andreivich, son of a family that had escaped from Soviet-dominated Poland and resettled with relatives in Olean. Their story had made quite a sensation in town. Jarek's English was pretty bad, but he was cute and he seemed nice. My English teacher asked Jarek if there was someone in the class he would like to help him learn his new language. I was delighted when he picked me.

Over the next three months, I saw Jarek almost every day and we be-came friends. My father, naturally, took an interest. His interest turned to alarm the first time they met after school one day. It was at Jarek's invitation.

"I and my parents are going to Canada tomorrow to see friends. Kay would enjoy the ride, I think. I would like her to come with us. My parents' English is not yet good and Kay could help me translate for them at the border. Can I ask her please to come? It will be Saturday and not interfere with school." He was very polite. His now pleasantly accented English was persuasive.

"We'll check with her mother," Dad said with equal civility. "Thank you." The three of us chatted for a while about Jarek's life in the United States and his parents' new freedom, then headed for home.

I knew Dad well enough to see tension others would miss. At home, he went right to the phone and called the FBI in Washington. It turned out that Jarek and his parents had been under surveillance since the day they reached Olean. "We've just been waiting to see what they were up to," the agent told Dad. "But we didn't think the kid had a job to do. We thought it was about the boy's father infiltrating the Dresser Corporation. By the way, they're Russian, not Polish."

"I thought so," Dad said.

"This looks like a setup for a grab," the agent said. "They are still very interested in you, too. We've spotted them watching. We've been waiting to see what direction they would take before alerting you. If you changed your behavior in response, it would have been a surveillance tell."

Dad thanked him and rang off.

On Saturday morning, I called Jarek to decline his invitation. "Maybe next time?" I said.

The following Monday night after dinner Dad asked me to join him for a little stroll up Van Buren beyond our house.

"You recall that invitation to Canada?"

"Sure," I said. "He wasn't in school today."

"Well, he was telling you the truth. He did go to Canada. My friends from the Bureau followed him. They learned a few useful things about his contacts up there. It turns out his contacts were at the Soviet Consulate. My friends at the Bureau brought me some sad news, though." My dad fell silent for a few paces. He looked down at the pavement.

"What was that?"

"They had a fatal accident on the way home."

I stopped in my tracks and stared at him.

"I had no choice in this matter," Dad said. "He was getting too close."

"For what?"

"Ultimately, it was going to be him or you. Him and his friends, that is. You would not have won."

By 1957, my father was conducting his business with the Dresser Corporation more like a consultant than an employee. Dresser was now part of his network of contacts in critical industries that built centrifugal compressor products and gas turbines. They were needed wherever oil and gas production, transmission, and refining were underway, worldwide.

In the summer of 1957, Dad took my family on a cruise to Europe. He, my mother, and my thirteen-year-old sister, Judy, spent nearly a month abroad that turned out to be both wonderful and strange.

I stayed home in Olean awaiting my first child. I had eloped to Pennsylvania one night with a man my father didn't like. I soon came to like him even less than my father did because of abuse I had not seen coming. Within two years, our marriage would be over, I would have two children, and I would be living with my grandmother.

In preparation for the trip, my father bought Judy a journal to record every day's travels—the cities, the historic sights, the people they met, and anything else she thought was interesting. Many years later, Judy shared that journal with me. She had noted the facts that she thought were most important, for example: The boys in Britain just stare; boys in Italy act thirteen; all the grass in Switzerland is short because the cows eat it, and in Switzerland girls all have big feet and they're ugly. Judy had also bought fifty-five souvenirs in forty-one places, and one tube of toothpaste. Her journal records were impeccably detailed.

For his part, my father must have judged that an innocent, naive record like Judy's would be free from his biases and slant, if he ever needed to prove the trip was nothing more than a family sightseeing tour.

Judy's journal began by describing the overnight train ride from Buffalo to Hoboken, New Jersey, the bus to Rockefeller Center in New York City, and the cab to the cruise ship in New York Harbor. They boarded at 9:45 on Wednesday morning, September 25. The ship sailed at 11:40, Judy took pictures of the skyline and the Statue of Liberty, and they all had tea and sweets at four. Nothing could be less clandestine than that, it would seem.

Luxury was the keynote of the cruise, beginning the next day with lobsters for lunch and filet mignon for dinner. Judy was delighted, and her parents enjoyed all the fineries in high style, except for an unexpected, mid-ocean course change to avoid Hurricane Frieda. The captain chose the re-route over rampant seasickness among the paying customers headed for London. It was all an adventure for Judy, duly recorded in day-by-day, wonder-struck detail.

Buried within Judy's journal, however, was an itinerary that, bit by bit, told a very different story when read with years of hindsight. The trip was marked with strangely coincidental meetings and improbable connections between people my father apparently just happened to meet while they traveled the continent.

While seeing as many of London's sights as possible in three days, they met a friendly British couple named Sally and Bernie Williams. They chatted, ate, drank together, and parted as if better friends had never met.

The next stop was Rome. Mr. and Mrs. Williams happened to be there, too. Judy took a picture of them dining together at one of Rome's finest restaurants of the day, Antica Biblioteca Valle—The Ancient Valley Library.[2] The restaurant had stayed open and popular for nearly seventy more years until it succumbed to the pandemic of 2020. The book-lined alcove where Judy took her picture remained unchanged during all those years. The conversation that evening seemed to Judy to cover areas of business that my father and Bernie shared and names of a few people they knew in common, even though they lived across the ocean.

After two days in Rome, they went to Genoa for two days, where my father had "things" to attend to in the city. After a one-night stay in Portofino, they traveled a few more miles to the nearby Mediterranean fishing village of Sestri Levante. They booked into the Hotel Mira. Judy noted that they were the only tourists to be found anywhere in the sleepy village or on its deserted beaches.

While there, my father dressed in a suit and tie each morning and "went to work" in a chauffeured car. At dinner both nights the family dined with Mr. and Mrs. Haug, tourists from communist East Berlin, an unusual origin for such well-dressed tourists in 1957, especially those visiting an obscure fishing village in Italy.

Next, a three-night stay in Florence took them to many interesting and historic places before going on to Venice. There they stayed at Hotel Dolder and had dinner with a couple they quickly befriended. The husband was an executive from a Texas branch of the Dresser Corporation, at whose Olean branch my father served as a consultant and had an elaborate office that was more like a small suite with a kitchen and bath. I had visited it on a number of occasions and decided that consultant was a pretty good job title. They didn't seem surprised to meet in Venice.

And the Texas couple had just arrived in Sestri Levante from a vacation in Soviet-controlled East Germany, a nation listed in very few tourist brochures.

The family then traveled to Zürich for a day, then Interlochen, and back to Zürich, where they met Mr. and Mrs. Hacket, also from Dresser in Texas. Finally, on the way back to London, they spent a day and night in Amsterdam at the Grand Hotel Krasnopolsky.

The European vacation ended on schedule on October 22 with a transatlantic flight from London to New York's Laguardia Airport, then an extravagantly expensive helicopter ride from Laguardia to the airport in Newark, New Jersey, and from there, a plane ride back to Buffalo.

Judy's journal recorded all of these apparently well-orchestrated "chance" meetings, lavishly funded, and often occurring in obscure locations. They involved people from the Soviet sphere of influence, a major US manufacturer of strategically important technology, and a connection to the United Kingdom, for all of which my father seemed to be a mysterious nexus of connections.

With a little more searching many years later, Judy and I discovered old, long-ignored photos and letters among our father's memorabilia. They revealed another of his homes-away-from-home in Beirut, Lebanon, complete with a chauffeur, a Lebanese man named Sammy who was also a bodyguard and interpreter. The Beirut home was elegant, a place of comfort and accommodation for Mideastern contacts, some of whom dressed in Western garb and others in the ancient manner of desert-dwellers.

Whether my father was working with the FBI or the CIA, acting as a commercial consultant to facilitate multinational projects that were supposed to fly under the radar of international regulations, or something entirely different, I have accepted that I may never know. My intuition and my father's occasional comments about those days, however, favor the FBI. My conclusion would be the same in any case: It all sounds like Dad—nothing ordinary, everything an adventure, and whenever possible just a little dangerous.

August 17, 1958, a Sunday afternoon at the Haven Theater, downtown Olean, New York[3]

This event coincides closely with another major aeronautical project my father was closely connected to. In that context, we present this as another close brush with those who saw me as a means of leverage and control. I had by then assumed a more active role in my own protection.

In 1957, Weldon Worth at Wright-Patterson Air Force Base near Dayton, Ohio, published research describing how a manned space plane could be built. Air force officials liked the idea and launched a project dubbed SR-89774 to design a reusable space plane. The program soon morphed into a plan for a Recoverable Orbital Launch System—ROLS. It was designed around a revolutionary new jet engine concept, a Liquid Air Collection Engine—LACE. It was not atomics-based, but LACE/ROLS also promised overwhelming tactical advantages.

An air force contract to develop a LACE system powered by pure oxygen extracted from the liquified air was placed with General Dynamics, Marquardt, and Garrett AiResearch. General Dynamics had contracted with my father as a consultant in the Nautilus days. This project was another leap forward in their cutting-edge, high-speed aviation program.

Meanwhile, rumors, scraps of intelligence, and even the popular press in the United States were hinting at more Soviet experiments in nuclear-powered aircraft. Some said they had already flown a prototype. The US program was still underway, too, and GE had developed a working, ground-test-based, atomic-jet engine anchored in their already proven jet technology.

The Soviet program of nuclear aircraft was planning a "Flying Nuclear Laboratory" test bed of their own.

My father's previous, and in some cases ongoing work with four of the principal spaceplane contractors—GE, General Dynamics, the US Army, and the US Air Force—and with the jet pioneers at Bell and Westinghouse, made him once again a nexus of valuable active connections and expertise in such advanced projects. Once again, he was a valuable humint target.

By now, Dad told me, the FBI was keeping close ears and eyes on his work. They detected rumors and communication traffic about proposed new Soviet contacts. Unfortunately, nothing was specific enough for a target date, place, or tactic. My father trained me in self-defense.

The need for it became all too real on the afternoon of August 17, 1958, a bright, sunny Sunday. The temperature was headed for ninety. It seemed a lovely time for a movie in an air-conditioned theater. My grandmother, as always, was delighted with a chance to babysit my one-year-old son so I could visit my dad and take my little sister to a movie.

"What are we going to see?" Judy asked.

Gigi. It was the biggest Hollywood splash of the year, so far. Maurice Chevalier and Leslie Caron played the starring roles. It was romantic and a little bit risqué, a definite must-see, according to my friends. Judy, now age fourteen, would love it, if Dad would let her go.

"We'll just tell Dad we're going to the movies," I said. "He'll be glad we're doing something and won't care what the movie is about. He probably won't even ask."

We found Dad working on something that looked complicated out in the garage. He had a solder gun in his hand. Whatever it was, it had a big copper kettle on the bottom, a long spiral coil of copper tubing coming out of the top, and a bunch of other metal and glass and crockery parts sorted out in neat piles on the floor. If Dad could build jet engines, this must be something important. After a moment I recognized some of the parts but I asked anyway.

"What's that, Dad?"

"Just a kind of experiment you might say. It's for fractional distillation of volatile liquids and selective, temperature-controlled condensation." He smiled as if the thing were his own baby. He patted its copper belly. "It's a new hooch cooker."

That part I understood. By now we knew Dad was a master at home distilling. He was proud of his elixirs. When he was playing humble, he simply said it was something "better 'n cough medicine." In general, though, he believed his smooth lightnin' needed enjoying, not naming. He put his tools down.

"So, what brings you ladies out here on such a fine summer day?" He looked us over, clearly appraising what we were wearing. "I see the heat calls for something skimpy today."

We were both wearing short shorts.

"It's the 'in thing,' Dad." I tried not to sound defensive.

"It sure makes you noticeable," he said. That was something he always wanted me to avoid. I usually thought of it as a protective papa kind of thing, but I knew there was more behind it.

"It's okay, Dad, don't worry," I said. "I'll keep an eye on Judy."

Dad laughed. "She's not the one I'm worried about, Trouble." He knew I liked it when he called me that. "Let me show you something first. Then she can go with you."

I learned later that the FBI had warned Dad about new Soviet interest. That made this afternoon the right time for another self-defense lesson. He enjoyed teaching me basic protective moves a young girl could use if necessary. He always started with: "Getting away is better than fighting. But if you can't get away, know how to fight."

"I'll show you a new move before you go. Girls in short shorts can attract more attention than they want."

"You mean . . ." I stopped without saying "the Russians?" Judy had never been told about them.

"Exactly," he said, hearing it anyway. "This move will be handy if somebody gets too close."

Dad opened two folding chairs, placed them side by side, and set a wooden skid on edge between them for an armrest. It made a good-enough mock-up of the Haven Theater seats.

"Sit here." He pointed to the right seat. "Put your left elbow on the armrest. I'll sit next to you on your left. Now imagine I'm a big guy, okay?"

"Sure!" I said, warming to the role. "Ugly and smelly?"

"Don't be too sure. Some of the worst people look real nice. Now imagine this guy puts his hand on your leg. Here's what you do." I loved this kind of stuff. He made a quick move that startled me. I was looking at him from the floor before I knew I was there, though he had gently slowed my fall. "That's my friend Ikky," he said. "It's a variation on an aikido move called ikkyo." I tried it on him a dozen times and soon it felt natural. "Not bad, Trouble," he said with a smile.

I saw with that simple move I could effortlessly use a man's elbow as a fulcrum, his hand as a lever, and shove his head almost anywhere I wanted, as long as I did it fast. If there was a seatback in front of him, like in a theater, he'd hit it hard. It favored leverage over strength. I loved it. The simplicity of a move I could make crippling in an instant astonished me. I hoped I'd never need it. On the other hand, I couldn't wait for some goon to make me try.

I looked at my watch. "The matinee starts in fifteen minutes. Coming, Judy?" I grabbed her hand before Dad could ask which movie we were going to see, and we almost knocked over Dad's copper and solder handiwork on the way out.

Sunday afternoon was a bad day at the box office for the Haven. Hardly a dozen people were scattered throughout the theater. I looked around while the MGM Lion roared at us from the opening screen. Frederick Loewe's "Gay Paree" filled the theater with romantic music. Then, as if on cue, I saw the silhouette of a young man come in from the lobby. He walked slowly down the middle aisle scanning the seats. About halfway he looked in our direction. In spite of hundreds of seats open all around, he selected our row. He stepped along the seats and sat down on my left, directly beside me.

Judy, on my right, looked past me wide-eyed. I nudged her and whispered, "Watch the movie. I've got this." I had a fearless nature, even when I should have known better.

The man settled into his seat and seemed to ignore me, but a few minutes into the story, I felt the softest touch beside my left knee. I did not react and the touch soon disappeared. Minutes later, the touch returned, but now with a caressing palm that moved slowly up my thigh. Again, I did not react. I reckoned that if I let him move his hand to just the right place, I'd have his elbow just where I wanted it.

I gently placed my hand behind his arm as if I was enjoying his touch. He stayed relaxed. Then, at just the right moment, I turned my touch into a vice grip and nailed his elbow to the armrest. Before he could react, I launched him face forward. His nose smacked the metal-edged back of the seat in front of him with a sickening crunch.

He rebounded to his feet, a jack-in-the-box on a broken spring. Something heavy clattered to the floor from his left hand and rolled away with a metallic sound. I saw the glint of polished steel and a blade with a wicked arc to its cutting edge. It disappeared beneath the next row of seats.

Both of his hands covered his face. Rivulets of blood ran between his fingers and down his chin. I heard him gasp out an agonized cry, which—probably made so by my own adrenaline rush—has stayed in my mind verbatim to this day, syllable for ugly syllable, exactly as he uttered it. The words were not English.

"*Chertovski suka!*" He spit out the words, spun away, stumbled up the row of seats, and out the door.

"What was that?" Judy gasped. "Did I really just see that?" Seventy years later her recollection of the event still matches mine, even though we've not talked about it in almost as long.

"That creep grabbed my leg," I said. "I wasn't having any of his funny stuff." She never knew the real story until many years later. She had been kept innocent of my father's escapades.

Later that afternoon, I told the whole story to my father and one of the FBI agents on sentry duty at our home.

"I thought the likelihood was low," my father said, "so I let her go without the usual tail. Safety and freedom are a tricky mix to calibrate with a feisty teenage girl."

The agent asked me, "Tell me again what the man said."

That sound had screwed itself into my mind. I didn't know what it meant. It just sounded nasty. I repeated it.

"*Chertovski suka!*" the agent repeated slowly after me with a growing smile. "I learned enough Russian when I was stationed in Berlin after the war to know that one." He turned to Dad with a crooked grin.

"This is one tough gal you've got here, Mr. Haas. Any little girl who can crush a Russian thug's nose like a raw egg is bound to get herself called . . ." He looked at me with an appraising glance and apologized for saying it. "*An F-ing bitch.*"

Those words rang proudly in my memory for years to come.

Friday evening, September 4, 1959. The Haas family home in Olean, New York

My parents came home to Van Buren Avenue with a nice tan. A couple of weeks in the Caribbean sun will do that.

In 1959, the *New York Times* ran an article featuring a palm-studded Cuban beach graced with a smiling bikini-clad sunbather. The story promised that Yankee tourists would now be treated like VIPs if they chose to visit the paradise-isle of Cuba. Dr. Castro, Cuba's new, revolutionary communist leader—as of New Year's Day, 1959—had issued all Americans a heartfelt invitation. He rolled out a red-carpet welcome. My parents accepted the invitation to take what I assumed was a vacation.

Cuba's tourist agency promised that anyone flying from Miami to Havana could fly home at half-fare if they stayed at the Habana Hilton or another top-of-the-line Havana hotel for four days. To top it off, the unspent airfare could be applied to the hotel bill. Castro allocated fifty million dollars to make American tourists feel welcome. His method was simple. He confiscated all the best hotels in Cuba, no matter who owned them, and then used them as he liked.

At the same time, Castro warned his people that the United States was about to invade Cuba. He promised the invaders their blood would flow in the streets, quoting Stalin, "Death is the solution to all problems. No man—no problem." He armed Cuban students for the expected combat. Cuba had become a Caribbean enigma, threatening mayhem against their invited guests.

Every nation and multinational corporation with business in Cuba worried that Cuba's new communist paradise would come at their expense. Castro claimed that foreigners had already enriched themselves at Cuba's expense for a century, so he was simply righting the ledger. He grabbed hundreds of millions of dollars in US assets, along with the assets of other capitalist nations, and thousands of their businesses.

My parents' Florida suntans were actually due to the largesse of at least one, and possibly all, of the American-owned oil companies operating in

Cuba. They included the Esso Oil Corporation (Standard Oil Company of New Jersey), Shell Oil, and Texaco, the Texas Oil Company. They all had the same agenda.

Beginning with the Suez Crisis, my father's consulting services with the world's major oil prospecting, pipeline distribution, and refining operations had made him a key player. He was most useful where behind-the-scenes, under-the-radar communications were needed. With a reputation for combining technical expertise and connections rumored to include US intelligence, he was tapped for back-channel negotiations between the oil companies and Cuba. He was not the only one recruited, but he fit a unique niche.

Miami was a good middle ground for both sides to meet, though safety could not be guaranteed even there. Too much power, prestige, and money were at stake. Castro threatened the "extortionist, exploitative monopolies which had drained the [Cuban] national economy and mocked the people's interests." He decried "the despicable interests of US monopolies which have hampered the growth of our economy, and the expression of our political freedom."[4] Castro was known to be a ruthless killer of all who resisted him. His bloody revolution had scourged his own homeland for the last six years.

Of added concern to oil companies, including the American "Big Three," was the hint geologists had recently detected in signs of enormous, new heavy-oil deposits under Cuba's northwest coast, just off-shore in La Habana and Matanzas Provinces.

Castro saw three options to capitalize on his new black gold. He could buy the wells, refineries, and pipelines or he could negotiate a better deal with existing operators, but he just stole them all. His new ties with the Soviet Union could also bring their oil exploration and reclamation teams precariously close—within ninety miles—to the United States.

Complexities multiplied and negotiations had gradually soured as trade goods like sugar entered the mix. Whatever intermediaries my father met with, and whatever quid-pro-quo offers passed between them, something apparently did not go right.

This time, my father may have been beyond his depth. It was possible he learned things he should not know, maybe angered the wrong power merchants, or unwittingly reopened issues festering within the NKVD since the Schevchenko days. Whatever the cause, and without my father's knowledge, something came home before him to lay in wait for his return.

The night my parents returned to Olean, they seemed relaxed, in good spirits, and not at all tired from their journey. Dad showed me a glossy, white folder decorated in elaborate, blue script, *Jack Lynch's Beachcomber Nightclub—Miami, Florida.*" It held a picture of him in a white tux and Mom in a ball gown, smiling, drinking champagne. Judy and I ooh'd and ahh'd over our glamorous parents. It is still one of the happiest pictures of our parents in the family album. So that night we were going to stay up late to hear all about their vacation. By about eleven o'clock, fifteen-year-old Judy had taken herself off to bed, though Mom, Dad, and I were still wide awake.

"Let's watch a movie," Mom said. It sounded like fun.

In our home, watching a late movie began with a simple ritual. Break out the snacks, ready the drinks, and make a quick potty-stop so everybody can sit through the entire movie. I had a pop, Dad had something on the rocks, and Mom, the only beer drinker in the house in those days, popped the cap off the only bottle of beer left in the refrigerator.

We had two bathrooms, built back-to-back. I closed the door to mine and I heard Mom close the door to hers. She must have been thirsty, or absent-minded, because I noticed she still had her beer in her hand on the way. A moment later I heard a loud thud through the wall and the floor shook beneath my feet.

"Mom? You okay?" I called.

No answer came back. I called again. No answer again. "Dad, come here," I called, while pulling up my pants and dashing out to the hallway. Suddenly I felt sure something was wrong.

We found Mom on the floor, eyes closed, barely breathing. Her beer was lying beside her, spilled across the bathroom floor. Dad could not rouse her.

"Go get Doc," Dad said. The urgency in his voice left me no doubt. I ran barefoot out the front door and across the street to Dr. Martino's house. He was a good friend, and just now by the luckiest chance, our closest neighbor.

"Come quick! Something's happened to my mom." Doc outran me home. Everything moved fast then. Within moments, Doc had carried Mom to his car, piled her motionless body into the front seat, and sped off down the hill to Olean General Hospital, less than a mile away. "Wait here," he called back to us on the way to the car, "I'll call you from the E.R."

About 1:30 a.m., he did call. Mom had died.[5] Doc came back to our house alone. All he said was, "Larry, let's talk." He walked into the kitchen and motioned for my father to follow, alone. I stayed in the living room with Judy now awake and wide-eyed beside me, listening as hard as we could round the corner and peeking in from time to time.

They talked for an hour with Mom's half-empty beer bottle sitting on the kitchen table between them. I saw Doc sniff the beer, wrinkle his nose, and give my dad a whiff. Dad fingered the bottle cap Mom had left there. Then I saw both of them inspect the scratch marks on the back-door latch.

"We can call it a stroke," Doc finally said, "if you don't want anybody to know what really happened. Some people will find it hard to believe at only forty-two, but such things do happen."

"Okay," Dad said. I couldn't believe how steady he seemed. I knew something much worse was going on inside, but his control was keeping it all down so he could make one more request.

"Make it stick, Doc. Too many questions, otherwise. We don't want any of them asked."

By 1966, I was twenty-seven years old, had been married, had two children, divorced their violent gangster father who my starry teenage eyes hadn't seen through soon enough, and then remarried far better. My father had also remarried. That was less than six months after my mother's death. Since then, he had continued his dizzying career with hardly an interruption. He traveled around the United States and overseas operating with remarkable ease across political, civilian, and military lines. He clearly continued to find his work satisfying and profitable. For two of those years, between about 1961 and 1963, I had been living in Mexico "out of harm's way."

Whether my father remained a person of interest to foreign agents, I no longer knew with certainty, though I would have bet on it. The world he lived in was too interesting to retreat from. We had remained close, though he had eventually moved from our home to another state.

In any case, I felt like it was time for me to introduce my youngest child, Missy, to her grandfather. He lived on a palatial estate named Farwood. It was hidden away in twenty-seven acres of deep woods across the state line. The chance for Dad and Missy to finally meet seemed well worth the many-hour drive.

If I had been a student of scientific and military news in 1966, I would have noticed three events in the world of aircraft, atomics, turbines, and submarines of special importance to my father.

On January 11, 1966, the first Lockheed SR-71 Blackbird jet landed at Beale Air Force Base in California. It was a long-range spy plane that could fly sixteen miles high at nearly 2,500 mph over targets like the Soviet Union.

The Blackbird was as much a target for Soviet espionage as it was for their anti-aircraft missiles. Their missiles couldn't reach it, but their spies had a better chance. My father had, naturally, long maintained his worldwide network of connections with aircraft that flew high, hot, and fast.

On October 5, 1966, an experimental reactor at the Enrico Fermi Nuclear Generating Station on Lake Erie in Michigan suffered a partial meltdown when its cooling system failed. My father's work with Flader and with General Dynamics on the Nautilus project prepared him for work as a nuclear safety consultant who instinctively and technologically understood the danger that what would someday come to be known as the China Syndrome.

In 1966, France signed a treaty for cooperation in nuclear research with the Soviet Union. Construction of France's first nuclear submarine, *Le Redoutable*, was then well underway and slated to launch in 1967.

Each of those events, in its own way, engaged Soviet interests. My father once again represented a nexus that almost exactly matched the ongoing work and the Soviets' intelligence targets.

My "Incident at Farwood" in 1966 may have been a coincidence, but I had long ago been sensitized to dark motives behind odd events. It may have been one last attempt to use me as a bargaining chip in "hiring" Larry Haas as an intelligence source.

Farwood Estate sat at the end of a quarter-mile drive off a little-traveled county road. Tall blue spruce guarded the way like brooding sentinels.

My visit with Missy and Dad was wonderful. Naturally, I had to end it too soon because the drive home would be long. By nine o'clock I was leaving the estate to head back. The beginning of the trip would take me along miles of narrow country roads, through deep woods and sparsely populated farmlands.

As I turned right out of the winding driveway, I noticed a dark-colored car parked back along the road behind me. It might have been my imagination, but the headlights seemed to come on just as I reached the county road. The vehicle slowly caught up with me and followed close behind for a number of miles. Eventually, we reached an intersection where the light was red. In my rear-view mirror, I saw the driver's door open behind me. A man stepped out and walked quickly toward my car.

He indicated by a cranking hand motion for me to roll my window down. Naturally wary of strangers on a dark road, I did not comply, but indicated I could hear him. Curiosity often outweighed caution, a trait I seem to have inherited, but this time caution at least kept my window up.

"Hello. I see you are from out of state," he said with a foreign accent I recognized as Russian. "This is a dark night." I looked up. He was right, the sky was moonless and overcast. "These roads turn many ways. If you follow me, I will show you a quicker route to where you are going."

"Really?" But how would he know where I was going?

"There is no sense taking this route," he said, probably taking my silence for indecision. "Turn here. Follow me. I will show you a good way." He motioned with his arm to indicate a right turn. "Yes?"

"Okay. Sure. Thank you." I gave him a pleasant smile and decided to give him the head start he wanted.

He smiled back, made an odd little bow, and walked back to his car.

I had studied my map carefully on the way down and knew the right turn he suggested would take me down miles of hinterland roads, past a few farms, and onward to a secluded reservoir.

When the light turned green, I rolled my window down and waved him around my car as if I would follow. He pulled around me and turned right onto the intersecting road. I inched around the turn slowly to let him gain a small lead. His tail lights receded into the distance. As he began to round a distant bend, I killed my lights, cut a hard U-turn, raced to the intersection, and turned back toward my home, and sped away.

I drove as fast as I dared the rest of the way home. I smiled remembering Peter Pan's age-old road map. "Second star to the right and straight on 'til morning."

Home Safe and Final Days

One cold January night in 1963, my father had invited me to his home, the one he built for all of us high up on Van Buren Avenue in Olean. He greeted me on the front steps with an odd statement.

"Time's almost up, Bunny."

"What time is that?"

"The time I can protect you. Your guards, your protectors, need to pull away because I . . ." He paused, looking for words he was almost never short of. "Well, let's just say 'because.'"

"Should I worry?" I didn't know if I was relieved or afraid.

"Nothing to be afraid of if you can get far enough away from me. You can't stay around here any longer. It just won't be safe. I've been dodging bullets for years, and not always well enough." He left unnamed the events neither one of us wanted to remember. "So, I have a plan."

"Uh oh!" I laughed. Dad's plans never lacked for excitement. They usually also had just enough danger to make them irresistible. "Tell me more."

"Nope." That mischievous grin was a tell. Something big was up. "Come with me."

I stepped into the house, hung up my coat and scarf in the front hallway, and followed him into the living room. A man was seated on the couch. He saw me and stood up. He looked seven feet tall with shoulders to match. His hands were enormous but they looked clean. Most remarkable, though, was his smile. I think I noticed it almost before I realized he was a giant.

"This is my friend Jerry," my father said.

"Hello, Kay," Jerry said. Before I could manage an obligatory "Pleased to meet you," he added, "Your father has told me a lot about you." He said it like it was a good thing.

I held out my hand to shake his and found mine engulfed in a firm but surprisingly gentle grip. I got the point. "Are you my new bodyguard?" I hoped it was true.

"No, Bunny," Dad said, "just a friend." But by that point in my life, I knew that if any dad introduces his daughter to "just a friend" who happens to be male, he's hoping for some good chemistry.

If that was his scheme, it turned out he was right. Those few words would change the rest of my life in ways I could not have imagined—not that he hadn't done that before in a hundred interesting ways. The remarkable hours of conversation that followed launched a new relationship entirely different from any I'd known before. Jerry's quiet presence took me in. I saw something unusually strong in him, but he was kind and gentle, both funny and wise. It seemed to surround him, and before long, me.

"Your father and I have known each other for a couple of years," Jerry said. "I trust him. It's not something I say often." His eyes told me it was true and it mattered to him.

The next forty-four years—beginning on a warm, spring evening only two months later in a secluded chapel in Olean, New York—became the best years of my life. They proved Jerry was right to trust Larry Haas, and I was right to trust Jerry. I often joked that if my dad had hoped for good chemistry, heaven had been on his side. The five children Jerry and I raised together proved the point almost magically.

We lived in seclusion in a forest home that Jerry and I built by ourselves. It was far from the nearest city and almost as far from the nearest paved road. In the nearby small, rural community everyone knew everyone. A stranger would have been spotted by the locals as quickly as a sixteen-point buck strapped to a car roof on opening day of deer season.

If those good, long years spent far from the modern world, far off the beaten track, were a kind of hiding, it worked. Except for my "Incident at Farwood," there never was another event like the ones that had kept me and my family on edge for so long. If the danger had passed long ago, that was okay, too. The house we built together in the forest was large and sturdy. The home we created there was even stronger.

My father's story, as it turned out, also came to a better ending. After his second wife—probably not his wisest choice so soon after Mom's death—died of a lingering illness, he married one more time, and once again within months. This time, he did it right. He married a wise and kind woman named Dolores Mae with whom he finally lived a "happily-ever-after" story of his own. With her, he rounded out many more years in reasonable contentment, though still with distant travels, intrigue, and, of course, living a little bit dangerously when it was the right thing to do.

A Personal Note from Kay Haas

If history were taught in the form of stories, it would never be forgotten.[1]
—Rudyard Kipling

They tried to kill me seven times.

I didn't really know if they were Soviet spies, American communists at their bidding, or the spy's family bent on vendetta. But I do know the world of secret agents plays by deadly rules. As Larry Haas's firstborn child, that birth order fact haunted me for the rest of my life. It was significant in the culture of my father's enemies.

My father[2] had secrets that others wanted. His refusal to cooperate made me a pawn played for coercion and maybe for revenge.[3] We spoke to no one about such things. The FBI wanted it kept quiet. While my father continued his own career, he worked with the Bureau, too, but always under that ongoing cover of silence.

———◆———

In his secluded cabin in the hills of Western Pennsylvania, near the end of a life of audacious plans tangled with unintended consequences, my father made a dire forecast about the world as he had come to know it. He predicted that the conflict between the world's greatest military powers—the Cold War between the United States and the USSR that had consumed most of his life—would not end in peace by the twenty-first century. Instead, the hostilities would move in ever more dangerous directions. He had watched the United States, the USSR, and other world powers wage proxy wars through opposing sides in regional wars. My father believed such wars merely shielded the superpower homelands from bloodshed on their own soil. The rest of the world would be their battleground—and booty for the victor.[4]

So, this story, played out between two men and two great powers, is really two stories separated by fourteen seconds. That's all the time it took for Andrei Ivanovich Schevchenko to utter his threat of vengeance. I became a means by which that threat was to be carried out. That made this my story, too, and I promised I would tell it. I am the last person alive who knows it.

In his last hours, on November 27, 1989, I sat beside Dad's bed with him and his wife of nearly twenty good years. In the fading twilight of that rainy Monday afternoon, as a cold autumn wind moaned among the treetops above his home, my father found a measure of comfort in proposing one last plan from his deathbed. It was no less audacious than all the others that had shaped his life.

"It's time to tell my story, Kay." He left his life in my hands.

I gave him my promise. And I kept it.

Notes on Compiling *The First Counterspy*

The First Counterspy fills gaps between known events. At times its main characters are quoted from sworn FBI interview records, Larry's accounts as recalled by Kay, Kay's children, her sister, Judy, and her cousins.[1] Other gaps are filled by logical inference based on documented surveillance, related evidence, and historical records. The most intriguing ingredient, however, remained the hardest to quantify—the personalities, emotions, and motives of the key players.

This is therefore a historian's—a storyteller's—creation based on the most thorough research possible, a product of investigation and intuition. A onetime lieutenant colonel in Soviet foreign intelligence once wrote, "Journalism, as concerns collecting information, differs little if at all from intelligence work."[2] That bright young officer later became the president of Russia, Vladimir Vladimirovich Putin.

Kay's research started when she decided to find a broader context for the many stories her father had told and the many odd, sometimes frightening events that seemed to follow him and his family for years.

Researching his life revealed fatal flaws in early Cold War espionage measures, countermeasures, and especially in the recruitment and training of both spy and counterspy. It was possible to observe the FBI "learn its way" into subsequent, full-scaled investigations of Soviet espionage, a practice at which it soon became highly skilled, though also notoriously devious in the practice as they saw the need.

By October 1945, for example, the Bureau was more than a year into the Schevchenko case, a complex cross-country investigation. But not until October 2 did Harvey Rath, a special agent at the FBI's New York City field office, decide to "check the records of the State Department for all information available about Andrei Schevchenko." The FBI, operating under the Department of Justice, was not automatically entitled or privy to

Department of State files in cases like this, and until this point agents had not even asked.[3]

Larry Haas's education paralleled the FBI's as he gained a broader perspective and deeper knowledge about the forces that were shaping the world.

The notion that Soviet espionage was a serious risk to the United States, for example, was still relatively new and underappreciated at higher echelons of the government during WWII. According to historian Sibley, "Early in WWII the FBI had no formal, comprehensive counterintelligence program" against Soviet espionage. A scholarly consensus that Soviet espionage was either nonexistent or of minor importance in the early 1940s was well entrenched in the public and academic mind. Sibley states, however, "Suspicion of Soviet espionage was palpable in the agency [FBI]."[4]

In the Schevchenko case, the FBI did evolve its prowess quickly and with remarkably few missteps. The Bureau had also benefitted from generous assistance by British intelligence and the rapid advancement in US cryptographic analysis. This development began while the FBI's workforce was growing explosively with little control over the quality of its newest recruits.[5] Hoover, on the other hand, placed the Haas-Schevchenko investigation in the hands of seasoned agents,[6] though even there the Bureau was sometimes hampered by its inept recruitment practices and by the very Washington bureaucracy to which it answered.[7]

Concerning the question of Schevchenko's true identity posed earlier (introduction), two additional items of evidence appear to be in conflict. On return to the Soviet Union on January 3, 1946, the FBI's inspection of Schevchenko's luggage on the dock just after boarding ship revealed a personally handwritten, self-addressed label in Russian: "A. I. Schevchenko, Moscow, U.S.S.R. Custom House of Moscow."[8] Addressing his own luggage to himself is, of course, not conclusive, but supports a presumption that the name was his. On the other hand, recent personal communication by one of us (WP) with officials at the Archives of the Federal Security Service of the Russian Federation (FSB) yielded a denial of any record of a Soviet citizen of that era named Andrei Ivanovich Schevchenko. Due to the vagaries and recognized inconsistent transparency of such archives, however, this is also not taken as conclusive.

As a result, in the absence of convincing evidence to the contrary we have accepted Schevchenko's full name as given along with the personal details of his origin, education, and family as accurate.

In the mid to late 1950s, Larry Haas started sharing his experiences with Kay and later with Kay's children. "Grandpa Larry" was the family raconteur. FBI reports confirm that Haas convinced Andrei that he would be a trustworthy sub-agent. In classic, old-Russian fashion, Larry survived many hard-drinking nights with Andrei[9] without revealing himself as a double agent. Andrei, however, under the influence of his own hundred-proof truth serum, sometimes gave up more than he should have. He revealed intriguing hints, and once in a while outright actionable intelligence, about the Soviet Trading Commission, *Amerikanskaya Torgovlya* (Amtorg[10]), where he ultimately served as vice president. In that capacity, he oversaw billions of dollars of Soviet wartime purchases under US Lend-Lease. He was also deeply embroiled in Soviet consular intrigue, tactics, and methods. Larry interpreted such disclosures as sometimes true, sometimes braggadocio, and sometimes a ploy to convince Larry to return the favor.

Larry once told Kay, "My tongue was sore from biting it. I must not have said anything too bad."

Larry Bell, founder of Bell Aircraft, and George H. Bucher, president of Westinghouse Electric and Manufacturing, are also quoted from historic records as they relate to Larry Haas. Haas had worked in key, highly sensitive positions under both men.

In addition, we present the personal experiences of Kay Haas from the 1940s through her father's death in 1989, especially the series of attempts on her life or security. Kay's memory of stories that her father told her is nearly as photographic as her father's recall appeared to be. Neuroscientists debate whether a truly photographic memory is hereditary or even exists, but Kay offers a hint in its favor. Her father made sure she understood matters that he insisted she never forget. Her safety and his legacy were at stake.

Kay's son, Denny, also offered intriguing hints from his grandfather's exotic tales. Many conversations in this book are quoted from Haas and Leona and Joseph Franeys' appearance before the HUAC hearings of June 6, 1949.[11] In addition, some specific personal (KH) documents provide new information on the case never before released.[12]

Nevertheless, history can also change over time in the simple act of transmission. The Haas-Schevchenko affair began to change almost immediately.

On June 7, 1949, for example, only one day after HUAC interviewed Larry Haas and the Franeys about the Schevchenko case, the *New York Times* published a long account by Clayton Knowles, special to the *Times*. That account already contained one significant error, one lie, and one flawed recollection.

In the *Times*, Bell's P-39 and P-63 airplanes—the Airacobras and Kingcobras—conventional propeller-driven aircraft skillfully flown by

Soviet pilots, were misidentified as the top secret P-59 Airacomet jet fighter, the plans of which Schevchenko was trying to steal.

In a December 1944 FBI report, written in collaboration with Haas only days after the event, Larry entered an error of his own into the HUAC record. Larry said he had originally asked Schevchenko for $50,000 in a misguided attempt to discourage Schevchenko's plan to buy Larry's invention. In Haas's HUAC testimony, however, he reported asking Schevchenko for $500,000. That number was then reported by Knowles. Whether the higher figure was an FBI typo (though Larry did sign the original interview transcription attesting to the lower figure) or a HUAC stenographer's typo in 1949 cannot be determined. The possibility also remains that between 1945 and 1949 Haas decided to make his request seem even more outlandish to prove he never meant it. Haas's motive and means, therefore, remain ambiguous—as he might have been himself.

Various historical accounts, including the *Times* story, cite Secretary of State Byrnes as adamantly denying that he blocked Schevchenko's prosecution, in spite of HUAC testimony in which FBI agents themselves blamed him. The October 2, 1945, top secret FBI memo sent by Director Hoover to all involved field offices, to all interested parties in Washington, and to President Truman, confirms Byrnes's denials, but at that time did not correct the public record. Hoover's blue bomb penned to Ladd in 1949 now finally resolves that question—Andrei Schevchenko had Attorney General Clark to thank for his freedom, as long as it lasted.

The *New York Times* is respected worldwide as a source of news and accurate historical records. Yet, within twenty-four hours of the HUAC hearings, one of its journalists had introduced ambiguity and misinformation into the historical record. These errors were undoubtedly accidental. On the other hand, some other errors, as published in the *New York Journal-American*, appeared to be purposeful and intentional.

The December 4, 5, and 6 front-page exposés in the *New York Journal-American* that revealed Schevchenko and his network were both correct and incorrect. Fictional elements were inserted in the true story to send a clandestine, coercive message to Schevchenko and to mislead his superiors. The stories had the effect of forcing Schevchenko into voluntary collaboration with the FBI as his only remaining safe haven. The news was manipulated to craft a historically unreliable record for the purpose of national security and to achieve an extrajudicial quasi-justice. Later commentaries based on those stories risk promoting that misinformation as fact.

Such dynamics when applied today—popularly dubbed "fake news"—could also unintentionally aid and abet conspiratorialists, dissidents, and recruiters for the most dangerous elements of international society. The story of Haas and Schevchenko is not unique in that regard. It illustrates again that reliance on a single source of news is ill-advised, as is the equally dangerous assumption that all news is accurate.

The source of the stories leaked to the *Journal-American* about Schevchenko has never been fully verified. Analysis of internal clues, inconsistent statements, and inaccuracies that seemed intentional, however, all lead back—as Andrei Schevchenko also concluded—to Larry Haas and FBI director J. Edgar Hoover. Hoover's proclivity for managing information and his exasperation with his superiors' refusal to prosecute Schevchenko make the Haas-Hoover collaboration plausible, the most likely bridge between the verifiable facts. The *Journal-American* exposés served both Haas and Hoover in ways that are hard to interpret as coincidental, accidental, or unintentional.

Concerning locale, all of the places where Kay, Larry, and Andrei lived are accurately described here, as are landmarks in and around the Buffalo area, Chester, Philadelphia, and New York City.

The tale of Ella Bull, Larry's Native American mother, and his status as a half-sibling, accurately recounts the family lineage as Larry told it to Kay, though some family members contest this. Larry's account of his ancestry, however, does appear credible, or at least defensible, based on the documented history of falsified family obituaries, a brother exiled into nonexistence, and a sister relegated to anonymity. Larry's invention of a false ancestry would serve no rational purpose. In further support of Larry and Kay's credibility are the myriad close parallels between their and their family members' stories when compared to voluminous, detailed FBI records.

The path Larry forged through the aircraft industry, from Chevrolet to Curtiss-Wright, from his "one big lie" at Bell to Westinghouse, and his later work with high-tech turbines, is well documented. Kay's family album of photographs and clippings independently support much of that history. Larry's later work in atomics with Flader and the Nautilus project are also reliably documented, though in less detail, and independently corroborated by other family members. Judy Haas's lengthy and detailed travel journal (only briefly summarized here) offers many more tantalizing but undeniable insights into the covert nature of Larry's international exploits. Judy reports today that she accompanied her parents to Europe on a number of other occasions, including many equally strange "coincidental" meetings and apparently clandestine rendezvous.

Larry was also the grandpa-raconteur who kept Kay's children spellbound for years afterward with tales of his adventures and travels. One of those stories was the kind that, in hindsight, made all the rest of his yarns and sagas seem more credible.

Grandpa Larry once told a grandson, Denny, about his work as a nuclear safety consultant during construction of one of America's first commercial atomic power plants. He had discovered that mistakes were made and then covered up by contractors—mistakes that could have blown up "a big chunk of the countryside" and spread fallout for a hundred miles in whatever direction the wind was blowing. It was a harrowing tale in which Larry found himself cast as a David standing up to an industrial Goliath behaving badly for its own profit.

More than three years later, nearly every detail of Grandpa Haas's story lit up the silver screen in the Academy Award–nominated movie *The China Syndrome.* Jane Fonda and Michael Douglas co-starred with Jack Lemmon (playing plant supervisor Jack Goodell), whose role almost precisely paralleled the story Larry had told Denny long before. Instead of being gunned down by a corporate thug as Goodell was in the movie, however, Larry was run off the road at high speed by a corporate security agent. In the movie, TV sound technician Hector Salas suffered that fate with fatal consequences. Larry, on the other hand, had survived the attempted assassination and escaped to Beirut for three years until he thought it was safe to come home.

The Schevchenko family's arrival in the United States and his background are taken from the FBI's reliance on the Soviet PR-1 biographical data submitted to the State Department. That single data source is echoed in all subsequent reports, including the official FBI historical commentary and critical analysis, "Shameful Years."[13] Those records include his Moscow training as an aeronautical engineer and his youthful experiences and romantic writings among the gypsy camps of the Caucasus. Andrei's elder son, Arseniy, retained in Moscow, is not independently verified, but is based on Kay's recollection of conversations with her father, and is plausible based on Stalin's well-known tactic of assuring loyalty through hostage-holding.

Schevchenko's role at the Bell Aircraft Plant in Buffalo is accurately depicted, as is his eventual promotion to vice president (alternatively translated as vice chairman) of Amtorg with billions of dollars' worth of Soviet purchasing power at his disposal. Schevchenko can be seen accompanied by Bell plant officials and Soviet Air Force officers inspecting Bell's P-39 and P-63 aircraft in YouTube documentaries transferred from Bell publicity films made at the time.

The names and specific roles of other Amtorg officials, such as Iskhak Abdulovich Akhmerov, are more obscure given the sometimes-opaque records of Amtorg and its legal and illegal operatives. Akhmerov was a highly decorated Soviet officer who served as both the chief illegal *rezident* in the United States, starting in 1942, and later the legal *rezident*, station chief, on the Soviet consular staff in New York City. Akhmerov was also chief of the NKVD in the United States during WWII and is known to have run a number of Soviet spy networks in the United States. But while it is plausible that he was Schevchenko's handler in 1945 based on dates and known circumstances, it has not been fully confirmed. His role as spymaster over Schevchenko is our speculation, but oversight of Schevchenko by someone with such skills and power within the Soviet apparatus is assured, given the hierarchy and accountabilities then in place. Some accounts also name Schevchenko as an NKVD officer while others do not.

The Soviet spy network in the United States before and during the war years was far more developed than was the FBI anti-Soviet surveillance. The FBI agents assigned to this case were learning Soviet spy craft on the job. Many of their early procedures lacked the sophistication for which they later became renowned. According to FBI Special Agent Robert J. Lamphere, in his book *The FBI-KGB War: A Special Agent's Story* (New York: Random House, 1986), Special Agent Don Jardine, Lamphere's colleague, was the agent "running [Haas and others] as double agents against the Soviets." Jardine's name is not found, though, in any of the four hundred pages of more than eighty declassified FBI documents made available for this account. Many places in those reports, however, display names redacted under black ink. This may reflect a policy to withhold certain key names to preserve undercover viability. As a result, with apologies, we may have inadvertently attributed some of Jardine's actions to other agents, but the substance of the actions remains unchanged.

Schevchenko's failure apparently revealed a serious error in Soviet spy craft of the day. He was by nature a man better suited to the life path he had chosen in science and engineering rather than to espionage. Much of his behavior as a spy seemed inept and forced against the grain.

Nevertheless, by 1952, the record of Schevchenko's failure already suffered from distortion and sneering commentary in a purportedly objective report to the Congress of the United States and the American people. In describing Schevchenko's intelligence gathering methods, the HUAC report[14] stated, "Actually, Andrei Schevchenko was paying for information which he could have secured from periodicals dealing with aeronautics. In fact, at that time his financial contributions were probably the only return of Lend-Lease that this country was receiving from Russia."

The prominence of M.I.C.E. in spy craft is classical, universal, and ancient. Whether known by other acronyms or more nuanced in application, it is always basically the same. The seduction formula described here is a composite of many descriptions of the art. It was first described to one of us (WP) by retired FBI agent Joseph Koletar, author of *The FBI Career Guide* (AMACOM, 2006) as the long seduction, a classical Soviet, and more recently Russian, technique for gaining human intelligence. Robert Greene's *The Art of Seduction* (Profile Books, 2003) also helped design a seduction formula that closely matched the (somewhat botched) game plan Schevchenko seemed determined to follow, though with some personal improvisation.

All sums of money that Andrei gave to Larry and the Franeys are accurately depicted here (all serial numbers recorded in the FBI archives), many of which were found to harbor fingerprints verified as Schevchenko's.

Colonel Milo Miller was the US Army Air Forces representative at Bell. He was authorized to approve such matters as P-39 and P-63 delivery schedules, equipment, and flight-test data. He interacted frequently with Schevchenko and the other Soviet military personnel visiting or stationed at Bell. Though reasonable, it cannot be verified that he was the third-party foil in Schevchenko's first- and second-date events. Miller would have been, however, a plausible choice for Schevchenko to use in depicting Schevchenko's urging of Larry toward an anti-military stance, and his depiction here served that dramatic purpose. Any negative light cast on the memory of the real Colonel Miller by this depiction is accidental and unintentional.

John Huston's *The Battle of San Pietro* documentary film is accurately depicted here. Various versions are available on YouTube.

The March 12, 1945, letter approving Larry's job change from Bell to Westinghouse is quoted verbatim here. War-critical industries were encouraged to share manpower in scientific and engineering areas, but such changes required government approval.

The injuries Kay suffered in her first abduction attempt resulted in the failure of her broken pelvis to ever heal properly. The damage led to a lifelong partial disability. By the early 2000s, increasing pain finally led to surgery for avascular necrosis of the pelvis and hip joint. A portion of one finger was also lost in the event, a lifelong scar she carries as an enduring memento.

The White House meeting at which President Truman was briefed by the major industrialists and military chiefs is accurately described for date, place, and attendees. Westinghouse's Bucher was in attendance. Haas's attendance, based on his own account, is not independently verified, but reasonably confirms Larry's re-persuasion, as FBI reports attest that Larry did have serious second thoughts and reservations about cooperating with the FBI. He envisioned and feared great danger in such work.

The correspondence quoted in "The Washington Hot Potato" chapter is all accurate, as are the handwritten notes by J. Edgar Hoover, including the note that reveals AG Clark as the party who refused to prosecute Schevchenko.

Schevchenko's apparent but unexpected reprieve by the Soviet apparatus after the *New York Journal-American*'s exposé—given one full month at liberty to shop, pack, and enjoy New York City during the Christmas season—is accurately depicted, though the Soviet motives for the short-term reprieve are presented only as reasonable surmise. That freedom would have allowed the NKVD to watch Schevchenko, trace his contacts, and observe signs he had been turned by the FBI.

Larry's secret trip to the White House is a re-creation of a meeting Larry described for Kay in detail on multiple occasions. We have, however, no independent corroboration of this event.

The packing of crates and boarding of the *Stalinabad* by Schevchenko and his family, followed by his immediate unavailability to take part in his luggage search, is accurately depicted. Many years later, Larry described to Kay the events onboard the *Stalinabad* that resulted in Schevchenko's death. It is Kay's recollection of that conversation with her father that we report. The route and location are our surmise based on calculations stated in the narrative. Credible records of Andrei Ivanovich Schevchenko's existence or career anywhere in the world after January 3, 1946, have not been found.

The FBI archival material used in writing this book is far more richly detailed concerning Schevchenko's activities with Larry and the Franeys than could be fully presented here. Many volumes of Bell Aircraft's *Bellringer* company magazine distributed to employees between 1943 and 1946 also support these events.

Concerning the HUAC investigations, all testimony is excerpted from the official transcript. Kay recalls numerous later contacts between her father and Richard Nixon, and on other occasions, Robert Oppenheimer, both of whom he met and befriended in connection with the June 6, 1949, HUAC investigation. Both Kay and Judy recall enjoying home visits from their "tall, handsome Uncle Bobby" [Oppenheimer]. Oppenheimer's HUAC testimony began on June 7, one day after Haas's testimony.

It is important to note that Larry Haas did not want this story told—and Kay did not tell it—merely to tell a good, tall tale. He meant it to show more specifically the unchanging nature of realpolitik at every level, from intensely personal to geopolitical.

John Adams, the second president of the United States, once said, "I must study politics and war that my sons may have liberty to study mathematics and philosophy."[15]

But the battlefield is not the only place where wars are waged, won, or lost. Larry Haas hoped writing about his part of the war would help people learn how to wage the next one—without fighting.

"To hold a pen is to be at war,"[16] Voltaire said. Perhaps that weapon will someday resolve what guns cannot.

Acknowledgments

By the time we started to write about America's first civilian counterspies, Kay Haas had spent many years amassing notes, clippings, volumes of declassified FBI documentation, and a small library of books that rarely contained more than glimmers of her father's role in the spy sagas of WWII. But Kay knew there was more to tell than historians yet knew. She and her father had lived it. First-person testimony of such events was rapidly disappearing beyond the horizon of living memory, and Kay began to fear that her father's story would soon fade into history's night as well. And she had a promise to keep—the promise she made at her father's deathbed—to tell the world about his life.

Her experiences in keeping that promise, however, had revealed that a complex tale like Larry Haas's, spanning years and myriad places, was unlikely to succeed through long-distance, impersonal relationships with writing and research partners. So our first acknowledgment goes to the Rotary International Club of Jamestown, New York, where we had met long before and shared many a luncheon and fellowship with our neighbors and community leaders. When conversation and a rough draft by Kay's husband, Lee, revealed that this small, dignified, and intelligent woman had once been thrown from a car by kidnappers, smashed the nose of a Russian thug, and survived a brief marriage to an underworld goon, there seemed only one possible path left—let's write the book. Rotary, it says in their Four-Way Test, builds better friendships, and that would be a place to start.

We also offer special thanks to the Niagara Aerospace Museum in Niagara Falls, New York, and its well-curated, carefully maintained Bell Aviation archives. Particular thanks go to archivist Ray Meissner, to Hugh Neeson, retired vice president at Bell Aircraft and museum education director, and to docent Walter Lechowski.

Additional information about Bell Aviation was generously provided by late friend Dick Harms, a longtime Bell engineer whose team designed and built the ascent engine that lifted *Apollo-11*'s crew off Tranquility Base on July 21, 1969. At 17:54:00 UTC (Coordinated Universal Time) that night. Dick's team notched another Bell milestone in flight in the same spirit that the Bell-GE team with Larry Haas had a scant quarter-century before.

We are also deeply indebted to many others who have researched and written about spies, Soviet and American in particular, and their spy craft during WWII and onward into the early Cold War years. Many have been generous with their time in lengthy conversations and careful reading and critique of selected excerpts and early draft material. They offered valuable insights and sources for additional enrichment of the final manuscript. Jack Barsky, author of the autobiographical book *Deep Undercover*, lived the secret life of a Soviet spy in the United States for many years. He helped us understand the severe handicap placed on Andrei Schevchenko by not training him—a man by nature unsuited to the task he had been given—and by the trauma of operating under the coercion typical of Stalinist-era intelligence gathering. Barnes Carr, also a scholar and author examining that era, offered many useful insights on the nature of Soviet espionage in the United States and other key players here and abroad. David Chambers, grandson of Whittaker Chambers, offered important insights on the nature of Soviet espionage networks and suggested key additions to our research concerning Schevchenko. John Earl Haynes shared recollections concerning Schevchenko, his network, and others of its kind in the United States during WWII based on his own extensive research. Katherine A. S. Sibley provided the most complete account of Haas's activities with Schevchenko and confirmed our finding that most resources concerning the Haas/Schevchenko case are sparse and incomplete. Larry Loftis shared his experience, similar to ours, in working from detailed archives and first-person accounts. As an acclaimed journalist, he offered valuable guidance concerning the authenticity of accurate quotations and its distinction from use and disclosure of dramatically reconstructed dialogue.

We also thank author and renowned bibliophile Arik Bjorn, for insightful and discerning analysis of draft manuscript material during the preparation of *The First Counterspy*. Thanks also to Bev Johnson (Quick Solutions) for preparing multiple draft manuscripts for first-reader reviews throughout the process.

Members of Kay's family—sister Judy, son Denny, cousin Caroline, nephew David McMahon, and husband Lee—all very generously contributed their time, reading, insights, and recollections, and especially their love for Kay, in compiling this work.

No book about aviation could be credible without a pilot's insights, especially one whose long and decorated career included flying the latest, hottest jet-powered warplane descendants of Larry Haas's child, the venerable Bell P-59. In our case, we thank good friend Commander John Watkins, USN (ret.), having flown from land, sea, and maybe most important of all, the Robert H. Jackson Airfield at New York's Chautauqua County-Jamestown Airport.

Early draft readers providing invaluable suggestions and critique included Walt's son, Dr. William Pickut; daughter, Dr. Catherine Lamberton; sister, Marianne Sorensen-Sack; and local writer-journalist Bob Houston. Most writers have a "day job," too, so special appreciation goes to Stacey Hannon, founder, owner, and publisher of the *Jamestown Gazette*, for adjusting the paper's rhythms as Walt stepped back from editor to contributing editor to devote more time and energy to Larry Haas's story.

Thanks also go to attorneys Greg Peterson and Byron Bilicki at the inception of this project. Colleagues at the Author's Guild (AG) and the American Society of Journalists and Authors (ASJA) have provided countless words of encouragement and resource suggestions for which we are grateful.

Of special importance and with great personal satisfaction, we also thank ASJA for facilitating our introduction to John Willig, an outstanding agent with a sure hand on the rudder who steered us to Gene Brissie at Rowman & Littlefield, where his staff brought this entire project to life.

And beyond thanks, Walt is grateful to his wife, Nancy, who with God's help, discovered levels of patience and wisdom without which Walt could not have completed this adventure.

Notes

Introduction

1. Alexander Feklisov, *The Man Behind the Rosenbergs* (New York: Enigma Books, 2001), 50.

2. Katherine A. S. Sibley, *Red Spies in America: Stolen Secrets and the Dawn of the Cold War* (Lawrence: University Press of Kansas, 2004), passim.

3. Don Whitehead, *The FBI Story—A Report to the People* (New York: Random House, 1956).

4. Ladd to Hoover, 100-340996-300, 6/9/49. Ladd wrote this office memorandum to explain, justify, deny, or otherwise illuminate the findings of two days earlier during the Hearings Before the Committee on Un-American Activities (HUAC), House of Representatives, 81st Congress, "Soviet Espionage Activities in Connection with Jet Propulsion and Aircraft," June 6, 1949.

5. Text of *Gorin v. United States*, 312 U.S. 19 (1941), passim. The conviction was based on the Espionage Act of 1917.

6. Conroy to Director, 100-340996-97, 10/2/45.

7. William C. Sullivan with Bill Brown, *The Bureau: My Thirty Years in Hoover's FBI* (New York: Norton Collection, 1979), 60–61.

8. Tim Weiner, *Enemies: A History of the FBI* (New York: Random House, 2012), 120.

9. FBI file number: 100-203581, Section 63, Part 1, Subject: Comintern Apparatus "The Comintern Apparatus is a phrase used by Soviet representatives and Communists generally to indicate the organisational [*sic*] setup within the Communist Party structure that is more or less under direct instructions from Moscow through Party and Soviet channels and which is utilized by Soviet representatives in this country [United States] for various special purposes including intelligence and related operations." It is also interesting to note in review of FBI file number: 100-17879, COMRAP, San Francisco, March 1946, www.fbi.gov, retrieved 02/12/19, that at the time of its original release, certain sections that probably referred to Loren G. Haas (based on references to events, dates, contact individuals, and the like) were redacted. This observation is consistent with, tends to confirm, Haas's claim that by mutual agreement with the FBI, his ongoing and all future work for and with the Bureau would remain incognito.

10. John Earl Haynes and Harvey Klehr, *Venona: Decoding Soviet Espionage in America* (New Haven, CT: Yale University Press, 1999).

11. Robert Louis Benson and Michael Warner, *Venona: Soviet Espionage and the American Response 1939–1957* (Washington, DC: NSA/CIA, 1996).

12. Over the course of 1945, Schevchenko and Haas met innumerable times at the Bell plant and almost always over ordinary matters of business. But meetings concerning the transfer of information, exposed microfilm, or other events relevant to espionage after which a post-contact interview was held totaled nine, not counting "social" meetings including Mrs. Schevchenko and Mrs. Haas. Haas, however, always reported on those meetings, too.

13. Some declassified as recently as 7/18/2011 and 8/25/2011.

14. HUAC, June 6, 1949.

15. Committee on Un-American Activities, US House of Representatives, 82nd Congress, Report No, 1229, Washington, DC, "The Shameful Years: Thirty Years of Soviet Espionage in the United States," January 8, 1952. The Committee on Un-American Activities is more commonly called the House Un-American Activities Committee (HUAC).

16. *COMRAP: Comintern Apparatus*, File Number: 100-203581, Section 63, Part 1, 153.

17. Current investigations continue to raise questions about this identity. These are discussed in the epilogue to this book.

CHAPTER 1: TWO NEW ARRIVALS

1. Milton had set fire to a Loblaw store near his Buffalo home. He then sat himself down on a tree stump to watch the show. To his delight, the firefighters fought the flames until only a field of smoldering rubble was left to mark their battle. A historian's entry in the archives of the Lackawanna (NY) Fire Fighters, International Association of Fire Fighters AFL-CIO #3166, recalls the event: "One of the costliest fires in the City's history struck the Loblaw store in the new L. B. Smith Plaza on Sunday, September 7, 1952, causing damage of $250,000 and injuring three firefighters. This ignited demands for a firehouse in the Fourth Ward." http://lackawannany.gov/wp-content/uploads/2017/07/HistoryLFD.pdf. Retrieved 1/21/18.

2. Ladd to Hoover, 100-340996-226, 12/17/45. The school and work details of Larry Haas's life in this chapter are taken from this source unless otherwise noted.

3. A conversation vividly recalled by Kay Haas based on her father's frequent recounting in later years.

4. Donald J. Norton, *Larry—A Biography of Lawrence D. Bell* (Chicago: Nelson-Hall, 1981), 97. In August 1941, Bell received an order from the US Army Air Forces for two thousand P-39s to be turned out at the unheard-of rate of five airplanes per day. Within about two years, Bell was rolling twenty of the planes off its assembly lines every day.

5. Stalin's radio broadcast to the Soviet people (July 3, 1941) [Subtitled]. https://www.youtube.com/watch?v=hSTQ7HTHMvo. Accessed 3/2/2018.

6. Among the many warnings delivered to Statin was one sent by Vasily Zarubin, later to become the *resident* in New York City. In the spring of 1941, Zarubin, an NKVD officer on assignment in China, learned from Walter Stennes, a high-ranking German adviser to Chiang Kai-shek, details of Hitler's plans for Operation Barbarossa, Germany's sneak attack on the USSR in mid-1941. This was among the many similar warnings Stalin inexplicably ignored.

7. Von Hardesty and Ilya Grinberg, *Red Phoenix Rising: The Soviet Air Force in World War II* (Lawrence: University Press of Kansas, 2012), 8–13, and personal communication with Grinberg (WP).

8. Rath to file, 100-78534, 10/2/45, and Ladd to Hoover, 100-340996-226, 12/17/45.

9. This account is based on Larry's detailed retelling of Andrei's story and supported by Schevchenko's position in the Directorate of Aviation. On more than one occasion, when he was frustrated with matters at Amtorg and the consulate, he succumbed to too much alcohol and Larry's listening ear. Andrei proudly explained how he was fighting for his homeland by working in the United States.

10. Hardesty and Grinberg, *Red Phoenix Rising*, 8.

11. Stalin's radio broadcast to the Soviet people (July 3,1941) [Subtitled]. https://www .youtube.com/watch?v=hSTQ7HTHMvo. Accessed 3/2/2018.

12. Rath to file, NY 100-78534, 10/2/45, and Ladd to Hoover, 100-340996-226, 12/17/45.

13. Ladd to Hoover, 100-340996-226, 12/17/45.

14. John Allen, ed., *One Hundred Great Lives—Revealing Biographies of Scientists and Inventors, Leaders and Reformers, Writers and Poets, Artists and Musicians, Discoverers and Explorers, Soldiers and Statesmen, Great Women* (New York: Greystone Press, 1944), 490. Leading intellectuals in the United States in the early 1940s often lionized Stalin. Here, Allen classes him with Buddha, Socrates, Churchill, and Sir Isaac Newton. His praise is nearly obsequious, exceeding in page count ninety of the other greats of history. After WWI and the Bolshevik Revolution, "It was Stalin, the builder, who carried through a reconstruction, a re-creation, such as history had never seen before . . . a man of steel . . . a patron of the arts on a scale the world had never known before." The faintest hint of negativity is easily dismissed. "He is ruthless—when he has to be . . . Only since Russia came into the war has the curtain gone up on a spectacle breathtaking in its scope and power." Though more muted in his acquiescence to Stalin's regime, President Franklin D. Roosevelt often clashed with Hoover's intense contrary stance on Stalin and Russia.

15. COMRAP. "A 'Legal agent' is one attached to the embassy, consular staff, or trade mission as a cover for access to the USSR's diplomatic channels of communication to Moscow." In addition, the Comintern dictates that "each Soviet citizen residing abroad is encouraged to gather information." "Encouraged" was understood to be a euphemism for "required."

16. Schevchenko was well suited to his assignment, as Haas learned while working with him.

17. COMRAP. Soviet agents (in the United States) operate within a network of informants, contacts, and sub-agents recruited from Soviet citizens, members of the Communist Party of the United States of America (CPUSA), and "others who can be bribed or coerced into doing the work." The FBI, and therefore Larry Haas, knew counterespionage against a Soviet agent was dangerous. Kay Haas reports that beginning in 1945 she apparently became the tool of coercion to force her father to reveal US military/industrial secrets.

18. On July 22, 1947, a HUAC hearing accepted the testimony of Victor Kravchenko, a Ukrainian-born Soviet defector, who said (through an interpreter) that "no person holding an important position in connection with the economic, political, or military organizations and arriving in the United States from the Soviet Union arrives without a special assignment as to the collection of secret information . . . every responsible representative of

the Soviet Union in the United States may be regarded as a possible economic, political, or military spy. I did not know of one department in the Soviet Purchasing Commission [Amtorg], whether it was aviation, metal, auto tractor, or other, which was not occupied in collecting secret information about its equivalent in American industry." Kravchenko was posted to the Soviet Purchasing Commission in Washington, DC, in 1943, defected to the United States in April 1944, and lived under a pseudonym after that in fear of assassination by Soviet agents.

19. Schevchenko's meetings with Haas are noted (decrypted) in Venona 205 New York to Moscow, May 18, 1943. Haas is also identified as "Shtamp" in Venona 1327, September 15, 1944. Indicating his importance to other Soviet agents, he is also noted in Venona 1607–1608, Anton (Kvasnikov) to Viktor (Fitin), November 16, 1944. It is also of interest to note that by 1952, the FBI was aware of a code-name Shtamp employee at Bell but still not aware it was Haas as noted in Director to SAC Buffalo, 65-2026, 3/21/52.

20. Kay Haas clearly remembers her father's attitude. "I hated that Russian from the first time I met him." She also recalls that her father described his feigned friendship under FBI direction as hard to keep credible, especially assuming Schevchenko was doing the same. Drinking heavily together both helped and jeopardized that pseudo-relationship.

21. Unless otherwise noted, all Franey narratives are taken from Rath to file, 100-78534, 10/2/45 passim and Ladd to Hoover, 100-340996-226, 12/17/45, passim.

22. Ladd to Director, 100-340996-96, 10/1/45.

23. Haynes and Klehr, *Venona*, 374–75, and Rath to file, 100-78534, 10/2/45. There is some indication that Leona had begun to supply Schevchenko with some of the technical data that he requested, refusing only to give him access to reports marked "Secret." On December 8, 1944, the FBI instructed her to extend her prohibition to include "confidential" and "restricted" documents. Evidence suggests she complied with the expanded range after this date. However, in testimony before HUAC in 1949, she denied giving anything at any time to Schevchenko that he was not allowed.

CHAPTER 2: ONE BIG LIE

1. Sibley, *Red Spies in America*, 100. The "man shortages" in WWII production "[demonstrate] how the war's need for qualified engineers clearly outdistanced security concerns."

2. *Bellringer*, February 1941, 16. Bell's success almost overwhelmed his resources. US government contracts and the rising demands of war forced the company to double its workforce almost overnight in response to a demand to raise annual aircraft production from ten thousand to twenty thousand per year.

3. Norton, *Larry*, 53–59.

4. Bell Aircraft company archives are maintained at the Niagara Aerospace Museum, Niagara Falls, New York.

5. III-B: Men with dependents, engaged in work essential to national defense, *Selective Service Regulations*, 1917.

6. Ladd to Hoover, December 18, 1945.

7. Robert A. Kilmarx, *A History of Soviet Air Power* (New York: Praeger, 1962), 211–12. This example of relatively lax security may not have been unique. Soviet technicians were later found to have obtained floor plans of the GE plant in Lynn, Massachusetts, and plans for the "first jet propulsion engine in the United States."

8. Ladd to Hoover, 100-340996-205, 12/18/45.

9. Ladd to Director, 100-340996-96, 10/1/45.

10. George Mellinger and Jim Laurier, *Soviet Lend-Lease Aces of World War 2* (Oxford, UK: Osprey Books, 2006).

11. Hardesty and Grinberg, *Red Phoenix Rising*, 197–98. Pokryshkin is credited with consolidating and adapting older air-tactical maneuvers into the VVS playbook. The result created a devastating and sometimes overwhelming advantage over Luftwaffe pilots. The details are clear in the tactic's name: "altitude, speed, maneuver, fire." It became known as the "Falcon Strike." Pokryshkin flew the first Bell P-39K ever delivered to Russia and was credited with more than fifty Luftwaffe kills.

12. Bill Gunston, *Aircraft of World War 2* (London: Octopus Books Limited, 1980).

13. Hardesty and Grinberg, *Red Phoenix Rising*, 31. Larry had learned of a heroic maneuver called the *taran* from one of the Russian fliers. A pilot refusing to quit the fight after his plane was damaged in battle sometimes chose to ram the German plane in midair to destroy it, then parachute to safety or attempt landing his crippled aircraft if possible. The outcome in *taran* was known to be questionable at best, but heroic in every case.

CHAPTER 3: FIRST MEETING

1. There are few FBI reports on Haas's initial impression and dislike of Schevchenko in their first meeting, though later FBI documents reflect on their early relationship. Kay, however, recalls her father's changing appraisal of the man as the case progressed. As a loan salesman, Larry had learned to take the measure of a person on first meeting. He did as much as he could to instill this ability in Kay and more than once used this story as a cautionary tale. This chapter dramatizes this event based on Larry's testimony, Kay's memory, and FBI documentation concerning the relationship that eventually developed. The date, time, place, and individuals involved are accurate and documented, as noted.

2. Schevchenko was much more than the man Bell introduced to Haas. His role encompassed logistics, finances, and aeronautical sciences. His ability and assignment to observe and report on anything of military-industrial and scientific value placed him in the category of technical intelligence agent, called the "XY line" in Soviet espionage jargon.

3. These two individuals were frequently noted as closely associated with Schevchenko at Bell, often pictured and quoted in various issues of Bell's in-house magazine, *Bellringer*, during 1943 and 1944. Schevchenko often referred to them when talking to Larry as "assistants," but Larry told Kay they seemed more like Andrei's keepers or watchers. In Soviet hierarchy the same individual could be a subordinate and a superior, depending on which table of organization was in effect, be it an individual's place in their legal work or their rank in the Soviet secret police structure. Kay does not believe her father was ever certain about Andrei's role with these two Soviet military officers.

4. Copy retained at Niagara Aerospace Museum, Archive Library.

5. Ladd to Hoover, 100-340996-226, 12/17/45.

CHAPTER 4: AN INVISIBLE NETWORK

1. HUAC, "Shameful Years," 30.

2. Arseniy is alternately transliterated as Arsenij. The latter spelling is Andrei (Andrej), Schevchenko's code name as found in Venona decryptions such as No. 1657, New York to

Moscow, November 27, 1944. The code name may represent an homage to Andrei's son. The existence and name of Andrei's son is based on Andrei's account to Larry. The use of family members as hostages was an established, common practice to assure faithful service by highly placed German and Soviet military officials.

3. Ladd to Hoover, 100-340996-226, 12/17/45, and Sibley, *Red Spies in America*, 106.

4. SAC Scheidt to Director, NY 65-15103, 10/18/49.

5. SAC Edward Scheidt New York to Director, 65-58801-8, 9/18/49. Zarubin operated under an alias of Vasilli Zubilin, a fact known to the FBI, but inexplicably as late as October 1949, he was still being referred to as Zubilin, Second Secretary of the Soviet Embassy in Washington, DC (100-203581-3702), in FBI communications that linked Schevchenko and Haas, with a suspicion that a Bell employee only known as "Professor" in 1943 to 1945 may have been approved by Zubilin to receive eighty thousand dollars for unspecified intelligence. Haas was not the prime suspect operating under the name "Professor," but as late as 1949 Haas still figured in FBI counterespionage cases. It is not clear whether Haas's bank activity was investigated for deposits of this magnitude. This investigation was part of the Jack Soble NKVD *spy ring* known as the *"Mocase."* This case was briefly reopened in 1957 but left the Professor's identity still unknown.

6. Pavel Sudoplatov et al., *Special Tasks: The Memoirs of an Unwanted Witness—A Soviet Spymaster* (Boston: Little, Brown and Company, 1994), 335.

7. Sibley, *Red Spies in America*, 178.

8. Sibley, *Red Spies in America*, 28.

9. Weiner, *Enemies*, 155.

10. John Earl Haynes, Harvey Klehr, and Alexander Vassiliev, *Spies: The Rise and Fall of the KGB in America* (New Haven, CT: Yale University Press, 2009), 374.

11. Venona, No. 1627, November 27, 1944. One Venona decrypt identifies that facility as "Arsenij's [Schevchenko's] plant," indicating Schevchenko's established role within the Soviet hierarchy.

12. Soviet agents engaged in espionage of a scientific/technical nature were called XY-operatives.

13. Haynes, Klehr, and Vassiliev, *Spies*, 373–74. Code names rarely relate to an easily identifiable profession or employment location, but they are usually colorful or distinctive. Schevchenko gave his ten contacts cover names: "Zero" (Franey at Bell); "Bugle"; "Ferro" (Petroff); "Thomas"; "Nemo" (Pinsly); "Armor" (Smeltzer); "Noise"; "Author"; "Bolt"; "Hong" (Haas); and "Arseny" (Schevchenko).

14. Special Collections at Wichita State University, Alexander Petroff Papers, MS 89-15.

15. Sibley, *Red Spies in America*, 144.

16. Hearings Before the Committee on Un-American Activities (HUAC), House of Representatives, 81st Congress, "Soviet Espionage Activities in Connection with Jet Propulsion and Aircraft," Executive Session. June 6, 1949. Confirmation of Fornoff's close, personal relationship with Schevchenko was offered by Franey and Haas in the Executive Session following the Public Session under the committee's sense that some public disclosures would be too damaging to Bell and the government if allowed into the public record.

17. Schevchenko obtained significant intelligence from Beiser. Sibley, *Red Spies in America*, 114.

18. HUAC, June 6, 1949. These words, or words to the same effect, are frequently cited as a standard Soviet enticement for Americans to collaborate in espionage as sub-agents.

19. Rath to file, NY-100-78534, 10/2/45.

20. Sibley, *Red Spies in America*, 114.

CHAPTER 5: THE LONG SEDUCTION

1. Based on known circumstances, we infer that Zarubin was Schevchenko's handler/mentor tasked with assuring that Schevchenko master certain rudiments of spy craft. Many of the harrowing details of these conversations that both instructed and terrified Schevchenko were related to Kay by Larry. These are based on "confidences" divulged by Andrei while under the influence of Andrei's "best American whiskey," which he kept amply stocked in his apartment at 4 West 93rd Street in Manhattan. Schevchenko's "truth serum" often backfired on him in this way.

2. John Simkin, http://spartacus-educational.com/Vasssily_Zarubin.htm.

3. As early as 1942, Akhmerov, while operating as an illegal, had reported to Moscow "that counterintelligence here [US] has become very flexible and farsighted." Such awareness on the part of all Soviet agents in New York City would have made Schevchenko's sharpening in spy craft an urgent matter for Zarubin.

4. Hardesty and Grinberg, *Red Phoenix Rising*, 342–43. Soviet aviation pioneers had been experimenting with the design of jet engines for years before WWII. The war, however, shifted priorities from experimentation to practical production of the better-developed, propeller-driven aircraft technology. The 1944 introduction of highly capable jet fighters into the war by the Germans forced Stalin and his war strategists to renew their quest for jet-powered fighters. Naturally, stealing technology could greatly accelerate development, given the exigencies of war.

5. Haynes, Klehr, and Vassiliev, *Spies*, 488.

CHAPTER 6: SEDUCING LEONA

1. Unless otherwise noted, these events concerning the Franeys between July and December 1944 are drawn from Rath to file, 100-78534, 10/2/45, and Ladd to Hoover, 100-340996-226, 12/17/45.

2. Hearings Before the Committee on Un-American Activities (HUAC), House of Representatives, 81st Congress, "Soviet Espionage Activities in Connection with Jet Propulsion and Aircraft," June 6, 1949.

3. Rath to file, 100-78534, 10/2/45. Filmed surveillance was a relatively new technology for the FBI at this time. It produced an almost unimpeachable record when compared to handwritten, voice-recorded, or photographed documentation.

4. The peculiarity of Andrei's sudden departure was heightened by FBI surveillance, which disclosed that no visitors arrived at Schevchenko's home that evening.

5. Ladd to Director, 100-340669-96, 10/1/45. Leona Franey told Andrei, "If you cannot get these reports by your own requests from the army authorities, I cannot give them to you without violating the espionage laws and being liable for prosecution." The fact that Schevchenko continued to ask for such material from Leona and from Larry Haas in the face of such clear rejection may be grounds to call his spy craft into question.

6. Ladd to Director, 100-340669-96, 10/1/45, and Conroy to file, 100-340996-97, 10/2/45. However, Schevchenko and his Soviet cohorts at Bell Aircraft requested such material on numerous occasions. "Soviet representatives knew this policy. As a result, there have been no formal requests by the Soviets for any information on documents related to these matters." The fact that Schevchenko was not granted diplomatic immunity on entry to the United States allowed him to ply his clandestine trade in a way that would be less likely to cause diplomatic embarrassment to the Soviet Union if he were caught. Andrei's guise as a naive illegal is consistent with a complaint that he once made to Larry that he was not protected by such immunity and therefore vulnerable. He posed his requests in the guise of "personal projects" rather than under a political or military justification, supporting this contention.

7. Ladd to Director, 100-340669-96, 10/1/45. Leona reported this request to her FBI contacts, who coordinated with the US Army Air Forces representative, who determined it was of a highly confidential nature and removed the only copy in the Bell Aircraft Technical Library from circulation.

8. The stage play *Rebecca*, adapted from a 1938 Daphne Du Maurier novel of the same name, enjoyed only twenty performances before closing on Broadway in January/February of 1945, but it remained popular based on a Hitchcock film adaptation that earned an Academy Award for Best Picture of 1940. This stage play is difficult to interpret as a communist parable of the kind Schevchenko often used to gauge the political sympathies of his proposed sub-agents. It might, however, have appealed to him on a more personal, romantic level based on the "gypsy vagabond" years of his youth, perhaps in an attempt to create a more amiable persona for working with Leona and her assistants in the library.

9. Ladd to Director, 100-340996-96, 10/1/45, and Rath to file, 100-78534, 10/2/45. The study Andrei requested is an example of documents whose title and number he learned from a source that was never clearly identified, though contacts at Wright Field in Dayton, Ohio, have been suspected.

10. Ladd to Director, 100-340996-96, 10/1/45, and Rath to file, 100-78534, 10/2/45. Leona would hear pleas of this nature on many occasions. Sometime later, Andrei told her that if the United States were at peace, he could purchase all the reports he wanted without any trouble, but that during wartime he had to be extremely careful.

CHAPTER 7: EVERYBODY'S ENEMY

1. https://www.wnyheritage.org/content/winter_of_1944-45, and https://liberation route.com, passim. Retrieved May 6, 2018.

CHAPTER 8: A MAN TO BE DEALT WITH

1. Kay Haas recounts this event in detail as her father considered it the event—the mistake—that changed his life. He told her the story more than once as a cautionary tale whenever Kay faced a situation that required careful, deliberate thought before speaking. This chapter is Kay's testimony of her father's account augmented by historical documentation. This incident is further corroborated in SAC Buffalo to file, 65-59543-88, 3/6/52.

2. *Kobrushka*, or *Kobra-shka*, names the Soviet fliers gave the P-39s, became a source of great pride to Bell Aircraft workers, the subject of great acclaim by the pilots as published in *Bellringer*, June 1944, 23.

3. Ian Darling, *Heroes in the Skies—American Aviators in WWII* (New York: Sterling, 2016), 85–86. The ALSIB route put up to eight thousand miles and twenty to twenty-five flying hours on each P-39 flown from Bell's Niagara Falls plant to various destinations in the Soviet Union. That "break-in" flight revealed defects, if there were any. In one case, for example, at sixteen thousand feet over Minnesota, one American transport pilot's P-39 that had been performing normally suffered a sudden, potentially explosive engine fire. The pilot barely managed a safe landing by finding a rustic airstrip near the Mayo Clinic. The repair crew reported the engine so badly burned it had turned black. The pilot, a civilian named Betty, decided not to tempt fate. She flew home on a commercial airline.

4. Hardesty and Grinberg, *Red Phoenix Rising*, 292. Rare instances were known, however, in which Airacobras had successfully harassed and attacked German bombers from as high as eighteen thousand feet, presumably by using hard-won altitude to gain speed and maneuverability in diving on their prey. German air ace Helmut Lipfert, following one such nearly fatal encounter, recorded grudging admiration of Russian Airacobra pilots. In his diary he later wrote, "there were Russians in the combat zone who could fly as well as we."

5. HUAC, "Soviet Espionage Activities," 6/6/49. At this point Larry found himself so carried away that he apparently conflated his two-bit fix with another that he also had in mind. He later explained to the HUAC members, "The particular item on which the fabulous sum was set was an item which was already in the hands of the Russian People. At that time, they had in their custody quite a number of obsolete B-17s. All of those had turbo-superchargers on them." Larry could have fixed everything the Russians needed, but he was prohibited by Bell from doing so.

6. Years later, describing this event during the HUAC hearings of 6/6/49, Larry described Bell's reaction euphemistically as, "Unfortunately, this brought perhaps a little bit of frowning from the management, since it was proposed to them previously that it be incorporated." But it was not adopted. Larry said he then found himself "on the 'outs' with my employers," a split Schevchenko decided to exploit.

7. This event, recounted in a much-abbreviated form in HUAC 6/6/49, nearly ended Bell's Lend-Lease commerce with the USSR. In Larry's words, after he admitted his invention would work, "[The Russians] insisted on knowing why it wasn't on their airplanes, and they became quite loud about it, and insisted there would be no more airplanes shipped to their government unless it was incorporated."

8. John Barron, *KGB Today: The Hidden Hand* (London: Hodder and Stoughton, 1984), 240. "Incentivization" for performance in the Soviet intelligence system was often based on lethal Stalinist discipline that resulted in intense performance competition and jockeying for privileged or even safe positions among coworkers.

9. Schevchenko frequently chose the Kenmore Theater as a meeting place. It was well-known and highly visible, but for those reasons possibly ill-chosen as a clandestine meeting spot. In its favor, a theater was a place where anyone or a crowd of people could hang out, loiter, or simply wait without being conspicuous.

10. When the Lend-Lease P-39s first reached Russia, Soviet pilots considered it "a strange new aircraft that was, at first glance, a challenge to understand and master." Nevertheless, air-historian V. Romanenko observed that "Soviet pilots [eventually] preferred the Cobra *despite some of its shortcomings* to any other aircraft received from the Allies, including the [British] Spitfire VB." (Emphasis added)

11. Norton, *Larry*, 95. In its initial configuration the P-39 could climb to 20,000 feet in five minutes at nearly four hundred miles per hour. After reconfiguring as the air forces required, they then rejected it for poor performance and Bell came to consider the plane's performance unsatisfactory anywhere above 10,000 feet. On the other hand, Bell later assured the British "up to an altitude of 16,000 feet where it is designed to fight, the Airacobra's performance surpasses that of the Spitfire, the [German] ME 109s, or the Focke-Wulf 190s."

12. Norton, *Larry*, 96. On January 8, 1941, a P-39 in its original configuration recorded a top speed of 620 miles per hour in a 21,000-foot power-dive from 27,000 feet, piloted by a reserve navy pilot named Andrew C. McDonough.

13. The technology Larry described is noted in Ladd to Hoover, 100-340996-226, 12/17/45.

14. HUAC, 6/6/49.

15. David Donald, ed., *American Warplanes of World War II* (London: Aerospace Publishing, 1995), passim.

16. John Golley, *Jet: Frank Whittle and the Invention of the Jet Engine* (Hampshire, UK: Datum Publishing, 2009). Passim.

17. This account may be apocryphal. It was recounted in a personal conversation (WP attending, 2019) at the Niagara Aerospace Museum (NAM) at Niagara Falls, New York. The museum houses Bell Aircraft's archives, many outstanding displays of aircraft, including an early P-59 engine. A number of NAM's current docents and officers worked at Bell, some in management, not long after the Haas-Schevchenko case became public. This story seems to have been "general knowledge" among Bell employees of the time, passed along through later years as corporate legend.

18. The statement "Secrecy is the enemy of human progress" was a common, ubiquitous "truth" espoused in Soviet propaganda aimed at scientists and technicians at that time.

19. Allen, *One Hundred Great Lives*, 499. The future Soviet utopia was being described by American intellectuals during WWII—persuaded by Soviet assertions like Schevchenko's—as a place where "the greatest rewards in money and honor are reserved for those who have made contributions by means of superior talent, higher education, or greater application—where the highest rewards of all are given to the great engineer, scientist, musician, artist, or writer." Schevchenko wanted Haas to see himself there.

20. Ladd to Hoover, 100-340996-226, 12/17/45.

21. HUAC, "Soviet Espionage Activities," 6/6/49. Larry is quoted as stating this figure in Ladd to Hoover, 100-340996-226, 12/17/45. But in HUAC testimony, Larry states $500,000. Whether this represents a later attempt by him to make the figure even more outrageous, therefore more absurd—indicating a nonserious offer—or whether it is a stenographic error in the testimony transcription is not known. Kay, however, recalls her father using the $50,000 figure.

22. Norton, *Larry*, passim. Larry Bell respected his employees. In 1937 he waived a representation vote for the United Auto Worker's (UAW) Local 501 and negotiated a good contract, heading off labor strife. With his men, he was known for being blunt but fair. With Bell, the workers knew where they stood.

23. Conroy to Hoover: FBI 100-78534. While the FBI agents began recording the serial numbers of all monies Schevchenko gave to informants as soon as they agreed to cooperate with the FBI, it was not until June 1945 that Conroy asked Director Hoover

for funds to give an equal amount of "clean" money back to Haas and Franey for the bills that the informants turned in, or to begin paying them a weekly sum in lieu of such a cash swap. FBI 100-340996-29, 6/13/45. On July 6, 1945, Conroy, having received no reply to his previous request, proposed to Director Hoover that Haas be paid $50 per week plus extraordinary expenses. Philadelphia office memo dated 11/13/45 states that Haas was paid $100 for services as an informant from October 15 to November 8 and notes authorization to pay Haas $50/week. Confirmed for record in SAC Philadelphia to Director, 100-340996-319, 10/20/53.

CHAPTER 9: FIRST DATE

1. SAC Buffalo to file, 651-59543-88, 3/6/52. Colonel Miller and Schevchenko frequently worked together on flight schedules for the P-39s and P-63s and in reviewing equipment test data. Miller would have been an ideal bridge between Andrei and Larry. This meeting required such a third party to engage Haas in certain military-industrial controversies. This file notes the presence of but does not name the third participant at this dinner meeting but circumstantial evidence suggests Colonel Miller as a most plausible candidate.

2. Allen, *One Hundred Great Lives*, 499. Haas suspected, on other occasions, that Schevchenko followed his leader's example. "[Stalin] starts off drinking the copious toasts on the same basis of the rest of the party; but not long after the opening rounds . . . the attendant begins filling his glass with a special concoction which allows him to stay right in on the toasts to the end and still not appear the worse for the wear."

3. This dinner was a favorite among Larry Haas's old stories when, as Grandpa Larry, he told Kay's children tales about "the Russian spy I once knew." He thought children should be taught irreverence toward any inflated ego, especially Stalin and his minions. Kay's memory informs this dramatized version of that night's dinner talk. She especially liked her father's version of the old "three guys enter a bar" line.

4. Also noted in Rath to file, 100-78534, 10/2/45.

CHAPTER 10: RETHINKING FLYING

1. Rainer Maria Rilke (1875–1926), Bohemian poet.

2. Boardman to Director, 100-340996-237, 5/9/46. On May 9, 1946, in a different setting, SAC L. V. Boardman at Philadelphia refers to a March 15, 1945, communication from SA Vincent M. Quinn at Buffalo stating, "Haas mentioned that Schevchenko at one time introduced him to General Piskounov [*sic*—actually Colonel S. A. Pisconoff] (Soviet Purchasing Commission Chief visiting Bell from the Soviet Embassy at Washington, DC), who apparently was aware of the dealings between Haas and Schevchenko . . . the Bureau and the Office of Origin might give consideration to this possible means of re-establishing Haas with the Russians." The suggestion was apparently unnecessary in that the connection between Haas and the Bureau was never officially severed and continued to bear fruit well into the ensuing years of the Cold War.

3. Conroy, 100-78534, 10/2/45. Andrei kept his promise to not ask about the P-59 and jet propulsion, but only until three months later on May 20. His other promises, however, never materialized, though Larry often wondered whether Andrei believed them himself.

4. The US Congress passed the Espionage Act on June 15, 1917, during the presidency of Woodrow Wilson. The law made it a crime for anyone to provide information of any kind with the intent of interfering with the US armed forces and their prosecution of war efforts or to promote the success of enemies of the United States. For an interesting discussion and insight into J. Edgar Hoover's early, zealous applications of this act, see: Weiner, *Enemies*, 13–16.

5. Ladd to Hoover, FBI 100-340996-226, 12/18/45.

CHAPTER 11: SECOND DATE

1. After additional editing out of an hour from Capra's ninety original minutes—described by some critics of the process as censoring—the film was released to the public on May 3, 1945, only two weeks after Haas and Miller saw Andrei's thirty-eight-minute cut. Capra had screened it for troops in Europe a month earlier, where its extreme realism was declared to resemble anti-war propaganda, unsuited for the troops and the public. The unflinching close-ups of the faces of dead soldiers, for example, even after editing, were previously unheard of in American newsreel footage.

2. Andrei's postscript to *The Battle of San Pietro* shocked Larry's senses in a memorable way. It set the stage Andrei had planned in order to widen the gulf between Larry's and Milo's worldviews. Here, Kay dramatizes the scene in dialogue based on her father's deep impression formed in this strange event and the subsequent dinner and drinks. He later said this series of events completely changed his appreciation for the power of well-planned propaganda. "This one even took me in!" he told Kay.

3. Alexander Orlov, *The Secret History of Stalin's Crimes* (New York: Random House, 1953), 216. Liquidation was the standard Soviet disciplinary measure for "wrong thinking" or for failure in the field. It was often administered by firing squad—*rasstrel'naya komanda*. Sibley, *Red Spies in America*, 64. In 1937, Stalin had more than three thousand supposedly unfaithful or failed KGB officers shot, a cautionary statement for all who followed.

4. Christopher Andrew, *The Sword and the Shield: The Mitrokhin Archive and the Secret History of the KGB* (New York: Basic Books, 1999), 93. Stalin was antagonistic toward agents who warned that Hitler was planning to attack the Soviet Union. For example, he dismissed alerts from Richard Sorge (stationed in Tokyo). Sorge was revered in Soviet intelligence as one of the finest, but Stalin accused him of spreading disinformation, calling him a lying "shit who has set himself up with some small factories and brothels in Japan." Stalin rejected all warnings from highly credible sources throughout his intelligence network worldwide.

5. HUAC, "Soviet Espionage Activities," 6/6/49, 120–22.

6. SAC Buffalo to file, 65-59543-88, 3/6/52. Because of Schevchenko's elevated position in the hierarchy of international commerce, especially in aircraft, he was often seen as a valuable job lead or reference. He was used to influencing both employers and employees about work placement. Bell Aircraft test pilot Brian Orville Sparks, for example, after breaking both legs in a plane crash, went to Amtorg to ask Schevchenko, with whom he had become friendly at Bell, for help getting a job at the Export-Import Company in New York City. Schevchenko's plan to influence Haas to transfer to Westinghouse was not unusual or ill-founded.

7. NSA/CIA, *Venona*, 732. As early as May 20 and September 14, 1944, the New York to Moscow coded radio channel carried technical information about Westinghouse's top secret jet engine research gathered by an agent code-named GNOME (William Perl, an American physicist). Schevchenko now wanted Haas at Westinghouse.

8. Robert C. Rubel, (2010) "The U.S. Navy's Transition to Jets," Naval War College Review: Vol. 63 : No. 2 , Article 6, 4. Available at: https://digital-commons.usnwc.edu/nwc-review/vol63/iss2/6. Retrieved 01/12/21.

9. David O. Woodbury, *Battlefronts of Industry: Westinghouse in World War II* (New York: John Wiley & Sons, 1948), 277–86.

10. Rubel, "The U.S. Navy's Transition to Jets," 1. retrieved 01/12/21.

11. Conroy to file, 100-78534, 10/2/45. At this time, Schevchenko was experiencing a cascade of important and welcome changes. One day after telling Larry of his promotion, he arrived at New York City at 8:45 a.m. the next morning, February 23, 1945, his last official date at Bell, and continued on to Washington, DC, on February 26, to confer with his superiors at the Soviet Government Purchasing Commission, 3355 16th Street, NW.

CHAPTER 12: THIRD DATE AND GOODBYE

1. СССР (Союз Советских Социалистических Республик) is a Russian abbreviation for the Union of Soviet Socialist Republics (USSR), the Soviet Union. CCCP is Cyrillic script equivalent to "SSSR" in Latin script.

2. In New York City, FBI surveillance became highly detailed. Schevchenko arrived alone on February 25 and departed for Washington, DC, the next day, where he stayed for an undetermined period. In transit, he stored one of two suitcases in a locker at Grand Central Station. Agents gained access and found it contained a pamphlet, "Gas Turbines and Jet Propulsion for Aircraft," by G. Geoffrey Smith, O.B.E., English-Russian and Russian-English dictionaries, and other popular literature on aircraft. Nothing of a secret or confidential nature was found.

3. Conroy to file, 100-78534, 10/2/45. Schevchenko arranged for a permanent residence at apartment 3D, 4 West 93rd Street, to which he brought his family from Buffalo on April 3. Within two weeks Schevchenko gave Mrs. Franey two hundred dollars and requested aeronautical information to be sent to him from Bell. The New York City office opened an individual case file on Schevchenko at that point and transferred surveillance from Buffalo.

4. Hoover to Vaughn, a friend and adviser of President Truman, November 5, 1946, "Soviet Government Purchasing Commission" (also March 29, 1946), FBI file, box169, OSF, HSTL.

5. Sibley, *Red Spies in America*, 25.

6. Conroy to file, 100-78534, 10/2/45.

7. Larry told Kay, "Those Russian pilots deserved a better backer at the plant than the one Schevchenko forecast. Andrei was smart, but that made him an exception." The true identity of Schevchenko's replacement, if there indeed was one, is not known, but his description was clearly intended to motivate Haas to move on.

CHAPTER 13: BIRTH OF A COUNTERSPY

1. This event was pivotal for Larry Haas, the FBI, and the entire Schevchenko case. It is documented where possible and partially reconstructed for dramatic purposes as dialogue from many sources, including FBI records, *Bellringer* magazine, and Kay's testimony concerning Larry's multiple retellings of this remarkable meeting.

2. *Bellringer*, July 1941, 8–9. The Bell Aircraft Security Service functioned as law enforcement at the plant with duties extending as far as espionage detection.

3. Robert J. Lamphere and Tom Shachtman, *The FBI-KGB War: A Special Agent's Story* (New York: Random House, 1986), 13. Robert J. Lamphere, a fourteen-year veteran of the Bureau, wrote, "We [agents] were constantly afraid of earning the displeasure of Hoover—who, we learned, could fire any of us at any time for any infraction of the multitudinous rules that governed the conduct of an FBI man, on or off the job. Unlike other government employees, we in the FBI were not covered by many civil service protections."

4. "Faded Glory: Dusty Roads of An FBI Era." http://historicalgmen.squarespace.com/. Retrieved 3/12/18.

5. For twenty-first-century comparison, this average, off-the-rack price represented 20 to 25 percent of an average American man's weekly pay. Hoover required dark, unadorned suits with white shirt and conservative tie for all agents at all times.

6. Haynes, Klehr, and Vassiliev, *Spies*, 375. One Soviet cable transmitted in late 1944 (decoded after the war) noted that Haas had already given Schevchenko detailed drawings of a jet engine then under development at Bell Aircraft, presumably of the General Electric J-31 that Haas was working on, for installation in the Bell P-59 aircraft. This material would have been classified as top secret. Haas, however, continued to deny this. The fact that Schevchenko continued to ask for such drawings throughout 1945 is consistent with Haas's denials.

7. Conroy to file, 100-78534, 10/2/45. Whether or not this was a real or sham offer remains in doubt. Conroy describes it as: "Haas attempted to sell a theory on jet propulsion to Schevchenko for $50,000." Ultimately, Haas describes the "attempt" as a sham and the item was not a theory but hardware.

8. HUAC, "Soviet Espionage Activities," 116–19.

9. Larry Loftis, *Code Name: Lise: The True Story of the Woman Who Became WWII's Most Highly Decorated Spy* (New York: Gallery Books, 2019), 52–53. In October 1941, a French resistance fighter named Jean Lucien "Kiki" Keiffer was arrested by the Nazi *Geheime Feldpolizei*, the Secret Field Police. Kiki quickly changed allegiance to work for the Germans. Illustrating a spy's Ego/Excitement motive, Kiki's interrogator, Hugo Masterman, wrote in a postwar report to the British MI5, "There are [spies] who have a natural predilection to live in that curious world of espionage and deceit, and who attach themselves with equal facility to one side or the other, so long as their craving for adventure of a rather macabre type is satisfied."

10. Rath to file, 100-78534, 10/2/45. At this point the New York City field office assumed responsibility to place this meeting under surveillance. Special Agents Harvey Rath, Francis X. Plant (identified in Lamphere, *FBI-KGB War*, 21, as "a walking archive of the identities, features and peculiarities of Soviet agents"), and others included photographic and movie records in their reports. This handoff with Philadelphia, however, was not yet perfect. It required better coordination between Philadelphia and New York City concerning the time and place of meetings. As a result, neither Schevchenko nor Haas were

under surveillance for their May 20, 1945, meeting. These were still early days of counterspy surveillance.

11. Rath to file, 100-78534, 10/2/45. Larry Haas's formal resignation from Bell Aircraft became effective on 3/14/45.

12. Conroy to file, 100-78534, 6/11/45. This agreement is further confirmed: "Informant Loren G. Haas has cooperated with the bureau and has furnished considerable information concerning his contacts with Schevchenko."

CHAPTER 14: MOVING THERE

1. Kay Haas was a personal witness and a participant in this event. The narrative is reconstructed from her memory, known events, and the key employment document still in her possession.

2. This leaflet can be found online as published by the War Manpower Commission. https://www.docsteach.org.

3. The original document, reproduced here verbatim, is in the possession of Kay Haas.

4. Fletcher to file, 100-30568, 7/27/45. This position placed Larry at the nexus of top secret design, development, and operation of the first fully US-bred jet engine and the navy fighter planes that would use them. It was also exactly where Andrei Schevchenko wanted him.

CHAPTER 15: A FIRST COLLABORATION

1. Kay inserts this New York cabbie vignette only to characterize her father for the reader. He spoke of New York City's "hack drivers" as a feisty breed, irascible, and cantankerous, but good at heart. This trip to New York City occurred, Kay says, so a cab ride like this must have, too.

2. HUAC, "Soviet Espionage Activities," 6/6/49. Larry described this event four years later to committee member Tavenner. "This date [March 18, 1945] actually is the one on which he [Schevchenko] approached me from the standpoint of obtaining for him highly secret turbojet engine data, drawings, reports, and other pertinent information. I agreed to do, upon the previous advice of the Federal Bureau." This took place less than two weeks after March 7, 1945, when Larry agreed to cooperate with the FBI.

3. Rath to file, 100-78534, 10/2/45. Such peculiar surveillance techniques fascinated Kay Haas, beginning with this one, which her father related in detail. His recollection differs in only one minor respect from the surveillance account, which states Larry and Andrei "walked leisurely around the midtown area for approximately 30 minutes, stopping leisurely for drinks." Larry described that leisurely walk as including another lesson in surveillance avoidance and a spirited discussion over drinks about future airplane factory designs, as described here, before meeting at Wivel.

4. At this point, as Larry related later in life after many more peculiar turns of events with Soviet intelligence, Larry said he had his first inkling that if Andrei could not get him to deliver key information to the Soviet Union, Andrei would have been delighted to deliver Larry himself as a willing new builder of the nascent communist utopia.

5. Lamphere, *FBI-KGB War*, 29–30. Wivel was known to the FBI as a favorite "watering hole for visiting Russians . . . there was still near-famine in Moscow . . . but the

smorgasbord was bountiful." Andrei once boasted to Larry that when scouting new locations for Amtorg—it had outgrown its present location—he had entertained New York's Mayor LaGuardia at Wivel.

6. Larry was charmed by the phrase, surely enhanced by its exotic place and manner of delivery. It and this delightful meeting with Thor's sister became a favorite bauble in the tales he later told from his personal folklore. Kay recalls him often repeating that phrase whenever a situation called for a charming, forgiving way to say "That's okay"—*"Det blir bra."* The following dialogue is a dramatic reconstruction based on Kay's recollection of her father's account and key topics Andrei seemed to think were important that day in beginning to recruit a valuable sub-agent. Soviet logic fascinated Larry. In his defense, he was known often to remind people, "To understand something or someone is not necessarily to agree."

7. The Yakovlev aircraft, notably the Yak-1, Yak-3, and Yak-7, are richly described in Hardesty and Grinberg, *Red Phoenix Rising*, passim.

8. Meeting reconstructed from Ladd to Director, 100-340996-96, Rath to file, 100-340996-97, 10/2/45, passim.

9. Rath to file, 100-78534, 10/2/45. Schevchenko resided at this address until renting an apartment on West 93rd Street to move into with his family. The rooming house typifies the close contact Soviet employees kept with each other, both for cultural comfort and mutual surveillance. A number of other Amtorg employees shared this rooming house.

CHAPTER 17: NEW PRIORITIES

1. Weiner, *Enemies*, 100–101. Within the FBI, "unlike other government agencies at the time, the Soviets were considered as much an enemy as the Germans." This was clear as early as the 1941 Ovakimian affair (see Sibley, *Red Spies in America*, 74). Gaik Balodovich Ovakimian was the chief of the New York Amtorg office but pardoned of propaganda violations and allowed to return to Russia as a diplomatic gesture of good will to the Soviet Union after the German invasion. Ovakimian was later found to have been a key spymaster before his departure.

2. Andrew, *The Sword and the Shield*, 112.

3. Arnold Beichman. "Roosevelt's Failure at Yalta" (Stanford University, Hoover Institution), October 30, 2004. https://www.hoover.org/research/roosevelts-failure-yalta. Retrieved 06/03/20.

4. Sibley. *Red Spies in America*, passim. Soviet espionage was a low priority for the Roosevelt administration. Sibley demonstrates that the FDR administration clearly did not make capturing of Soviet spies a priority during the war.

5. Venona decrypt No. 1469, October 17, 1944, is one of many that refer to Roosevelt by the code name Kapitan, one of the few Soviet intelligence code names that can be interpreted as respectful in deference to his office, possibly reflecting his softer attitude toward the Soviets. A similar case of code name matching a Soviet characterization was the code name Nabob given to Henry Morganthau Jr., the US Secretary of the Treasury under Roosevelt, in supposed mockery of his wealth and haughty behavior. Venona 1838, New York to Moscow, 12/29/44.

6. Magnuson, Ed, "The Truth About Hoover," *Time*, December 22, 1975, 14.

7. Timothy Miscamble, *From Roosevelt to Truman* (Cambridge: Cambridge Univ. Press, 2007), 51.

Chapter 18: Trying Again

1. Ladd to Hoover, 100-340996-226, 12/17/1945. To establish his importance and credibility in the eyes of the Franeys, Schevchenko boasted of lavish spending and moving into a prestigious apartment recently vacated by the chairman of Amtorg.

2. Address confirmed in Rath to file, NY-100-78534, 10/2/45.

3. Spring tabs are controls that are placed on airplane ailerons, elevators, or rudders. They control the longitudinal stability of a plane. They primarily correct defects in a plane's design. The Bell Aircraft Corporation never used any spring tabs on its airplanes. Reports on such technology at the Bell library were contained in confidential memoranda from NACA on practically all fighter planes produced in the United States and a few bombers.

4. Rath to file, NY-100-78534, 10/2/45.

5. This was an Oscar-nominated drama starring Bette Davis playing a schoolteacher determined to bring formal education to a Welsh coal mining town despite strong local opposition. For Andrei—following the communist playbook of persuasion—this is another parable of the unrecognized dignity and strength of the working class in capitalist society and the valor of rare upper-class people who nurture heroes of the underclasses. It was a clear attempt to gauge the Franeys' political sensitivities as potential fellow travelers and co-conspirators. Their response to Andrei on this occasion is unknown but they continued to cooperate with the FBI against him.

Chapter 19: A New Beginning

1. This excerpt from Truman's May 8, 1945, radio speech announcing Germany's unconditional surrender to the war-weary American public should also be understood in the context of his well-known anti-communist convictions and his growing knowledge of the Soviet Union's increasing espionage efforts in the United States and its designs on eastern Europe. www.americanrhetoric.com. Retrieved 2/14/2020.

2. Margaret Graver, *Letters on Ethics: To Lucilius (The Complete Works of Lucius Annaeus Seneca)* (Chicago: University of Chicago Press, 2017).

3. Figures vary depending on definitions, for example whether half-tracks are counted as trucks or separately, or whether tanks and tank chassis are counted together, but the unprecedented, enormous magnitude of production is beyond dispute. US government statistics can be found at https://www2.census.gov/prod2/statcomp/. Retrieved 8/14/19.

Chapter 20: Into the Spider's Lair

1. This account of Saturday, May 19, is based on, Ladd to Director, 100-340996-96, 10/1/45, Rath to file, 100-78534, 10/2/45, Ladd to Hoover, 100-340996-226, 12/17/45, and on aspects of these personal experiences related to Kay by Larry Haas.

2. https://www.poetrybyheart.org.uk/, retrieved 12/4/18.

3. Andrei had given Larry sixty dollars for Dorothy's travel expenses.

4. The events of May 20 and the following night are drawn from Fletcher to file, 100-30568, 7/27/45; Ladd to Hoover, 100-340996-226, and recollections of Kay Haas.

5. HUAC, "Soviet Espionage Activities," 6/6/49. Larry later related that "in that time of war there were scarcities, among which were cigarettes and good scotch. Mr. Schevchenko's apartment lacked nothing. He had a complete array of liqueurs and cigarettes and food and money. He had everything one could desire."

6. This movie was a 1945 box office hit and a tale of class struggle. It inspired Americans who saw the Soviet experiment in communism as a harbinger of a classless paradise. It was also Andrei's attempt to gauge his new friends' political views. This entire day's events are documented in SA Fletcher to file, FBI 100-30568, 7/27/45.

7. This event illustrates Andrei's convoluted and sometimes artless scheming to engage Larry in a way that might elicit collaboration. This particular evening, however, deepened the rift between Larry and Dorothy in a way that Kay later heard about from both her father and mother with remarkable similarity in both accounts. Many children—Kay included—sometimes hear reciprocal parental complaints.

8. Hardesty and Grinberg, *Red Phoenix Rising*, 32. The early Yakovlev series, the Yak-1, -2, and -3, were a heroic and largely successful improvement over pre-Barbarossa vintage VVS aircraft, but a few problems remained to be solved after rushing them into service against the Luftwaffe, including chronic fuel leaks, cockpit canopy defects, and shortages of critical components for repair and maintenance.

9. Andrei was trying to make Larry feel complicit in his scheme. Guilt by association was still a tenuous gamble, though. Andrei may instead have been trying to create a sense of credit by association for a plan with good prospects for success.

10. Obtaining the right camera was not a trivial matter. In a January 4, 1945, Venona decrypt (Reissue T210.2 and 211, No. 18-19) AL'BERT (Akhmerov) is urgently asking for a CONTAX camera. "It is extremely difficult to get one here [New York]." He requests help from L. A. Tarasov (a Soviet diplomat in Mexico, a better source).

CHAPTER 21: FINAL DOUBTS

1. This meeting of the Interim Committee in Washington, DC, is factual. George Bucher is known to have attended, though Haas's attendance is not documented in the FBI files available. Haas would have been an observer, not a committee attendee. Larry Haas described this event to Kay as "one of the most remarkable experiences in my life."

2. *New York Times*, February 24, 1938. Headline: "Bucher Promoted by Westinghouse; Former Assembly Worker in Pittsburgh Plant Elected President of Company."

3. Lamphere, *FBI-KGB War*, 21. Retired Special Agent Robert Lamphere called Rath "a gem." Agents were selected by the FBI for intelligence and ingenuity, among other traits also valued in industry. The FBI eventually lost Rath to industry, Rath having invented a "baby crib gadget" while recuperating from an illness at home. A toy company, impressed with his "gadget," offered him better pay and less risk.

4. The meeting described here became an indelible memory and a defining moment for Larry Haas, though he was ordered by Bucher to "forget you attended." Haas's attendance was sub-rosa. This Interim Committee was formed at the urgent request of leaders of the Manhattan Project. Larry later told Kay this was the first time he met President Truman. The second meeting, described later, was cloaked in deeper secrecy. A complete transcript of this June 1, 1945, meeting, including attendees, is available from archivists at http://nuclearfiles.org/. Retrieved 1/3/2020. (http://nuclearfiles.org/menu/key-issues/nuclear-weapons/history/pre-cold-war/interim-committee/interim-committee-informal-notes_1945-06-01.htm)

5. The following dialogue is both quoted from the transcribed content of the meeting and in places paraphrased for brevity faithful to the content, with the exception of Truman's

conversation with Haas, given here in a dramatic reconstruction based on Haas's description and Kay's memory of his stories about this event.

6. According to National Archives: Daily Appointments of Harry S. Truman, Friday, June 1, 1945, the president would have been between appointments with a Mr. Philip Buck at 3:30 and US Army General Mark W. Clark at 3:45. Though Clark would not be privy to Manhattan Project deliberations, he was soon to take an important role in negotiations with the Stalinist regime and its minions in Europe. The work of Soviet agents like Schevchenko would have been relevant. Clark had been promoted to four-star rank on March 10 and led the 15th Army Group in the Spring 1945 offensive that ended the war in Italy. He accepted the German surrender in Italy and delivered unconditional surrender terms to German forces there and in West Austria, becoming commander in chief of US Forces of Occupation in Austria at the end of the war. Truman's growing caution toward communist activities can be seen in his back-to-back conversations with Haas and Clark on the same day. See https://www.trumanlibrary.gov/. Retrieved 2/4/2020.

CHAPTER 22: LOSING HIS GRIP

1. FBI 100-340996226, 12/17/45.

2. This was most likely a symmetrical airfoil, a design well suited to precision aerobatic planes, possibly in Schevchenko's estimation for highly maneuverable fighters, as well as the V1-style missiles he mentioned.

3. This event may have been a further reflection of pressure on Schevchenko for performance and intelligence from across his network. While Bell had no involvement with Japanese aircraft, others in Schevchenko's network probably did. Confusing sources with each other under pressure would have been both dangerous and embarrassing for him. Unsuited by nature and poorly trained in clandestine work, Andrei's stability was being challenged.

CHAPTER 23: READING MATTER TO DIE FOR

1. Ladd to Hoover, 100-340996-226, 12/17/45.

2. Conroy to Director, 100-340996-29, 6/13/45.

3. This is a direct quote repeated by Kay in describing her father's many explanations for joining and staying with his FBI collaboration over the years, though this was the only lighthearted one he ever admitted to.

4. Weiner, *Enemies*, 27. As early as 1919, Hoover was aware of dirty money and blood money funding Soviet espionage and sabotage in the United States. In the earliest days, such funding also included gold and diamonds smuggled from overseas. "The Comintern was trying to underwrite its American allies with smuggled gold and diamonds."

5. Conroy to Director, 100-340996-22, 6/15/45, in response to FBI Urgent teletype.

6. Reconstructed from Kay's testimony of her father's account and from FBI documentation of key points of the ensuing conversation at Schevchenko's apartment in New York City.

7. Fletcher to file, FBI 100-30568, 7/27/45. This unusual reluctance to drink shows Andrei's rising caution shading toward paranoia.

8. Sibley, *Red Spies in America*, 114. Soviet intelligence agents had detected closer monitoring by the FBI. The Soviet Consulate found itself under "increasing surveillance."

Schevchenko was advised by NKVD *rezident* Stepan Apresyan to photograph documents at his apartment to avoid detection at the consulate, where many of the agents brought material for photographing.

9. Conceivably, Andrei was working with his Republic Aircraft rocket engineer contact code-named B on his own version of the JB-2 Robot bomb that would have the weapons capability of the German V-1 buzz-bomb.

10. Conroy to Director, 100-340996-49, 7/6/45. Andrei's wish list had changed again. Whether this reflected changing demands from the Soviet researchers Andrei was supposed to feed information to or Andrei's search for weak spots in Westinghouse's classification system is unclear, but his requests were escalating.

11. Fletcher to file, 100-30568, 7/27/45. The phrase "if you can go along" quoted here is as close as Andrei ever came to a direct request for Larry to enlist as a sub-agent.

12. Fletcher to file, FBI 100-30568, 7/27/45. Andrei was sharing the rental of a residential home with Amtorg's president but calling it a dacha, probably in a bid to impress Larry. A dacha is a Russian seasonal or year-round cottage or second home, usually in the country or near a beach. It is unlikely that Andrei could afford a dacha in Rye, New York, on his own. The Soviet Consulate used the home for visiting dignitaries and officers. This kind of self-aggrandizement by Andrei was common.

13. Fletcher to file, 100-30568, 7/27/45. If money was supposed to be addictive to a capitalist man like Larry, Andrei was glad to be the pusher. He would try to create a useful dependency.

14. Conroy to Hoover, 100-340996-48, 6/27/45.

15. SAC EE. Conroy to Director, 100-340996-29, 6/13/45.

16. Conroy to Hoover, 100-340996-49, 7/6/45. Nearly every procedural question raised by the FBI in this investigation had, as yet, no routine answer. Deliberations sometimes delayed and jeopardized progress. In such cases, Conroy sometimes "managed up" his chain of command in this way. Later, Hoover can be seen attempting the same toward the Department of Justice. The Schevchenko case helped initiate the FBI's subsequent anti-espionage playbook. Another request on the topic, dated 7/14/45, was sent by Conroy to the director (apparently redirected to Assistant Director D. M. Ladd for action) in an FBI teletype marked URGENT. It stated in part: "Answer to my letter requested immediately, so that the informants [Haas and Franey] may intelligently meet subject [Schevchenko] ... and so that a definite procedure may be followed concerning money paid to informants by subj."

17. Ladd to Director, 100-340996-272, 12/19/46. Payment to Haas succumbed to indecision. A December 19, 1946, memorandum from Ladd to Director, Ladd states, "In connection with the services rendered by this informant it is pointed out that Loren Haas was active as an informant for purely patriotic reasons and that at no time did he receive regular reimbursements for his services." SAC Philadelphia to Director, 100-340996-319, 10/20/53 however, states Haas was paid $50 per week (one month, 1945).

CHAPTER 24: A PROFITABLE VACATION

1. The following Franey account is drawn and reconstructed from Rath to file, 100-78534, 10/2/45, Ladd to Director, 100-340996-96, and 10/1/45, HUAC, June 6, 1949, passim. Larry had also recounted parts of this event, as he later heard it from Leona, retold derisively of Schevchenko.

2. Considering Andrei's frequently noted suspicion that his apartment was bugged, quite possibly by his own Soviet secret police, this was most probably an attempt to listen for clues concerning the Franeys' loyalty or disloyalty to Andrei's schemes.

3. This odd sequence of events exposed the Franeys to the intense rivalry for control of valuable assets and the stifling environment of surveillance within the Soviet system. Since Wivel was a favorite of Soviet agents in New York City, Andrei's nervousness may have reflected orders for him to place the Franeys under more watchful eyes and ears by taking them there. Andrei's insistence that they occupy his apartment alone quite probably placed them under audio surveillance by the microphone bugs that always prompted him to play loud music to cover conversations with his guests. The People's Paradise transplanted its Orwellian nightmare to wherever Soviet citizens worked, whether at home or abroad.

4. Rath to file, 100-78534, 10/2/45. Andrei was clearly on a charm offensive aimed at wowing the Franeys. Toots Shor's Restaurant was an iconic New York City landmark habituated by the famous and the powerful. It was owned and operated by Bernard "Toots" Shor, who often hosted Frank Sinatra, Marilyn Monroe, Yogi Berra, Judy Garland, Ernest Hemingway, Orson Welles, and many more of that ilk. Years later, old friends mounted a plaque at the site of the restaurant inscribed: "Where the 'crumb bums' who played sports and the 'crumb bums' who wrote about them got together with those who rooted for them and read them, especially Toots."

5. Throughout Andrei's negotiations with the Franeys and Larry Haas, he often framed his requests as important on a personal level, hence including Antonina, rather than on a military level. He apparently hoped to disarm notions and suspicions of aiding an ally that was slowly revealing itself to be a rival, if not an enemy. The personal avarice that Andrei tried to display would supposedly be more acceptable to a capitalist citizen than would be his zeal for a militarist ideal. The Franeys had not displayed sufficient sympathy to Andrei's ideology to place them in his camp as fellow travelers. He targeted them with the M in MICE—money—rather than the I—ideology.

6. Rath to file, NY-100-78534, 10/2/45.

7. This would serve two related purposes. First, it would assure Andrei that Joe Franey, the agreed-upon photographer for this and subsequent assignments, had mastered the camera. Second, it was a "safe" request intended to begin getting Leona accustomed to obtaining information. It would be a prelude to requesting minor confidential items that would only bend a rule for pay. Once comfortable with that, Leona could be persuaded that more confidential items were really no worse. Having bent, then broken the rules, no matter how slightly, Leona could supposedly be controlled to give Andrei anything he wanted under threat of exposure and/or loss of the income. The camera was the gate at the top of a slippery slope that Soviet intelligence operatives used expertly. This would also be a test of Andrei's ability to master the technique. It did not, however, adequately account for Leona's and Joe's patriotism and integrity.

CHAPTER 25: SPY CRAFT IN EXECUTION

1. Conroy to Hoover, 100-304996-34, 7/20/45. For this meeting there seems to have been some confusion between the Philadelphia and New York FBI field offices concerning whether or not surveillance of this meeting would be made. SAC Conroy sent an urgent, coded teletype to Director Hoover on 7/20/45 requesting guidance. Surveillance was

ultimately approved on "an extremely discrete basis." This kind of near-miss on surveillance was rare in this investigation.

2. The average monthly apartment rent in New York City through the 1940s was about fifty dollars, with many adequate living spaces priced considerably lower.

3. Conroy to Director, 100-340996-34, 7/20/45. This is from a handwritten note found on an urgent FBI teletype in which Conroy requested the NYC office be advised of Haas's upcoming meeting with Schevchenko on 7/21–7/22 in case surveillance coverage is desired. In such a case "Philadelphia should furnish [to Conroy] all details concerning the meeting." This once again illustrates that in the Haas-Schevchenko case, the FBI was still developing its methods for its new counterespionage initiative against the Soviets.

4. Rath to file, 100-78534, 10/2/45.

5. Rath to file, 100-78534, 10/2/45.

6. Fletcher to file, 100-30568, 7/27/45.

7. Conroy to Hoover, 100-78534, 7/6/45. This is the earliest request in the Haas-Schevchenko files seeking permission from the Joint Chiefs and "a technically qualified Bureau representative" to clear technical documents that Haas could give to Schevchenko, "and to assist in proving any violations of the espionage statutes by Schevchenko." Special reference is made to technical reports on "compressor fuel pumps and turbines of jet propulsion planes."

8. The threat of disclosure in this way, akin to a blackmail threat by the accused, implicit in this case rather than stated, was called "graymail," no less a danger than blackmail.

9. This comment was prescient. Larry and Hoover would make good use of it after all else failed.

Chapter 26: Invisibility, Bombs, and Victors

1. The argument reconstructed here between Andrei and Larry concerning the most likely victor to be declared in the Pacific War was recounted many times by Larry to Kay, friends, and family as a source of amazement at the hubris of the Soviet side. Subsequent historians, however, do find that a more nuanced and complex explanation describes the event better than either side's version alone. The accounts of Andrei's surveillance detection and evasion are taken from accounts in numerous personal and FBI post-contact interviews with Larry, many of which he found quite humorous.

2. Wilcox to Director, 100-9708, 10/18/45. Leona gave the postcard to Agent Quinn. It had been postmarked July 31, 1945, 12-PM, Grand Central Annex. The front bore a diagram of the Statue of Liberty, the Rockefeller Center, and the Empire State Building. Though addressed to Joe Franey, the note on the back began "Hello Leona." It ended "Andrei."

3. This camera was clearly a top-of-the-line model that Andrei obviously thought was perfect for the application he had in mind. It had a 4.5 F, two-inch telephoto kino plasmic lens built by Hugo Meyer & Co., a yellow filter 2X, and an onteca shield with a lens.

4. Ladd to Director, 100-340996-96, 10/1/45. This total of $240 is the largest payment Schevchenko is known to have paid to the Franeys or Haas at a single time, though payments to other sources in his network are unknown.

5. Rath to file, 100-78534, 10/2/45.

6. Athodyd thrust refers to the function of a ramjet, the "flying stovepipe." Athodyd (*aero thermodynamic duct*) powered planes were being studied by the Luftwaffe near the end of WWII, as well as US researchers. They were jet engines with essentially no moving parts, promising high thrust, high speed, and relatively simple manufacturing.

7. The times and movements of this meeting between Schevchenko and the Franeys were confirmed as a cross-check of their post-contact interview by photographic surveillance. The Franeys consistently proved to be accurate and truthful reporters in all ways that could be verified by physical surveillance. This level of observation and confirmation shows that throughout the FBI investigation of the Haas-Schevchenko case FBI skills and procedures continued to evolve in a positive direction.

8. Rath to file, 100-78534, 10/2/45. This brief but peculiar event and the subsequent meeting between Schevchenko and Haas was photographically recorded by Special Agent Rath. In Larry's recollection of Andrei's surveillance detection/evasion lesson in the park on this occasion, it was described to Kay as an example of Schevchenko's misplaced confidence in his ability to detect surveillance.

9. Ladd to Hoover, 100-340996-226, 12/17/45.

10. This account is based on Fletcher to Hoover: FBI 100-304966-50, 8/23/45, Fletcher to Hoover: FBI 100-30568, 10/24/45, and elements of these events that were recounted to Kay by her father.

11. "'Tooey' Spaatz: Bomber of Japan," *Life Magazine*, August 20, 1945, 11, 25. In this issue Spaatz is quoted as asking the rhetorical question that still resonates more than seventy-five years later. "Wouldn't it be an odd thing if these were the only two atomic bombs ever dropped?" Haas recounted this brief episode as offering a lighter moment while waiting for the agents and practicing elements of surveillance detection and evasion. He had kept a copy of this *Life Magazine* (since lost) and quipped that the general deserved another star just for tolerating the nickname.

12. Ronald Schaffer, *Wings of Judgment: American Bombing in World War II* (New York: Oxford University Press, 1985), 13.

13. Kay recalls that her father, though never averse to beer and spirits, complained about his own tendency later in life to sometimes drink too much, blaming it on a habit and a perverse "taste for more" that he had gained through many hard-drinking nights with "that crazy Russian" Schevchenko. As he grew older, he found it difficult to refrain at times, though he denied lapsing into alcoholism, a mostly successful restraint that Kay confirms.

14. SAC Philadelphia to Hoover, 100-340996-62, 8/31/45 and Rath to file, 100-78534, 10/2/45. The letter is transcribed from Fletcher to file, 100-340996-119, 10/24/45. This meeting was observed by Rath. Motion pictures were taken by Special Agent Smith. Quotations and actions in this account are taken from this file.

15. Considering the scarcity and expense of the cameras that Schevchenko gave to Leona Franey and Larry Haas, Schevchenko's decision to give Leona Franey (8/12) rather than Larry Haas (8/27) the first one is of interest in light of the impatience he soon expressed to Haas. Bell was reducing its personnel with the end of hostilities in view, so Andrei may have tried to make the best use of her remaining time. He may also have been cultivating Joe for his value at Hooker, especially if Leona soon became useless.

16. Fletcher to file, 100-340996-119, 10/24/45. Andrei's growing dissatisfaction with his role in the United States became more understandable when, during this visit, he told Larry that all of his and Antonina's belongings and their home had been burned in the

battle of Leningrad. He said, "Larry, I like your country and may be here for quite a long time." He was thinking of buying a home in the United States. This stands in contrast to his earlier request to be recalled to Russia and it exposes his ambivalence and chronically unsettled sense of purpose. Andrei added, however, that his colleagues at Amtorg were considering purchase of prefabricated homes to rebuild the city, but Andrei was not of that mind for rebuilding his own home.

17. Conroy and Rath to Hoover, 100-78534, 9/17/45. Larry's post-contact interviews with FBI agents were always cross-checked by surveillance of which Haas was sometimes unaware. On the twenty-seventh, surveillance reports indicate that Haas was seen to enter Schevchenko's apartment carrying no packages and with no bulges in his pockets, but on leaving he was seen to have "a large bulge in his left coat pocket ... The object in the pocket appeared to be weighty inasmuch as his coat was pulled down on the left side ... [it] was covered by a white handkerchief or white tissue paper."

CHAPTER 27: THE ALL-IMPORTANT *IF*

1. At the FBI's request, Leona Franey made up a list of thirteen documents of a type she thought would be of interest to Schevchenko. They ranged from unclassified, to restricted to confidential. Two were not under army control but were classified by other government agencies. Of the remaining eleven, four were unclassified and the army had no objection to having them photographed. The remaining seven were classified and deemed highly undesirable for release to Schevchenko. Three of those contained precisely the performance data he sought.

2. Pieper to Hoover, 100-25265, 8/27/45.

CHAPTER 28: THE WRONG RIDE TO SCHOOL

1. This is a first-person account by Kay Haas concerning a traumatic childhood event that left her with permanent injuries and scars, both physical and emotional.

2. When I had asked in the past about black cars with men sitting in them, my father only said the men in those cars were his friends. I never heard names mentioned and I did not think to ask. Somehow, I had the impression they were like faraway babysitters or maybe guards watching our neighborhood. Years later, I learned they were assigned to watch me and our family through some kind of arrangement my father had made through the FBI because some of his work with them could have placed us in danger. The FBI was new at using civilians in such a risky role and had to keep a close eye on us. They were part of my life for years after this event.

CHAPTER 29: ACCUSATIONS AND RENEWED ALLIANCE

1. This meeting is reconstructed for dramatic purposes from Kay's account of her father's later testimony. Some of her injuries from the abduction attempt left lifelong disabilities requiring surgery as long afterward as sixty years. Some of her scars remain as emotional as well as physical. As an adult, she insisted on her father's full and detailed explanation, especially his subsequent decision to continue working with the FBI.

2. Fletcher to Hoover, 100-340996-91, 8/31/45. A penciled note on this communication dated 9/6/45 adds that since Westinghouse is under contract to the US Navy for the

development of jet propulsion, "Col. S. K. Forney [sp? poorly legible] appraised bulletin in question is a navy document and any clearance will have to come from the navy." The chain of command through which approvals had to move was labyrinthine and slow. A copy of these notes, sometimes called "the manual" or "the booklet" in subsequent FBI communications, is in the possession of Kay Haas.

CHAPTER 30: THE WASHINGTON HOT POTATO

1. This sequence of correspondence is disclosed in Ladd to Director, 100-340996-96, 10/1/45, Conroy to file, 100-340996-97, 10/2/45, passim, and others.

2. Weiner, *Enemies*, 151. Not the least of Hoover's frustrations was the fact that President Truman continued to hold a negative view of Director Hoover's perceived resistance to oversight. Two years later, on May 2, 1947, White House counsel Clark Clifford recorded in notes of a meeting with the president that Truman was "very strongly anti-FBI." The president "wants to hold the FBI down." That sentiment had started to develop before the Schevchenko-Haas affair.

3. Ladd to Director, 100-340996-226, 12/18/45. This is the cover letter to the forty-four-page summary dated 12/17/45 carrying the same file number.

4. Hoover to Attorney General, 100-340996-84, 10/2/45. In this memorandum Hoover reminds the AG of his previous five memoranda on this subject dated August 31, September 12, 18, and 21, and October 1, 1945.

5. Mumford to Ladd, 100-340-996-81, 9/21/45. As of 9/21/45 the navy had returned "the booklet" to the New York Bureau office without authorization to release it to Schevchenko. Special Agent J. K. Mumford (NY) then informed Assistant Director Ladd that "an answer concerning clearance might be expected from the military authorities late this afternoon." Mumford then advised Mr. Fletcher to have the material returned to Special Agent Hartzenstein at the Philadelphia field office. The importance of maintaining a record of this convoluted chain of possession was heightened by Haas, who said that such confidential information was essentially only on loan to him. Westinghouse could recall all copies of any such confidential material at any time.

6. Fletcher to Hoover, 100-340996-83, 9/26/45.

7. Fletcher to Hoover, 100-340996-83, 9/26/45.

8. Mumford to Ladd, 100-340-996-81, 9/21/45.

9. This private library was fictitious, invented solely to explain why Larry would not fulfill Andrei's requests without unpredictable, lengthy delays. Such delays would actually be due to ongoing bureaucratic delays in obtaining the permissions Larry needed for release of key documents to Andrei.

10. It was never ascertained or recorded that Antonina was an NKVD officer or one who could be questioned by Andrei's superiors—an arrangement that would not have been unusual for one in Andrei's position—but this odd request for privacy with Larry in a darkened park may reflect Andrei's heightening suspicions about all people in his sphere of operations.

11. Director to Caudle, 100-340996-268, 11/21/46. The identity of these individuals was not disclosed, but this was approximately when a Russian operative named Zhukov had arrived in New York from Russia to serve as general manager at Amtorg. The relationship between Schevchenko as vice president and Zhukov as a new general manager may

have been unsettled, heightening the internal competition over assets, jurisdictions, and authority.

12. This referred to both ram jet propulsion and jet propulsion.

13. This date suggests that he wanted everything on aluminum alloys after the date Larry left Bell, suggesting Larry might have provided it based on P-39 and P-63 construction practices to which Andrei would have been permitted access. See also item number 7 on Andrei's list.

14. Hoover to Attorney General, 100-340996-84, 10/2/45.

15. Fletcher to file, 100-340996-119, 4/24/45.

16. Fletcher to Director, 100-340996-128, 10/15/45.

17. Fletcher to file, 100-340996-119, 4/24/45. On further examination the agents found that all of the films Andrei gave to Larry and the Franeys was reloaded into previously used cassettes. None of the film was Kodak of any kind.

18. Fletcher to file, 100-340996-119, 10/24/45.

19. Fletcher to Director, 100-340996-111, 10/17/45.

20. Wilcox to Director and SAC New York, 100-340996-126, 10/22/45.

21. Hoover to SAC Buffalo, 100-340996-120, 10/23/45.

22. 100-340996-234 cited in Director to Attorney General, 100-340996-292.

23. Ladd to Hoover, 100-340996-226, 12/17/45.

24. Only three weeks earlier, on October 2, the warden of the Federal Reformatory at El Reno, Oklahoma, had mailed Truman's famous inmate-made desk sign to Truman at the request of Truman's friend Fred Canfil, US Marshal for the Western District of Missouri. It was just what the Schevchenko Hot Potato case needed. https://www.trumanlibrary.gov/. Retrieved 2/1/18.

25. Ladd to Tamm, 100-340996-124, 10/25/45. Office memorandum at 12:15 p.m. The 7:55 p.m. approval was recorded in a handwritten note at the bottom of this memo.

26. Tamm to Ladd FBI Office Memorandum File * * * 100-340996124. Westinghouse Electric Corporation Report A176, prepared under Navy Contract No. NOa(S1289), Section 3, Item 2 (f), entitled "Design Study of Control and Regulating System, ModelX915A Engine," which was issued to the Bureau of Aeronautics on September 22, 1945. A copy of this document remains in the possession of Kay Haas.

27. Whitson to Ladd, 100-340996-125, 10/26/45.

28. Ladd to Hoover, 100-340996-226, 12/17/45.

29. Ladd to Director, 100-340996-272, 12-19-1946. Zhukov was a name well known to US military intelligence, but the individual carrying the letter clearly could not have been Marshall Georgi Konstantinovich Zhukov, who was a battlefield hero of the USSR's defenses throughout WWII. On just about the date of this strange visit to the Franey home, Marshall Zhukov had claimed illness in declining an invitation to the United States from President Eisenhower. Sibley, *Red Spies in America*, 175. The man at Leona's front door was most surely not that Zhukov. The man did, however, remain an important target of the FBI's investigations of Schevchenko's known associates through September 1946, having returned to Russia and re-entered the United States on at least one more occasion. December 1946 FBI communications used the French transliteration of the Cyrillic characters of his name as Joukov, perhaps to better disambiguate the individuals.

30. Letter, Hoover to Acheson, 11/2/45.

31. Fletcher to Director, 100-340996-159, 11/7/45.

32. Fletcher to Director, 100-340996-136, 11/2/45.

33. Rath to file, 100-340996-207 (100-78534), 2/1/46.

34. Conroy to Director, 100-340996-148, 11/27/45. The communication links in surveillance were still not fully developed. The Buffalo field office was strongly criticized by SAC Conroy in a letter to Hoover. Buffalo had failed to adequately instruct the Franeys that every contact with Schevchenko should be reported immediately so that every office involved could establish the needed surveillance. This lapse "occasioned a considerable waste of effort and time in the attempt to locate the subject and the informant in New York City."

35. F.B.I. Teletype. Urgent. Conroy to Director, 100-340996-166, 11/26/45.

36. Sibley, *Red Spies in America*, 92, 115. "Even when the FBI was given a specific mandate to find communists ... it received limited cooperation from other government departments." Sibley adds that Hoover faced "daunting hurdles counterintelligence officials faced in apprehending even those agents for whom they had compelling evidence of spying." The Haas-Schevchenko case was one of the most egregious instances of this dichotomy between intelligence and enforcement.

37. William C. Sullivan, with Bill Brown, *The Bureau: My Thirty Years in Hoover's FBI* (New York: Norton Collection, 1979), 60–61. Doling out sensational news stories to reporters also had the benefit of creating an obligation on the part of the press to return the favor by publishing favorable news about the FBI, Hoover, or someone to whom Hoover owed a favor. At its best, it was a useful symbiosis. At worst, improper and underhanded.

38. Intelligence Activities, Senate Resolution 21, Hearings Before the Select Committee to Study Governmental Operations with Respect to Intelligence Activities of the United States Senate, 94th Congress, First Session, Volume 6, Federal Bureau of Investigation, November 18, 19, December 2, 3, 9, 10, and 11, 1975. Washington: 1976.

CHAPTER 31: TRIAL, PROSECUTION, AND THREAT

1. Haynes, Klehr, and Vassiliev, *Spies*. Only three months earlier, Andrei Schevchenko had collaborated with Leonid Kvasnikov, a renowned Soviet scientist with expertise in aeronautics, atomics, and other scientific fields, serving in New York City under diplomatic cover as deputy to the *rezident*. Andrei and Leonid, both leading XY (science and technology) line officers of the NKVD New York station, crafted a detailed report on the Manhattan Project, the US atomic bomb program (code-named Enormoz by Soviet intelligence), to Vsevolod Merkulov, head of the Soviet secret police, intelligence, and counterintelligence force in Moscow. It is not clear how Rushmore learned about Schevchenko's connection to Enormoz espionage, though years later Larry Haas told Kay that during one long night of drinking late in 1945 Andrei had divulged his role, perhaps through his attempts to gain information from Joseph Franey's work at Hooker Chemical. This further supports Haas/Hoover as the source of the "unauthorized leak." The evening before the 6/6/49 HUAC hearing, a reporter named Edward K. Nellor, writing for the *Buffalo Courier-Express*, interviewed Haas, the Franeys, and a fourth, unnamed Bell employee whom Schevchenko had tried to recruit. Nellor stated, "The evidence, obtained last night, points to a 'leak' in the Department of Justice." *Buffalo Courier-Express*, "Flight of Russian Jet-Plane Spy Hints Justice Department Leak." 6/6/49.

2. Noting that Rushmore's story had also been published in other national newspapers, Nebraska Senator Kenneth Wherry read major portions of the stories into the December 10, 1945, Congressional Record and used the case as fuel for his repeated calls for investigation of the State Department for subversive and overly liberal influences.

3. Ladd to Hoover, 100-340996-226, 12/17/45. "Except for the statement regarding the seizure by the FBI of documents in a 36th Street rooming house in July of 1945 and the presenting of the case to the State Department at that time, all of which is completely erroneous, the general allegations in the article are correct." This revelation could have created the impression with Schevchenko's superiors that, because he had not reported such an incident to them, he had kept it secret because he had been co-opted by the FBI into collaboration, in other words, become a double agent against the Soviet Union.

4. For a detailed discussion and the testimony of Budenz on a wide range of Soviet anti-American activities, see HUAC June 20, 21, 27, 1945, passim, and HUAC November 22, 1946, 1–49, passim.

5. Haynes, Klehr, and Vassiliev, *Spies*, 533. Boris (patronym and surname unknown) was an NKVD officer working at the Soviet Consulate under Pavel Ivanovich Fedosimov, acting *rezident*, or chief, of the New York station. Schevchenko had previously mentioned a "Boris" to Haas as a rather ominous figure within the consulate and Amtorg hierarchy.

6. Dialogue in this section is a dramatic re-creation based on known events, circumstances, and the character of the participants, though not specifically documented.

7. Rath to file, 100-340996-207 (100-78534), 2/1/46.

8. Haynes and Klehr, *Venona: Decoding Soviet Espionage in America* (New Haven, CT: Yale University Press, 1999), 267. Pavel Ivanovich Fedosimov was an NKVD officer with extensive experience running American sub-agents, most notably in the Manhattan atomic bomb program. He was apparently well aware of the need for proper selection and training of intelligence workers and expressed a need for patience and possibly some degree of leniency when such preparations had not been taken. One of those was Robert Owen Menaker, identified by cryptographers in sixteen Venona messages under the code names BOB and CZECH. Fedosimov reported to Moscow on one occasion in 1944 when Menaker had botched an important assignment that "allowances should be made working with Menaker since he had not been thoroughly trained or screened prior to assignment." The Schevchenko case illustrates the same degree of forbearance by Fedosimov. Another advantage of this attribute was that allowing Schevchenko some degree of freedom and largesse after his exposure might allow NKVD surveillance to detect any subsequent contacts he would make with the FBI, if he actually was a collaborator or had been turned.

9. Rath to file, 100-340996-207 (100-78534), 2/1/46.

10. Rath to file, 100-340996-207 (100-78534), 2/1/46.

11. The text of this card is found in SAC, Philadelphia to Director, 100-340996-190, 12/29/45. On receipt of this card Haas contacted Agent Ring to report its receipt and contents. Fletcher to file, 100-340996-202, 1/22/46.

12. 100-340996-206, 2/1/46. FBI Laboratory investigation confirmed by comparison to known samples that the handwriting on the card was Schevchenko's.

CHAPTER 32: THE THREAT DELIVERED

1. Edward Winter, "A Nimzowitsch Story." Retrieved 4/2/19.

2. This day changed the course of Larry Haas's life. He relived it many times for Kay and her mother in later years. A threat by a Soviet spy, especially one who had been named "one of the most dangerous spies ever sent to the United States," cannot be forgotten. This account is dramatized based on Kay's testimony, a first-person witness of her father's many-times retold story, though no account of this incident remains in FBI files to which we have access. For the FBI, this event signaled a notable failure, especially in its first-ever Soviet anti-espionage case. In addition, it illustrates tactics Hoover would likely not publicize. Historian Tim Weiner later described certain FBI counterespionage methods. "The [intelligence] division conducted uncounted break-ins and buggings . . . the routine destruction of FBI files ensured that no accurate account existed." Weiner, *Enemies*, 192–93. This is further supported by Max Lowenthal, *The Federal Bureau of Investigation* (New York: Harcourt Brace Jovanovich, 1950), 433–34, citing Howard B. Fletcher's memorandum to D. M. Ladd, 11/7/49, both of whom played key roles throughout this Schevchenko/Haas case. Concerning the later Coplon case, Fletcher advised "that all administrative records in the New York [City] office covering the operations of this informant be destroyed." Haas was the informant in the present case and the absence of an FBI record of "The Threat" in no way diminishes the veracity of Larry and Kay Haas's personal testimony and experiences.

3. http://historicalgmen.squarespace.com/agents-of-the-30s-biographie. Accessed 3/18/18. SAC Conroy, known in the Bureau as "E.E.," headed the New York City field office during World War II. Though anti-Soviet counterespionage was new to him, during his tenure the Bureau captured many Axis spies, including four Nazi saboteurs delivered to Long Island by a German submarine. Not one act of enemy sabotage occurred in the New York City area while under Conroy's command.

4. SAC Philadelphia to Hoover, 100-340996, 12/29/45. This FBI interoffice memo contains a copy of the Christmas letter dated December 17, 1945. The memo also requests handwriting verification as Schevchenko's; later confirmed.

5. Howard Rushmore, "Red Spy Paid for Jet Secrets: Bribed US Engineers for Blueprints of Planes," *New York Journal-American*, December 4, 1945; Rushmore, "Red Courier System Bared: Soviet Ring Uncovered in Spy Hunt," December 5, 1945; Rushmore, "Wherry Pushes His Demand for State Dept. Quiz," December 6, 1945. All three stories ran on the front page.

6. Weiner, *Enemies*, 157–58, 192. FBI director Hoover held intensely anti-communist views and made his position known to both the Roosevelt and Truman administrations. Often frustrated by Washington's unwillingness to act—due to diplomatic and political considerations rather than legal—Hoover, highly skilled in manipulation, sometimes turned those skills toward "influencing" reluctant politicians, reporters eager for stories, and radio and television personalities. Hoover sometimes waged his war on communism behind the scenes using intelligence for influence and coercion. And "Hoover's intelligence operations . . . ranged to the edge of the law."

7. The year 1945 had been disastrous for Soviet espionage. A number of high-profile defections had already made headlines for American and Canadian Soviet agents renouncing the Soviet Union and Stalin. This internationally embarrassing cascade of collapsing espionage networks now threatened to end with Andrei Schevchenko at the crest of that wave. In addition to journalist Rushmore's defection, Louis Budenz, a Soviet espionage agent heading the *Buben Group* of spies in the United States, defected and became a vocal anti-communist testifying in court against others. On September 5, 1945, Igor Gouzenko,

working at the Soviet Embassy to Canada in Ottawa, defected to reveal Soviet atom-bomb espionage. On November 7, only one month before Schevchenko's newspaper exposé, Elizabeth Bentley, an American Soviet agent, had revealed the names of 150 Soviet operatives in the United States. Schevchenko now felt forced to join the ranks of those infamous defectors—or face the wrath of his superiors in Moscow for allowing yet another exposure of sabotage against their wartime allies. These prior disgraces were clearly in Schevchenko's mind when he told Haas, "You made me look like a fool in the eyes of my country."

8. Lamphere, *FBI-KGB War*, 23. A colleague of Schevchenko, another (unnamed) Amtorg employee, had been under pressure to defect, this time by FBI Special Agent Don Jardine in New York City. The man said he knew that the disgrace of his failure in the United States promised punishment and possible execution on his deportation. Nevertheless, he chose deportation over cooperation with the FBI, stating he doubted he could "make it" in a capitalist society. Schevchenko's enraged reaction may have tangled with similar conflicts.

9. Weiner, *Enemies*, 142–43.

10. Robert W. Stephan, *Stalin's Secret War: Soviet Counterintelligence against the Nazis, 1941–1945* (Lawrence: University Press of Kansas, 2004). Andrei would have been quite clear about the fate of a Soviet citizen who had failed in his assignment, thereby opening himself to an accusation of acting as an anti-Soviet agent. Stalin's SMERSH (Motto: "Death to Spies"), the Soviet military internal counterintelligence agency—though it concentrated on Nazi spies—punished failure anywhere in the world with brutal certainty.

CHAPTER 33: ANOTHER NAME FOR JUSTICE

1. This event is a dramatic recreation of Larry Haas's testimony to Kay, friends, and family, retold in cinematic detail many times over subsequent years by Larry. Arguably, no White House record of this sub-rosa meeting would have been kept. This, however, is Larry Haas's account.

2. Letter to James Byrnes, Harry S. Truman, January 5, 1946. Years later, Larry told Kay that President Truman had read to him from notes concerning a message the president was "preparing for Secretary of State Byrnes." Excerpts from such a letter, dated just before Larry's clandestine White House visit, are used here to reflect the event as Larry later described it. https://teachingamericanhistory.org/library/document/letter-to-james-byrnes/.

CHAPTER 34: LOST AT SEA

1. Conroy to Director and SACs. Urgent. 100-340996-205, 12/20/45. On December 20, Conroy alerted Hoover and SACs on the northeast coast of the Soviet ships in harbor from Baltimore to New York City, making special note of the *Stalinabad* on the New Jersey side of New York Harbor, scheduled to sail on Christmas Day. He advised searching Schevchenko's luggage if he should attempt to board any of those ships. By December 29, it was clear that Schevchenko and his family would board the *Stalinabad*, and Hoover asked the Attorney General's permission to search Schevchenko's hand luggage. The AG approved. Memorandum, Hoover to Attorney General, 100-340996-200, 12/29/45.

2. Rath to file, 100-340996-207 (100-78534), 2/1/46.

3. Conroy to Director, 100-340996-222, 2/5/46. On February 1, 1946, SAC Conroy informed Hoover that the Schevchenko case had been placed on a pending inactive status. Schevchenko had departed the United States with "no indications that he will return."

4. This event, as in chapter 33, "Another Name for Justice," is also a dramatic re-creation of Larry Haas's testimony to Kay, friends, and family, retold in cinematic detail many times over subsequent years by Larry. This, once again, is Larry Haas's account. Attempts to detect any record of Andrei Ivanovich Schevchenko after this event in January 1946 have been fruitless. NKVD archivists in 2020 also deny (to WP) records of Schevchenko activities.

5. Ladd to Director, 100-340996-267, 11/20/46. A month after the *Stalinabad*'s departure, E. E. Conroy wrote to Hoover, "In the event that Schevchenko does not return, an opportunity may arise for the further use of the services of informant Haas ... it is possible that contact may be established between Haas and some other Russian representative who may have been assigned to carry on Schevchenko's work in this country."

CHAPTER 35: METAMORPHOSIS

1. Boardman to Director, Special Delivery, 100-340996-237, 5/9/46, and SAC Philadelphia to Director, 100-340996-265, 11/6/46.

2. Ladd to Director, 100-340996-267, 11/20/46.

3. SAC Philadelphia to Director, 100-340996-263, 11/14/46.

4. Boardman to Director, Special Delivery, 100-340996-237, 5/9/46.

5. Wilcox to Director, 100-996340-275, 1/3/47. Buffalo's SAC Wilcox eventually approved a payment of three hundred dollars by SA Edwin F. Dooley, who then retained the camera at the Buffalo Field Division office. Larry, however, complained that the FBI had "chiseled him out of fifteen dollars" on the deal and withheld its lens, claiming it had been a separate gift from Andrei. Larry demanded and got ten dollars for the lens.

6. Director to SAC New York, 100-996340, 4/7/1947.

7. SAC Buffalo to Director, 100-340996-281, 4/17/47.

CHAPTER 36: THE POWER NEXUS

1. Photographs taken at Westinghouse show Haas wearing his signature fedora and rolled-up shirtsleeves. At one time he is seen directing a Grumman F6F Hellcat, a carri-er-based propeller-driven fighter aircraft, through the Westinghouse plant gate, mere inches wider than the plane, surrounded by a street-level throng of civilian and plant onlookers. It would be used to model wing folding for the Westinghouse/USN new jet program.

2. SAC Buffalo to file, 65-59543-88, 3/6/52. Schevchenko's network of sub-agents had brought him hints of Flader's reach into strategically important technologies. In the latter part of 1945, Schevchenko encouraged Haas to seek employment with Flader. Haas did not reveal that he already knew the man.

3. A letter dated 1 March, 1950, addressed to Larry Haas at Frederick Flader, Inc., Laskey Road, Toledo, Ohio (in personal collection of Kay Haas), written by G. R. Rusk of the Freeman Supply Company of Toledo, thanks Mr. Haas for speaking to a meeting of the American Foundryman's Society. Rusk thanks Haas for "an interesting evening, discussion, on timely subjects" and asks him to "visit 1 or 2 of their plants."

4. SAC Philadelphia to Director, 100-340996-265, 2/6/46. In February of 1946 Larry Haas informed ASAC William C. Hinze Jr. at the Philadelphia field office that he would resign from Westinghouse to accept a position at Frederic Flader, Inc., Air and Power Research Engineers on 2/15/46 in North Tonawanda, New York (Greater Buffalo area).

5. SAC Buffalo to Director, 100-340996-281, 4/17/47. Flader's work as a contractor under NEPA was sufficiently strategic that his employees, including Haas, required top-level security clearance by the Atomic Energy Commission.

6. This is enshrined in the Haas family archives.

7. SAC Buffalo to Director, 65-59543-86, 2/28/52. During an interview with agents of the Buffalo field office on 2/19/52, Haas developed information concerning a previous coworker at Flader who revealed that she had known Schevchenko. She showed Haas a camera Schevchenko had given her, identical to the one he had given Haas, and disclosed a close, personal knowledge of both Andrei and Antonina Schevchenko. This (name redacted) person had remained employed in atomic research with Flader and was subsequently investigated under the provisions of the Atomic Energy Act of 1946. This record is one of the few but telling indications that Larry Haas remained actively engaged in FBI counterespionage work into the 1950s. Also: SAC Buffalo to file, 65-59543-88, 3/6/52. On 3/6/52, Haas is also noted as contributing to an FBI inquiry into Schevchenko's prior interest in the Republic-Ford JB-2 surface-to-surface tactical missile system, knowledge of which Haas disclaimed.

CHAPTER 37: HUAC AND THE BLAME GAME

1. https://www.brainyquote.com/authors/hubert-h-humphrey-quotes. Retrieved 10/10/20.

2. In addition to a transcript of these proceedings, a transcript of the succeeding—same day—behind-closed-doors Executive Session investigating matters of national security not to be made public has also been used extensively in this narrative of the events of June 6, 1949.

3. The letters summoning him and Dorothy to HUAC remain in Kay Haas's possession.

4. Dooley Memo to file, 100-340996-289, 5/5/49. The men at the Haas's home that night also said that the FBI files were closed to them, so they had to rely on testimony of first-person witnesses like Larry Haas and the (unnamed) Franeys. It is well known that Hoover and HUAC formed a tight force against communist infiltration and espionage but had to maintain a certain distance—as exemplified by unshared files—for political, administrative, and intelligence reasons, as well as for "credible deniability" when necessary.

5. Nixon was known as a witness interrogator with a skill for crafting incisive questions that probed core issues and yielded unequivocal answers. In this case, two questions containing a mere forty-five words appear to have completely exonerated Haas of a major intelligence breach. Kay Haas recalls a long friendship that later grew between Haas and Nixon.

6. HUAC, "Soviet Espionage Activities," 6/6/49. Whether or not he knew it, Tavenner had already addressed Larry's most deeply hidden concern that this hearing might raise questions about Schevchenko he would not want to answer. Tavenner's opening comments had revealed "[Schevchenko's] present whereabouts and occupational assignment are unknown."

7. "Soviet Espionage Activities in Connection with Jet Propulsion and Aircraft," Hearings Before the House on Un-American Activities, House of Representatives, Eighty-first Congress—Executive Session. June 6, 1949.

8. That moment kicked off a friendship and mutual admiration society that lasted through many years to come, as Kay recalls.

9. Judy Haas, Kay Haas's younger sister, confirms Kay's recollection that Oppenheimer was an occasional, if not frequent, visitor at the Haas residence. They thought he was quite handsome and recall calling him Uncle Bobby.

10. HUAC, "Shameful Years," 42.

11. It is curious that in this important government document, Schevchenko's name is given as Andrei V. Schevchenko though his patronym is Ivanovich. Historic records sometimes change by an accumulation of infinitesimal errors, though, as will be noted later, in the Schevchenko case some more significant reporting errors entered the record almost immediately.

CHAPTER 38: A COVER-UP EXPOSED

1. *Hamlet*, Act 3, Scene 2, 222–30.

2. Ladd to Director, 100-340996-300, 6/8/49.

3. Ladd to Director, 100-340996-96, 10/1/45.

4. Three years later and two days after the HUAC hearing, Hoover revisited the situation with Ladd. Among other topics, they re-evaluated the decision on whether or not the FBI's double agent should go to Schevchenko in New York empty-handed on Saturday, October 27, 1945. In that conversation, Ladd reminded Hoover that his reaction to the AG had become somewhat nuanced. Hoover did not want to lose track of Schevchenko, but the means to that end were unclear. On June 8, 1949, Ladd wrote to Hoover, "You will recall that following your meeting with the Attorney General and the Undersecretary of State on October 25, 1945, you issued the following instructions: 'I desire that there be no arrest made of Schevchenko this Saturday, but that steps be taken to see that the informants do not deliver to Schevchenko any documents at that time. If possible, I would like to have the contact maintained, even though I know it will be particularly difficult, but at least we ought to keep a close contact on Schevchenko, even though he loses all confidence in the informants. He would then very likely try to establish other contacts.'" Nevertheless, Hoover said FBI supervisor Lish Whitson "went too far" in directing Wilcox to have Franey concoct an excuse for a no-show on Saturday, and by relaying Hoover's reasoning to Wilcox. Hoover wrote another blue bomb, *There was no reason to give details to SAC. H.* In the Fall of 1945, some aspects of the Schevchenko case had apparently run ahead of Hoover's and his field agents' ability to manage them with a sure hand. In the absence of a transcript of the 10/25/45 meeting, it may be conjectured that Clark saw weaknesses in Hoover's case and was justified in blocking the arrest.

5. Hoover to Clark, 100-340996-292, referring back to 100-340996-234, 10/31/45. Hoover informed AG Clark, "Mr. Acheson stated that in view of the very delicate situation then prevailing with Russia internationally concerning the Japanese problem, which at that time was in such a state that Russia had refused to attend a forthcoming meeting the following Tuesday in Washington on Pacific affairs unless prior to that time agreement was reached including Russia in the administration of affairs in Japan, that any incident such as the Schevchenko matter might aggravate the situation and make it even more difficult from an international point of view." Unless stopped, the Schevchenko/Haas case was on the verge of derailing the realignment of world powers in the Pacific.

CHAPTER 39: KILLING ME SEVEN TIMES

1. *Olean Times Herald*, "Witness in Red Spy Drama Puts Olean as Possibility in Scene," June 8, 1949. Haas reported that on occasional trips to visit friends and family in Dorothy's home town, Olean, New York, "it was quite probable that they [he, Dorothy, and Kay] had been tailed by Russians on some of those trips [with] sinister Russian spies, lurking in Olean's peaceful, tree-shaded streets as they played their grim roles in one of the greatest espionage dramas of the Second World War. The Haas family had been "living for more than three and one-half years under the 'round-the-clock scrutiny of Soviet espionage." Haas was aware of this scrutiny through his ongoing anti-Soviet collaboration with the FBI. The incident related here detailing the break-in at her home in Olean describes the ongoing nature of that Soviet surveillance and the threat they posed.

2. https://www.yelp.com/biz/antica-biblioteca-valle-roma.

3. http://cinematreasures.org/theaters/14634.

4. *Cuba Debate*. Cuba nationalizes US companies. August 10, 2015. http://en.cuba debate.cu/news/2015/08/10/cuba-nationalizes-us-companies/. Retrieved September 20, 2019.

5. More than sixty years later Kay demonstrated her nearly photographic memory and reliability by recounting this event precisely as recorded on Dorothy's official death certificate received from the City of Olean only after preparing this account.

A PERSONAL NOTE FROM KAY HAAS

1. Rudyard Kipling, *The Works of Rudyard Kipling: All Eight Volumes* (Oxford: Benediction Classics, 2011).

2. "Loren 'Larry' Haas," *Simpson's Leader-Times*, Kittanning, Pennsylvania, November 28, 1989. Loren George Haas: April 27, 1917, to November 27, 1989.

3. FBI files document ongoing connections between Haas and he FBI through 1957. Personal documents retained by the family and personal experiences relevant to such involvement extend at least ten years beyond that date.

4. Andrew Mumford, "Proxy Warfare and the Future of Conflict," *RUSI Journal*, 158:2 (2013): 40–46. The nature of proxy warfare is important to understand in both historic and current international relations. Mumford offers a brief and informative discussion.

NOTES ON COMPILING *THE FIRST COUNTERSPY*

1. Personal interviews with all of these family members, along with their mementos, writings, and clippings, have contributed to this book.

2. https://quotely.org. Retrieved 12/08/19.

3. Rath to file, 100-78534, 10/2/45.

4. Sibley, *Red Spies in America*, 4, 5, 243.

5. Weiner, *Enemies*, 13–16. In 1940 the Bureau employed 898 agents. By 1943, Hoover had swelled the ranks to 4,591 agents and 7,422 staffers, yet a vanishingly small number had foreign language ability or knew their way around foreign countries.

6. Many excellent, often pithy, and candid biographical sketches of agents named in this book can be found in "Faded Glory: Dusty Roads of An FBI Era." http://historicalgmen .squarespace.com/. Retrieved 3/12/18.

7. Max Lowenthal, *The Federal Bureau of Investigation* (New York: Harcourt Brace Jovanovich, 1950), 316.

8. Hoover to SAC NY, 100-340996-194 and -204, 1/22/46.

9. Ladd to Hoover, 100-340996-226, 12/17/45, passim.

10. The United States established diplomatic relations with the Union of Soviet Socialistic Republics (USSR) in November of 1933, but trade had already been under way for almost a decade through USSR's Amtorg Trading Corporation, which was established in New York State on May 24, 1924. Amtorg was formed by merging two previous Soviet entities, Products Exchange and Across-America, Inc. According to "Shameful Years" (p. 6), "With the founding of Amtorg the Soviet Union had for the first time a legitimate cover for its espionage activities in the United States." In secret Soviet communications decrypted by Venona code breakers, Amtorg was known as "Magazin."

11. HUAC, "Soviet Espionage Activities," 6/6/49, passim.

12. Ladd to Hoover, 100-340996-226, 12/17/45, passim. A comprehensive forty-four-page FBI interoffice memorandum titled "Andrei Ivanovich Schevchenko." Also, Ladd to Hoover, 100-340996-96, 1/10/45, passim. A slightly different but consistent set of details on the "Subject Schevchenko" case.

13. HUAC, "Shameful Years," 41.

14. HUAC, "Shameful Years," 42.

15. https://www.amazon.com/Decor-Poster-study-politics-Inspiring/dp/B01MY 91T3L. Retrieved 4/29/19.

16. https://libquotes.com/. Retrieved 4/29/19.

Selected Bibliography

Barron, John, *KGB Today: The Hidden Hand* (London: Hodder and Stoughton, 1984).

Barsky, Jack, *Deep Under Cover: My Secret Life & Tangled Allegiances as a KGB Spy in America* (Carol Stream: Tyndale, 2017), and personal communication (WP).

Bray, Jack, *Alone Against Hitler—Kurt Von Schuschnigg's Fight to Save Austria from the Nazis* (Guilford: Prometheus Books, 2020).

Carr, Barnes, *Operation Whisper: The Capture of Soviet Spies Morris and Leona Cohen* (Lebanon: University Press of New England, 2016), and personal communication (WP).

Greene, Robert, and Joost Effers, *The Concise Art of Seduction* (London: Profile Books, 2001).

Hardesty, Von, and Ilya Grinberg, *Red Phoenix Rising: The Soviet Air Force in World War II* (Lawrence: University Press of Kansas, 2012), and personal communication with Grinberg (WP).

Haynes, John Earl, Harvey Klehr, and Alexander Vassiliev, *Spies: The Rise and Fall of the KGB in America* (New Haven, CT: Yale University Press, 2009), and personal communication (WP).

Haynes, John Earl, and Harvey Klehr, *Venona: Decoding Soviet Espionage in America* (New Haven, CT: Yale University Press, 1999).

Koletar, Joseph W., *The FBI Career Guide* (New York: American Management Association, 2006), and personal communication (WP).

Lamphere, Robert J., and Tom Shachtman, *The FBI-KGB War: A Special Agent's Story* (New York: Random House, 1986).

Loftis, Larry, *Code Name: Lise: The True Story of the Woman Who Became WWII's Most Highly Decorated Spy* (New York: Gallery Books, 2019), and personal communication (WP).

Lowenthal, Max, *The Federal Bureau of Investigation* (New York: Harcourt Brace Jovanovich, 1950).

Miscamble, Wilson D., *From Roosevelt to Truman: Potsdam, Hiroshima, and the Cold War* (Cambridge: Cambridge University Press, 2007).

Rubel, Robert C. (2010) "The U.S. Navy's Transition to Jets," *Naval War College Review* 63, no. 2, Article 6. Available at: https://digital-commons.usnwc.edu/nwc-review/vol63/iss2/6.

Sibley, Katherine A. S., *Red Spies in America: Stolen Secrets and the Dawn of the Cold War* (Lawrence: University Press of Kansas, 2004), and personal communication (WP).

Turner, William W., *Hoover's FBI* (New York: Thunder's Mouth Press, 1993).

Weiner, Tim, *Enemies: A History of the FBI* (New York: Random House, 2012).

Whitehead, Don, *The FBI Story—A Report to the People* (New York: Random House, 1956).

Woodbury, David O., *Battlefronts of Industry—Westinghouse in World War II* (New York: John Wiley & Sons, 1948).

FBI surveillance data, investigative reports, memoranda, and correspondence between agents, Hoover, the Joint Chiefs, Cabinet Secretaries, and President Truman, relevant to the case:

7 Nov. 1949	SAC NY to Dir
18 Oct. 1949	SAC Scheidt NY to Dir
28 Feb. 1952	SAC Buffalo to Dir
6 Mar. 1952	Buffalo report
21 Mar. 1952	SAC Buffalo to Dir
11 June 1945	SAC Conroy NY report
15 June 1945	Ladd NY to Dir URGENT
13 June 1945	SAC Conroy to Dir
12 July 1945	SAC NY (see 13 Apr) to Dir
14 July 1945	NY (see 6 July) to Dir URGENT
20 July 1945	SAC Conroy NY to Dir and SAC
27 July 1945	SAC Fletcher Phila report
7 Aug. 1945	SAC Conroy NY to Dir
11 Aug. 1945	SAC Conroy NY to Dir
23 Aug. 1945	SAC Fletcher Phila to Dir
27 June 1945	SAC Conroy NY to Dir
6 July 1945	Phila to Dir (partial record)
31 Aug. 1945	SAC Fletcher Phila to Dir
21 Sept. 1945	J. K. Mumford to D. M. Ladd
17 Sept. 1945	SAC Conroy and SA Rath NY report
26 Sept. 1945	SAC Fletcher Phila to Dir
2 Oct. 1945	Dir Attorney to Atty. Gen.
27 Aug. 1945	Sac NJL Pieper San Francisco to Dir
12 Sept. 1945	SAC Fletcher Phila to Dir URGENT
31 Aug. 1945	SAC Fletcher Phila to Dir
31 Aug. 1945	SAC Fletcher Phila to Dir
1 Oct. 1945	D. M. Ladd to Dir
2 Oct. 1945	SAC Conroy NY to Dir Report
2 Oct. 1945	SAC Conroy NY to Dir
15 Oct. 1945	SAC Fletcher Phila to Dir
18 Oct. 1945	SAC J. B. Wilcox Buffalo to Dir

5 Nov. 1945	SAC Fletcher Phila to Dir
30 Nov. 1945	Dir (signed) to SAC Buffalo
27 Nov. 1945	Dir to SAC Buffalo
2 Nov. 1945	Dir to Dean Acheson (Und Sec State)
24 Oct. 1945	NY Report
23 Oct. 1945	SAC J. B. Wilcox Buffalo from Dir (URGENT)
2 Oct. 1945	SAC J. B. Wilcox Buffalo to Dir & SAC Conroy NY
25 Oct. 1945	D. M. Ladd to E. A. Tamm
26 Oct. 1945	Lish Whitson to D. Ladd
8 June 1949	D. M. Ladd to Dir
10 Nov. 1955	W. G. Eames, Mr. Nichols (HUAC Transcript)
14 Nov. 1946	SAC Phila to Dir
15 Nov. 1945	NY Report
7 Nov. 1946	NY Report
6 Nov. 1946	SAC Phila to Dir (Haas Westing. → Flader)
20 Nov. 1946	D. M. Ladd to Dir
21 Nov. 1946	Dir to T. L. Caudle (Asst AG)
3 Jan. 1947	SAC J. B. Wilcox Buffalo to Dir
13 Jan. 1947	SAC Buffalo to Dir
9 May 1946	SAC L. V. Boardman Phila to Dir (spec deliv.)
5 May 1949	Dir (and SA Edwin F. Dooley Buffalo) to AG
17 April 1947	SAC Buffalo to Dir
7 April 1947	SAC NY to Dir
19 Dec. 1946	D. M. Ladd to Dir
20 Oct. 1953	SAC Phila to Dir
14 Nov. 1945	FBI Lab to SAC Fletcher Phila
8 Nov. 1945	SAC Phila to FBI Lab
17 Dec. 1945	SAC Phila Report
22 Jan. 1946	SA Thomas F. Ring Phila Report
1 Feb. 1946a	SA Wm. Hinze Phila Report
22 Jan. 1946	SAC Conroy NY
20 Dec. 1945	SAC Conroy NY
5 (?) Feb. 1946	(1 Feb. SA Harvey E. Rath) SAC Conroy NY to Dir
26 Nov. 1945	SA Harvey E. Rath NY Report

26 Nov. 1945	NY to Dir URGENT
27 Nov. 1945	SAC Conroy NY to Dir
18 Dec. 1945	D. M. Ladd to Dir (full forty-four-page summary)
18 Dec. 1945	D. M. Ladd to Dir (intro to summary)
3 Jan. 1946b	SAC Phila to Dir
29 Dec. 1945	Dir to AG
1 Feb. 1946	SA Rath NY Report
7 Nov. 1945	SAC H. B. Fletcher Phila to Dir
29 Dec. 1945	SAC H. B. Fletcher Phila to Dir
3 Jan. 1946	J. C. Strickland to D. M. Ladd
22 Mar. 1957	SAC NY to Dir
21 May 1949	Dir to Atty. Gen
20 Nov. 1945	Lab Work Sheet
5 Feb. 1945	SAC Conroy NY to Dir

Index